Deconstructions

From the same publishers

The Feminist Reader   *Edited by Catherine Belsey and Jane Moore*
New Historicism and Cultural Materialism   *John Brannigan*
Postmodern Narrative Theory   *Mark Currie*
Literary Theory from Plato to Barthes   *Richard Harland*
Marxist Literary and Cultural Studies   *Moyra Haslett*
Renaissance Drama and Contemporary Literary Theory   *Andy Mousley*
Twentieth-Century Literary Theory   *K. M. Newton*
Literary Feminisms   *Ruth Robbins*
Deconstruction – Derrida   *Julian Wolfreys*
Literary Theories   *Edited by Julian Wolfreys and William Baker*
Applying: To Derrida   *Edited by John Brannigan, Ruth Robbins and Julian Wolfreys*

Deconstructions

A User's Guide

Edited by

Nicholas Royle

palgrave

First published 2000 by
PALGRAVE
Houndmills, Basingstoke, Hampshire RG21 6XS and
175 Fifth Avenue, New York, N.Y. 10010
Companies and representatives throughout the world

PALGRAVE is the new global academic imprint of
St. Martin's Press LLC Scholarly and Reference Division and
Palgrave Publishers Ltd (formerly Macmillan Press Ltd).

ISBN 0–333–71760–0 hardback
ISBN 0–333–71761–9 paperback

This book is printed on paper suitable for recycling and
made from fully managed and sustained forest sources.

A catalogue record for this book is available
from the British Library.

Library of Congress Cataloging-in-Publication Data
Deconstructions : a user's guide / edited by Nicholas Royle.
    p. cm.
  Includes bibliographical references and index.
  ISBN 0–333–71760–0—ISBN0–333–71761–9 (pbk.)
    1. Deconstruction. I. Royle, Nicholas, 1963–
PN98.D43 D424 2000
149—dc21   00–059130

10 9 8 7 6 5 4 3 2 1
09 08 07 06 05 04 03 02 01 00

Printed and bound in Great Britain by
Creative Print & Design (Wales), Ebbw Vale

Contents

Preface

This book is intended as a user's guide to deconstruction across a range of topics and discourses. There are essays on cultural studies, drugs, ethics, feminism, fiction, film, hermeneutics, love, poetry, postcolonialism, psychoanalysis, technology and weaving. But each of these essays has more than one focus, exploring or opening onto further and other deconstructions. The chapter on feminism, for example, is in a sense just as much, also, about visual art; the chapter on fiction as much, also, about confession; the chapter on the postcolonial as much, also, about the Jewish–Algerian–French 'origins' of deconstruction. And so on. *Deconstructions* has been put together in the hope of demonstrating the ceaselessly multiple and altering contexts in which deconstructive thinking and practice are at work, both within and beyond the academy, both within and beyond what is called 'the West'. The book starts with an introductory piece, 'What is Deconstruction?', before moving on to a series of more specifically focused essays, each of them specially written for this volume. It was proposed at the outset of this project that each essay should have a title beginning 'deconstruction and . . .'. The final essay, by Jacques Derrida, is concerned with the 'and' itself. As he remarks at the beginning of that essay, in the beginning there is the 'and'. Inaugural and supplementary, 'and' affirms the irreducible opening of, and to, deconstructions. The index at the end of the book suggests, under the heading 'deconstruction and . . .', at least some of its innumerable other possibilities.

Acknowledgements

The editor and publishers would like to thank Jenny Holzer for permission to reproduce four of her works:

Raise Boys and Girls the Same Way, from *Truisms* (Sony JumboTRON video sign, Candlestick Park, San Francisco, 1987);

Arno, nine LED signs (Museo Guggenheim, Bilbao);

I Am Awake in the Place Where Women Die, from *Lustmord*; photograph of handwriting on skin;

With You Inside Me Comes the Knowledge of My Death, from *Lustmord*; human bone and engraved and etched silver (Galerie Rähnitzgasse der Landeschauptstadt, Dresden, 1996).

The editor would also like to thank Pauline Morgan for her help with compiling the index, and Maxwell Royle for his help with proofreading.

Notes on the Contributors

Derek Attridge is Leverhulme Research Professor at the University of York. He is the editor of Jacques Derrida's *Acts of Literature* (1992) and the author or editor of several books on poetics, deconstruction, James Joyce, and South African literature.

Geoffrey Bennington is Professor of French at the University of Sussex, where he is also Director of the Centre for Modern French Thought. He has written extensively on the work of Jacques Derrida, and his books include *Jacques Derrida* (1991) (written with Derrida himself) and *Interrupting Derrida* (2000).

David Boothroyd teaches cultural studies at the University of Teesside. He is a co-founding director of *Culture Machine* (http://culturemachine.tees.ac.uk) and his work in cultural theory and philosophy has appeared in several edited collections and scholarly journals. His forthcoming book is entitled *Culture on Drugs: Narco-Cultural Studies of High Modernity*.

Timothy Clark teaches at the University of Durham. He works in literary theory, especially Romantic and post-Heideggerian poetics. His books include *Derrida, Heidegger, Blanchot* (1992) and *The Theory of Inspiration* (1997). He is currently working on a study of Heidegger's poetics, and he is co-editor of the *Oxford Literary Review*.

Jacques Derrida has for more than thirty-five years been one of the most faithful *users* of 'deconstructions'. But he is not and has never wished to be – nor even to supply – a *guide* to them.

Diane Elam is Professor of English Literature and Critical and Cultural Theory at Cardiff University. She is the author of *Feminism and Deconstruction: Ms en Abyme* (1994) and *Romancing the Postmodern* (1992), as well as co-editor with Robyn Wiegman of *Feminism Beside Itself* (1995).

Maud Ellmann is University Lecturer and Fellow in English at King's

College, Cambridge. She is the author of *The Hunger Artists: Starving, Writing and Imprisonment* (1993) and editor of *Psychoanalytic Literary Criticism* (1994).

Rodolphe Gasché is Eugenio Donato Professor of Comparative Literature at the State University of New York at Buffalo. His books include *Die hybride Wissenschaft* (1973), *System und Metaphorik in der Philosophie von Georges Bataille* (1978), *The Tain of the Mirror: Derrida and the Philosophy of Reflection* (1986), *Inventions of Difference: On Jacques Derrida* (1994), *The Wild Card of Reading: On Paul de Man* (1998) and, most recently, *Of Minimal Things: Studies on the Notion of Relation* (1999). He is currently completing a booklength study on Kant's aesthetics.

Peggy Kamuf is Professor of French and Comparative Literature at the University of Southern California (Los Angeles). Her most recent book is *The Division of Literature, or the University in Deconstruction* (1997). She has translated numerous books and essays by Derrida, and is the editor of *A Derrida Reader: Between the Blinds* (1992).

J. Hillis Miller is UCI Distinguished Professor of English and Comparative Literature at the University of California, Irvine. He is the author of many books and articles on nineteenth- and twentieth-century literature and on literary theory. His most recent books are *Reading Narrative* (1998) and *Black Holes* (1999).

Caroline Rooney is Lecturer in English and a member of the Centre for Colonial and Postcolonial Research at the University of Kent. Her forthcoming book is entitled *Literature, Animism and Politics*.

Nicholas Royle is Professor of English at the University of Sussex. His books include *Telepathy and Literature* (1991), *After Derrida* (1995), *The Uncanny* (forthcoming), and (with Andrew Bennett) *An Introduction to Literature, Criticism and Theory* (2nd edition, 1999). He is co-editor of the *Oxford Literary Review*.

Robert Smith used to be a Prize Fellow of All Souls College, Oxford. During that period (1990–98) he published several texts exploring other texts – by Freud, Pascal, Wim Wenders, J. H. Prynne, Heidegger, etc. – including a book on Derrida, *Derrida and Autobiography* (1995). He is executive editor of the journal *Angelaki*, as well as series editor of the Angelaki book series called *Angelaki Humanities*. Currently, he is completing a book under the working title of *Remains Unknown: Forms of Death in Literature, Freud and Philosophy*.

Gayatri Chakravorty Spivak is Avalon Foundation Professor of the Humanities at Columbia University. Her books are *Myself Must I Remake* (1974), *In Other Worlds* (1987), *The Post-Colonial Critic* (1988), *Outside in the Teaching Machine* (1993), *A Critique of Postcolonial Reason* (1999) and *Red Thread* (forthcoming). She has translated Jacques Derrida's *Of Grammatology* (1978), and Mahasweta Devi's *Imaginary Maps* (1994), *Breast Stories* (1997) and *Old Women* (1999).

Robert J. C. Young is Professor of English and Critical Theory at Oxford University and a Fellow of Wadham College. He is the author of *White Mythologies: Writing History and the West* (1990), *Colonial Desire: Hybridity in Culture, Theory and Race* (1995), *Torn Halves: Political Conflict in Literary and Cultural Theory* (1996), and *Postcolonialism: An Historical Introduction* (2000). He is also General Editor of *Interventions: International Journal of Postcolonial Studies*.

1

What is Deconstruction?

Nicholas Royle

Dear Madam/Sir,

I love your dictionary. It is the most wonderful single-volume dictionary of the English language. I am even willing to give serious consideration to the thought, expressed by you on the front cover, that it is 'The AUTHORITY ON ENGLISH TODAY'. *Chambers Dictionary* has long had a special place in my heart. I picked up a copy of the 1993 edition more or less the day it was published. I should have written to you at the time. For it was that edition which contained, for the first time, an entry for the word 'deconstruction'. Now with the latest edition (1998) I see that the entry is unchanged and I just have to write to you about it. I can no longer contain myself. You define it as follows:

> **deconstruction** n. a method of critical analysis applied *esp* to literary texts, which, questioning the ability of language to represent reality adequately, asserts that no text can have a fixed and stable meaning, and that readers must eradicate all philosophical or other assumptions when approaching a text.

This definition seems to me, if you will permit me to say so, awful beyond words. It is so bad that I hardly know where to begin to vent my lexico-graphical sadness and spleen. Such venting, however, must also be one of laughter, since this definition of 'deconstruction' is also terribly funny. Think about it. What would it be like if readers were to 'eradicate all philosophical or other assumptions when approaching a text'? According to you, 'deconstruction' requires that everyone must become as mad as hatters, or madder – for, of course, even Lewis Carroll's Hatter is full of assumptions, philosophical or otherwise, for instance about the sexual identity of 'Time', about Alice not knowing what he means, or about what it means to know and speak to Time:

> 'If you knew Time as well as I do,' said the Hatter, 'you wouldn''t talk about wasting *it*. It's *him*.'

1

'I don't know what you mean,' said Alice.

'Of course you don't!' the Hatter said, tossing his head contemptuously. 'I dare say you never even spoke to Time!'   (Carroll, 1960, p. 69)

How could one possibly 'eradicate all assumptions', and not only eradicate them but *at the same time* still manage to know what and where a text was and what it would mean to 'approach' it?

I offer a hypothesis: your definition is haunted by the anxiety that, with deconstruction, the very possibility of a dictionary explodes. After all, how could one have a dictionary if, as you put it, 'no text can have a fixed and stable meaning'? The very possibility of defining any words at all appears to shatter. No, the prospect of deconstruction is apparently too much to think about, even if it does seem necessary to retain the word in your authoritative new edition. Deconstruction is ridiculous. You don't say this, but you imply it through the use of the verb 'to assert': deconstruction '*asserts* that no text can have a fixed and stable meaning . . . .' Of course you cannot possibly believe that such an assertion is true or has any value. But then why bother to offer such a self-evidently absurd definition? One thing at least seems clear: there is to be no eradication of certain basic assumptions on the part of the Editor of *Chambers Dictionary*, including the assumption (which I must admit I find incomprehensibly baffling) that it is possible for 'language to represent reality adequately'. What on earth do you mean? In the beginning there was reality, after a while along came language in order to represent it, and lo, over all the lands and waters there was adequateness (adequacy of language and also, one must suppose, adequacy of languages and between languages). What is this 'reality' you are talking about? How can 'language' be simply separate from it? I imagine you will be telling me next that you dare say I never even spoke to reality! Convinced I must, after all, have been hallucinating, I go back to check your definition once again – but there it is, the very words I have cited. I tremble at this gobbledegook. I don't know where to turn.

What is deconstruction? Allow me, if you will, to quote one or two other dictionary definitions in order to try to clarify matters. As I said, 'deconstruction' does not appear in *Chambers* prior to 1993: it is absent from the 1988 edition. But it is at around that time that 'deconstruction' (in the senses with which we are concerned here) 'enters the language', as the saying goes; for the word does appear in the 1989 new edition of the *Oxford English Dictionary*, where it is defined as follows:

deconstruction   [f. DE + CONSTRUCTION]
a.   The action of undoing the construction of a thing.
b.   *Philos.* and *Lit. Theory.* A strategy of critical analysis associated with the French philosopher Jacques Derrida (b. 1930), directed towards

exposing unquestioned metaphysical assumptions and internal contra-
dictions in philosophical and literary language.

Now this seems to me a much better definition than your own. The *OED*
definition at least makes some sense – which, sadly, is more than can be
said for the *Chambers* effort. It is useful, too, in that it draws attention to
the fact that the word has a history and has different meanings: the older
sense of 'deconstruction' as 'undoing the construction of a thing' dates
back, says the *OED*, to at least 1882.

But there are other ways in which their definition strikes me as preferable to your own. First, the *OED* does well, I think, in suggesting that
'deconstruction' in its more contemporary usage is best understood in
terms of its association with the writings of Jacques Derrida. Many others
have written deconstructive texts, many others have contributed towards
the continuing elaboration of what is called deconstruction, but Derrida
remains the key figure for an understanding of what deconstruction is
about. It will be especially to his writings that I shall refer in the remainder of this letter, when and where it seems helpful. Secondly, *Chambers*
sees deconstruction as a 'method', whereas the *OED* defines it as 'a strategy'. Thirdly, *Chambers* describes deconstruction as something that is
'applied', whereas the *OED* defines it as an 'analysis'. And finally,
Chambers sees deconstruction as concerned especially with literary texts,
whereas the *OED* associates it more broadly with philosophy and literary
theory.

Now all this may seem to you like quibbling, but if lexicographers are
not concerned with the details of definitions, who else can be expected to
be? Of course you would be quite justified in claiming that *Chambers* is not
the *OED*: you don't have pages and pages in which to expatiate and furnish details and examples of when and where the word 'deconstruction'
has been used or mentioned (or undecidably used *and* mentioned, as
deconstructive thinking would invite us to consider). Fair enough. But the
differences are still there, even if one is simply comparing the *Chambers*
definition with the one that appears in the so-called *New Shorter OED*.
(That title raises curious questions, don't you think? A dictionary can be
shorter and yet still the 'same' dictionary? How short could it be and still
be the same dictionary? Might it be limitable to a single entry, for example 'deconstruction'? *The Shortest of All OEDs. . . .*) In any case, slipped in
somewhere between 'decongestion' and 'decontamination', here is the
definition given in *The New Shorter Oxford English Dictionary* (1993):

deconstruction   n. 1. The reverse of construction; taking to pieces. *rare*,
L19. 2. A strategy of critical analysis of (esp. philosophical and literary)
language and texts which emphasizes features exposing unquestioned
assumptions and inconsistencies. L20.

Impossibly, I want to do justice to these different definitions. (There, in passing, is another definition, perhaps: deconstruction is the attempt to come to terms with the fact that justice necessarily 'exceeds law and calculation', that it cannot be programmed but comes from the future, and that 'one must always say perhaps for justice': see Derrida, 1990a, p. 971.) If I say that the *Chambers* definition is less accurate, less responsible than the longer or shorter *OED*'s, this does not mean I find the *OED* definitions unproblematic. I want to spell out what is just plain *wrong* about your definition; but I also want to suggest that none of these definitions is finally perhaps very useful.

As I was saying, on the subject of your definition of deconstruction as 'a method . . . applied *esp* to literary texts': one of the most lucid and concise texts that Derrida has written on the subject of 'what is deconstruction?' is 'Letter to a Japanese Friend'. (A letter, like the one you are reading at the moment: I believe there is some significance in this fact of letter writing, I mean to do with the nature of deconstruction. Letter writing is strangely lonely, alone but not alone. It is singular – just me writing, for example, to just you – but also general, in the sense that a letter must in principle be readable in our absence, even after our deaths. Finally, letter writing will have been an experience – the experience and experiment of a writing in which I do not readily know what I am going to say. In another epistolary text, called 'Telepathy', Derrida appropriately recalls Flaubert observing, in a letter to Louise, 'Only just up, I am writing to you without knowing what I am going to say' (Derrida, 1988b, p. 12). This also makes me think of *Aspects of the Novel* (1927), where E. M. Forster recounts the anecdote about the old lady who is 'accused by her nieces of being illogical' and who exclaims: 'How can I tell what I think till I see what I say?' (Forster, 1976, p. 99). Deconstruction is about precisely this sort of tension with the unpredictable and unforeseeable. I'm sorry, perhaps I appear to have drifted off the point: in any case, I hereby suspend this parenthesis.)

In his 'Letter to a Japanese Friend' Derrida flatly and simply declares: 'Deconstruction is not a method and cannot be transformed into one' (Derrida, 1991, p. 273). His point is that deconstruction is not a method that can be applied to, say, a literary text (or to a philosophical or any other text, including a dictionary, or to film or weaving or feminism or drugs or psychoanalysis or love, etcetera and so on). Richard Beardsworth offers a good gloss on this:

> Derrida is careful to avoid this term ['method'] because it carries connotations of a procedural form of judgement. A thinker with a method has already decided *how* to proceed, is unable to give him or herself up to the matter of thought in hand, is a functionary of the criteria which structure his or her conceptual gestures. For Derrida . . . this is irresponsibility itself. (Beardsworth, 1996, p. 4)

The term 'method' also suggests something systematic and closed, a procedure that comes to an end. The *OED*'s use of the words 'strategy' and 'analysis' is preferable, so long as one is trying to reckon with these as *interminable*. I don't want to appear disingenuous: I can't pretend that there haven't been people who have sought precisely to present deconstruction as a method, as if it were possible to apply it to this or that. Indeed there's recently been an entire volume, entitled *Applying: To Derrida* (1996), devoted to exposing this error of supposing that deconstruction was something to be simply *applied*. As Geoffrey Bennington acidly notes, in the opening essay of that volume: 'The demand for application . . . in fact reinforces the structure which means that nothing ever gets applied and that we spend our time theorizing about the more or less tragic or culpable failure to apply' (Brannigan et al., 1996, p. 6). Suffice to say – and I hope you will forgive the bluntness of my phrasing – deconstruction in that sense was never of much use to anyone at all. That was a principally North American version of 'deconstruction', in vogue in the late 1970s and early 1980s, the sort often (though often too quickly and misleadingly) identified with the so-called 'Yale School' in the United States, the sort of formalistic deconstruction that was later so brilliantly and devastatingly criticized by Rodolphe Gasché (1986) and Geoffrey Bennington (1988). Little more than an updated version of American New Criticism, this was deconstruction as the close reading of mainly literary texts, concerned with foregrounding moments of indeterminacy, paradox and inconsistency.

When deconstruction first took hold (like a virus or parasite) in North American and Western European universities in the late 1970s and early 1980s, it was generally associated with the idea of a strategy concerned with conceptual oppositions (speech/writing, presence/absence, inside/ outside, and so on), and more particularly with acknowledging that such oppositions always entail a 'violent hierarchy' (Derrida, 1981, p. 41): one of the poles of the opposition (speech, for example) is, in a specific context which must itself be demonstrated, privileged over its supposed opposite (writing, for example). Deconstruction involves an overturning of this hierarchy and a reinscription or transformation of the basis on which the opposition functioned in the first place. It always sounds stupidly formalistic when it is put like this, and that is where I can appreciate the difficulties you must have been in (and, I must add, you still are in) as regards how to define 'deconstruction'.

It was this formalistic sense of deconstruction that no doubt led Derrida to say, in 1980, that 'deconstruction' 'is a word I have never liked and one whose fortune has disagreeably surprised me' (Derrida, 1983, p. 44). His dislike is instructive. On the one hand, it is a good example of the fact that deconstruction does not belong to anyone, it is not something anyone (you or I or Derrida) can control, it has a strange viral, parasitic or ghostly life of its own. On the other hand, Derrida has not given up in despair and stopped using the word 'deconstruction': on the contrary, he has persisted in using it and indeed persisted in helping to transform and multiply the contexts in which it takes place. These contexts would include but would certainly not be confined to, for example, architecture, legal studies, nursing, computers and technology, poetry and fiction, ethics, hermeneutics, cultural studies, postcolonial studies, drugs, ghosts, et cetera. Indeed, throughout the 1990s deconstruction just went on multiplying, showing up almost everywhere and anywhere, but above all *keeping moving:* its status or stability is, if you will, that which is essentially destabilizing, on the move. As Derrida observes in 'Afterword' (as it happens, once again, a text written in the form of a letter), first published in 1988, deconstruction is above all

> this destabilization on the move in, if one could speak thus, 'things themselves'; but it is not negative. Destabilization is required for 'progress' as well. And the 'de-' of *deconstruction* signifies not the demolition of what is constructing itself, but rather what remains to be thought beyond the constructivist or destructionist scheme. (Derrida, 1988a, p. 147)

Deconstruction, Derrida says, 'is just visiting' (Derrida, 1995, p. 29): it *apparitions itself* everywhere. Deconstruction is a sort of ghost-effect inscribing 'things themselves'. 'The logic of spectrality', he remarks, is 'inseparable from the very motif . . . of deconstruction' (Derrida, 1994, p. 178).

So, am I beginning to make sense when I say that you cannot say that deconstruction is 'a method'? Richard Beardsworth's point is that 'method' is misleading because deconstruction has to do with what cannot be formalized or anticipated. Deconstruction has to do with the unforeseeable, the incalculable, indeed the impossible. As Timothy Clark stresses: 'Since deconstruction cannot be anticipated or programmed it is indeed *impossible,* in the strict sense of not falling within the realm of the possible or calculable' (Clark, 1992, p. 190). This in turn calls to mind what Derrida himself has described as 'the least bad definition' of 'deconstruction', namely 'the *experience of the impossible*' (Derrida, 1992, p. 200). This definition involves a notion of necessity, he says, which is no longer opposed, or in contradiction, to the impossible. It is, for example, a necessary possibility that a letter can fail to reach its destination: this necessity, which is part of the very structure of writing as telecommunication, means that any letter, any text is haunted by this possibility of non-arrival. For instance, this letter that you are reading at the moment. It is not simply a question of an inefficient postal system in a supposedly literal sense, but rather to do with a sense that we can never be quite sure that any letter, any text, has ever completely, fully, finally arrived. This element or characteristic of writing or reading is not thinkable: Derrida has on occasion called it '"death"' or 'the nonpresent *remainder*' (Derrida, 1988a, pp. 8, 10). As Bennington has succinctly phrased it, 'deconstruction is not what you think' (Bennington, 1989, p. 84). This is why the question 'what is deconstruction?' is itself evidence of a serious naivety, for deconstruction *is*, above all perhaps, a questioning of the 'is', a concern with what remains to be thought, with what cannot be thought within the present.

This is also where I have to say that the *OED* gets things just as wrong as *Chambers* does, because what all of these dictionary definitions fail to register is that deconstruction is not restricted to so-called 'philosophy and literary theory'. Deconstruction has to do with identity and experience in general. Permit me to attempt a very brief explanation of this in terms of the notion of the text. A widespread misunderstanding – one that you share with the editors of the *Oxford English Dictionary* and many others – is that deconstruction has to do, not with experience or real life or 'reality' (as you call it), but with language and, in particular, with texts.

The misunderstanding of deconstruction as 'textual', a 'method' or style of writing or reading texts, will no doubt last as long as deconstruction 'itself' (as if one could say such a thing: deconstruction is always different from itself, always deconstruction*s*). But, as I said, I want to try to do justice – however impossible that may be – to what I believe is going on with this strange word, concept, phenomenon, experience: deconstruction. Consider what is, in this context, perhaps Derrida's most famous proposition: 'There is nothing outside the text' (*il n'y a pas de hors-texte*)' (Derrida, 1976, p. 163). Bennington comments on this in his short aphoristic essay, 'Deconstruction is not what you think':

'Text' is not quite an extension of a familiar concept, but a displacement or reinscription of it. Text in general is any system of marks, traces, referrals (don't say reference, have a little more sense than that). Perception is a text . . . . Deconstruction does not have a place for language over here, and a world over there to which it refers. Elements in the language refer to one another for their identity, and refer to non-linguistic marks which refer in turn to their identity and difference. There is no essential difference between language and the world, the one as subject, the other as object. There are traces. (Bennington, 1989, p. 84)

Deconstruction has to do with traces, with the logic of the 'nonpresent remainder', with a much broader and more ghostly conception of language than, for example, your dictionary definition might seem able to tolerate.

What Derrida has done with 'text' is to have demonstrated how it opens onto what he calls 'unbounded generalization' (Derrida, 1983, p. 40). As he puts it, in 'Living On: Border Lines', a text is

> no longer a finished corpus of writing, some content enclosed in a book or its margins, but a differential network, a fabric of traces referring endlessly to something other than itself, to other differential traces. Thus the text overruns all the limits assigned to it so far (not submerging or drowning them in an undifferentiated homogeneity, but rather making them more complex, dividing and multiplying strokes and lines) – all the limits, everything that was to be set up in opposition to writing (speech, life, the world, the real, history, and what not, every field of reference – to body or mind, conscious or unconscious, politics, economics, and so forth).   (Derrida, 1979, p. 84)

If deconstruction has to do with sorts of 'conceptual breakthrough' such as this, the consequences for dictionary editors are no doubt challenging. As Derrida has phrased it:

> Every conceptual breakthrough amounts to transforming, that is to say deforming, an accredited, authorized relationship between a word and a concept, between a trope and what one had every interest to consider to be an unshiftable primary sense, a proper, literal or current usage. (Derrida, 1983, pp. 40–1)

Imagine an edition of *Chambers Dictionary* which, under every entry, would offer a definition of what is currently taken as being a word's 'unshiftable primary sense', its 'proper, literal or current usage', and then, immediately supplementing that, would offer an extensive exposition of the 'unbounded generalization' of that same word. What a user's guide that would be! Interminable: the experience of the impossible.

Permit me to summarize all this by trying to say something about what is called constative and performative language. Indeed, this is perhaps the most useful way of starting to think about deconstruction. (Doubtless that is where I should have begun, or did begin but without explicitly remarking it as such. And I might have commented on the words of address with which I began: 'Dear Madam/Sir . . . .' I might have said something about the loving affirmation, the singular but general *affection* signalled in the word 'Dear', about the 'Dear' as apostrophe, as the figure of address which inaugurates the singularity of this letter while at the same time remarking its belonging to the generality of the genre of letter-writing. I might have said something also, perhaps, about my uncertainty concerning who you are, for instance whether a man or a woman – for your dictionary only specifies 'the Editor' (*Chambers*, 1998, p. vii), without identifying her or him by name. All of this in any case will have been at work through this letter, scattering its effects.) Constative language is language when it is supposedly simply stating something: your language, the discourse of the dictionary, is a conventional and very powerful example of this. 'Deconstruction', you say, is such-and-such. This is an apparently constative statement, a statement of fact or at least definition. You define it as follows: '*Adj* **constative** (of a statement) that can be true or false; that implies assertion rather than performance. – *n* such a statement (opposed to *performative*)'. Performative language, on the other hand, is language when it is not simply saying, but *doing* something *by saying*. Again, to quote your own definition: '*adj* **performative** of a statement or verb that itself constitutes the action described', '*n* such a statement (*opp* of *constative*)'. The example you give, and which I have always found so touching, ironic and beautiful, is: '*I confess my ignorance*'. Other examples of performative statements would be promises, threats, acts of naming or instituting, pronouncing someone dead, et cetera. (You may care to note in passing that this notion of language as performative immediately and irrevocably complicates the idea that language could be assumed to 'represent reality adequately': performative language does something, in actuality, *in reality, with reality*.)

In a wide range of texts, including 'Signature Event Context', 'Limited Inc a b c . . .', 'Envois' and 'Psyche: Inventions of the Other', Derrida has demonstrated how the relationship between the constative and the performative is one of mutual contamination: any so-called constative statement will have a performative element, if only in so far as it is readable or intelligible, in other words in so far as it calls for an event or experience of reading, listening or whatever, that must in itself be susceptible to the unforeseeable or incalculable. Thus every definition in a dictionary is not simply constative but performative, generative, in collusion with chance, one might say – except that this collusion can never be simply foreseen or calculated. What I have been saying to you here in this letter is itself a demonstration (a very poor one, perhaps, but a demonstration nevertheless) of the performative effects of your definition of 'deconstruction', of the fact that definitions do not merely state things but have effects. I had to write to you, like I said. On the other hand, any so-called performative statement will have a constative element: one cannot name a baby or make a promise or inaugurate a new institution without this event being recognizable, in other words without conforming to the *constative* nature of conventions, rules or laws.

In performative fashion, deconstruction seeks to take as fully into account as possible the ways in which all performatives are necessarily haunted by a nonpresent remainder, by what remains to be thought, calculated or experienced: it tries to engage, for example, with the consequences of the fact that every performative can only be what it is in so far as it is structured by the necessary possibility that it fails or goes astray.

But deconstruction is also undecidably performative *and* constative in its concern with producing new effects, new languages, new institutions, new forms of politics, friendship, democracy, internationalism and so on. As Derrida has remarked:

> Deconstruction is inventive or it is nothing at all; it does not settle for methodical procedures, it opens up a passageway, it marches ahead and leaves a trail; its writing is not only performative, it produces rules – other conventions – for new performatives and never installs itself in the theoretical assurance of a simple opposition between performative and constative.   (Derrida, 1989, p. 42)

So, let me reiterate, in case it hasn't been clear: it is not a matter of saying we can or should get rid of dictionaries. We must have dictionaries, especially ones like yours: I will always love *Chambers Dictionary*. And the concepts of the constative and performative (which you define with such elegance and economy) are invaluable. We must have constative statements, definitions that aspire to having the authority of truth. Take, for example, the following definitional, constative statement by Derrida:

> Deconstruction is neither a theory nor a philosophy. It is neither a school nor a method. It is not even a discourse, nor an act, nor a practice. It is what happens, what is happening today in what is called society, politics, diplomacy, economics, historical reality, and so on and so forth. Deconstruction is the case. I say this not only because I think it is true and because I could demonstrate it if we had time; but also to give an example of a *statement*.   (Derrida 1990b, p. 85)

There you go then, another definition of deconstruction: 'It is what happens, what is happening today'. Imagine using that as your dictionary definition. It would seem a bit vague, I suspect. But in a sense Derrida's statement here strikes me as true as well as useful: if there were one word for describing the late twentieth century, for summarizing what at the start of the twenty-first century has been happening and is continuing to happen, both in the so-called Western world and beyond, it might be 'deconstruction'. (To put it like that is no doubt a little provocative, I know – it has to be understood on the proviso that, as I've been trying to stress, deconstruction has to do with what is *not* present, for example with what makes every identity at once itself and different from itself, haunted, contaminated, set beside itself. I also wish passionately to drive home to you the fact that, as a sort of parasite or foreign body, deconstruction is not concerned with *destroying* its host. As Derrida has emphasized: 'the idea that a deconstructive discourse might come to command and replace other practices, discursive or not, is a kind of madness or comedy that doesn't interest me in the least' (Derrida, 1993, p. 229). End of another parasitical parenthesis.)

Now the 'example of a *statement*' I quoted a moment or two ago – from a text with a title that would put the wind up any lexicographer ('Some Statements and Truisms about Neo-Logisms, Newisms, Postisms, Parasitisms, and other Small Seismisms') – was originally given as a lecture in 1987, at a symposium entitled 'The States of "Theory"', at the University of Southern California at Irvine. It is a definition of deconstruction that is marked by the singularity of that occasion. Despite its constative, statemental status, it is also *doing something* in the process, and this something is not only different from what went before (no one had ever before defined deconstruction in quite this way, in quite this context), but also different in so far as it remains to be thought, it remains to be reckoned with by, for example, you.

Please forgive me for having taken up so much of your valuable time. Perhaps I should have tried, like the mad Hatter, to speak to time. In any case, I can't help wondering what you are going to make of all this. If I appear to have been going on so much about deconstruction in relation to language, I'm sorry: it's just that you are the editor of a dictionary and I really wanted to get some basics sorted out. Basics would include, as I have tried to make clear, a sense of deconstruction as what goes beyond language, certainly beyond any ordinary sense of the word 'language'. If you want a few summary suggestions for a definition of deconstruction in the future, I humbly propose some or all of the following:

> **deconstruction**   n. not what you think: the experience of the impossible: what remains to be thought: a logic of destabilization always already on the move in 'things themselves': what makes every identity at once itself and different from itself: a logic of spectrality: a theoretical and practical parasitism or virology: what is happening today in what is called society, politics, diplomacy, economics, historical reality, and so on: the opening of the future itself.

I add that last definition as a sort of postscript. It is Derrida's phrase, another phrase for deconstruction:

> the opening of the future itself, a future which does not allow itself to be modalized or modified into the form of the present, which allows itself neither to be fore-seen nor pro-grammed; it is thus also the opening to freedom, responsibility, decision, ethics and politics, so many *terms* that would therefore have to be withdrawn from the deconstructible logic of presence, conscience or intention.
>
> (Derrida, 1992, p. 200)

That's it. I have to stop. It will be obvious to you by now that I cannot send this. I ask myself: what would it mean to suppose that a letter like this could reach its destination? I ask you, dear, anonymous reader.

WORKS CITED

Beardsworth, Richard (1996), *Derrida and the Political* (London: Routledge).

Bennington, Geoffrey (1988), 'Deconstruction and the Philosophers (The Very Idea)', *Oxford Literary Review*, **10**, pp. 73–130; reprinted in Geoffrey Bennington, *Legislations: The Politics of Deconstruction* (London: Verso, 1994).

Bennington, Geoffrey (1989), 'Deconstruction Is Not What You Think', in *Deconstruction Omnibus Volume*, ed. Andreas Papadakis, Catherine Cooke and Andrew Benjamin (London: Academy Editions), p. 84.

Brannigan, John, Ruth Robbins and Julian Wolfreys (eds) (1996), *Applying to Derrida* (London: Macmillan).

Carroll, Lewis (1960), *Alice's Adventures in Wonderland* and *Through the Looking-Glass* (New York: Signet).

Chambers English Dictionary (Edinburgh: Chambers, 1988).

The Chambers Dictionary (Edinburgh: Chambers, 1993).

The Chambers Dictionary (Edinburgh: Chambers, 1998).

Clark, Timothy (1992) *Derrida, Heidegger, Blanchot: Sources of Derrida's Notion and Practice of Literature* (Cambridge: Cambridge University Press).

Derrida, Jacques (1976), *Of Grammatology*, trans. Gayatri Chakravorty Spivak (Baltimore, MD: Johns Hopkins Press).

Derrida, Jacques (1979), 'Living On', trans. James Hulbert, in Harold Bloom *et al.* (ed.), *Deconstruction and Criticism* (New York: Seabury Press), pp. 75–176.

Derrida, Jacques (1981), *Positions*, trans. Alan Bass (London: Athlone Press).

Derrida, Jacques (1983), 'The Time of a Thesis: Punctuations', trans. Kathleen McLaughlin, in *Philosophy in France Today*, ed. Alan Montefiore (Cambridge: Cambridge University Press), pp. 34–50.

Derrida, Jacques (1987), 'Envois', in *The Post Card: From Socrates to Freud and Beyond*, trans. Alan Bass (Chicago, IL: Chicago University Press), pp. 1–256.

Derrida, Jacques (1988a), 'Signature Event Context', trans. Samuel Weber and Jeffrey Mehlman; 'Limited Inc a b c . . .', and 'Afterword: Toward an Ethic of Discussion', trans. Samuel Weber, in *Limited Inc.* (Evanston, IL: Northwestern University Press).

Derrida, Jacques (1988b), 'Telepathy', trans. Nicholas Royle, *Oxford Literary Review*, **10**, pp. 3–41.

Derrida, Jacques (1989), 'Psyche: Inventions of the Other', trans. Catherine Porter, in *Reading de Man Reading*, ed. Lindsay Waters and Wlad Godzich (Minneapolis, MN: University of Minnesota Press).

Derrida, Jacques (1990a), 'Force of Law: The "Mystical Foundation of Authority"', trans. Mary Quaintance, *Cardozo Law Review*, **11**, 5/6, pp. 921–1045.

Derrida, Jacques (1990b), 'Some Statements and Truisms about Neo-Logisms, Newisms, Postisms, Parasitisms, and other Small Seismisms', trans. Anne Tomiche, in *The States of 'Theory': History, Art and Critical Discourse*, ed. David Carroll (New York: Columbia University Press), pp. 63–95.

Derrida, Jacques (1991), 'Letter to a Japanese Friend', trans. David Wood and Andrew Benjamin, in *A Derrida Reader: Between the Blinds*, ed. Peggy Kamuf (London and New York: Harvester), pp. 270–6.

Derrida, Jacques (1992), 'Afterw.rds: or, at least, less than a letter about a letter less', trans. Geoffrey Bennington, in *Afterwords*, ed. Nicholas Royle (Tampere, Finland: Outside Books).

Derrida, Jacques (1993), 'Politics and Friendship: An Interview with Jacques Derrida', in *The Althusserian Legacy*, ed. E. Ann Kaplan and Michael Sprinker (London: Verso).

Derrida, Jacques (1994), *Specters of Marx: The State of the Debt, the Work of Mourning, and the New International*, trans. Peggy Kamuf (London: Routledge).

Derrida, Jacques (1995), 'The Time is Out of Joint', trans. Peggy Kamuf, in *Deconstruction is/in America: A New Sense of the Political*, ed. Anselm Haverkamp (New York: New York University Press), pp. 14–38.

Forster, E. M. (1976), *Aspects of the Novel*, ed. Oliver Stallybrass (Harmondsworth: Penguin).

Gasché, Rodolphe (1986), *The Tain of the Mirror: Derrida and the Philosophy of Reflection* (Cambridge, MA: Harvard University Press).

The New Shorter Oxford English Dictionary on Historical Principles, ed. Lesley Brown, 2 vols (Oxford: Clarendon Press, 1993).

The Oxford English Dictionary, 2nd edn, prepared by J. A. Simpson and E. S. C. Weiner, 20 vols (Oxford: Clarendon Press, 1989).

2
Deconstruction and Cultural Studies: Arguments for a Deconstructive Cultural Studies

Gayatri Chakravorty Spivak

> The urge to put Derrida 'to use' in such critical discourses as New Historicism and Cultural Studies only underscores the resistance to the truly philosophical nature of deconstruction.
>
> Stuart Barnett, *Hegel After Derrida*

Derrida's copious teaching notes, published these days almost as is, remind us that teaching is no more than a 'who wins loses' style game against its own destined errancy.[1] A teacher will say, everyone knows this. I am not sure. Aristotle's class notes, Hegel's class notes, Saussure's class notes seem to have frozen into orthodoxies of various kinds. 'Culture' is learned without teachers, even as it is taught by parents and elders, of both genders, in different ways. 'Cultural Studies' is a terrible misnomer, now that it has been around long enough for people to have forgotten that it was originally a study of the politics of those who claim dominant culture. 'Civilizational competence' is learned by those ambitious to enter the discourse of the masters, even if to destabilize it. The institutionalization of Cultural Studies has something like a relationship with the missed crossings between errant tendencies. This essay runs after them, necessarily in vain.

I CLAIMING ANCESTORS AND TELEOPOESIS

Let us first recite the divided origin of what is metropolitan Cultural Studies today: in the sixties in Britain, Richard Hoggart publishes *Uses of*

14

Literacy; Stuart Hall founds Cultural Studies in Birmingham; the first group of students produce *Empire Strikes Back*, a manifesto; *Women Take Issue*, the feminist supplement, appears in 1978.[2]

Also in 1978, in the United States, Edward W. Said's *Orientalism* brings forth a scholarly interest in the constitution of the conquered stranger as other. (The general difference in mood between UK and US Cultural Studies can be observed in the difference between Paul Gilroy's two books, *There Ain't No Black in the Union Jack* (Gilroy, 1987) and *The Black Atlantic* (Gilroy, 1993), the latter in the company of Martin Bernal, Ivan Van Sertima, Jack D. Forbes, all in the Said tradition.) A related but different story is also part of the account of US cultural studies. Lyndon Johnson had lifted the alien quotas with the new immigration act of 1965, and thus ushered in an enormous rise in Asian (including Indian) immigration. A proportion of their children, who may loosely constitute an upwardly mobile model minority, begin to inaugurate varieties of 'national origin' or 'hybridist' Cultural Studies. Already existing Pan-Africanist tendencies within the upwardly mobile sections of the beneficiaries of the Civil Rights movement feed into these tendencies, *mutatis mutandis*. Chicano/as, Latino/as, straddling two imperialisms (the Spanish and the American), become more starkly visible in this growing field. We learn of Rodolfo Acuña's *Occupied America* and Mario Barrera's *Race and Class in the Southwest*'s theories of internal colonization.[3] Asian-Americans early cathect a diversified history. Maxine Hong Kingston's *The Woman Warrior* inaugurates that thematic.[4] The oppressed autochthone, coming late to this collective claiming of 'culture' as an object of study, hits the mainstream with Leslie Marmon Silko's *Almanac of the Dead*.[5] The legacy of the Sioux Ghost Dance, celebrated in Silko's novel as the beginning of a revised cultural politics reactive to the encounter with the foreigner – French and British – dates back to the end of the previous century, of course. Curiously enough, it is to this legacy that Jacques Derrida, and therefore deconstruction, quietly allies him/itself in *Specters of Marx*: 'the past as absolute future.'[6]

By this reckoning, deconstructive Cultural Studies would also be a claiming of ancestors. In *Specters*, Derrida claims Marx in a common legacy of Abrahamic messianicity. 'There is no culture without a cult of ancestors, a ritualization of mourning and sacrifice . . . The very concept of culture may seem to be synonymous with the culture of death, as if the expression "culture of death" were ultimately a pleonasm or a tautology. But only such a redundancy can make legible the cultural difference and the grid of borders' (Derrida, 1993, p. 43).

The power and mutating foundation of metropolitan Cultural Studies can be read as the movement of the colonized towards the colonizer, with a reversal-displacement of the 'cultural difference [across a] grid of borders' that had been laid down as impassable political frontiers by the col-

onizing powers – rememorizing a history legitimately inherited only by
the latter. In the process, that *topos* of *postcolonial* writing that insists that
colonialism imposed a new civilization upon colonized space without
proper burial rites for the earlier one is turned around. Cultural Studies
calls the glass half full and reclaims a transformed history, ancestors-in-
poesis – imaginatively Janus-faced.

I was a student of English Honours at the University of Calcutta, where
the curriculum was straightforward 'Brit. Lit'. If we thought of the study
of culture, we thought of neighbouring Shantiniketan, where
Rabindranath Tagore had established his experimental school, college
and University. Tagore was among the first thinkers of Cultural Studies
in India. As he wrote of Viswa-Bharati, the University, three years before
his death: 'Gradually another idea entered the school – India's connection
to the world upon the terrain of culture'.[7] This confident nationalist invocation of an eclectic high culture is not necessarily what we understand by
Cultural Studies today. Yet this impulse, like nation-think itself, can be
found in other guises in metropolitan Cultural Studies today. The lineaments of the earlier idea are to be seen in Mnouchkine's gorgeous work,
or Peter Brook's noble production of the Indian epic *Mahabharata* (1985).
    In the New York production of the Brook epic, at the inception or the
high point of the epic battle, a group of East Asians burst into *hingshay
unmotto prithhi* – 'the world is mad with violence' – accompanying themselves on the harmonium. Tagore had made lyric music available to the
Bengali middle class, in order that they may take the 'best of the colonizing culture'. The harmonium is ubiquitous in middle-class households. In
the Bengali context, such a song sung to the harmonium is hopelessly
kitsch. Lacking this cultural information, Brook connects to Tagore's original impulse, including his effort to welcome the high cultures of China
and Japan into his Cultural Studies project. Watching this (for me) contradictory moment at the Brooklyn Academy of Music, I thought precisely of Tagore's words – India's connection to the world upon the
terrain of [high] culture. *Shanskriti* (Bengali) or *samskrti* (Sanskrit) – the
word Tagore uses for 'culture' – carries within it an implication of refine-
ment.
    Although the local 'tribal' Santals of Bolpur and a general imaginary of
rural India provided colour for many of the thematics of the new school
at Shantiniketan, the 'tribals' were not Tagore's partners. For *Cultural
Studies*, Tagore looked mostly up at the ancient Hindu philosophical non-
dualistic *Upanisads* and out at 'the world'. Those were his ancestors and
his kin. If, by contrast, we include the Santals (and the other ninety million 'tribal' or 'aboriginal' peoples) in our claim for ancestry and kinship,
we would get something like the following:

India's wide range of altitude, rainfall and geological conditions has given rise to an enormous diversity of ecosystems supporting some 81,000 recorded animal species and 45,000 plant species. Such biological diversity has nurtured cultural diversity . . . The country has 4,365 distinct ethnic communities, 325 languages, six major religions and dozens of smaller independent faiths, and ways of life ranging from hunting and gathering through farming and herding to craft working and industrial processing. The last century, however, has seen a sharp decline in biological and cultural diversity throughout India, the rate of loss accelerating in the last few decades as the development process has taken hold.[8]

It is interesting that during the very century that nationalist intellectuals were laying the foundation for an elite and international 'Indian' culture that still survives in peculiar transformations, subaltern cultural diversity, according to the authors (all from the Indian Institute of Public Administration) of the passage above, suffered a sharp decline. I will suggest later that, in globalization, this pre-text is once again important; and ignored by Cultural Studies because of its suppression at the origin. The point where Cultural Studies in India (or anywhere in the South) touches Cultural Studies in the metropolis is around the issue of multiculturalism. Ecology has no part to play there.

It is by problematizing the connection between debates such as the one over secularism in India [writes Partha Chatterjee] and those within liberal-democratic theory in the West that it might be possible to fight the attitude, present even in the hallowed precincts of philosophical discourse, which Arjun Appadurai has described as 'Intelligent multiculturalism for us, bloody ethnicity or mindless tribalisms for them'.[9]

It is my conviction that the Tagorean variety of Cultural Studies, not necessarily so well institutionalized as Tagore's educational experiment, can be located elsewhere as well under the auspices of the colonialisms of the last century; and that it provides a sort of discontinuous prehistory for much US Cultural Studies today. It is a directedness towards the imaginative component in other 'cultures', among whom the imaginative members of the colonizing 'culture' are prominently included. Although the connection is not often made public in the mainstream, its vector directs much of the US Cultural Studies initiative. Fanon's resistant writing got its first impulse from a foiling of this hope, held only by the indigenous colonial elite: the colony's connection to the world upon the terrain of culture. How would the ghost of such a composite ancestor think the future? The word 'culture' is a name for a complex strategic situation in a particular type of society. And the prayer to be haunted by this hybrid ghost is a robust acceptance of the fact that the old civilization of the colonized had been suppressed without proper funeral rites.[10]

The colonized intellectual claims a culturally differentiated common humanity with the colonizer. This is the condition of possibility of mimicry: to be different yet same. This is the description of the hybrid: a mixture of difference and sameness.[11] The failure of this vector – the assimilated Christian Martiniquais treated like a Negro in France – writes Fanon's desire for Africa, a ghost cleansed of hybridity, given an essentiality that the spectre cannot furnish. The dynamics of the vector makes the early DuBois write: 'I sit with Shakespeare and he winces not' (DuBois, 1970, p. 51).

This is imagination speaking, *poesis* not *istoria*.[12] This version of Cultural Studies does not check the historical Shakespeare's proclivities towards racism. Latterday claims for varieties of destabilizing subalternities can be read within this template.

At about the same time as Tagore's Shantiniketan in India, this heliotropic gesture comes into its own, most dazzlingly, in the United States, in the heritage of modern slavery where the ancestor is not merely unmourned but the pulse of ancestry is annihilated. It flowers in the Harlem Renaissance. DuBois claims that 'there are today no truer exponents of the pure human spirit of the Declaration of Independence than the American Negroes', and Alain Locke, of whom more later, writes:

> a more highly stylized art does not exist than the African. If after absorbing the new content of American life and experience, and after assimilating new patterns of art, the original artistic endowment can be sufficiently augmented to express itself with equal power in more complex patterns and substance, then the Negro may well become what some have predicted, the artist of American life.[13]

Another example, though on a different register, is the heritage of the Sioux religion of the Ghost Dance, mentioned above. Here Cultural Studies reverse and displace foundations of a transformed ancestor-claim: 1. the Sioux religion and the first battle of Wounded Knee (1890) ⇨ 2. the ghost dance 'cited' at the uprising of the second Wounded Knee (1973) ⇨ 3. a 'literary citation' in Leslie Marmon Silko, *Almanac of the Dead* (1991). James Mooney's contemporary account of the Ghost Dance religion shows how far the first impulse went towards a human embrace of the foreigner.[14] The Sioux Ghost Dance religion was already a desire to claim a 'poetic' common ancestry for all native Americans that would give the lie to mere 'history'. The step towards the foreigner, the attempt to claim a hybrid ancestry, is where I place Sitting Bull with the forerunners of metropolitan cultural study, figures like W. E. B. DuBois and Rabindranath Tagore.

A deconstructive cultural study would locate other such figures, and would note, not only the kinship, but the differences. Indeed, DuBois himself attempts such an analysis of sameness in difference under various colonial systems and acknowledges their deep ambiguities, in 'The Negro Mind Reaches Out'.[15] In 'The Shadow of France' section of his essay, for example, he asks: 'is Boineuf [of Martinique] an exception or a prophecy?' Such speculations help us understand the chiastic constitution of a figure such as Frantz Fanon, born the year DuBois wrote the essay.

Another deconstructive move can be recalled here. Introduced in Derrida's *Politics of Friendship*, it is the thinking of *teleopoesis* – 'generation by a joint and simultaneous grafting, without a proper body, of the performative and the constative'.[16] Derrida's example here is Nietzsche, who reverses Aristotle's alleged remark 'O my friends, there is no friend' to 'O my enemies, there is no enemy'. He at once *states* (or cites) the earlier remark, for it is specifically upon that remark that he grafts. But he also, of course, performs it in its *reversal*. Imaginative making at a distance – *teleopoesis*. Thus when the bondsman affects and reverse-performs the lord by claiming ancestry, that is *teleopoesis*, an important part of metropolitan Cultural Studies. This imaginative grafting is in the name of a new kind of 'perhaps', 'the possibilization of [an] impossible possible [which] must remain at one and the same time as undecidable – and therefore as decisive – as the future itself' (PF, p. 29). We cannot decide it, and therefore it remains decisive, the unrestricted gamble of claiming the metropolis as (reversed) ancestor.

Just as this 'perhaps' is perhaps an overwriting of Derrida's earlier articulation of ethics as an 'experience of the impossible', so also may this grafting of the performative and the constative be an overwriting of an earlier deconstruction of constitutions as rusing the performative in the constative. The constituted subject is performed by the act of the declaration of independence, yet it signs the declaration as if it was (con)stated beforehand: a ruse. But now a more enabling idea: a grafting. The rusing is the birth of a new nation, the grafting the gesture of the foreign body in the nation: postcoloniality and Cultural Studies – the 'and' a supplement.

There is, then, a performative–constative founding ruse in all constitutions. The specific constitution desired by Nelson Mandela relates to this generality in both similarity and difference by virtue of the asymmetry of historical interest.[17] This is a relationship that entails a judgement. Cultural Studies cannot be a disinterested pursuit. As such, it runs the risk of most things taken under deconstructive advisement – the risk of describing every human science as an ethico-political forcefield whose lineaments are made visible, never fully, through scrupulous close reading. It can be particularly useful for Cultural Studies when it is a study of the politics of who claims dominant culture.

And yet, is this not the occupational hazard of every disciplinary position? To view all that is in terms of the constitutive element of one's discipline, as molecules, as force fields, as philosophemes, as narratemes. . . .

Such a positioning constitutes itself by bracketing, of course, but also by tacitly keeping its constituted opposite at bay. By virtue of being constituted as an opposite, the domesticated difference is also a relationship of sameness. We ask this question, then, of all that we wish to constitute as itself. What does it keep at bay as its constituted opposite? What, for instance, might a Cultural Studies, at the end of the Cold War, keep at bay?

We already have that potted history in hand: migrants in the metropolis as well as a connection with a colonial past, not necessarily interconnected. Indeed, if we want to pursue the second track – tales of conqueror and conquered gradually coming to claim a shared ghost – we will lose ourselves in the temporizing of 'the world' in the displacement of peoples. Such an exploration would redo all the human sciences within a cultural studies paradigm. But that is a collective agenda. I can only look at US Cultural Studies as a discipline seeking to define itself, this being the indefinite nature of all disciplinarity. From what does it seem to be distancing itself today?

If we keep ourselves confined to US tertiary education, the fields that Cultural Studies infiltrates by distancing are, first, Area Studies; secondly, Comparative Literature and, finally, History and Anthropology.

II CROSSING DISCIPLINES

Area Studies in the US were founded in the wake of the Cold War and funded by federal grants, backed up by the great foundations, especially Ford. The United States needed to know foreign countries in order to keep its status intact as a competing superpower. The connection between power and knowledge could not have been clearer. 'To meet the demands of war, scholars of diverse disciplines [of many areas of the globe which had been inadequately studied] were forced to pool their knowledge in frantic attempts to advise administrators and policy maker', says the Introduction to the 'national conference on the study of world areas', which was held in New York on November 28–30, 1947. Language and Area Centers between 1959 and 1968 were authorized by Public Law 85–864, the National Defense Education Act of 1958 (as amended), Title VI. The great foundations are now considering rethinking the area studies mandate after the Cold War. Can deconstruction help?

The geopolitical aim of Area Studies has been an open secret for the last fifty years, although a restricted notion of academic freedom – the disinterested nature of 'the essence of knowledge as knowledge about knowledge' – has allowed the custodians of knowledge to disavow their relationship to the instruments of power.[18] The plea that Derrida made in the eighties, that with students and the research community, in every operation we pursue together (a reading, an interpretation, the construction of a theoretical model, the rhetoric of an argumentation, the treatment of historical material, and even mathematical formalization), we argue or acknowledge that an institutional concept is at play, a type of contract signed, an image of the ideal seminar constructed, a *socius* implied, repeated or displaced, invented, transformed, menaced or destroyed

(Derrida, 1992c, p. 22)

remains as important today as it was then.

Area Studies were mostly committed to the Social Sciences – though 'culture' entered through the soft focus of non-quantitative 'history', especially Art History; and through efficient language learning. For reasons that are not far to seek, the most important Area Studies initiatives were in the areas of East Asia and Latin America. South Asia and the African theatre – the remains of the most recent European imperialisms – were engaged without typical Area Studies mediation. They were uneasily divided between colonial history and Anthropology. The Centers for South Asian Studies were few (Harvard, Berkeley, Pennsylvania), Sanskrit-focus, and German-model. Paradoxically, Southeast Asia, being more directly part of the US empire, was constructed with a more anthropological focus.

This is a rudimentary account of the complex Area Studies phenomenon, which obviously did not stay in one place.

One noticeable thing about Area Studies was high quality combined with openly conservative or 'no' politics. Because they were tied to the politics of power, their ties to the power elite in the countries studied were strong, the quality of their language-learning was generally excellent, and the processing of data often sophisticated, extensive and intensive. Academic 'Cultural Studies', as a metropolitan phenomenon originating in the radical fringes of English Departments, opposes this with no more than English-language based political convictions, in-house debates about expanding the canon, often with visibly foregone conclusions that cannot match the implicit political cunning of Area Studies at their best; and earns itself a reputation for 'lack of rigor', and for politicizing the academy. Can deconstruction help?

As it leaves the cosy shelter of the English department – everything in translation – Cultural Studies must necessarily find its being in the literary shadow of Area Studies, ostensibly well separated from it. This shadow is called 'Comparative Literature'. Area Studies related to foreign 'areas'. Comparative Literature was made up of the literatures of Western European 'nations'. This distinction, between 'areas' – non-European – and 'nations' – European – infected Comparative Literature and Area Studies from the start.

If the 'origin' of Area Studies was the aftermath of the Cold War, the 'origin' of US Comparative Literature had something like a relationship with the events that secured it: European intellectuals fleeing 'totalitarian' regimes. In the 1940s and 1950s, Comparative Literature in the US rose to unprecedented intellectual eminence with a large influx of prominent 'comparatists' (to research the Euro–US transmogrifications in an already existing disciplinary formation would make this relationship visible) seeking refuge from such regimes in Europe, including such men as Erich Auerbach, Leo Spitzer, René Wellek, Renato Poggioli and Claudio Guillén. One might say that US Comparative Literature was founded on inter-European brotherhood, even as Area Studies had been spawned out of inter-regional vigilances. It has been noticed by many and asserted by Derrida that deconstruction found a home in 'Comparative Literature' rather than in 'Philosophy' in the United States. Derrida may have been partly a beneficiary of its originating impulse. It may have kept deconstruction moored to its European provenance, even in its radicalism. It has also kept deconstruction's interest in sexual difference at an uneasy distance from the male-dominated centre of high comparativism. Thus the imperative to re-imagine Comparative Literature is also an imperative to re-imagine deconstruction.

As graduate students of Comparative Literature in the early sixties, we were made to read fantasmatic origins split between Germany and France: Goethe's notion of *Weltliteratur* as a mirror for ourselves and Van Tieghem in the Que-sais-je series giving us a run-down of the French version.[19] We read René Etiemble's *Comparaison n'est pas raison* to get a sense of controversy. We leaned to scoff at influence-studies, referring to them collectively as *Rousseau en Angleterre*. Some of the source texts were Auerbach, Poulet, Curtius, Heller.[20] René Wellek was one of the major movers. I received my degree in Comparative Literature (English, French and German) and went on to teach at the Program in Comparative Literature that Professor Wellek had founded at the University of Iowa. In ten years I was its Chair, was about to bring out *Of Grammatology*, and met Wellek, the grand old man. 'Do you teach oriental languages?', he asked me. He worked on 'national' language Comparative Literature, I was clearly from an 'area'.

One way that this divide is being filled up is by destabilizing the 'nation'-s – introducing Francophony, Teutophony, Lusophony, Anglophony, Hispanophony within the old 'national' boundaries – the biggest winner being 'Global English'. This is so often contested by vested interests that I state my reservations hesitantly. Yet it must be said that this restricted destabilization effort, recalling the initial Birmingham model, is to put some black on the Union Jack or, to put a spin on Jesse Jackson's slogan, to paint the red, white and blue in the colours of the rainbow. You can give it a deconstructive name by 'naturalizing' hospitality and the *arrivant*, give it a Levinasian aura by 'naturalizing' the 'other'. Perhaps deconstruction does have some role to play in providing the heritage of imperialism some metropolitan legitimacy. This too is a matter of claiming ancestry, after all.

But deconstruction also provides a check for this tendency towards totalization. You mark your place in the text, as far as you can, so that you don't feel like offering your thoughts as a totalizable generalization, which, by the presuppositions of deconstruction would be a 'transgression'.

This is one aspect of deconstruction that is often overlooked. Derrida says it simply in an interview: 'the reference to a critical function of literature, in the West, remains very ambiguous. The freedom to say everything is a very powerful political weapon, but one which might immediately let itself be neutralized as a fiction. This revolutionary power can become very conservative' (Derrida, 1992a, p. 38). In *Politics of Friendship*, Derrida writes that we must read carefully precisely because all decisions are made in urgent non-knowledge (PF, pp. 78–9). In *Of Spirit*, even as he cautions that in all opposition, we are unilateral, he also says that 'the question of knowing which is the least grave of these [unilateral] forms of complicity is always there – its urgency and its seriousness could not be over-stressed' (Derrida, 1989, pp. 39–40).

Deconstruction, in other words, is limited by the undecidability of the empirical, of decisions, of the future – the 'perhaps' decides. To ignore this limit is to transcendentalize systems, including 'social constructions'. Derrida's example of systemic construction is Saussure's view of language: '[L]anguage always appears as a heritage of the preceding period. . . . Everything that pertains to a linguistic system, is . . . a fortuitous and involuntary result of evolution'.[21] 'Since language', Derrida writes in 1968,

> which Saussure says is a classification, has not fallen from the sky, the differences have been produced, are produced effects, but they are effects which do not have as their cause a subject or substance. . . . If such a presence were implied in the concept of cause in general . . . we then would have to speak of an effect without a cause, which very quickly would lead to no longer speaking of effects. I have attempted to indicate the direction [*tenter d'indiquer la visée*] out of the closure of this loop [*schème*] via the 'trace' which is no more an effect than it has a cause, but which in and of itself, extra-textually [*hors-texte*], is not sufficient to operate the necessary transgression.[22]

An effect that seems to have no subject can seem to lose its status as effect. We must not think of 'culture' as such an effect. Think of it as a 'trace' – something that structurally signals at the absence of its 'source', but to a particular absence, not absence in general. Thus a trace is caught in text or weave and cannot become 'an effect without a cause' leading to 'no effect at all'. No grin without a specific cat.

One cannot of course identify this general thought of the trace with some specific critical move. But surely there is something like a relationship between this warning (in the general sense) and the gesture that opens Derrida's conversation with Derek Attridge (in the narrow sense). In answer to the question – 'Could you expand upon that statement concerning your primary interest in literature', Derrida asks the interviewer to situate his own 'stereotype' of himself; and engage in a textual weaving of the production of his preferences in adolescence and early career, that would be as indecisive as any tracing (see Derrida, 1992a, pp. 34–7). No general systemic pronouncing on 'deconstruction and literature', as, for us, there cannot be a general systemic pronouncement on 'deconstruction and culture'. This is where Cultural Studies must forever rehearse the cultural subject's 'politics of exodus': middle passage, exile, indenture, migration . . . ? From where do you stereotype yourself? How is this different from mere historicizing? In that there is never a closure here. The trace is also an effort to indicate intentionality [*tenter d'indiquer la visée*], not a cause or effect.

Some years later, when even seeing one's own text as a seamless text seemed too 'naturalizing' a metaphor, Derrida writes of 'the textile metaphor': 'it remains more natural, originary, proper than that of sewing . . . Sewing . . . *betrays*, it exhibits that which it should hide, dissimulacras that which it signals.'[23] This passage could be a description of the technique of *Glas* where, twenty-five years ago, Derrida had tried to get the blasting-effect of placing what we would today call 'queer culture' in metonymic positioning with hegemonic straight male culture; attempting to graft performative and constative.

Can we describe, transcode, transmit, and institute the relationship (perhaps) resulting from deliberate positioning, as a method? Is this not also the question of Cultural Studies? To this Derrida's answer might be, not only: 'Here again I do nothing other, can do nothing other than cite . . . only to displace the syntactic layout [*agencement*] around a physical world, real or fake, which signals and makes forget the other'; but also this imperative to anyone who would learn deconstruction to keep that question alive, not just short-circuit it: 'all the examples can be cut out [*se découpent*] thus. Regard the holes if you can.'[24]

Let us now look at Anthropology and History as Cultural Studies' antonym. Those disciplines have undergone changes in the direction of Cultural Studies, although factoring in 'culture' without textuality is not much use. I am treating such changes as part of the 'Cultural Studies' initiative towards reforming its antonyms.

Both of these disciplines, in their pristine forms, deny the cultural 'other' the subjectship or agency of unmediated academic knowledge.

'Subaltern Studies', inspiring itself from Gramsci, took its brief of rewriting Indian colonial history by looking for insurgent agency below the progressive bourgeoisie.[25] However, since the initial practitioners of Subaltern Studies had no interest in legitimizing their own civil status in the name of 'culture', their work stands as an important element in the prehistory of 'Cultural Studies' that is counter to the Tagore/DuBois/Fanon line. The first flush of British Cultural Studies is unmarked by the subalternist impulse. To the extent that Cultural Studies in the United States attempts to come to terms with the indigenous subaltern as an inhabitant of an originary hybrid space, it has had to be deconstructive of notions of autochthonous origin. I am thinking specifically of the work of groups such as the Public Culture collective. Everyone is from somewhere else, and the queer is askew.

But even so, these attempts have perhaps not interested themselves sufficiently to 'regard the holes if you can'. Let us consider what such an injunction might mean.

First, to consider, not the continuity of a concatenation (I lean here upon the French where the word for argument is *enchaînement*) in the text, but the gaps that have had to be supplemented by citation. And, in order to regard them responsibly, to work at the aporia of exemplarity. In so far as the cited fillers are 'examples' of your argument, they are not identical with and self-sufficient unto themselves and cannot constitute your hybridity. When we choose something as an example or counter-example, we are obliged to deny its singularity by subduing it to our argument. In fact this aporia contains as it denies all understanding, not merely deliberate citation. The ethical gesture towards the other of my understanding may be simply a scrupulous methodological reminder that all our understandings are bound by a future anterior that will have happened because we speak and in spite of our speech. The most logical practical acknowledgment of the aporia at the origin is to beg the question, to take as demonstrated that which we set out to prove. You assume your hybridity in order to cite its examples. 'I sit with Shakespeare and he winces not'. The hybrid I is constituted to state the programme of hybridity. The performative ruses the constative. Or, perhaps, grafts them without a proper body – a trace, a stereotype, the ingredients of our work.

Shifting again to the concept-metaphor of a patchwork from that of grafting, we consider the injunction to regard the holes as holes cut from anterior texts, themselves not originary.[26] Those cuts bleed. Thus the affect and passion of the cut must be felt in terms of that anteriority if possible. This possibility is related to the prayer to be haunted by a past, for the unanticipatable periodicity of a haunting, that can only be described as a 'perhaps'. And here, the rupture with the past, willed or unwilled, of the subject of Cultural Studies, the metropolitan migrant or the candidate for globalization, is such that the ancestors claimed are some version of the Euro–US, straight up or reversed: Straight up: 'I sit with Shakespeare and he winces not', reversed: the subaltern only speaks in the native languages of the Southern hemisphere.[27]

What would Deconstruction and Cultural Studies look like if the hospitality/*arrivant* figure were twisted [*retorse*], as a subject for historical or anthropological investigation? In other words, taking account of the earlier impulse (a fold in the fabric of hospitality), to be imaginatively hospitable to the colonizing culture, even as it contested the right to colonize, what if we ceased imagining the object of hospitality only as the begging stranger at the door, and the subject of hospitality only as the arch-European dominant, Periclean Greece or its contender, Jerusalem? What if we supplemented Derrida's *De l'hospitalité* with a history that relates with a twist to the democratic tradition? It is with this question in mind that I approach *Gora*, a novel by Tagore, perhaps a response to Kipling's *Kim*, where the presuppositions are based in the species of colonial Cultural Studies I have described above.[28]

The point I am trying to make, I suppose, is that we cannot use deconstruction if we borrow no more than its thematics:

> What we will thus be concerned with here is the very possibility of thematic criticism, seen as an example of modern criticism, at work wherever one tries to determine a meaning through a text, to pronounce a decision upon it, to decide that this or that is a meaning and that it is meaningful to say that this meaning is posed, posable, or transposable as such: a theme . . . [I]f we can begin to see that the 'blank' and the fold cannot in fact be mastered as themes or as meanings, . . . then we will precisely have determined the limits of thematic criticism itself. (Derrida, 1981, pp. 245–6)

Derrida's concept-metaphor is the fold of the hymen. The sustaining argument of my essay is in the fold of minoritarian or postcolonial claims upon an unproblematic history or ancestry, as marked in Cultural Studies. A reading that ignores the first fold, the located Cultural Studies impulse produced by the colonial subject, focuses thematically on migration as the bottom line of culture.[29]

During the Indian Mutiny (the First Battle of Indian Independence, 1857), the Irish widow of an Irish soldier killed in battle dies in childbirth at the home of an Indian civil servant, in the employ of the Crown. The child is brought up by the Indian couple and becomes a heroic Brahmin-identitarian Hindu nationalist. When his (foster) father is dying, the secret of his birth is revealed to him because, not being by birth a Brahmin, he cannot perform the funeral rites. It is after this knowledge that he becomes a 'true' Indian. The novel celebrates the not-quite-not-colonizer (Irish-as-British) as hybrid. This is *Gora*.

The question in *Gora* does indeed come from abroad [*de l'étranger* H, p. 11]. What would it be to be hospitable to the invader: Sitting Bull's question. *Gora* attempts to imagine the *xenos* – the foreigner (H. p. 11) from below. (Strictly speaking, the above of the below, the colonized elite, a category not thinkable when we conceive of Socratic Greece in an opacity that conceals an oligarchy supported by an upwardly mobile slave population, an agist caste-bound queer population, and an instrumentalized female population.[30]) I am not sure why Derrida quotes the stranger in Plato's *Sophist* who, contradicting old Parmenides, does not wish to be considered a patricide (H, p. 12). But in the heritage of slavery or postcoloniality, the question of patricide is the first question of teleopoesis – enemy into friend. In *Gora*, for example, agency is displaced into the subjected. The foreigner can only be welcomed by (forgetting) the murder of the fathers: Gora's biological Irish/British father and his collectivity. Derrida's rich text moves to ask if all laws of hospitality are not obliged to transgress *the* law of hospitality: to offer the newcomer an unconditional shelter. To Derrida's list of the indeterminate newcomer (H, p. 73) Tagore adds the impossible category of a member of the imperial race as one to whom a singular hospitality can be shown by the spirit of the subject nation, by a nationalist of the subject-nation. This singular fictive hospitality is shown in the embrace of the Indian (foster) mother, who is, strictly speaking, foreign to the foreigner. Such hospitality puts the father's murder under erasure, only for the space of the book. To generalize it is to forbid resistance. Yet surely such a welcome is upstream from the political – a depoliticization that deconstructs the genealogical (PF, pp. 104–5). The violent death of the biological father is finally obliterated in the novel by the banal failed death of the querulous and unwilling adoptive father, the colonized host.

This impossible colonizing foreigner, being, in history, though not in consciousness, part of the colonizing group, is the Law of forced entry *as* Law that he questions.

Marx had complimented Aristotle but exempted him from understanding quantification as *telos* – the capitalist value-form.[31] The Platonic Socrates maybe thus forgiven by restoring him to his 'trace', forgiven from understanding the upstairs/downstairs twist of modern colonial hospitality. *Gora* stages the unknowing 'Law' giver (Gora, the white man), disgusted by an Indian colonial subject, whom he mistakenly considers to be bound to himself by a greater Law (G, pp. 47–9); scorning a white Magistrate, mistakenly considering him to be on the other side, a mere 'Law' giver (G, pp. 179–81); and, finally, the real encounter, the real invitation to teleopoesis, the furtive silence at the foster-father's bedside, when he knows he is Irish. The European doctor enters with the Bengali family physician. Gora is still dressed in ritual clothes, with the marks of ritual upon his face and body. The doctor looks at him and thinks: 'Who is this person? 'Before this Gora would have felt a resentment', Tagore continues, 'at the very sight of an English doctor. Today he kept looking at him with a special eagerness [*bishesh ekta outshukyer shohit*] as he examined the patient. He kept asking himself the same question again and again "Is this man my closest kin here?"' (G, p. 472).

My apologies for this hasty cobbling of two important texts. It is simply to suggest that a 'deconstructive' Cultural Studies cannot stop at undoing Area Studies by the migrant's celebration of herself as the other. Then it amounts to excluding 'the rest of the world', as it was compellingly articulated in that 1981 address 'Geopsychoanalysis: . . . "and the rest of the world"'.[32] In this courageous essay, protesting the policy of the International Psychoanalytic Association towards political torture, the graphic of the exclusion of the arriver, more dominant today as 'a messianicity without messianism' and 'hospitality', resonates with the earlier themes of ethnocentrism and, more important for our argument, the irrelevance of our institutional behaviour for large areas of the contemporary world – naming 'Latin America' as the space of paradox in-between – a note increasingly submerged in the varieties of globalizing triumphalism, which sees the in-between only as celebratory:

> What will from now on be called the Latin America of psychoanalysis is the only area in the world where there is coexistence, whether confrontational [*s'affrontant*] or not, between a strong psychoanalytic institution on the one hand and a society on the other (civil society or State) that engages in torture on a grand scale that no longer limits itself to its brutally classical and easily identifiable forms. (GΨ, pp. 228–9; translation modified)

Without deconstructive care, metropolitan Cultural Studies can institutionally ignore such coexistences and complicities, precisely because it is metropolitan, precisely because claiming hybridized ancestry can cut both ways. It will not acknowledge that the cuts bleed.[33] How can 'the rest of the world' be acknowledged?

In his *Specters of Marx*, Derrida proposes a New International which is, crudely put, the Human Rights initiative with an economic consciousness. In a certain sense, this request has been kept by the United States. 'Human Rights' are now almost inevitably exercised within a trade paradigm.

But I think it can be safely argued that this is not what Derrida meant. As to what he did mean one must of course and always only conjecture. Let us say he meant that, when we consider human rights infringements by governments, we should also consider the economic exploitation urged upon those governments by the Group of Seven, through trade-related economic restructuring, as practices to be measured upon their people. If that is so, Derrida's urging remains astute and has gone increasingly unheeded.

This is a good thought, to which I would add that the reverse is also true. Because the question of Human Rights has been so often confined within trade-related political paradigms, it can only be approached if culturally diversified ethical systems are studied. Pedagogically speaking, such studies are much more successful through language-based literary investigation than through evidence from interested cultural informants. History and Anthropology must approach the language of the other not only as 'field languages'. In order to crack this one, we need to move from Anglophony, Lusophony, Teutophony, Francophony, et cetera. We must take the languages of the Southern hemisphere as active cultural mediums, rather than as objects of cultural study by the sanctioned ignorance of the metropolitan migrant. I cannot dictate a model for this from my New York City office, or Derrida from Irvine or Paris. I can only qualify myself and my students to attend upon this as it happens elsewhere. Here and now, I can only caution against some stereotypes: that such an interest is anti-hybridist, culturally conservative, 'ontopologist', 'parochial'.[34] Other stereotypes are correct but irrelevant; namely, that attention to the languages of the Southern hemisphere is inconvenient and impractical.

Inconvenient. There are, after all, only a few hegemonic European languages and innumerable Southern hemisphere languages. The only answer to that, asked to write on so potentially pretentious a topic as 'Deconstruction and Cultural Studies' is: 'too bad'. Think of the many texts where Derrida has commented on the separate trajectories of French and English, too many to count. In *Given Time*, circulating around the necessary impossibility of thinking (that there is an unaccountable) gift (in the beginning), Derrida writes as follows in Chapter Two, 'The Madness of Economic Reason', before plunging into the reading of a French text in the rest of the book:

> Let us not accumulate these examples [of idiomatic differences]; they will be numerous but different from one language to another. Let us merely draw from them a *conclusion* (which is that the essential link from the thought of the gift to language, or in any case to the trace, will never dispense with [*faire l'économie des*] idioms) and a *doubt* (is it not impossible to isolate a concept of the essence of the gift that transcends idiomatic difference?).   (Derrida, 1992d, p. 54)

Do such things apply only to French and German? Does the story of aporias vanishing if 'shibboleth' be pronounced right only apply to Hebrew (see Derrida, 1992b, pp. 390–400)? India has long laboured under Weber's denial of philosophy, Africa under Hegel's denial of humanity. Latin America, indeed all the settler colonies, fall into a similar pit if one gets off the Ariel–Caliban debates. Can the serious international scope of something called Islam be diversified or unmarked? At the end of 'The Madness of Economic Reason', after meticulous readings of two poems by Mallarmé, when Derrida quotes Mauss quoting 'a beautiful Maori proverb' (see Derrida, 1992d, p. 67), should we remember his conclusion and his doubt as we read the concluding paragraphs and footnotes to his chapter? Can the 'native informant' ever become the subject of a 'Cultural Study' that does not resemble metropolitan language-based work? If one asks these questions, one sees that the neat reversal (often called destabilization) must exclude much for its own convenience.

Engagement with the idiom of the global other(s) in the Southern hemisphere, uninstitutionalized in the Euro–US university structure except via the objectifying discontinuous transcoding tourist-gaze of anthropology and oral history, is the displaced lesson of Deconstruction and Cultural Studies. This is not remedied by the re-territorialized desire of the metropolitan migrant to collaborate with the South, through the mediation of the class, increasingly produced by globalization, that is sufficiently out of touch with the idiomaticity of non-hegemonic languages. This is the flip side of the databasing of so-called indigenous knowledge undertaken today by the globalizing agencies directly, without accessing the cultural idiom of the Aboriginal from the position of the subject. I remind the reader of the aboriginal diversity ignored by the Tagorean version of Cultural Studies. Today, a deconstructive cultural study must ponder the ruse between the necessary yet impossible constative thought of *gift* at the origin and the unquestioning performative of 'data' (*given*-s) at the end, opening the way to a quantification (value-form) whose translation into qualitative good is again in the mode of the necessary/impossible. The move from money to data as the general equivalent is the move from industrial to finance capital, world trade to globalization, economic questions to questions, seemingly, of 'culture'.[35]

What I am suggesting may sound discouraging. And perhaps deconstructive Cultural Studies' battle against the cultural imperialism of metropolitan multiculturalism takes it clear out of the academic enterprise.[36] I hate to use this word, but perhaps it gives us a certain kind of honesty.

In other words, Cultural Studies must open up from the inside the colonialism of European national-language based Comparative Literature and the Cold War format of Area Studies, and infect History and Anthropology with the 'other' as producer of knowledge. But from the inside, acknowledging complicity. No accusations. No excuses. Only, learning the protocol of those disciplines, turn them around, laboriously. This is the new politics of reading Derrida outlined in *The Ear of the Other* (Derrida, 1985).

III RECIPROCITY, PERHAPS: FIELD WORK WITHOUT
TRANSCODING, THERE: CARE IN THE CLASSROOM, HERE

Doing this carefully will surely reveal how we, the metropolitan new immigrants who provide the major motor of Cultural Studies and provide others the models to teach with, are complicit, folded together, with the very disciplines we invade and transform; if only because we inherit the same institution, nestled in the ideology of a political economy that we too act out, at best interrupting it with gestures that are subsumed within the nation. We too, like Goethe, want to see our own face in the world. We are in the country that has won the Cold War. Redoing the Cold War we want to globalize, disavowing an exodus.

Ours is a commercializing culture, not the best subject position for undertaking cultural study. A glance at the day's newspaper shows that older folks' sports and grandparents' christmas ornaments are now big business.[37]

We redesign for Cultural Studies, keeping this 'in view'. Subaltern 'cultures' of the South cannot give rise to a Cultural Study continuous with the institutions of the North.

Not ever? Perhaps not.

Let us play Alain Locke's thought of 'reciprocity' off Jacques Derrida's thought of the 'perhaps'.

Locke faced the cultural 'globalizing' of Pan-Africanism in the twenties and offered us this model of reciprocity, surprisingly close to today's mainstream, yet with an enlightened view of cultural exchange:

[U]nless we approach Africa in the spirit of the finest reciprocity, our efforts will be ineffectual or harmful. We need to be the first of all Westerners to rid ourselves of . . . the insufferable bias of the attitude of 'civilizing Africa'. . . . On the other hand, the average African of the enlightened classes has his . . . pride of blood and bias of clan. . . . [I]t must be recognized that for the present the best channels of cooperative effort lie along economic and educational lines . . . America offers the African his greatest educational opportunity; Africa offers the Afro-American his greatest economic opportunity. (Locke, 1924, p. 37)

This is a project to transform African subalternity, inside and outside, through education and economics. With no example of hybridity accessible to him but 'the Afro-American', in the political atmosphere of 1924, before the spate of *de jure* decolonizations, Locke cannot imagine that a literature can arise out of anything but a national base. He risks the statement of a counter-internationalizing nationalism that is distinct from celebrations of subalternity: 'It is contemporary criticism, not contemporary art, which is at fault through obscuring the progressive cultural nationalisms of the future with the reactionary political nationalisms of the past.'[38] Yet, the question that he asks has strong resonances today: 'does the internationalization of culture imply for art more or less of the spirit which we admit is now its animating breath and inspiration?' Let us supplement it with Derrida's question: 'Would there be in the concept of *eudoxia* [to be found in a Platonic discussion of democracy] (reputation, approbation, opinion, judgement), and in the concept of equality (equality of birth, *isogonia*, and equality of rights, *isonomia*) a double motif that might, *interpreted otherwise* [*autrement*], remove [*soustraire*] democracy from autocthonous and homophilic rooting?' (PF, p. 104; emphasis mine; translation modified). Deconstruction is one name of interpreting otherwise; Locke's argument can take it on board.

Locke repeatedly recommends the training of a readership – *eudoxia* (Derrida), if you like, or 'educate the educators' (Marx, Third Thesis on Feuerbach):

> Not cultural uniformity, but cultural reciprocity is needed. . . . If criticism could somehow in an effective modem way achieve this spirit and attitude, the art which today seems so hopelessly sectarian would appear in transformed values as essentially international and universal. . . . Our real step toward a permanently broadened cultural attitude has been the realization of the crossing of cultures as after all the fundamental source of unusual cultural developments. . . . The only consistent attitude with such a situation is the cultural reciprocity which we think to be the basis of the soundest possible internationalization of culture.   (Locke, 1925, pp. 75–6)

This combination – reciprocity, training of the imagination to recognize a counter-internationalizing rather than essentializing nationalism, accompanied by a clear-eyed acknowledgement of the contaminated foundations of metropolitan agency – stages a step forward that is also a restraint, the deconstruciive *pas*, itself caught in French, 'step' and 'halt!' at once. We are traced in those contaminated foundings. We have already seen that Derrida advised trace-thinking to restrain the loop of arguing out production as causeless effect. That would be to halt. But we are now assured that 'no context can determine meaning to the point of exhaustiveness. Therefore the context neither produces nor guarantees impassable borders, thresholds that no step could pass . . .' (Derrida, 1993, p. 9). Step halting, then, halt stepping.

This compromised moment of the 'perhaps' is what a deconstructive cultural studies re-inscribes. This is where Derrida is indeed a Franco-Maghrebin, as Locke is an 'Afro-American'. I re-cite a move from Virginia Woolf here to show that the opening of this 'perhaps' for readers to come is not confined to some essentialized or naturalized hybrid. ' "I" is only a convenient term for somebody who has no real being', Woolf writes in one of her most persuasive texts. 'Lies will flow from my lips, but there may *perhaps* be some truth mixed up with them; it is for you to seek out this truth and to decide whether any part of it is worth keeping.'[39]

Woolf places us in the classic paradox – 'I will lie' – and writes the reader in the 'perhaps'. It is in this mode that she gives a random name to that 'I' that is merely a convention: Mary Beton or Mary Seton. And it is also within this mode that she acknowledges the compromised foundations of metropolitan agency. Mary Beton owes her £500 to imperialism, her eponymous aunt 'died by a fall from her horse when she was riding out to take the air in Bombay', and she herself sees money as a better alternative to democracy (RO, p. 37). In the final movement, Woolf takes us into the impossible possible of the 'perhaps', only as fiction can. She puts Mary Beton to rest (RO, pp. 104–5) and speaks 'in my own person' (RO, p. 105). She inaugurates a ghost dance, asking all aspiring woman writers to be haunted by the ghost of Shakespeare's sister, and quite gives up the 'room of one's own and £500 a year' in her closing words: 'I maintain that she would come if we worked for her, and that so to work, *even in poverty and obscurity*, is worth while' (RO, p. 114).

A Room of One's Own has become a hastily read cult text and Alain Locke is not part of mainstream Cultural Studies. We add the cynicism of the last seventy years, remind ourselves that no place on earth has been able to practise an inner-directed 'responsible' reciprocity where the exchange with the subaltern has altered itself as a result of the impetus from the other side. And, offering Cultural Studies nothing more plausible than a fieldwork without the goal of transcoding for the academy, let us think 'perhaps'. Let us think teleopoesis: 'generation by a joint and simultaneous grafting, without a proper body, of the performative and the constative'.

Fieldwork without transcoding: an alteration perhaps happening to the imagination of a fieldworker rather than a difference claimed by the ethnographer. At the extreme edge of Cultural Studies, where the critique of Anthropology/History/Comparative Literature begins to fill itself with content, this silent work can stand guard. We can keep teaching its cautionary practice in the deconstructive classroom. This instruction, *mutatis mutandis*, applies even to so-called South–South Cultural Studies.

It seems to us now that the idea of a collectivity without organization – that may seem hopelessly impractical at first glance as suggested in *Specters of Marx* or *Politics of Friendship* – is actually the figure of a classroom. To demonstrate this, I read two paragraphs of *Politics of Friendship*.

In the Foreword to the book Derrida tells us that the entire book is an account of but one session of the seminar on the topic of the politics of friendship that he had taught in 1988–9 (PF, p. vii). He tells us further that in each session the same questions had been repeated, permutations and combinations played, in many different ways.

> In the course of the academic year 1988–89, each session opened with these words from Montaigne, quoting a proposition [*propos*] attributed to Aristotle: 'O my friends, there is no friend'. Week after week, its voices, tones, modes and strategies were tried on, to see if its interpretation could then be sparked. . . . This text, taking its time, replays, *represents*, only its first session.   (PF, pp. vii–viii)

Reading the book, we should imagine the iteration in the classroom. A few chapters in, after reminding us what happens if we simply act on the philosophy of the perhaps (a passage we have already quoted), Derrida insists that, in spite of this, the philosophy of the perhaps must be repeatedly rehearsed in the classroom.

In *Politics*, the un-organized, un-collectivized practitioners of the New International of *Specters* are re-inscribed as figures who can re-cite an alleged saying of Aristotle's through many relays across the centuries. For the duration of the book, the possibility of such a company – 'How many are we?' is reiterated – is the invocation of that absent class. And a single teacher's students, flung out into the world, is surely a better real-world example than one named the New 'International', which immediately brings Marxist organization to mind. In the context of the earlier book, perhaps the lesson was that the presuppositions of the text of Marx should be internalized (learnt) by as large a group as possible – so that practice is changed upstream from the party line – rather than be the means of metonymically collectivizing people whose other differences will inevitably bring the 'collectivity' down.

This is clearly not the place to discuss the idea in the context of Marx and Marxism. But in the context of deconstructive Cultural Studies the idea is worth considering. If we teachers try to learn and teach the limit to our institutional Cultural Studies as the subject-position of our 'other' in subaltern Southern culture, even as we rigorously disassemble the presuppositions of traditional Anthropology, History, Area Studies, Comparative Literature, we can, 'perhaps', hope not to drown a good thing in the quick fix of triumphalism.

Derrida has strongly and subtly questioned the efficacy of multiplying 'warnings . . . such as these typical and recurrent syntagms: "relation without relation", community without community . . . "inoperative" community, "unavowable" communism or community, and all the "X without X" whose list is, by definition, endless, finite in its infinitude'. If 'a political history or philosophy . . . attempted to read all the apparently contradictory possibles . . . that these "sophisticated discourses" recall [*rapellent*] . . . they could do very little, almost nothing' (PF, p. 81). Put crudely, they offer the ability of quick fixes while we eat our cake and have it too. Let us teach a resistance to mere theoreticism in the classroom.

IV   CONCLUSION

In a more extended study, I had chosen the diachrony and synchrony of a South Asian religious minority as 'A Compromised Example', where the US classroom played a mobilizing electronic role. I had passed to the question of woman and advanced the following suggestion in the end: The epistemological undertaking of constituting a general gendered will for globalization is an object of deconstructive cultural study. This is the female client of micro-credit. If the colonial subject was classed, and the briefly appearing postcolonial subject raced, the subject of globalization is gendered. It was in view of globalization and virtuality that I offered a gloss on mere 'transnational literacy'.

For globalization is not only transnationalization. The day for learning the agency of the letter (literacy) is over. The task is to wrench Marx from Judeo-Christian messianicity and the apparent failure of his Eurocentric discourse of progress as we see the triumph of the spectrality of capital as Reason. (Deconstruction taught us long ago to call it keeping 'the economic under erasure'.[40] But the day for thinking capital as merely economic is over as well.) The task, further, is to wrench deconstruction from its proper home in 'Comparative Literature', to let it loose in 'Cultural Studies' so that it can transform its nice nursery of hybrid plantings to reveal the saturnalia of an imagined counter-globalization. An unrestricted Hegelianism, undoing Hegel's Eurocentric teleologies:

> During saturnalia, order was overturned; the law transgressed itself: time of debauchery, of licentiousness, of drunkenness, spasmodic revolution in the course of which, says an anachronistic treatise of mythology, 'the social classes were topsy-turvy', the masters becoming the slaves of their slaves. . . . *Sa* [Absolute Knowledge]'s saturnalia would then be intimately bound up with a disordering [*dérèglement*] of the *seminarium*.[41]

As for wrenching deconstruction from 'true' philosophy, deconstruction itself gives us a guarantee for it, *pace* the epigraph to this essay.

'Deconstruction' might be the name, the textual figure, of a great messy change, not confined to the metropolis. The academic activities undertaken in the name of deconstruction, including this one, inevitably, manage that mess. Perhaps we will become the object of some future 'Cultural Studies' as the organic intellectuals of the first wave of deconstruction.

We must remain open to the scrutiny of the improper. Perhaps this is the last lesson of deconstruction for the proper investigation of culture.

NOTES

1. I thank Deborah White for a perceptive first reading of this essay.
2. Richard Hoggart, *The Uses of Literacy: Aspects of Working-Class Life, with Special Reference to Publications and Entertainments* (New York: Oxford University Press, 1970); Stuart Hall, 'Cultural Studies and the Centre: Some Problematics and Problems', in Hall et al. (eds), *Culture, Media, Language* (London: Hutchinson, 1980), pp. 15–47; *The Empire Strikes Back: Race and Racism in 70s Britain* (London: Hutchinson, 1982); *Women Take Issue: Aspects of Women's Subordination* (London: Hutchinson, 1978).
3. Rodolfo F. Acuña, *Occupied America: The Chicano's Struggle Toward Liberation* (San Francisco, CA: Canfield Press, 1972), and Mario Barrera, *Race,.and Class in the Southwest: A Theory of Racial Inequality* (Notre Dame: Notre Dame University Press, 1979). The colonial line was Antonio Gramsci, 'Some Aspects of the Southern Question', in Gramsci, *Selections from Political Writings, 1921–1926*, trans. Quintin Hoare (New York: International Publishers, 1978), pp. 441–62. Postcolonially, the source for the notion was Samir Amin, *Unequal Development: An Essay on the Social Formation of Peripheral Capitalism*, trans. Brian Pearce (New York: Monthly Review Press, 1976). The internal colonization debate in the African-American context, recounted in Philip S. Foner and James S. Allen (eds), *American Communism and Black Americans: A Documentary History, 1919–1929* (Philadelphia, PA: Temple University Press, 1987) was an earlier formation which arose anew with Stokeley Carmichael and Charles V. Hamilton (eds), *Black Power: The Politics of Liberation in America* (New York: Vintage, 1967).
4. Maxine Hong Kingston, *The Woman Warrior: Memoirs of a Girlhood Among Ghosts* (New York: Knopf, 1976).
5. Leslie Marmon Silko, *Almanac of the Dead* (New York: Simon and Schuster, 1991).
6. Jacques Derrida, *Specters of Marx: The State of the Debt, the Work of Mourning, and the New International*, trans. Peggy Kamuf (New York: Routledge, 1994), p. 35. See also Ken McMullen's 1983 film *'Ghost Dance'*, made for Channel Four (London), where Derrida makes a cameo appearance, playing himself.
7. Rabindranath Tagore, *Rabindra Racanabali* (Calcutta: W. Bengal Govt. Press, 1961), vol. 11, p. 801; translation mine.
8. Ashish Kothari, Saloni Suri, and Neena Singh, 'People and Protected Areas: Rethinking Conservation in India', *The Ecologist*, **25**.5 (Sept/Oct 1995), p. 188. The difficulty of calling the supposedly pre-Indo-European autocthonous groups uniformly 'aboriginal' or 'tribal' is precisely that India is an ancient settler colony.
9. 'Religious Minorities and the Secular State: Reflections on the Indian Impasse', *Public Culture*, **8**.1 (Fall 1995), p. 13. It should perhaps be mentioned that this piece is a typical case of the locationist problem in Cultural Studies. It was published in the US without the introductory section (*Economic and Political Weekly*, 9 July, 1994, pp. 1768–77), which applies to India alone.
10. I have discussed this in greater detail in 'Academic Freedom', *Pretexts*, **v**, i–ii (1995), pp. 117–56.
11. The concept of hybridity owes most to the work of Homi K. Bhabha. Its most

powerful recent articulation is in 'Border Lives: The Art of the Present', in Bhabha, *Location of Culture* (New York: Routledge, 1994), pp. 1–18.

12. Aristotle, *The Poetics*, trans. W. Hamilton Fyfe and W. Rhys Roberts (Cambridge, MA: Harvard University Press, 1991), p. 35.

13. DuBois, *Selected Writings*, p. 57. Alain Locke, 'The Legacy of the Ancestral Arts', in Alain Locke (ed.), *The New Negro: An Interpretation* (New York: Arno Press, 1968), pp. 256–8. I thank Brent Edwards for mentioning Alain Locke to me.

14. James Mooney, *The Ghost-Dance Religion and the Sioux Outbreak of 1890* (Lincoln: University of Nebraska Press, 1991).

15. DuBois, 'The Negro Mind Reaches Out', in Locke, *New Negro*, pp. 392–7. The next quoted passage is from p. 397.

16. Derrida, *Politics of Friendship*, trans. George Collins (New York: Verso, 1997), p. 32; translation modified. Hereafter cited in text as PF, with page reference following.

17. In spite of the important critique of Anne McClintock and Rob Nixon in 'No Names Apart: The Separation of Word and History in Derrida's "Le Dernier Mot Du Racisme"', in *'Race', Writing, and Difference*, ed. Henry Louis Gates, Jr (Chicago: University of Chicago Press, 1986), pp. 339–53, the reading of Nelson Mandela's autobiography in 'The Laws of Reflection: Nelson Mandela, in Admiration', in *For Nelson Mandela*, ed. Jacques Derrida and Mustapha Tlili (New York: Seaver Books, 1987), pp. 11–42, remains a model of postcolonial cultural studies. Mandela, a Christian legalist who repeatedly claims 'conscience' over an unjust law and is brutally thwarted from entering that tradition honourably, reclaims his own ancestry by inscribing his 'village in the Transkei' as the seed-bed of 'a revolutionary democracy' (primitive communism: Marx), rather than 'custom' (colonial powers). See Terence Ranger, 'The Invention of Tradition in Colonial Africa', in Eric Hobsbawm and Terence Ranger (eds), *The Invention of Tradition* (Cambridge: Cambridge University Press, 1983), pp. 211–62, and, in greater detail, Mahmood Mamdani, *Citizen and Subject: Contemporary Africa and the Legacy of Late Capitalism* (Princeton, NJ: Princeton University Press, 1996).

18. Derrida, 'Mochlos; or, the Conflict of the Faculties', in Richard Rand (ed.), *Logomachia: The Conflict of the Faculties* (Lincoln, NB: University of Nebraska Press, 1992) is an extended critique of this vision of knowledge. Derrida's lecture was delivered at Columbia University in 1980.

19. 'National literature is now rather an unmeaning term; the epoch of World literature is at hand, and everyone must strive to hasten its approach. But, while we thus value what is foreign, we must not bind ourselves to anything in particular, and regard it as a model. . . . [I]f we really want a pattern, we must always return to the ancient Greeks. . . . All the rest we must look at only historically, appropriating to ourselves what is good, so far as it goes' (January 31, 1827), Johann Wolfgang von Goethe, in John Oxenford (trans.), *Conversations with Eckermann* (Washington, DC, Walter Dunne, 1901), p. 175. With hindsight, it would be interesting to descend from the sublime to the ridiculous and compare this 'structure of feeling' with the appropriative multicultural menu under the master-pattern of Thanksgiving in Gopinathan, 'With Justice', quoted in note 77. The *metaphora* of Cultural Studies must make odd connections. Paul Van Tieghem, *Le Mouvement romantique (Angleterre-Allemagne-Italie-France)* (Paris: Vuibert, 1923) is the other book cited in my text.

20. René Etiemble, *The Crisis in Comparative Literature*, trans. Herbert Weisinger and Georges Joyaux (East Lansing: Michigan State University Press, 1966); Erich Auerbach, *Mimesis: The Representation of Reality in Western Literature*,

trans. Willard R. Trask (Princeton, NJ: Princeton University Press, 1953); Georges Poulet, *Studies in Human Time,* trans. Elliott Coleman (Westport, CT: Greenwood Press, 1979); Ernst Robert Curtius, *European Literature and the Latin Middle Ages,* trans. Willard R. Trask (Princeton, NJ: Princeton University Press, 1973); Erich Heller, *The Disinherited Mind: Essays in Modern German Literature and Thought* (New York: Barnes & Noble, 1971).

21. Ferdinand de Saussure, *Course in General Linguistics,* trans. Wade Baskin (New York: McGraw-Hill, 1959), pp. 71, 86.

22. Derrida, 'Differance', in *Margins of Philosophy,* trans. Alan Bass (Chicago: University of Chicago Press, 1982), pp. 11–12; translation modified. 'Loop' is bold, but it catches exactly the implication of the passage; at the time of the writing of which this particular meaning was not available in colloquial American English.

23. Derrida, *Glas,* trans. John P. Leavey, Jr and Richard Rand (Lincoln, NB: University of Nebraska Press, 1990), pp. 208b, 209b; translation modified.

24. *Ibid.,* pp. 215b, 210b; translation modified. The sentences are not consecutive in Derrida's text.

25. Ranajit Guha et al. (eds), *Subaltern Studies: Writings on South Asian History and Society* (Delhi: Oxford University Press, 1982–), vols 1–11.

26. 'Concept-metaphor' mutely marks the closing argument in Derrida's 'White Mythology: Metaphor in the Text of Philosophy': '. . . to explode the reassuring opposition of the metaphoric and the proper, the opposition in which the one and the other have never done anything but reflect and refer to each other in their radiance' (Derrida, *Margins,* pp. 270–1).

27. For the latter position, see Ramachandra Guha, 'Subaltern and Bhadralok Studies', *Economic. and Political Weekly,* **30.33** (19 August, 1995), p. 2058, and Harish Trivedi, 'India and Postcolonial Discourse', in Harish Trivedi and Meenakshi Mukherjee (eds), *Interrogating Post-colonialism: Theory, Text and Context* (Shimla: Indian Institute of Advanced Study, 1996), pp. 231–47.

28. Rabindranath Tagore, *Gora,* trans. Sujit Mukherjee (New Delhi: Sahitya Akademi, 1997); Derrida, *De l'hospitalité* (Paris: Calmann-Lévy, 1997). Hereafter cited in text as G and H respectively, with page reference following. I have given a more extended reading of *Gora* in an anthology being edited by Ato Quayson and forthcoming from Cambridge University Press.

29. Christopher Bracken plays interestingly with Derridian concept-metaphors, despite a slight tendency towards unmediated thematizing of philosophemes, in *The Potlatch Papers: A Colonial Case History* (Chicago, IL: University of Chicago Press, 1997), especially pp. 5–31.

30. Assia Djebar's impulse towards placing Delacroix, or the French Captain who occupied Algiers, into teleopoesis, shares something of this impulse from the above of the below, but she foregrounds that subject-position as a woman: see 'Forbidden Gaze, Severed Sound' in *Women of Algiers in their Apartment,* trans. Marjolin de Jaeger (Charlottesville, VA: University of Virginia Press, 1992), pp. 136–40; and *Fantasia: An Algerian Cavalcade,* trans. Dorothy Blair (London: Quartet, 1985), pp. 6–8.

31. Marx, *Capital: A Critique of Political Economy,* trans. Ben Fowkes (New York: Vintage, 1976), vol. 1, p. 52.

32. Derrida, 'Geopsychoanalysis: . . . and the rest of the world', trans. Donald Nicholson-Smith, in *American Imago* **48.2** (summer 1991), pp. 199–231. Hereafter cited in text as GΨ, with page reference following.

33. To some it may seem incorrect that I say nothing about the use of psychoanalytic vocabulary in Cultural Studies. Over the years, I have often indicated my discomfort with it. To do no more than signal the nature of that discomfort,

and to link it with metropolitan thematizing discourses on 'deconstruction [postmodernism] and politics' by analogy, I will content myself here with quoting a passage from 'Geopsychoanalysis': 'despite all the commotion over such issues as "psychoanalysis and politics", despite the deluge of discussions on this kind of topic that we have witnessed over the last ten or twelve years at least, it has to be acknowledged – indeed all this agitation actually signals the fact – that at present there exists no approach to political problems, no code of political discourse, that has in any rigorous way incorporated the axiomatics of a possible psychoanalysis [to tap the history of the subject responsibly in order to restore agency?] – if a psychoanalysis is possible. . . . I am speaking of discourses emanating from non-analysts as well as others, that of psychoanalysts or crypto-analysts operating in the psychoanalytic milieu and using psychoanalytic terminology' (GΨ, p. 214; translation modified).

34. For 'ontopologist' see Derrida, *Specters*, p. 82. In a recent issue of *The New Yorker* (June 23 and 30, 1997), Salman Rushdie refers to all the literatures of India not in English as 'parochial'.

35. For money as the 'general equivalent', see Marx, *Capital*, vol. 1, pp. 162–3.

36. A text for meditation: 'The decision of thought cannot be an intra-institutional event, an academic moment'. See Derrida, 'The Principle of Reason: the University in the Eyes of its Pupils', *Diacritics*, **13.3** (Fall 1983), p. 19.

37. These two examples are from *The New York Times*, 28 December 1998 (Richard Weir, 'Pay for Play: Aging Athletes Can Still Find Competition in Sports Leagues Run for Fun and Profit', and Kimberley Stevens, 'Snapped Up: Tinsel Trees and Ornaments of Yore', *The City*, pp. 4–6). But examples are every-where, every day, of course.

38. Locke, 'Internationalism – Friend or Foe of Art?' in *The World Tomorrow* (March, 1925), p. 75. The next quoted passage is from the same page. Here I can only signal the importance of this set – cultural and political nationalisms. See Joseph Stalin, *Marxism and the National-Cultural Question: A Collection of Articles and Speeches* (San Francisco, CA: Proletarian Publishers, 1975); and V. I. Lenin, *Imperialism: The Highest Stage of Capitalism* (New York: International Publishers, 1993). Although Stalin constantly invokes Lenin in order to legitimize himself, Lenin is speaking of the Northwestern European single nation empires and their connections to the march of Capital, whereas Stalin is speaking of the Russian, Ottoman and Habsburg empires, and the manipulation of their cultures and identities in the interest of forming some-thing like a new empire. Thus their lines lead toward finance capital and lin-guistic and cultural politics respectively. In this essay, I attempt to show how deconstruction can undo this polarization. For the Indian case, the difference signalled by Locke may be seen in the contrast between '*Mera Bharat Mahan*' – 'my India is great', a politically nationalist slogan – and the music video 'I love my India', written by an Indian woman located, as it happens, in the subcon-tinent. Corresponding undoings proliferate in globalization, generally with a national-identity tag, under erasure, as that which remains – *ce qui reste*. The sheer usefulness of a deconstructive habit of mind is undeniable here, even as deconstruction questions its usefulness, as in Derrida, 'Passions: "An Oblique Offering"', in David Wood (ed.), *Derrida: A Critical Reader* (Oxford: Blackwell, 1992), pp. 5–35. If I needed a logo for this footnote, I would choose the Canadian artist Karma Clarke-Davis's 'Untitled', from *Corner Buddha – Karma. Om . . . The Walk of a Nomad*, colour photograph employed in video (final illus-tration, catalogue, 'Tourists in Our Own Land(s)', Gallery 44 (Toronto), 9 July–8 August 1998) – lit-up outline of part of a bridge against a dark sky, and the oblique neon sign 'OPEN'. . .

39. Virginia Woolf, *A Room of One's Own* (New York: Harcourt, 1929), pp. 4–5, emphasis mine. Hereafter cited in text as RO, with page references following.
40. Gayatri Spivak, *In Other Worlds: Essays in Cultural Politics* (New York: Methuen, 1987), p. 168.
41. An unrestricted Hegelianism without a recognizable political agenda was announced as early as 1967 in Derrida, 'From Restricted to General Economy: A Hegelianism without Reserve', in *Writing and Difference*, trans. Alan Bass (Chicago, IL: University of Chicago Press, 1978), pp. 251–77. The quoted passage is from Derrida, *Glas*, pp. 232–3a. If it is hard or incorrect to analogize the philosopheme, it is altogether risky with *Glas*. I offer nonetheles my dry reduction: deconstruction can not only undo Hegel's Eurocentric teleologies, but deconstructive Cultural Studies can aspire to undo the hybrid as *telos*; and at least in theory make us aware of the myriad resistances that cannot be conveniently catalogued.

WORKS CITED

Acuña, Rodolfo F. (1972), *Occupied America: The Chicano's Struggle Toward Liberation* (San Francisco, CA: Canfield Press).

Amin, Samir (1976), *Unequal Development. An Essay on the Social Formation of Peripheral Capitalism*, trans. Brian Pearce (New York: Monthly Review Press).

Aristotle (1991), *The Poetics*, trans. W. Hamilton Fyfe and W. Rhys Roberts (Cambridge, MA: Harvard University Press).

Auerbach, Erich (1953), *Mimesis: The Representation of Reality in Western Literature*, trans. Willard R. Trask (Princeton, NJ: Princeton University Press).

Barrera, Mario (1979), *Race and Class in the Southwest: A Theory of Racial Inequality* (Notre Dame, IL: Notre Dame University Press).

Bhabha, Homi (1994), 'Border Lives: The Art of the Present', in *Location of Culture* (New York: Routledge), pp. 1–18.

Bracken, Christopher (1997), *The Potlatch Papers: A Colonial Case History* (Chicago: University of Chicago Press).

Carmichael, Stokeley and Charles V. Hamilton (eds) (1967), *Black Power: The Politics of Liberation in America* (New York: Vintage).

Chatterjee, Partha (1994), 'Religious Minorities and the Secular State: Reflections on the Indian Impasse', *Economic and Political Weekly* (9 July), pp. 1768–77.

Chatterjee, Partha (1995), 'Religious Minorities and the Secular State: Reflections on the Indian Impasse', *Public Culture*, **8.1** (Fall).

Curtius, Ernst Robert (1973), *European Literature and the Latin Middle Ages*, trans. Willard R. Trask (Princeton, NJ: Princeton University Press).

Derrida, Jacques (1978), 'From Restricted to General Economy: A Hegelianism without Reserve', in *Writing and Difference*, trans. Alan Bass (Chicago, IL: University of Chicago Press), pp. 251–77.

Derrida, Jacques (1981), 'The Double Session', in *Dissemination*, trans. Barbara Johnson (Chicago, IL: University of Chicago Press), 173–286.

Derrida, Jacques (1982) 'Differance', in *Margins of Philosophy*, trans. Alan Bass, (Chicago, IL: University of Chicago Press).

Derrida, Jacques (1983), 'The Principle of Reason: the University in the Eyes of its Pupils', *Diacritics*, **13.3** (Fall).

Derrida, Jacques (1985), *The Ear of the Other: Otobiography, Transference, Translation*, trans. Peggy Kamuf (New York: Schocken Books).

Derrida, Jacques and Mustapha Tlili (eds) (1987), 'The Laws of Reflection: Nelson

Mandela, in Admiration', in *For Nelson Mandela* (New York: Seaver Books), pp. 11–42.

Derrida, Jacques (1989), *Of Spirit; Heidegger and the Question*, trans. Geoffrey Bennington and Rachel Bowlby (Chicago, IL: University of Chicago Press)

Derrida, Jacques (1990), *Glas*, trans. John P. Leavey, Jr and Richard Rand (Lincoln, NB: University of Nebraska Press).

Derrida, Jacques (1991), 'Geopsychoanalysis: . . . "and the rest of the world"', trans. Donald Nicholson-Smith, in *American Imago*, **48.2** (Summer) pp. 199–231.

Derrida, Jacques (1992a), 'This Strange Institution Called Literature', in *Acts of Literature*, ed. Derek Attridge (New York: Routledge), pp. 33–75.

Derrida, Jacques (1992b), 'Shibboleth', in *Acts of Literature*, ed. Derek Attridge (New York: Routledge), pp. 399–400.

Derrida, Jacques (1992c), '*Mochlos*; or, the Conflict of the Faculties', in *Logomachia: The Conflict of the Faculties*, ed. Richard Rand (Lincoln, NB: University of Nebraska Press), pp. 1–34.

Derrida, Jacques (1992d), *Given Time: I. Counterfeit Money*, trans. Peggy Kamuf, (Chicago, IL: University of Chicago Press).

Derrida, Jacques (1992e), 'Passions: "An Oblique Offering"', in *Derrida: A Critical Reader*, ed. David Wood (Oxford: Blackwell), pp. 5–35.

Derrida, Jacques (1993), *Aporias*, trans. Thomas Dutoit (Stanford, CA: Stanford University Press).

Derrida, Jacques (1994), *Specters of Marx: The State of the Debt, the Work of Mourning, and the New International*, trans. Peggy Kamuf (New York: Routledge).

Derrida, Jacques (1997a), *Politics of Friendship*, trans. George Collins (New York: Verso).

Derrida, Jacques (1997b), *De l'hospitalité* (Paris: Calmann-Lévy).

Djebar, Assia (1985), *Fantasia: An Algerian Cavalcade*, trans. Dorothy Blair (London: Quartet).

Djebar, Assia (1992), 'Forbidden Gaze, Severed Sound', in *Women of Algiers in their Apartment*, trans. Marjolin de Jaeger (Charlottesville, VA: University of Virginia Press), pp. 136–40.

DuBois, W. E. B. (1968), 'The Negro Mind Reaches Out', in *The New Negro: An Interpretation*, ed. Alain Locke (New York: Arno Press), pp. 392–7.

DuBois, W. E. B (1970), *The Selected Writings* (New York: Mentor).

Etiemble, René (1966), *The Crisis in Comparative Literature*, trans. Herbert Weisinger and Georges Joyaux (East Lansing, MI: Michigan State University Press).

Foner, Philip S. and James S. Allen (eds) (1987), *American Communism and Black Americans: A Documentary History, 1919–1929* (Philadelphia, PA: Temple University Press).

Gilroy, Paul (1987), *'There Ain't No Black in the Union Jack': The Cultural Politics of Race and Nation* (London: Hutchinson).

Gilroy Paul (1993), *The Black Atlantic: Modernity and Double Consciousness* (Cambridge: Harvard University Press).

Goethe, Johann Wolfgang von (1901), *Conversations with Eckermann*, trans. John Oxenford (Washington: Walter Dunne).

Gramsci, Antonio (1978), 'Some Aspects of the Southern Question', in *Selections from Political Writings, 1924–1926*, trans. Quintin Hoare (New York: International Publishers), pp. 441–62.

Guha, Ramachandra (1993), 'Subaltern and Bhadralok Studies', *Economic and Political Weekly*, **30.33**, 19 August.

Guha, Ranajit, et al. (eds) (1982), *Subaltern Studies: Writings on South Asian History and Society*, vols 1–11 (Delhi: Oxford University Press).

Hall, Stuart (1978), *Women Take Issue: Aspects of Women's Subordination* (London: Hutchinson).

Hall, Stuart (1980), 'Cultural Studies and the Centre: Some Problematics and Problems', in *Culture, Media, Language*, ed. Hall *et al.* (London: Hutchinson), pp. 15–47.

Hall, Stuart (1982), *The Empire Strikes Back: Race and Racism in 70s Britain* (London. Hutchinson).

Heller, Erich (1971), *The Disinherited Mind: Essays in Modem German Literature and Thought* (New York: Barnes & Noble).

Hoggart, Richard (1970), *The Uses of Literacy: Aspects of Working-Class Life, with Special Reference to Publications and Entertainments* (New York: Oxford University Press).

Kingston, Maxine Hong (1976), *The Woman Warrior: Memoirs of a Girlhood Among Ghosts* (New York: Knopf).

Kothari, Ashish, Saloni Suri and Neena Singh (1995), 'People and Protected Areas: Rethinking Conservation in India', *The Ecologist*, **25.5** (Sept/Oct.)

Lenin, V. I. (1993), *Imperialism: The Highest Stage of Capitalism* (New York: International Publishers).

Locke, Alain (1968), 'The Legacy of the Ancestral Arts', in *The New Negro: An Interpretation*, ed. Alain Locke (New York: Arno Press), pp. 256–8.

Locke, Alain (1924), 'Apropos of Africa', in *Opportunity* (February).

Locke, Alain (1925), 'Internationalism – Friend or Foe of Art?', in *The World Tomorrow* (March).

Mamdani, Mahmood (1996), *Citizen and Subject: Contemporary Africa and the Legacy of Late Capitalism* (Princeton, NJ: Princeton University Press).

Marx, Karl (1976), *Capital: A Critique of Political Economy*, vol. 1, trans. Ben Fowkes (New York: Vintage).

McClintock, Anne and Rob Nixon (1986), 'No Names Apart: The Separation of Word and History in Derrida's "Le Dernier Mot Du Racisme"', in *'Race', Writing, and Difference*, ed. Henry Louis Gates, Jr (Chicago, IL: University of Chicago Press), pp. 339–53.

McMullen, Ken (1983), *'Ghost Dance'*, a film made for Channel Four (London).

Mooney, Jarnes (1991), *The Ghost-Dance Religion and the Sioux Outbreak of 1890* (Lincoln, NB: University of Nebraska Press).

The New Yorker 23 and 30 June 1997.

Poulet, Georges (1979), *Studies in Human Time*, trans. Elliott Coleman (Westport, CT: Greenwood Press).

Ranger, Terence (1983), 'The Invention of Tradition in Colonial Africa', in *The Invention of Tradition*, ed. Eric Hobsbawm and Terence Ranger (Cambridge: Cambridge University Press), pp. 211–62.

Saussure, Ferdinand de (1959), *Course in General Linguistics*, trans. Wade Baskin (New York: McGraw-Hill).

Silko, Leslie Marmon (1991), *Almanac of the Dead* (New York: Simon and Schuster).

Spivak, Gayatri Chakravorty (1987), *In Other Worlds: Essays in Cultural Politics* (New York: Methuen).

Spivak, Gayatri Chakravorty (1995), 'Academic Freedom', *Pretexts*, **V** pp. i–ii, 117–56.

Stalin, Joseph (1975), *Marxism and the National-Cultural Question: A Collection of Articles and Speeches* (San Francisco, CA: Proletarian Publishers).

Tagore, Rabindranath (1961), *Rabindra Racanabali*, vol. 11 (Calcutta: W. Bengal Govt. Press).

Tagore, Rabindranath (1997), *Gora*, trans. Sujit Mukherjee (New Delhi: Sabitya Akademi).

Tieghem, Paul Van (1923), *Le Mouvement romantique (Angleterre-Allemagne-Italie-France* (Paris: Vuibert).

Trivedi, Harish (1996), 'India and Postcolonial Discourse', in *Interrogating Postcolonialism: Theory, Text and Context*, ed. Harish Trivedi and Meenakshi Mukherjee (Shimla: Indian Institute of Advanced Study), pp. 231–47.

Woolf, Virginia (1929), *A Room of One's Own* (New York: Harcourt).

3

Deconstruction and Drugs: A Philosophical/Literary Cocktail

David Boothroyd

Nick had a deprecating little laugh that he used for punctuation. Sort of an apology for talking at all in the telepathizing world of the addict . . .

William Burroughs, *Naked Lunch*, p. 170

'You're feeling it, aren't you?'
'Yeah, I am actually.'
'It's quite impossible to describe, isn't it?'
'Yeah, it is.'

Martin Amis, *Dead Babies*, p. 87

Sometimes ah think that people become junkies because they sub-consciously crave a wee bit of silence.

Irvine Welsh, *Trainspotting*, p. 7

He couldn't tell at first but he was dancing like a maniac . . . they were all going crazy.

Irvine Welsh, *Ecstasy*, p. 27

No doubt we should have to make some distinction between . . . drugs, but this distinction is wiped out in the rhetoric of fantasy that is at the root of the interdiction: drugs, it is said, make one lose any sense of true reality.

Jacques Derrida, 'The Rhetoric of Drugs', p. 236

Short-circuiting the exasperating detour of communication, or more generally suspending the pro-active expenditure of the will's energy as it works to fuel its own consciousness, is the mark of an urge to a junkie-like descent into a silence which few people at some point in their lives wouldn't admit to craving – if not at some point every day. But drugs and their effects are always a matter of the mix, the concoction or recipe, the purity and the impurities, as well as of the 'set and setting', as Leary and his coterie never tired of saying; and with street drugs, there is also the matter of all the unknown ingredients, the precipitates of amateur chemistry, or whatever was to hand to give bulk to the stuff as it changed hands on its way to market. It is such contingencies as these which determine whether drugs intoxicate, narcotize, energize, silence, make a person withdrawn and dreamy, talk their head off, suffer genital retraction or an inconsolable erection or just go plain crazy.

If you are reading this book, you are probably familiar with the fact, or may know from personal experience, that 'recreational' or 'lifestyle' drug-use is a pandemic phenomenon and 'addictive' drug-use is becoming increasingly widespread in all Western societies. As Noel Gallagher infamously commented, taking (illicit) drugs is for the 'chemical generation' like having a cup of tea, a part of 'normal' daily life. If you turned to this chapter first, you may well regard the rethinking of the recreation/addiction and the use/abuse dichotomies within the wider discussion of drugs, to be an urgent matter, one for which deconstruction seems unprecedentedly appropriate. Clearly the network of discourses organizing the 'drugs debate', and, ultimately, the logistics of the 'war on drugs', too, if only for their crass 'binaryisms', are potential sites of deconstructive interventions of one sort or another. You may be anticipating that the outcome of this thematic conjunction, 'deconstruction and drugs', might at least go towards a re-ordering of the controlling distinctions operating in the world(s) of drugs and drug taking. That is, after all, surely what is hinted at in Derrida's remark (cited above) about the 'rhetoric of fantasy' and the 'rational' rejection of the pleasures gained from drugs, which are generally assumed to be enjoyed in the absence of any 'truth'. We would want, at the very least, to remake some governing distinctions.

But even more crucially, 'truth' and 'the truth about drugs' (which would somehow have to contain the truth about truth drugs, too) cannot avoid cross-contamination: they can never be entirely unaffected by each other. The 'truth about drugs' is distributed and presented in a spectrum of well-known and lesser-known drug literatures, ranging from those expressed in terms of 'mental experiences', 'rushes' and 'highs', through pharmaco-anthropological studies of mystical tribal rituals, to text books recording the medical and legal classification of drugs. Such discourses and narratives figure yet more widely, in innumerable cultural forms, as different from each other as 'great modern literature' and school playground chat. However, when *the* so-called 'truth about drugs' is marshalled to serve as a rhetorical weapon in the armoury of prohibitionism, one can be sure that this involves a degree of conflation and confusion of elements of the many possible drug discourses and narratives. As Derrida once pointed out, 'there is not a *single* world of drugs . . . to conflate such differences in a homogeneous series would be delirious, indeed narcotizing' and he asks whether one could in any case 'ever condemn or prohibit without also confusing' (Derrida, 1995, p. 237). The 'truth about drugs' is always exactly what it thinks it is not: it is itself a particular kind of discursive cocktail and not at all the drug-free, uncontaminated, sober, pure of heart and mind, objective, legitimate regulator of drugs.

A deconstructive engagement with the 'truth about drugs' authorizing all current delimitations of 'drugs', offers the prospect of rethinking our relation to the alterity of drugs. In what ways might it be possible to exploit drugs to disrupt the attempts to contain them? Could deconstruction 'take drugs' in order to inaugurate a cultural 'new deal' on drugs, one that would be ethical in so far as it would enable our culture to get along with drugs – whose ubiquity in every sense is never in doubt – *otherwise* than we currently do? Such questions are of course 'theoretical', but they are directed at the possibility of discovering alternative 'drug practices'. Such practices could never simply be derived from a better understanding of drugs, in the traditional sense of possessing new 'knowledge'. They could only emerge out of a double-science which attempts to think together the theoretical as well as the practical aspects of what Avital Ronell has called the modernity of *being-on-drugs* (Ronell, 1992, p. 59). It is modernity's 'intersecting cut' between drugs, freedom and what Ronell calls 'the addicted condition' of being-on-drugs that must be subjected to an 'interminable analysis' (p. 59).

This essay will attempt to mix (and no doubt risk mixing up) 'drugs' and 'deconstruction', and to discern in the course of this experiment the nature of the peculiar relation between them. It will show that the theme of 'drugs' is as useful a way to elucidate the workings of 'deconstruction' as is deconstruction a means of reworking our understanding of drugs and their effects. Each would be a user's guide to the other. Disciplinary propriety would ordinarily demand that it be made clear at the outset what 'type' of drugs this chapter brings into conjunction with the subject of deconstruction. It would insist on a preliminary compliance with one or another, or several, determinations of the object as such. But, as the nature of this 'complicity' with supposed drugs expertise (and typologies in general) is precisely a theme here, and because the deconstruction of anything has to begin by means of a partial suspension of the metaphysical conceptual determination of something as 'something', any such demand must also be subject, by the same logic, to a strategic suspension. This discussion of 'deconstruction and drugs', coming as it does after decades of critical elaboration of deconstruction, will assume at least (if only out of habit) the efficacy of the strategy of the *sous-rature* ('under erasure'). This could be said to be deployed from the outset in anticipation of a new 'sense' for 'drugs'.

We may begin, in any case, with the 'rhetorics' of use and abuse, and with the hard stuff: Derrida uses this metaphor to describe deconstruction itself as 'an abusive investigation which introduces beforehand what it seeks to find'. The present essay, in fact, has just done this in turn, by introducing beforehand 'the foreign substance of a debate' (Derrida, 1978, p. 154). Deconstruction is no stranger to abuse. It is 'parasitically' abusive in relation to the tradition of Western philosophy, and, as is so often the case in relation to discussions of deconstruction, the theme at hand – the 'abuse' in question – is doubled-up in it: deconstruction itself has often been made an object of abuse for its alleged irresponsibility, its 'nihilism'. It has, nonetheless, always recognized the importance, even the necessity, of 'abuse' in another sense: as a tactic in its strategic underminings, loosenings, erosions, subversions and (one might add and add . . .) its '*et ceteras*'. All of which are abusive in the conventional sense, from the perspective of those orthodoxies, authorities, institutions, etc., which underwrite the 'truth' about *everything*. But, without some sort of 'abuse' somewhere along the line, without some sort of break with regulation and with modernity's decision of the meaning of 'drugs', without some sort of upset regarding 'propriety' in general and with respect to anything in particular (not just drugs), nothing would ever happen. Without experimentation, without acting on the urge to excess, without 'aggressions' and 'infidelities', in *whatever* cultural forms these take – and here we are talking not only of philosophical and literary modes of experimentation, but of all 'heresies' and even half-formed heretical impulses – there would never have been anything worthy of the name 'culture'. Any culture identifiable on the basis of its *interdictions* only stands to confirm this.

What is abusively introduced beforehand here is the idea that there is an affinity between deconstruction and drugs. This is, of course, directly remarked in several ways and in several places, more or less explicitly, in Derrida's writings. In particular, in relation to his discussions of the *pharmakon* in the essay 'Plato's Pharmacy', in relation to supplementarity, undecidability, play, repetition; in other words, right at the heart of deconstruction's thinking of writing and textuality. As 'drug', *pharmakon* carries the sense of both 'antidote' and 'poison', but it is also (in Plato) a metaphor for writing. Derrida's account of the *pharmakon* (in this instance the text of Lysias's speech), with regard to the opening scene of *Phaedrus*, undermines the possibility of its representing, or offering up, an 'unveiled' or 'naked' truth (Derrida, 1981b, p. 71, citing Plato 230d–e). The difference between deconstruction as *writing* and 'drugs' is seen as reducible, though never quite entirely to zero: 'writing is not only a drug' (Derrida, 1995, p. 234). They *copulate* as Bataille might have said, rather than converge at a point of unity. By attempting to think the 'drug' as 'writing" and vice versa, the concepts of 'drugs' and 'writing' are made to operate in Derrida's writings, each in the guise of the other – allowing each to participate in alternative systems of substitutions. They are each thereby made available for reinscription; their recuperation, by the system which controls them and distinguishes them, is deferred. In this play, 'drugs' become approachable in their 'undecidability', as not-yet-decided, not locked into traditional, orthodox, institutional, normative and prescriptive systems of reference. Playing with drugs, experimenting with them, engaging with them, by means of an 'incessant tropism' (Harvey, 1992, p. 215) or by other experimental means, and in other senses: this is what is made possible in their conjunction with deconstruction.

SAYING YES TO DRUGS . . .

Yes to deconstruction, yes to drugs. In everyday life and on different cultural plateaux today, countless people are saying yes to both deconstruction and drugs, some of them undoubtedly to both. But what is the significance of these affirmations and what is the nature of the connection between them here? There may be many instances of yea-saying to both deconstruction and drugs, literally in the same head, but this chapter's real concern is not with what goes on inside heads but with the 'yes' which can be said to the 'and' in the title 'deconstruction *and* drugs'. It engages in an experimental affirmation of the reciprocal supplementarity of deconstruction and drugs, and seeks to discover whether drugs can serve as an 'ally' in the general deconstruction of the rational normality Reason asserts.

What, then, is the point? To say that deconstruction is 'like a drug'? Yes. That drugs figure in the thinking which attempts to approach the limits of Reason? Yes. To supplement all previous delimitations of 'drugs' with an account of the unthought, unthinkable, pharmakon of 'drugs', and to find that the values of purity and sobriety etc., are merely rhetorical, antithetical mythologies figuring in a system of oppressions? To see that contamination is a more useful trope for thinking about our 'narcotic modernity', that the addiction/recreation dichotomy needs greater attention than it has received in other approaches to drugs? . . . Yes, yes, yes, yes.

> I say the *yes* and not the word 'yes', for there can be a yes without the word, which is precisely our problem. . . . What is it that is spoken, written, what occurs [*advient*] with *yes*? (Derrida, 1991a, p. 590)

Derrida's meditation on the *yes* as 'before language, in language, but also in an experience of the plurality of languages' (Derrida, 1991a, p. 590) is helpful here. The expression, *yes*, of the rush or onset of the effect of a drug introjected (ingested, inhaled, imbibed, etc.) into the body, or of deconstruction into the corpus of metaphysics, is the occasion of a certain 'coming' (*advient*). This reminds us of two important things: firstly, that experience is (something) other than the particular language (*parole*) which expresses it, but also, secondly, that this difference, between the two yesses, is in no way independent of the system of representation which 'feeds-back', determining the understanding of experience. In other words, experience is always structured, organized and 'experienced', on the condition of its contamination by the marks of language (*langue*), of one 'yes' by another 'yes'.

This all really began with a simple observation: both deconstruction and drugs are to be found at work everywhere, changing, in one sense or another, the way that our culture relates to, sees, thinks, perceives and represents *everything*. The bigger theme of *totality and its transgression*, is what has prompted this framing of their conjunction. For this to begin to take effect, we must now specify the drug (or text) this essay is really on. The other ingredient, or *pharmakon*, taken here as a point of focus, is *The Major Ordeals of the Mind* (1974/[1967]) by the French poet and essayist Henri Michaux. In it he writes up an account of his experimental explorations of the limits of human reason through the use of drugs. The first section, entitled 'Disorientations', opens with the following:

> I want to lift the veil from the 'normal', the unrecognized, unsuspected, incredible, enormous normal. The abnormal first acquainted me with it, disclosing to me the prodigious number of operations which the most ordinary of men performs, casually, unconcerned, as routine work, interested only in the outcome and not in the mechanisms, however marvellous, far more wonderful than the ideas he sets such store by, which are often so commonplace, mediocre, unworthy of the matchless instrument that reveals and plies them. I want to lift the veil from the complex mechanisms which make man, first and foremost, an operator.
>
> (Michaux, 1974, p. 3)

Michaux finds that the psychotropic drugs he uses 'brilliantly dramatize' these 'operations' which give rise to 'normality'. *The Major Ordeals of the Mind* consists of a series of reports recorded within the drama of his being-high which are interwoven with more sober reflections, footnotes and asides. In a number of respects, this interweaving parallels the effects of deconstruction as it works away at the limits of metaphysics, exposing the instability of its foundations and promoting its auto-destruction. Both deconstruction and these reflections of Michaux, which record, often in a style which mimics empiricism, the struggle of consciousness to retain control of its thinking at the point at which 'thought is short-circuited and left behind' (Michaux, 1974, p. 39), involve an onslaught on Reason. They

undertake de-systematizations of systems of organization, both egological and ontological: the institutions of Reason and 'good sense' are
approached in their various states of ruination. As we shall see, for
Michaux, the loosening grip on 'reality' which the drug (mescaline) facil-
itates, engenders, most interestingly, an experience with language.
Michaux shows how what is soberly regarded as the grip *on* reality can
also be seen as the grip *of* normality. For him, drugs (rather than any
philosophical poetics) are able to transport thinking to the limit at which
the operation and force of the normalizing rhetorics orchestrated by
Reason can be scrutinized. Drugs are Michaux's means of entry to this
scene of destruction, both of the ego and its representations. It is from
amongst the wreckage of the machinery of normalization that he articulates his claim to go beyond what 'the metaphysicians' are able to think.

> More than the all too excellent skills of the metaphysicians, it is the
> dementias, the backwardnesses, the deliriums, the ecstasies and ago-
> nies, the breakdowns in mental skills which are really suited to 'reveal'
> us to ourselves.   (Michaux, 1974, p. 7)

But, despite their shared interest in and distrust of the delimitations of the
thinking authorized on the basis of the 'all too excellent skills of the metaphysicians', no one would deny that doing deconstruction and doing
drugs, in this sense, are two very different things. Their respective relationships to Reason and modern rationality, for example in their
approaches to the *abyssal* (whether in terms of 'logic' or 'experience'), are
as different as Newtonian experiments and bungee-jumping, when used
as means of exploring the earth's gravity. And yet . . .

. . . SAYING YES TO DECONSTRUCTION

> [T]he farther we go the more the question of drugs seems inseparable
> not only from such tremendous questions as 'the concept', 'reason',
> 'truth', 'memory', 'work'', and so forth, but also from the centres of
> urgency where all these things appear to gather symptomatically.
>   (Derrida, 1995, p. 248)

The vast literature around the 'theory of deconstruction', concerning
what deconstruction is and what it can do – for example, as a way of reading texts, of re-reading tradition, of restaging the ancient question of the
relationship between philosophy and literature, or reason and madness,
and so on – is now increasingly *supplemented* by deconstructive applica-
tions in a wider cultural and political domain. Indeed, deconstruction is
increasingly being used as the framework for an ethics of *response* and a

rethinking of the political in relation to, for example, friendship, or democracy and its institutions. This is nowhere more evident than in Derrida's own recent work, which continues to provide a lead on several of these fronts.

This represents a significant development beyond the early reception of deconstruction in the disciplines in which it was first extensively taken up, for example in philosophy and literary studies, where emphasis was largely on these disciplines' intra- and inter-disciplinary concerns. Since then, the more disseminatory legacy of its radical understanding of the 'text', beyond the disciplinary borders of philosophy, literary theory and 'Derrida Studies', has become evident. This development was, in a sense, as predictable as the general semiology which Saussure correctly antici-pated on the basis of his theory of language as a system of signs. What is often understood as deconstruction's parasitical relation to 'metaphysics' is inversely reflected in deconstruction's need to be fuelled by the 'foreign substance of a debate'. As the development of deconstruction continues, it is, and will further be, marked by the elaboration of themes – such as 'drugs' – which have hitherto been delimited by, and in a sense *lost to*, dis-ciplinary knowledges such as economics, criminology, health and addic-tion studies, all of which, according to their respective rhetorics and schemas, attempt to anchor drugs and their effects in the 'normal'.

For Michaux it is psychotropic drugs themselves, and not their figural-cum-conceptual displacement, which prove to be the supplement which effectuates a closure of what he refers to as 'normality'.

> In quite different ways, in many ways, the drug catches out, discovers, unmasks mental operations, injecting consciousness where it had never been, and at the same time dislodging it from places where it had always been: a queer case of drawers that can function only alternately – *some must be closed before others may open*.   (Michaux, 1974, pp. 5–6, my emphasis)

Deconstruction's engagement with (the theme of) 'drugs' is twofold. Firstly, it calls for the deconstruction of the discursive totalities which frame a 'drug world' in which drugs are made the scapegoat for a series of oppressions, too numerous to mention, but ranging (at the end of a lengthy chain of substitutions and inscriptions concerning, above all, the determination of the drug as 'toxic substance') from the murder of Colombian peasants to the normalization of the casual violence of the strip-search. As Derrida asks: 'How can one ignore the growing and undelimitable, that is, worldwide power of those super-efficient and properly capitalist phantom-States that are the mafia and the drug cartels on every continent?' (Derrida, 1994, p. 83). This aspect of the deconstruc-tion of drugs could be described as the ethico-political dimension of the general deconstruction of drug rhetorics. Secondly, and at the same time, deconstruction presents the possibility of a transfigurative opening and an alternative thinking of the relation to 'drugs'. Having recognized that 'Every phantasmatic organization, whether collective or individual, is the invention of a drug or of a rhetoric of drugs' (Derrida, 1995, p. 247), drugs may be taken *otherwise* – in a sense for which there is as yet no concept, on the basis of a non-authoritarian, deregulated understanding of their *multiple* effects, in *several* senses. In other words, the force of dominant drug rhetorics may be countered by the deratiocinatory force of a reinscribed notion of drugs. Could there be a *measure* for drugs, unfettered, for example, by such rhetorics as those of authenticity and inauthenticity, of health and illness, of use and abuse, etc? This is the key question deconstruction enables us to ask in a meaningful way, and is itself a certain sort of measure of its own distanciation from those very rhetorics it 'brings to closure'. Where it might take us is not yet clear, but this possibility is something very real, not just a moment in a *closed* circle of substitutions: it signals more than a return to the same set of alternatives concerning drugs; it signals more than an inversion of traditional, hierarchical, binary evaluations.

These two elements of the deconstructive engagement with drugs, the dismantling of rhetorics and the generative openness to 'semantic' (and ontological) transfiguration, are not distinct; they are certainly not separated in time, and both the drug-user and drugs discourse are always in reality caught up in both of these systems, which govern our thinking and the discursive practices structuring everyday life (including the practical pursuit of chemotechnological pleasures and escapes). And just as this 'double-science' of deconstruction never *wholly* exceeds metaphysics, the deconstruction of drugs can never be *wholly* separated, either, from being-high. Deconstruction and being-high encounter one another by means of a kind of *tropic* blurring of which Michaux's psychotropic experiments are both an *example* and a *part(aking)*.

The deconstruction of 'drugs' actually involves action on both of these fronts: it deconstructs the multiple rhetorics of drugs, but at the same time directs thinking to that other, transfigurative, moment in which the deconstructive potency of drugs, taken in *any one* of their many possible senses, has another kind of effect; *an effect related to their alterity*. Michaux is principally concerned with this latter aspect, with what he refers to as the 'alienating' and 'defamiliarizing high', and in this sense he fails to relate his own drugged-discourse to a wider sense of rhetorically constructed drug worlds. Which is not to suggest that the poet on drugs should particularly concern himself with the politics, legality or justice of the drugs-bust which could storm in on him at any moment, but rather to acknowledge that in the emphasis his thinking *on* drugs attaches to being-high, it remains resolutely blind to the conditions of *its own* rhetorical construction (i.e. the rhetorical construction of the discourse of highs, rushes, disorientations and transcendences, etc). Thinking *between* the two is central to Derrida's critique of what he calls the 'shared axiomatics' of prohibitionist anti-drug rhetoric and the libertarianism of 'atheist poets' of intoxication and excess (Derrida, 1995, p. 240). As he puts it:

> In the end, or in the very long run (for by definition there will never be any absolutely final term), a thinking and a politics of this thing called 'drugs' would involve the simultaneous displacement of these two opposed ideologies in their common metaphysics.
>
> (Derrida, 1995, p. 266)

The point here is that deconstruction can no more disqualify *being-high* or disregard its potential usefulness with respect to the transfigurative moment, than can those who suppose, all too uncritically, that being-high is the bearer of its own truth, and do not address the complexities, or even see the necessity, of its being called to account.

Deconstruction repeatedly acts as a sort of referee whose function is to remind the players in this game of order vs. excess of the dangers of being entrenched in either camp. Derrida, furthermore, seeks to stress that the desire and pursuit, by any means, of the dual perspective of seeing things from the supposed border between them, is also impossible, and moreover a characteristic trait of the 'liminal' intellectual, artist or writer, or drug-taker.

> In certain always singular circumstances, the recourse to dangerous experimentation with what we call drugs may be guided by the desire to think the alleged boundary from both sides at once. . . . This experience (one to which artists and thinkers occasionally devote themselves, but which is by no means the unique privilege of those who claim or to whom we grant such status), this experience may be sought with or without 'drugs', at least without any 'narcotic', 'classified' as such by the Law. We will always have unclassified or unclassifiable supplements of drugs or narcotics. (Derrida, 1995, p. 245)

The point here is not that drugs are of no special significance to deconstruction, but rather that they are of *singular* significance. We are therefore 'provoked' by deconstruction to seek in the deconstructive engagement with the drug-text, the *pharmakon*, both its possibilities and its limitations with respect to transgression. 'Dangerous experimentation' with 'drugs' is, to be precise, *figuratively* advocated – to the extent to which anything can be regarded as a 'drug', and therefore any activity as 'drug-taking'. And it is meaningless or otherwise inconsequential to be for or against this.

Michaux's text has been taken into the body of this essay as a *pharmakon*. From Michaux's own perspective, psychotropic drugs 'themselves' have a decisive role to play in the experimental deconstruction of 'the normal'. Consequently, he approaches the subject of limits from the perspective of being on drugs in the 'normal' sense.

> Not until insidious derangement by a drug had brought this mechanism to a halt did I at last, quite late in life, realize experimentally so vital, almost omnipresent a function, whose incessant action had just ceased.   (Michaux, 1974, p. 4)

The 'insidious derangement' Michaux recalls here is achieved, he suggests, by a prosthesis whose role is entirely passive. The drug is a technology for switching *off* the machinery which keeps 'normality' and normal thinking going. This use of drugs to supplement the totality of the normal, results not in a vision of transcendence, of another reality, but in a zone of deferral; a kind of reduction or bracketing of traditional systems governing what Michaux refers to as 'mental' orientation. On drugs he enters the zone of the '*yes* without the word', with which we began this discussion. At least for a moment, he enters what Derrida once referred to as 'the element of the *Pharmakon* . . . the combat zone between philosophy and its other. . . . An element that is *in itself . . . undecidable*' (Derrida, 1981b, p. 138). Michaux's affirmation coincides with the rush, or hit, of the *undecided* drug, which is then brought under control by his thinking and naming of it as an 'insidious derangement', by the act of referring this being-high to the ordered arrangement it displaces.

REJECTING TRANSCENDENCE

By the very necessity of its being *written*, Michaux's account of this 'experience' is never simply a representation of some other 'place'. Despite his enthusiasm for 'insidious derangement' and the discoveries this allows him, being high is ultimately not inhabitable territory for the poet who would actually write. Control, come-down and being straight have a logical as well as pharmacological relation to writing. The following remark of Derrida is one of many which articulates the same idea in terms of en/closure:

> Even in aggressions and transgressions, we are consorting with a code to which metaphysics is tied irreducibly, such that every transgression re-encloses us – precisely by giving us a hold on the closure of metaphysics – within this closure . . . One is never installed within transgression, one never lives elsewhere.   (Derrida, 1981a, p. 12)

That drugs cannot be a means of transcendence, of passage to an 'else-where', is not only made clear in everything Derrida has said about the *pharmakon*, but is echoed again in his discussion of 'drugs' in 'The Rhetoric of Drugs' (1995/1983). To propose that they *can* be only amounts to a feeble repetition of the *theme* of transcendence; such thinking takes us back to an unaltered state. Michaux resoundingly rejects the return of nor-mality in any of its many inverted forms, of which transcendence is just one, and he is at pains, in a number of his sober reflections, to distinguish his own drug-taking experiments from the activities of others, experi-ments which leave them 'enclosed', in one sense or another. Michaux writes: 'Those who have taken a powder with quasi-magical effects and consider themselves quite unfettered, entirely liberated, out of this world perhaps, are still running on tracks' (Michaux, 1974, p. 105). And con-versely:

> Those who take drugs in order to surrender themselves to collective release and emotional abandon need not read further. There is nothing here that is meant for them. We do not speak the same language . . . The observer of psychic experiences has to be 'entrenched'. (Michaux, 1974, p. 156, fn 2)

'Entrenchment', for Michaux, is a narco-methodological principle. The 'entrenched' observer is the one who is able to straddle the limit between exuberant abandon and systematic recollection. And although, as already noted, Michaux's recollections are clearly caught up in the discourse of psychic experiences, he makes use of his being high to anchor his think-ing, and in part his writing, within experiences of dissolution, derange-ment, alienation and psychosis.

The problematics of locating this or any other kind of experiment with drugs in relation to the collective 'knowledges' of drugs and drug-taking, on the one hand, and the supposed experience of the 'other side', on the other, creep back in at this point and indicate a further aspect of Michaux's own rejection of transcendence. It is perhaps in the *difference between* his sober self-commentaries and footnotes and the deranged para-graphs to which they are appended, between what comes in madness and what comes as the thinking of the limit, that an affinity, or 'allegiance', between drugs and (deconstructive) *transgression* is to be discerned:

> there is one possible way to abort madness . . . there exists a possibility of transforming the scattering, dissipating, dislocating, devastating, breaking, tearing, dis-coordinating convulsiveness into an ally . . . (Michaux, 1974, p. 156)

This *possibility of transforming* is engendered by the drug, but what it shows is that 'taking drugs' is something which can never simply be limited to what *it* ('drug taking') *is taken for* (i.e. to mean, or, to bring about). Drugs can be taken for many different reasons and what drug taking *is*, within the nascent deconstructive logic of Michaux's double writing, is a rethinking of the liminal. He takes drugs to supplement the 'marvellous normal'; they enable him to 'think the micro-phenomenon . . . its numerous meshings, its many silent micro-operations of dislocation of alignment, of parallelism, of displacement, of substitution' (1974, p. 5). In principle, deconstruction can be brought to bear on anything, but in order convincingly to carry out the substitution by which *it* proceeds – rendering supplementary or 'liminal' the matter at hand – the matter at hand must, so to speak, present itself in a condition of ruinous auto-deconstruction. Deconstruction in the first instance just highlights the liminality of 'drugs': the 'drug' *deconstructs itself* (cf. Derrida, 1991b, p. 274). In other words, drugs could not be made an 'object' of deconstruction if they were not, from the outset, a marker of the rips and tears, resulting from the 'infidelities and aggressions', in the general metaphysical diktat by which Reason attempts to assert its authority over Unreason, madness, intoxication, etc. In taking Michaux's text here as an object of deconstruction, taking it as a *pharmakon*, we expose, in part, the degree to which it is attentive to the drugged-up condition of its production. Approaching a text in deconstruction involves becoming attentive to the manner in which each of the meanings it might be considered to bear is possible only on the basis of what remains unthought and yet within it.

The deconstruction of the modernity of being-on-drugs is not aimed at reviving or re-establishing an alternative form of 'the normal'. It must therefore, in addition to the deconstruction of drug 'rhetorics' which Derrida emphasizes, also deal with drugs in such a way as to exploit their (implicit) liminality and what they enable one to observe with respect to the *abyss* – '. . . if (indeed) the word "observe" applies to an abyss into which one is flung and from which nothing any longer separates you' (Michaux, 1974, p. 93). In order to figure how the *abyssal* in Michaux relates to the chiasmic *sous-rature* of deconstruction, we can go by way of the example which 'drugs' are here held to be.

TAKING DRUGS FOR EXAMPLE

Is there any possible justification for bringing 'drugs' to the 'premises' of deconstruction, or are we now heading for a run-in with the law? What is the basis here for making them serve as an *example* of deconstruction in general and including them in that deconstructive project which is aimed at 'the greatest possible totality' Derrida, 1974, p. 46)? If deconstruction were a new 'system of thought', for example a 'Derridean system of thought', then the following might, in principle, be all the authorization required:

> The example itself, as such, overflows its singularity as much as its identity. This is why there are no examples while at the same time there are only examples . . . The exemplarity of the example is clearly never the exemplarity of the example. We can never be sure of having put an end to this very old children's game in which all the discourses, philosophical or not, which have ever inspired deconstructions, are entangled even by the performative fiction which consists in saying, starting up the game again, 'take precisely this example'.
>
> (Derrida, 1992a, p. 15)

But given that such examples, or elements, of 'the system' of deconstruction do not stand as part to whole, nor can ever be solidly aggregated into a system, deconstruction remains a slippery notion. Slippage rather than control is the name of the game, and we are actually compelled to think 'deconstruction' *always* via the example.

Where writing, which is after all a kind of 'pharmacy', is 'the game' and deconstruction the stalling of its *closure*, it is only the example of deconstruction which props open the closing jaws of metaphysics. Deconstruction is like a pill held between the lips of tradition, on the brink of ingestion; it is a foreign substance which produces an infinitesimal alteration, but one that may change everything. To ingest or not to ingest, what is the difference? What does taking drugs contribute to the thinking of the limit? These questions do not at all displace others concerning the *theorization* of the closure, as such, but rather conjoin with them: the *difference* between the theory in general, or 'doing deconstruction', and the example, 'doing drugs', is all a matter of *closure* (*of the mouth* as much as of anything else).

And then, the decision to say yes to the *pharmakon* – to do deconstruction/to do drugs – having been taken . . .

> Diffuse agitation. Difficulty in thinking. Thinking according to my previous tendency, the point of view I had. . . . The point of view I am led to abandon. I am overwhelmed by a current to the point where my thoughts move with this hyperactive, torrential, rushing 'something' which I feel flowing by. . . . Ideas which, beyond my intervention, no longer control themselves, *aspire to transgression*.
>
> (Michaux, 1974, p. 45)

Deconstruction is the scene of precisely such an aspiration, it oscillates between the thought of transgression and retention of the foothold in metaphysics which anchors its very sanity (and reserves its place in the

institution). The dosage required to balance on the edge of this disinte-
gration is not subject to any expert prescription, it is entirely to be determined by the experiment itself. Too much and you slip over into the
telepathizing 'silence' of the uncontrollable gigglers, the mystics or the
comatosed. Too little and you just don't get off at all.

Examples never succeed in arriving at their destinations, as if, for
instance, *différance* were the object of a deduction based on them: they are
without any exemplar. The example is neither central nor exorbitant. Its
non-paradigmatic status in deconstructive thinking must therefore be
acknowledged. Examples are always, precisely, *supplementary* and operate across strategic conjunctions, which are thereby rendered non-hierar-
chical. This amounts, in effect, to the dislocation of the metaphysical
understanding of exemplarity. The 'deconstruction of metaphysics' proceeds on the basis of a series of examples, such as those comprising the
present volume, in which any 'deconstruction *of* . . .' is marked by the
double genitive, which unsettles the distinction between what belongs to
deconstruction in general and what belongs to the example. So there is no
suggestion here that 'drugs' are in any sense exceptional, or present us
with an exceptional insight into deconstruction. They are, however, 'singular'. It is ultimately this 'logic' which permits the deconstruction *of*
drugs, and all attempts to think drugs in relation to their undecidability,
rather than Derrida's own *exemplary* deconstruction of that undecidable
drug in 'Plato's Pharmacy', the *pharmakon*. It is because the drug will
always be apprehended as both antidote *and* poison that it is intrinsically
undecidable, liminal *and* transgressive. But because there are no pure
exemplars, there are no narcotic means of transcendence either. What
deconstruction presents 'positively' is an opportunity to disrupt the prescriptions and proscriptions of supposed pharmaceutical authorities, and
to do so on the basis of its own alternative 'pharmakology'.

What is it then that deconstruction gets off on? The undecidable *pharmakon* is the 'drug' deconstruction is on, and taking it as a supplement is
the means to a rewriting of the 'drugs script' as currently defined by
drugs 'knowledge' and drugs 'expertise'. Taking drugs into the orbit of
deconstruction's 'incessant tropism' is what any deconstruction of totality
must do whilst bearing in mind the need for some sort of *measure*.
Deconstruction offers a kind of controlled slippage: it remains wary of the
line between an effective and a toxic dose of whatever it is on (or about)
at any given time.

Irene Harvey's sober analysis of the question of exemplarity in deconstruction, in which she finds Derrida's writings to foreclose *the question* of
exemplarity (Harvey, 1992, p. 216), retraces this foreclosure, but by stop-
ping short of the 'intoxicated' extension of deconstruction to its other supposed moment, the opening of thought onto the alterity which exceeds
metaphysics, itself becomes an example of the sobriety characteristic of

rational thought. Rodolphe Gasché, too, has articulated an ethos of deconstructive restraint: he is a principal critic of the reception of Derrida's philosophy in which it is 'more often than not construed as a license for
arbitrary free play in flagrant disregard of all established rules of argumentation, traditional requirements of thought, and ethical standards
binding upon the interpretative community' (Gasché, 1987, p. 3). Even
Michaux articulates a similar reserve with respect to the interpretation of
drug experiences, as was noted above – but then, everyone decides to
draw the line somewhere.

These concerns with *measure* (rather than propriety) serve to emphasize
that it is precisely the problem of the *in-between* of sobriety and intoxication that this entire reflection is aimed at. I am in agreement with such
expressions of the need for a *measure* of control, which any deconstructive
thinking calls for. I would certainly concur also with the view that deconstruction is more than the promotion of 'licentious free-play, nihilistic cancelling out of opposites, abolition of hierarchies' (Gasché, 1987, p. 3). But I
have also attempted to show (of necessity, by means of a certain exemplarity), that the project of 'grasping' deconstruction 'in all its specificity'
(Gasché, 1987, p. 3) would itself also be limited to deconstruction's *metaphysical* moment. To be hooked on such a project is to be caught up in a
circle of bad repetition. And it is a form of bad repetition which characterizes modernity's experience of being-on-drugs, which is marked, as
Avital Ronell has described this, by our 'addicted condition' but also by
''the exposition of our modernity to the incompletion of *jouissance*' (Ronell,
1992, p. 59). Perhaps more importantly, we would have to ask at this point
whether the urge to redress the 'incompletion of *jouissance*' which, in
Ronell's analysis, fuels the circuit of addicted repetition, adequately
addresses the singularity of Michaux's experiments with the hallucinogen
mescaline as opposed to opiates; whether a general theory of narcotic
modernity misses the singularity and specificity of the drug and by extension Michaux's text. Here we touch upon the issue of whether there could
be a general theory of deconstruction rather than just a series of examples.

The 'addicted condition' has its counterpart in the holier-than-thou
preference for being-straight and 'drug free', which is no better nor worse
than its arch-enemy, being but an inverted form of the drugged madness
which Michaux, who attempts to *take drugs well*, recognized was, no matter how apparently exotic, still no more than a 'modulation' of *the same*:
being straight and being blasted both tend to give rise to ideas that are
'made up of similar elements, they are capable only of modulations'
(Michaux, 1974, p. 105). The deconstruction of drugs should, therefore,
neither remain fixated on the sober moment of providing an alternative
logos for them – a new 'pharmakology' – nor should it be averse to the
auto-deconstructive possibilities presented by partaking of drugs, as
Michaux's usage exemplifies.

REWRITING THE DRUGS TEXT AND TAKING DRUGS OTHERWISE

When Derrida expressed the idea of the text in deconstruction by saying that there is no 'outside-text' (*Il n'y a pas de hors-texte*), it was widely suspected that deconstruction was a sophisticated denial of 'experience' and 'the real', and therefore lacked seriousness. Experience was seemingly rejected in favour of an irreducible discursivity and open-ended textual play. Since then, the relevance of deconstruction as an approach to 'the text', particularly in the literal sense of reading literary, philosophical, historical texts, has found comparatively wide acceptance in the academy. However, the truly *speculative* import and the challenge of Derrida's early provocative remark, which urges the thinking of *everything* as text, still presents a serious affront to common sense as well as to philosophical thought. As David Wood has noted, the strategic generalization of the concept of the text as the 'articulation of differences' was never to be 'opposed to consciousness and experience', for these themselves 'display its primitive structures – differentiation, deferral' (1990, p. 63). So there never was any *denial* of consciousness, subjectivity, exteriority and the real world. Deconstruction represents the attempt to think from the limit of the inside/outside distinction, and in a manner which resists its own immediate reduction to a *liminology*: this is what deconstruction attempts in any particular context.

> If deconstruction takes place everywhere it [*ca*] takes place, where there is something (and is not therefore limited to meaning or to the text in the current and bookish sense of the word), we still have to think through what is happening in our world, in modernity. (Derrida, 1991b, p. 274)

The task of such a 'textualization' is the *re-inscription* of an exteriority always delimited correlative to (a prior) *inscription*. Gasché has usefully described inscription as what contextualizes rather than engenders (1986, pp. 157–8). Effectively, this means crossing (that is, chiasmically placing under erasure the difference between) constitution and meaning: deconstruction attempts to think *from the limit*, precisely, the non-difference between 'the life-world' and 'the text'. This move is not a totalizing attempt to think a 'unity', but it does aim at a kind of sublation of the phenomenological into what could be described as post-phenomenological textualization of difference. It stresses that thinking's 'other side' is the in-your-face (and off-your-face) reality of the quotidian – that plane which neither deconstruction nor drugs ever enables anyone to leave.

CONCLUSION: LIVING ON THE MARGINS OF THE UNFORGETTABLE

A deconstructive reading of Michaux's poetical narrative of intoxication seeks to do much more than expose the metaphysical presuppositions which lie behind its production. It also needs to consider, from the outset, its own shared fascination with Michaux's above-mentioned 'observations', at least in their focus upon the dysfunctional moments in systems of thought, be they conceptual or lived. Something of significance is evidently to be discerned in the 'breakdowns' Michaux explores. Whenever and wherever this thought of interruption and alterity finds its expression, it is associated also with moments of 'delirium', 'agony', 'ecstasy', 'surprise', 'overflowing', which are never simply 'figures' but always also moments of 'life'.

Such 'experiences' of alterity are real enough, as is the destruction of normality Michaux records in his accounts of what he calls his 'ordeals' (*épreuves*). In any case, with what motives would anyone be *principally* concerned to discredit the claimed insights of intoxication and the experience of the limit it represents, other than as an agent of normalizing power? It is more important to recall here that deconstruction 'begins wherever we are' (Derrida, 1974, p. 162); that its beginnings are multiple and that being-high is as much a place to begin as any other. Deconstruction has no interest in repeating the metaphysical exclusion of being-high in favour of sobriety, for this is simply to remain within the regime of metaphysical oppositions.

It is in the form of an intertextual, deconstructive engagement with Michaux's drug text that the case can be made, *contra* the metaphysicians, that exploding consciousness and raking over the debris of thought may find its relevance with respect to that sobriety-orientated other strategy, the patient archeology of conceptuality and reasoned argumentation of philosophy. Taken well, drugs, too, can undermine the conceptual authority of 'the normal' in general. For Michaux, it is in the mind's grievous moments, for example, when 'monstrously excited from the effects of large doses of mescaline' (Michaux, 1974, p. 5), that a trip to the limits of normality occurs as a poetic event, an encounter with language in which the difference between writing and experience is magically unmade. It is not surprising that such moments are clearly also expressed in terms of an experience with language. His thinking is overwhelmed at times by an almost Beckettian play of language:

> Words come. Words. Not the words I want. Not properly linked. Not in the right order. Forming only the fragment of the sentence I am searching for, scraps, pieces. . . . Yet I continue to write, to add words blindly aiming at the astonishing phenomenon. . . . *I seem to be writing*

not in order to get closer to what is to be said, but in order to get away from it.
                              (Michaux, 1974, pp. 27–31; my emphasis)

Does this 'astonishing phenomenon' cohabit with that 'experience of the impossible' so frequently invoked by Derrida as 'the least bad definition of deconstruction' (Derrida 1992c, p. 200)? Certainly, the arbitrariness of the normality in which the rational mind was at home with itself is exposed on the basis of the *destruction* of its regular order. But Unreason or madness, as such, only *reflects* normality, being made up of its elements. Deconstruction pushes beyond this truth to recover the sense in which the grievously intoxicated mind is no longer *wholly native* nor yet *wholly alien*.

There is no romanticism, either, in Michaux's trips to the borders of the normal. Due to his 'difficulties' with language, due to the ordeal of the 'mental excess' he has to struggle with, he inevitably gets little written down whilst he is high (Michaux, 1974, p. 46). What he learns is that in order to write, he must be a writer of the border. This, too, is a kind of ordeal, one which anyone writing on drugs today must face: such a writer must reject the seductions of both tripped-out mysticism and instrumental reason, evade the police, hide from the psychiatrists, risk being sold poison or placebos, and negotiate all other forces of control which strive to determine the meaning of 'drugs' and even prevent her/him from taking drugs (seriously) at all. From his risky, newly found, liminal perspective, Michaux learned of the 'scandalous forced *identity*' he was obliged to readopt on his return – when he came down (Michaux, 1974, p. 47).

With deconstruction, what goes up comes down elsewhere and somehow altered. The contingency of the 'normal' is now undeniable in a way in which it was not before prior to deconstruction's incessant tropism conjoined with Michaux's 'psychotropism'. Taking drugs (as a theme) has not given rise to nonsense, madness or ranting. A deconstructive approach to drugs exposes the hapless generality of thinking drugs in terms of the false alternatives of either panacea or panapathogen. This reading has emphatically not sought to go along with Michaux's text concerning what drugs 'reveal', as he puts it, of 'ourselves to ourselves'; it has sought, rather, to show how deconstructing his drug narrative can direct us towards alternative recipes for 'drugs', recipes better suited to a culture 'living on the margins of the Unforgettable' (Michaux, 1974, p. 170).

WORKS CITED

Amis, Martin (1975), *Dead Babies* (Harmondsworth: Penguin).
Burroughs, William (1993), *Naked Lunch* (London: Flamingo).
Derrida, Jacques (1974), *Of Grammatology*, trans. G. C. Spivak (Baltimore, MD: Johns Hopkins Press).

—— (1978), *Writing and Difference*, trans. A. Bass (London: Routledge and Kegan Paul).

—— (1981a), *Positions*, trans. A. Bass (Chicago: Chicago University Press).

—— (1981b), *Dissemination*, trans. B. Johnson (Chicago: Chicago University Press).

—— (1991a), 'Ulysses Gramophone: Hear Say Yes in Joyce', in *Between the Blinds*, ed. P. Kamuf (Hemel Hempstead: Harvester Wheatsheaf).

—— (1991b), 'Letter to a Japanese Friend', in *Between the Blinds*, ed. P. Kamuf.

—— (1992a), 'Passions: "An Oblique Offering"' in *Derrida: A Critical Reader*, ed. D. Wood (Oxford: Blackwell).

—— (1992b), 'This Strange Institution Called Literature: An Interview with Jacques Derrida', in *Acts of Literature*, ed. D. Attridge (London: Routledge).

—— (1992c), 'Afterw.rds: or, at least, less than a letter about a letter less', trans. Geoffrey Bennington, in *Afterwords*, ed. Nicholas Royle (Tampere, Finland: Outside Books).

—— (1994), *Specters of Marx: The State of the Debt, the Work of Mourning, and the New International*, trans. Peggy Kamuf (London: Routledge).

—— (1995), 'The Rhetoric of Drugs' in *Points . . .* , ed. E. Weber, trans. M. Israel (Stanford, CA: Stanford University Press).

Gasché, Rodolphe (1986), *The Tain of the Mirror* (Cambridge, MA: Harvard University Press).

—— (1987), 'Infrastructures and Systematicity', in *Deconstruction and Philosophy*, ed. J. Sallis (Chicago, IL: Chicago University Press).

Harvey, Irene (1992), 'Derrida and the Issue of Exemplarity', in *Derrida: A Critical Reader*, ed. D. Wood (Oxford: Blackwell).

Michaux, Henri (1974), *The Major Ordeals of the Mind*, trans. R. Howard (London: Secker and Warburg), originally published as *Les grandes épreuves de l'esprit et les innombrables petites* (Paris: Gallimard, 1966).

Ronell, Avital (1992), *Crack Wars* (Nebraska: University of Nebraska Press).

Welsh, Irvine, (1993), *Trainspotting* (London: Secker & Warburg).

—— (1996), *Ecstasy* (London: Jonathan Cape).

Wood, David (1990), *Philosophy at the Limit* (London: Unwin Hyman).

4

Deconstruction and Ethics

Geoffrey Bennington

Deconstruction cannot propose an ethics. If the concept – all the concepts – of ethics come to us, as they do, as they cannot fail to, from the tradition it has become commonplace to call 'Western metaphysics', and if, as Derrida announces from the start, deconstruction aims to deconstruct 'the greatest totality',[1] the interrelated network of concepts bequeathed to us by and as that metaphysics, then 'ethics' cannot fail to be a theme and an object of deconstruction, to be deconstructed, rather than a subject of its admiration or affirmation. Ethics is metaphysical through and through and can therefore never simply be assumed or affirmed in deconstruction. The demand or desire for a 'deconstructive ethics' is in this sense doomed to be disappointed.

And yet, through the naivety of certain reactions to deconstruction which have wished to present it as more or less straightforwardly ethical, as though the burden of deconstruction consisted in delivering us from metaphysical illusion into the clear light of ethical felicity and self-right-eousness,[2] we might also detect a certain truth worthy of elaboration. Deconstruction deconstructs ethics, or shows up ethics deconstructing (itself), in deconstruction, but *some* sense of ethics or the ethical, something archi-ethical, perhaps, survives the deconstruction or emerges as its origin or resource. Deconstruction cannot be ethical, cannot propose an ethics, but ethics might nonetheless provide a privileged *clue* for deconstruction, and deconstruction might provide a new way of thinking about some of problems traditionally posed by ethics.

The form of this argument is familiar from other deconstructive movements. Writing, for – the perhaps most famous – example, is itself a metaphysical concept which nonetheless, through its very metaphysical determination, provides important resources for the deconstruction of metaphysics. Similarly for the concept of the sign or of metaphor. Concepts constitutively 'secondarized' by metaphysics can be shown to be paradoxically primary, constitutive themselves of the very primary concept (and in the end, always, 'presence') from which they cannot fall to appear to be derived. In this sense, 'ethics' too always might provide deconstruction with resources repressed or left unexploited by its metaphysical determination, and these resources might then be shown to be in some way 'more powerful' than that metaphysical determination, in excess of it. In which case deconstruction might after all be describable as ethical, and perhaps as ethics itself. In 'Force of Law', Derrida famously and mysteriously claims that justice (as distinct from right or law) is the undeconstructible condition of deconstruction, and it seems that this must have some ethical resonance if it is to be intelligible.[3]

There is of course at least one salient difference between writing and ethics as potential deconstructive resources, and that is their very different status in metaphysical thought. Writing is at best a secondary concept in a domain (that of language) itself made secondary in traditional thinking, whereas ethics is, from the start, one of the basic divisions of philosophy, one of its major branches. It might then be expected that it will be a more complex and differentiated notion than was 'writing', and provide a concomitantly harder task for deconstruction. And further, whereas 'writing' is used explicitly and consistently in Derrida's work as a means into deconstructive thinking, exhaustively unpacked in both its traditional and its deconstructive guises, 'ethics' is never treated in such a way, and indeed, as we shall see, its *explicit* incidence in Derrida's work is essentially concentrated in his discussions of the work of Emmanuel Lévinas, whose thought is precisely dedicated to displacing the traditional metaphysical sense of ethics in the name of a redefined notion of metaphysics. It is these discussions of Lévinas that will provide us with our guiding thread.

On the other hand, if Derrida has been at all successful in carrying out or promoting the deconstruction of 'the greatest totality', then we would be right to expect that his thinking *in general* will not fail to have effects in the philosophical domain traditionally called ethics, and indeed that it would not be false to spread a discussion of 'deconstruction and ethics' across his work as a whole (the notes here will try to give a sense of this possibility). And indeed we shall see that this is the case: the very general concept of the 'originary trace' as developed in *De la grammatologie* in fact *immediately* engages with the 'relation to the other' which we can follow Lévinas in seeing as the basis of the ethical. This will have two distinct consequences: (1) deconstructive thought *in general* has an ethical import just because of this status of the originary trace, and (2) deconstructive thought will have *specific* interventions to make in the traditional metaphysical vocabulary of ethics, around concepts such as responsibility, decision, law and duty.

The non-ethical opening of ethics can be seen straightforwardly and yet intractably in the fact of reading, for example this, here, now.[4] Any text, 'before' affirming or communicating anything at all, is constituted as an appeal to a reading always still to come.[5] No text can make any particular reading of itself *necessary* (the text of laws is perhaps the clearest example here: laws attempt to exclude any reading other than the one 'intended' by the legislator, to constrain reading to *only this one* reading, but show up in the extraordinary textual efforts this involves the very impossibility of the task), but equally no text can open itself up to *just any* reading (no text is *absolutely indeterminate* with respect to its reading). Texts appeal to reading, *cry out for reading*, and not just for any reading, but leave open an essential latitude or freedom which just is what constitutes reading *as* reading rather than as passive decipherment. There would be no practice, and no institutions of reading, without this opening, and without the *remaining* open of this opening. (Hermeneutics is the dream of closing that opening.) Any reading at all, however respectful of the text being read (however respectful, that is, of the way the text reads itself) takes place in this opening, and this is why texts are not messages, and why the classical concept of 'communication' is unhelpful in discussing them. It follows that reading has a duty to respect not only the text's 'wishes' (the reading of itself most obviously programmed into itself) but also the opening that opens a margin of freedom with respect to any such wishes, and without which those wishes could not even be registered or recognized. Readers recognize those wishes (traditionally thought of as the 'author's intentions') only by opening themselves to the opening which constitutes the very *readability* of the text – however minimal that readability may be in fact – and that readability is, as such, already in excess of those wishes. A text is a text only as at least minimally readable in this sense, and that means it always can be read *differently* with respect to the way it would wish to be read. An *absolutely* respectful relation to a text would forbid one from even touching it. The ethics of reading would, then, consist in the negotiation of the margin opened by readability.[6]

Derrida on occasion formulates this situation in terms of legacies or inheritance. Here, for example, in *Specters de Marx*:

> An inheritance is never gathered, it is never one with itself. Its presumed unity, if there is one, can only consist in the *injunction to reaffirm by choosing. You must* [il faut] means you must filter, select, criticise, you must sort out among several of the possibilities which inhabit the same injunction. And inhabit it in contradictory fashion around a secret. If the legibility of a legacy were given, natural, transparent, univocal, if it did not simultaneously call for and defy interpretation, one would never have to inherit from it. One would be affected by it as by a cause – natural or genetic. One always inherits a secret, which says 'Read me,

will you ever be up to it?'   (p. 40 [16])

and a little later:

> Inheritance is never a given, it is always a task. It remains before us, as
> incontestably as the fact that, before even wanting it or refusing it, we
> are inheritors, and inheritors in mourning, like all inheritors. In partic-
> ular for what is called Marxism. *To be* . . . means . . . . *to inherit*. All ques-
> tions about being or what one is to be (or not to be) are questions of
> inheritance. There is no backward-looking fervour involved in recalling
> this fact, no traditionalist flavour. Reaction, reactionary or reactive are
> only interpretations of the structure of inheritance. We *are* inheritors,
> which does not mean that we *have* or that we *receive* this or that, that a
> given inheritance enriches us one day with this or that, but that the
> *being* we are *is* first of all inheritance, like it or not, know it or not.
>
> (p. 94 [54])

The concept of inheritance also appears at a key moment in a text on
Nelson Mandela: having pointed out Mandela's admiration for the
European tradition of parliamentary democracy, Derrida goes on:

> But if he admires this tradition, does that mean he is its inheritor, sim-
> ply its inheritor? Yes and no, according to what one understands here
> by inheritance. One can recognise an authentic inheritor in he who con-
> serves and reproduces, but also in he who respects the *logic* of the
> legacy to the point of turning it back on occasion against those who
> claim to be its holders, to the point of showing up against the usurpers
> the very thing that in the inheritance, has never yet been seen: to the
> point of bringing to light, by the unheard-of *act* of a reflection, what had
> never seen the light.[7]

It follows from this situation that reading-as-inheritance is not only itself
an ethical relation, but that it can be taken to *exemplify* the ethical relation
as asymmetrical relation to an unmasterable and unassimilable other.
That other is not *absolutely* other (if it were, the text would be unrecognizable as a text, would not even call for reading) but its otherness (the
insistence and ultimate indecipherability of the *call* for reading, the fact
that reading is not just a tranquil act of deciphering) is irreducible.[8] In this
situation in which one's duty is to read in respect for what makes reading
possible (i.e. for the very thing that makes it impossible for reading to be
mere deciphering, the thing that reading can never read as such), one's
duty, or the duty of that duty, is to be *inventive*. Being inventive means not
being merely *dutiful*. A dutiful (for example scholarly) reading never
begins to fulfil its duty, in so far as it tends to close down the opening that

makes reading possible and necessary in the first place:[9] and indeed this logic can be extended to the concept of duty in general – Kant famously says that I must act not just *in accordance with* duty but *from* duty, for the sake of duty (otherwise I always might simply be aping what I take to be dutiful conduct)[10], but the further logic of this is that I must in fact, in the name of duty, act not just *from* duty, but *out of* duty in the sense of inventing something that falls outside what duty might be taken to dictate or prescribe. Simply following one's duty, looking up the appropriate action in a book of laws or rules, as it were, is anything but ethical – at best this is an *administration* of rights and duties, a *bureaucracy* of ethics. In this sense an ethical act worthy of its name is always *inventive*, and inventive not at all in the interests of expressing the 'subjective' freedom of the agent, but in response and responsibility to the other (here the text being read). For I am, after all, reading the other's text, not simply attempting to 'express myself': and this situation is general. I can in fact 'express myself', exercise my freedom, only in this situation of response and responsibility with respect to the always-already-thereness of the other text as part of a 'tradition' to which I am always already indebted.

This 'ethics of reading' informs Derrida's formulations from his early work. In discussions of Freud or Lévi-Strauss, for example, it is clear that there is no escaping from 'complicity' with the tradition (it alone provides us with all our concepts and vocabularies), so the issue becomes one of rigorously and inventively negotiating that necessary complicity (what we have here been calling inheritance or just reading). 'Freud and the Scene of Writing', for example, begins by seeming to condemn Freud on the grounds that all of his concepts are inherited from the metaphysical tradition, and cannot therefore be as radical or as new as is often thought. But Derrida immediately goes on to recognize that *in itself* this situation of inheritance cannot be a ground for complaint or criticism, just because this situation is unavoidable: everyone must of necessity inherit their concepts from the tradition, so the ground of complaint is displaced, and the objection to Freud becomes the fact that he 'never reflected the historical and theoretical necessity' of this situation.[11] Similarly, in the famous early essay on 'Structure, Sign and Play in the Discourse of the Human Sciences', Derrida rapidly establishes around Lévi-Strauss the inevitability of a certain 'complicity' with the tradition: and, given that inevitability, the issue becomes one of how it is negotiated and reflected upon. Like Freud, Lévi-Strauss cannot do other than inherit his concepts from the tradition; what he might have been expected to do (and this, then, is an ethical complaint) is to reflect on that very inevitability. Only thus, the argument goes, would there be a chance of doing something about, and with, the inheritance one cannot choose not to take on.[12]

This situation of reading, then, provides a certain *matrix* for thinking about the inherited nature of concepts in general, the obligation (not a necessity, so at most what Derrida would call a *chance*) to read and thereby to give oneself the possibility of displacing them. On this construal, a certain apparent *irresponsibility* (what I have been calling reading) opens the possibility of responsibility as response to the other as necessarily not absolutely other. But if this situation is general, and places one's conceptual dealings in general in a *milieu* that might reasonably appeal to a displaced (responsibly read) sense of ethics to describe it,[13] that sense of ethics *doubles up* when the specific conceptuality being read and inherited is that of ethics itself. For Derrida's work does not just reflect, in a way we might want to call ethical, on the relation to the traditionality of thought *in general*, but also, on occasion, within that *milieu*, reflects on the traditionality of ethical concepts in particular, and indeed has done so increasingly in recent years. This more explicitly ethical reflection can rapidly be characterized as taking place in a space between a 'phenomenological' critique of the traditional division of philosophy (including the place that division gives to the ethical), and a Lévinasian attempt to retrieve a sense of the ethical as 'first philosophy'. Derrida wants both to register the force of Husserl's or (more radically) Heidegger's suspicion of the place of ethics in the traditional figuring of philosophy,[14] and Lévinas's powerful claim that ethics be re-considered as *first* philosophy, prior to what he calls ontology. The reference to Lévinas seems almost as essential to Derrida as the reference to Heidegger, and one way of tracking a path through Derrida's work is to follow the three great essays devoted to Lévinas.[15] We have already seen some of the doubts raised in 'Violence and Metaphysics' about Lévinas's basic conceptuality, and used 'En ce moment même . . .' to establish a certain originary ethicity in the textuality itself: let us now turn to 'Le mot d'accueil' for an elaboration of some more 'positive' ethical moments in Derrida.

The central argument of this text goes as follows: according to Lévinas, ethics begins in the welcome or reception of the other, who 'appears' non-phenomenally in the *face*.[16] This primary receptivity defines the ethical relation as the face-to-face, a non-symmetrical dual relation. Lévinas argues very forcibly that only this relation, as essentially ethical, provides the possibility of *sense* in a situation which is otherwise one of *disorientation*.[17] This face-to-face relation with the other is marked as asymmetrical by the other's transcendence, which in this context means that the other has a radical prior claim on me, or even allows 'me' to exist as essentially responsibility to and for the other. I do not exist first, and then encounter the other: rather the (always singular) other calls me into being as always already responsible for him.[18] In 'Le mot d'accueil', Derrida insists on how this dual (if asymmetrical) relation is from the start affected by the *third party*. This possibility of the third party (another other, the other's other) haunting my face-to-face is immediately the place of response and responsibility, the third party is the possibility of raising questions about that response and responsibility (p. 63). Reading beyond the obvious intention of Lévinas's text, Derrida wants to say that this originary presence of the third party haunting the face-to-face with the other may appear to compromise or contaminate the purity of the properly ethical relation, but that that possible contamination, that compromise of purity, is *necessary* if the ethical relation is to avoid the possibility of an absolute violence of that purity itself.[19] For if the singular encounter with the other in the face-to-face were not always already compromised by this haunting third party (and, therefore, by communicability, intelligibility, but also institutionalization and politicization), then the supposedly pure ethical relation always might be that of the worst violence:

> The third party does not wait, his illeity calls from the moment of the epiphany of the face in the face-to-face. For the absence of the third party would threaten with violence the purity of the ethical in the absolute immediacy of the face-to-face with the unique. No doubt Lévinas does not say it in this form. But what is he doing when, beyond or through the duel of the face-to-face between two 'unique beings', he appeals to justice, affirms and reaffirms that justice 'is necessary' [*il faut*]? Is he not, then, taking into account this hypothesis of a violence of pure and immediate ethics in the face-to-face of the face? Of a violence potentially unleashed in the experience of the neighbour and of absolute uniqueness? Of the impossibility of discerning good from evil, love from hatred, giving from taking, desire for life and death drive, hospitable welcome from selfish or narcissistic enclosure?
>
> The third party would thus protect against the vertigo of ethical violence itself. Ethics could be doubly exposed to this same violence: exposed to suffer it, but also to exercise it. Alternatively or simultaneously. It is true that the protective or mediating third party, in its juridico-political becoming, in turn violates, at least virtually, the purity of the ethical desire for the unique. Whence the terrifying fatality of a double constraint.   (p. 66)

This analysis, which in typical deconstructive style pushes the text read beyond its own explicit claims, but in so doing respects the logic of the text's own economy and answers to the 'ethics of reading' scenario we have sketched out above, generates a situation which can be found in all deconstructive situations: one of an essential *contaminability* which aims to account *both* for the possibility of any purity whatsoever, *and* for the *a priori* impossibility of the (even ideal) achievement of any such purity.

The logic here, which is just what is elsewhere formulated as the *quasi-trancendental*, states in general a complicity (even an identity) between conditions of possibility and conditions of impossibility, such that the *necessary possibility* of the failure, compromise or contamination of the supposedly (or desiredly) pure case is sufficient to justify the thought that that purity is *already* compromised in its very formulation. The very thing which is supposed to protect the purity in question is the thing that compromises it.[20] In this case, the ethical relation of the face-to-face constitutes itself *as* ethical only by protecting itself from itself in the figure of the third party: but that same figure will always prevent the ethical being quite the pure relation it was supposed to be, and to that extent casts doubt on its priority *as* ethical.

The paradoxical or aporetical consequences of this situation are considerable, but it is in them that we can find the core of deconstructive thought about ethics. For example, it follows from the situation just described (through and beyond Lévinas, in a version of Lévinas that already appeals to the third party beyond for its legitimacy) that justice finds its condition of possibility in what Derrida calls *perjury*. The ethical nature of the primary ethical relation in the singular face-to-face with the always unique other depends on that ethic's being protected from itself by the appeal to, and of, the third party: but appealing to that third party means that I am *eo ipso* being unfaithful to the other, failing in my implicit promise of an unconditional fidelity and respect. Ethics has a chance of being ethical only in this becoming-justice which is already also the becoming-right of justice, the becoming-formal of the absolutely non-formal relation of the face-to-face, the becoming-institutionalized of the preinstitutional 'absolute anteriority' of the relation to the other, and thus in the betrayal of my primary engagement to the other *as this* singular other. Ethics begins with this archi-betrayal or archi-perjury which functions as its condition of possibility and (therefore) of impossibility:

> Lévinas never designates this double bind in this way. I shall however take the risk myself of inscribing its necessity in the consequence of his axioms, axioms established or recalled by Lévinas himself: if the face-to-face with the unique engages the infinite ethics of my responsibility for the other in a sort of oath [*serment*] before the letter, a promise of respect or unconditional fidelity, then the ineluctability of the third party, and with him of justice, signs a first act of perjury . . .
>
> Thereafter, in the deployment of justice, one can no longer discern fidelity to one's promise from the perjury of false witness, but primarily one can no longer discern betrayal from betrayal, always more than one betrayal. One ought then, with all the necessary analytical prudence, to respect the quality, the modality, the situation of the failings with respect to this 'original word of honour' before all oaths [*serments*].

But these differences would never erase the trace of this inaugural perjury. Like the third party who does not wait, the agency [*l'instance*] that
opens both ethics and justice is, in them, in a situation [*en instance de*] of
quasi-transcendental or originary, even pre-originary, perjury.   (p. 68)

Ethics, then, is ethical only to the extent that it is originarily compromised
or contaminated by the non-ethical. According to a logic laid out more
than thirty years earlier in 'Violence and metaphysics', the chance of
avoiding the worst violence is given by a compromise involving an acceptance of, and calculation of, the lesser violence.[21] As with all other apparently purely positive concepts analysed deconstructively, ethics in this
Lévinasian sense can be made coherent only by allowing that it protect
itself from itself by a necessarily risky innoculatory contamination of itself
by its apparent other(s). In this case, Derrida will say that ethics is essentially *pervertible*, and that this pervertibility is the positive condition (to be
affirmed, then) of all the 'positive' values (the Good, the Just, and so on)
ethics enjoins us to seek.

This affirmation of pervertibility as a positive condition of what
appeared to be opposed to it (so that, for example, a positive condition of
promising is that I always might not keep my promise, for without such
a necessary possibility, if the object of my promise necessarily followed
from my promising it, my promise would not be a promise at all, but a
necessary causal sequence[22]) does not of course commit one to welcom-
ing *actual* perversions of ethical values. Saying that a positive condition of
ethics is an inaugural – structural – perjury does not mean that I am
henceforth ethically bound to *approve* actual acts of perjury. This production of a condition of possibility is the aspect of the analysis that prompts
its qualification as transcendental. But its specifically *quasi*-transcendental
character means that, as always in deconstructive thought, it is impossible rigorously to separate the transcendental from the factical or the
empirical,[23] and this entails that, uncomfortably, I cannot use the transcendental aspect of the analysis to provide *a priori* knowledge of which
empirical cases, which events arriving, in fact constitute acts of perversion
or perversity. The positive necessary possibility of perjury affects, in the
modality of necessary possibility, all empirical acts of promising or
swearing, for example, but leaves open the singular judgement each time
as to the actual perversity of this or that act. The quasi-transcendental
analysis opens up, as a condition of ethics, the possibility of the perjury or
perversion of ethics. The necessary possibility of the worst is a positive
condition of the (unconditionally demanded) better. The necessary possibility of what Kant called radical evil is a positive condition of the good.
The non-ethical opening of ethics, as 'Violence and Metaphysics' called it,
consists in just this: that the *chance* of ethics (i.e. its necessary possibility
as nonnecessary[24]) lies in its hospitality to the possibility that the event to

come is the worst, that the primary 'yes' it says to the other, the stranger,[25] the *arrivant*,[26] *always might* be a welcome to something or someone who will simply blow away my home, my welcome, the threshold at which I extend the greeting and the offer of food and drink in the primary ethical gesture according to Lévinas. Ethics means, then, on this view, that I know *a priori* that ethics is constitutively pervertible, but that I *never know* in advance when it is perverted in fact. As we saw earlier, any *knowledge* in this respect would immediately evacuate the specificity of the ethical in favour of an administrative or bureaucratic application of cognitive rules.

This situation appears to promote what might be called a *decisionistic* view of ethics. Without the sort of supposedly binding prior *test* of what is ethical provided by the so-called Kantian formalism, and without the sort of securities offered by the sort of ethical thinking that grounds ethics unproblematically in a particular *ethos* or even ethnos,[27] it looks unavoidable that ethics come to be a matter of singular decisions taken on the occasion of singular events. And, as is also the case with Carl Schmitt's decisionism in the realm of political theory, this always might seem to run the risk of promoting a particular understanding of the sovereignty of the deciding subject.[28] It is not hard to see that Derrida's doubts about Lévinas's granting primacy to the other in the ethical relation, with its concomitant (and attractive, seductive) demoting of the subject from its classical voluntaristic position, always might seem to risk returning to a sort of subjectivism without any doctrine of subjectivity to back it up. It is, then, of the utmost importance that Derrida explicitly and quite consistently argues that the logic of decision called for by the position we have summarized here is more powerful than the resources of the classical doctrine of the subject. For what would a decision that simply deployed my own subjective, egological possibilities be, if not a refusal of the very event of alterity that is here being radicalized as the (non-ethical) condition of the ethical? If 'decision' simply meant the expression of my subjective will, then it would be no decision at all, but again, in a different register, the mere application of given possibilities to a situation which consists precisely in a certain challenge to what is merely possible.[29] Derrida argues that the concept of responsibility, which is one way into what is here being described, exceeds the resources of the concept of the subject to such an extent that the subject functions as a *de-responsibilizing* concept, a concept which closes off the infinite nature of responsibility which it is Lévinas's strength to bring out so forcibly. And if Derrida's 'defence' of Husserl in 'Violence and Metaphysics' seemed to run the risk of reinstating the primacy of the subject against Lévinas's more audacious insight, 'Le mot d'accueil' makes clearer what the economy of the earlier text might have obscured a little: if we are to talk intelligibly of decisions and responsibilities, then we must recognize that they take place *through the other*, and that their taking place 'in me' tells us

something about *the other (already) in me*, such that, following another
'axiom' of deconstructive thought, 'I' am only in so far as I already harbour (welcome) the other in me, if only, as we pointed out at the beginning of this sketch, in so far as to be me I must accept as mine the alterity
of the 'tradition' (minimally in the form of the language I speak but never
chose to speak,[30] and under the name I am given but have never given
myself[31]). Here too, Derrida is explicitly extending (and thereby also,
respectfully, contesting) Lévinas:

> If one pursues them with the necessary audacity and rigour, these con-
> sequences ought to lead us to an other thinking of the responsible deci-
> sion. Lévinas would no doubt not say it like this, but can one not claim
> in that case [Derrida has just been quoting Lévinas to the effect that: 'It
> is not I – it is the Other who can say *yes*'] that without exonerating me
> in any way, decision and responsibility are always of the other? That
> they always come back down to the other, from the other, be it the other
> in me? For would it really be a decision, an initiative that remained
> purely and simply 'mine', in conformity with the necessity which yet
> seems to require, in the most powerful tradition of ethics and philoso-
> phy, that the decision always be 'my' decision, the decision of one who
> can freely say 'I', 'me', *ipse, egomet ipse*? Would what comes back down
> to me in this way still be a decision? Does one have the right to give this
> name 'decision' to a purely autonomous movement, be it one of wel-
> come and hospitality, which would proceed only from me, myself, and
> would merely deploy the possibilities of a subjectivity that was mine?
> Would we not be justified in seeing in that the unfolding of an egolog-
> ical immanence, the autonomical and automatic deployment of the
> predicates or possibilities proper to a subject, without that tearing that
> ought to advene in any so-called free decision?   (pp. 52–3)

This radicalization by Derrida of Lévinas's thought consists in a way of no
more than a rigorous unwrapping of the concept of alterity which it is
Lévinas's immeasurable merit to have brought out as the constitutive
moment of the ethical. That 'radicalization' can always look (and to
Lévinasians has often looked) like just the opposite, a reduction of the
radicality of Lévinas's own thinking, in so far as it seems to protest
against Lévinas's absolutizing of the other, and to that extent make the
other *less other* than is the case in Lévinas. But in this paradoxical domain
we should be wary of such a linear logic: Derrida's construal of alterity as
always less than absolute in fact constitutes a thought of the other as *more
other than the absolute other*. This apparent 'less is more' logic flows from
Derrida's earliest insights into the notion of difference, and the quasi-con-
cept of *différance* which I have suggested elsewhere can helpfully be
thought of as a name for the non-absolutizability of difference.[32]

Différance is what saves a thought of difference from the Hegelian arguments about absolute difference collapsing into indifference and absolute identity, or rather affirms the difference *in* indifference and absolute identity as not amenable to the dialectical resolution Hegel thinks inevitably follows from the truth of difference supposedly residing in opposition and contradiction. The apparently maximal thought of difference as contradiction in fact always leads to a reaffirmation of identity beyond difference, whereas the apparently minimal thought of difference *this side of* opposition and contradiction releases a more radical and intractable concept of difference which is not to be teleologically or dialectically gathered up in a greater identity.[33]

In the present context, the consequence of this thinking of difference or alterity as non-absolute is what saves Derrida from Lévinas's attempt to situate the ethical as such as 'first philosophy', against ontology, and also from the ultimate piety of the appeal to God as the almost inevitable figure of absolute alterity, and thereby as the truth of the singular face of the other which grounds ethics, gives sense, and supposedly saves us from disorientation. But it also, and this too is a general feature of deconstructive thought, makes it difficult to maintain with any confidence the inherited metaphysical distinctions between, for example, ontology, ethics and politics. Derrida's radicalizations of Lévinas in the first part of 'Le mot d'accueil' tend to complicate the distinction between ontology and ethics,[34] and the second part goes on to suggest that Lévinas will be unable, in spite of himself, to maintain the sorts of distinctions between ethics and politics which are, however, crucial to his philosophy, at least from the opening paragraph of *Totality and Infinity*.[35]

Derrida's point derives from what we have just seen about the figure of the third party: for if the third party makes possible the ethical relation as such by instigating an originary and necessary contamination of its purity, then the defining feature of the ethical (the dual figure of the face-to-face, however asymmetrical) tends to be lost in the perspective of a multiplicity of relations introduced by the opening to the third party in general. In which case we might want to say that we are as much in the domain of politics as of ethics.

This disturbing pluralization and even scattering of the figure of the other (to which Lévinas appealed to secure a principle of sense in a situation of distressful disorientation) gives rise, in other recent essays by Derrida, to the striking formula *tout autre est tout autre*.[36] This formula, translated by David Wills as 'Every other (one) is every (bit) other', introduces simultaneously a certain irreducible *singularity* and a certain *plurality*. One of the challenges of Derrida's thought has always been to grasp together singularity and plurality or multiplicity, and this challenge can be followed in recent work both through the questioning of Kierkegaard's distinction between the ethical and the religious in 'Donner la mort', and through the attempt to rethink the concept of democracy in *Politiques de l'amitié*. The principle whereby the very (irreplaceable) singularity of the other (the principle of its difference) is thinkable only in the context of that singularity's potential equalization with every other singularity (the principle of its indifference) will pose difficult challenges to our thinking for some (incalculable) time to come. In the context of 'deconstruction and ethics', it is this principle that ensures the possibility both of the ever-singular 'ethical' relation and of its perpetual transgression and dispersion in 'political' multiplicity.

NOTES

1. Jacques Derrida, *De la grammatologie* (Paris: Minuit, 1967), p, 68 [46].
2. See Derrida's comments on this prospect in *Passions: l'offrande oblique* (Paris: Galilée, 1983), pp. 13–15 [12–14]. Quoted at some length by Simon Critchley in 'The Ethics of Deconstruction: An Attempt at Self-criticism', and by Robert Bernasconi in his remarkable article 'Justice without Ethics', p. 58. Critchley's book *The Ethics of Deconstruction* (Oxford: Blackwell, 1992) remains in many ways a helpful introduction to the issues.
3. *Force de loi* (Paris: Galilée, 1994), p. 35 [945].
4. Derrida's second text on Lévinas, 'En ce moment même . . .', in *Psyché: Inventions de l'autre* (Paris: Galilée, 1987), makes much of instances in Lévinas's writing where he appeals to the present moment of writing or reading in the text itself, showing how such moments are dislocated repetitions of each other, where the text both interrupts itself and gathers up its interruptions into its texture. The inscrutability or indeterminability of deictic or indexical terms in written texts is one of Derrida's favourite features of writing, and the point from which the ambitions of phenomenology are systematically undone: *La voix et le phénomène* (Paris: PUF, 1967) already made the pronoun 'je' and the effects of its repeatability a crux of its analyses.
5. The following reflections on reading are summarized from the longer presentation at the beginning of my piece 'Lecture – de Georges Bataille', in *Georges Bataille – après tout*, ed. D. Hollier (Paris: Belin, 1995). Compare Critchley's somewhat different account of 'clôtural reading' in *The Ethics of Deconstruction*.
6. The 'ethics of reading' adumbrated here bears an obvious relation of respectful inheritance (and distance) to the description Heidegger gives in §35 of the *Kantbuch*, but could not quite accept Heidegger's justification of what he sees as the inevitable violence of interpretation by 'the force of an inspirational Idea'. I discuss this in relation to Kant in *La frontière* (forthcoming). See too J. Hillis Miller, *The Ethics of Reading* (New York: Columbia University Press, 1987).
7. 'Admiration de Nelson Mandela', in *Psyché* (Paris: Galilée, 1987) p. 456; cf. too pp. 471–2, and *Du droit à la philosophie* (Paris: Galilée, 1990) pp. 82 and 449.
8. This is the point of some of Derrida's objections to Lévinas in 'Violence and Metaphysics', in *Writing and Difference* (Chicago: Chicago University Press, 1978): Lévinas opposes to Husserl's difficulties in the *Cartesian Meditations* with the problem of the other the sense that the other is *absolutely* other than me, and Derrida defends Husserl on the grounds that the alterity of the other has a chance of being registered only to the extent that that other is in some sense the *same* as me. The other is only really other to the extent that he, she

or it does not simply fall back into the status of the sort of alterity the objects of the external world can have: the alterity of the other in Lévinas's sense depends, according to this early analysis, on the fact that the other is presumed to be enough like me for its otherness (as 'another origin of the world' in phenomenological parlance) to become salient. Derrida here finds himself in a curious position: *La voix et le phénomène* suggested (without producing detailed analysis) that this issue of the analogical appresentation of the other was, along with the temporal issues attaching to terms in 're-' (repetition, representation, retention), one of the points at which Husserl's phenomenology was at its most vulnerable. In 'Violence and Metaphysics' he appears to be defending Husserl on just this issue, on the grounds that Husserl allows the real alterity of the other to emerge just because of the impenetrability to me of what is nonetheless manifestly an *alter ego*, the *same* as me. The possible coherence of these two gestures is no doubt given by Derrida's complex thinking about 'the same' as constitutively non-identical. Derrida does leave open the possibility of criticizing Husserl on this point ('Violence and Metaphysics', p. 194, n. 1), as indeed he does in *La voix et le phénomène*, and returns briefly to it in 'Le mot d'accueil' in *Adieu* (Paris: Galileé, 1997), p. 96.

9. I argue this in the particular context of the journal *French Studies* in a paper presented to that journal's 50th annual conference in 1997: 'Faire semblant', probably not forthcoming in *French Studies*.

10. See for example Kant, *Critique of Practical Reason* (Cambridge University Press, 1997), p. 69: 'The concept of duty, therefore, requires of the action *objective* accord with the law but requires of the maxim of the action *subjective* respect for the law, as the sole way of determining the will by the law. And on this rests the distinction between consciousness of having acted *in conformity with duty* and *from duty*, that is, respect for the law, the first of which (legality) is possible even if the inclinations alone have been the determining grounds of the will whereas the second (*morality*), moral worth, must be placed solely in this: that the action takes place from duty, that is, for the sake of the law alone.' The Derridean rewriting of this into an obligation to act inventively *out of* duty would position that for the sake of which we should so act not as the law, but as justice, in the sense appealed to in *Force de loi*, where justice (beyond any formalization of it as law or right or institution) is presented as the 'undeconstructible condition of deconstruction', or even as deconstruction itself (p. 35 [945]). The apparent ethical pathos generated here needs to be tempered by the necessary possibility of the sort of aping Kant is concerned to exclude: my supposedly deconstructive invocation of justice as that for the sake of which I act *always might* be a mere simulacrum, and indeed always will be in the absence of invention. Derrida's regular appeals to the need for invention in the fields of ethics or politics necessarily disappoint: we would obviously like to be told what to invent – at which point we would be released from the responsibility of invention . . .

11. I discuss this gesture in the specific context of Derrida's relation to Freud in 'Circanalyse – la chose même', forthcoming in *Depuis Lacan*, ed. Patrick Guyomard and René Major.

12. 'The quality and fecundity of a discourse are perhaps measured by the critical rigour with which this relation to the history of metaphysics and of inherited concepts is thought through' (*L'écriture et la différence* (Paris: Seuil, 1967), p. 414 [282]).

13. On the question of responding and responsibility, see Gasché's *Inventions of Difference* (Cambridge, MA: Harvard University Press, 1994) and my reservations in 'Genuine Gasché (perhaps)' (*Imprimatur*, **1**, 2–3 (1996), pp. 252–7).

The displacement responsibility operates on ethics probably means that it is at least as compelling to call this a political situation, and one of the points of 'Le mot d'accueil' is to question the distinction between ethics and politics.

14. In 'Violence and metaphysics', Derrida associates Husserl and Heidegger at least in that they share (1) a commitment to the essentially Greek source of philosophy; (2) a demand for a transgression or reduction of metaphysics, and (3) 'the category of the *ethical* is here not only dissociated from metaphysics, but related to something other than itself, an earlier and more radical instance. When it is not, when the law, the power of resolution and the relation to the other come back to the αρχη, they lose their ethical specificity there.' [Derrida's footnote: Husserl: 'Reason does not tolerate being distinguished into "theoretical", "practical" or aesthetic, etc.'. Heidegger: 'Even such names as "logic", "ethics", and "physics" flourish only when original thinking comes to an end'] 'Violence et métaphysique', p. 121.

15. These are, equally spaced at intervals of sixteen years: "Violence et Métaphysique' (1964), 'En ce moment même dans cet ouvrage me voici' (1980), 'Le mot d'accueil' (1996).

16. Lévinas characterizes the face at length in section III, 'The Face and Exteriority', of *Totality and Infinity* (trans. Alphonso Lingis, 1969).

17. See the important essay 'La signification et le sens' ('Meaning and Sense', trans. Alphonso Lingis, Dordrecht: Martinus Nijhoff, 1987). The notions of orientation and disorientation appear insistently in this text: see for example pp. 34, 36, 39, 40, 42, 43, 44, 60 [91, 93, 97, 99]. It would be possible to show, in a parallel reading of Kant's short 1786 text 'What is it to Orient Oneself in Thought?', that the appeal to orientation makes sense only in a prior context of disorientation, so that orientation always retains the trace of the very disorientation it is supposed to overcome. See too Derrida's reflections on the notion of a 'heading' in *L'Autre cap* (Paris: Minuit, 1991).

18. I use the masculine pronoun to recall the fact that Lévinas has a specific and complex thinking around sexual difference and the feminine. Derrida draws attention to this at the very end of 'Violence et Métaphysique' (p. 228, n. 1), and devotes a large part of 'En ce moment même . . .' to discussion of it (pp. 192–8); see too 'Le mot d'accueil', pp. 71–85, on Lévinas's figuring of domestic space as feminine.

19. Lévinas himself introduces this notion of the 'Il', of *illeity*, to describe the 'beyond being' from which the alterity of the other issues (cf. 'La signification et le sens', p. 65, recalled in passing by Derrida in 'Le mot d'accueil', p. 74, n1: Derrida also points out that this co-originarity of the third person is clear in Levinas from *Totalitié et infini* onwards (pp. 111–12)). It is this dimension that allows the transcendence of the other to provide an orientation and to be related to God, and it is crucial for Lévinas to conceive of a 'God not contaminated by being', as he puts it in the 'Preliminary Note' to *Autrement qu'être*. But for Derrida, just this illeity is the principle of contamination, and just this will ensure that any 'orientation' it might be said to provide must be taken in the context of a greater and more encompassing disorientation. See the explicit commentary on the necessity of contamination in 'En ce moment même . . .' (p. 182).

20. This is a generalizable structure in deconstructive thought, perhaps most easily grasped in the arguments about life and death in the context of Freud: life is life only to the extent that it protects itself to some extent from itself (pure or unprotected life would be instant death) in an *economy of death* ('Freud et la scéne de l'ecriture', pp. 300–1 [202]). The same logic works the analysis of the relationship between pleasure and reality principles in 'Spéculer – sur

"Freud"', in *La Carte Postale de Socrate à Freud et au-delà* (Paris: Aubier-Flammarion, 1979) pp. 303–11.
21. Cf 'Violence et métaphysique', pp. 136 n1, 172, 191. These remarks should not be taken as implying that such a calculation is simple, nor even that we already know what violence is.
22. This 'necessary possibility' argument (that a promise is only a promise if it is necessarily possible that it be broken, only if there is the threat that the promise not be kept), suggests that the distinction between a promise and a threat is harder to grasp than might at first appear: the earliest hint of this thinking in Derrida's work appears to be in *Limited Inc.* (Paris: Galileé, 1990), pp. 141–2.
23. The quasi-transcendental argument (the transcendental pendant, as it were, to the quasi-logical argument about necessary possibility) which is *quasi*-transcendental just because of this complication of the levels of empirical/factical and transcendental, is already put, rather discreetly it is true, in Derrida's first published work: see his 'Introduction' to Husserl's *Origin of Geometry*, pp. 168–9 [150–1]. Cf. my attempt to formalize this situation in 'Derridabase', in G. Bennington and J. Derrida, *Jacques Derrida* (Paris: Seuil, 1991) pp. 248–63 [267–84].
24. See Derrida's explicit appeal to a notion of chance in the context of Lévinas (and of reading) in 'En ce moment même . . .' p. 175, and more generally in 'Mes chances . . .' which develops something like an ethics of 'giving chance its chance'.
25. See the short paper 'Nombre de oui', dedicated to Michel de Certeau, which, in *Psyché*, begins with the untranslatable sentence 'Oui, à l'étranger' ('Yes to the stranger' or, as the context goes on to suggest, 'Yes, abroad').
26. The figure of the *arrivant* arrives in *Apories* (Paris: Galileé, 1993) as a name for the absolute unpredictability of the event to come. See too Derrida's more informal elaboration of this issue in discussion with Alexander García Düttmann, 'Perhaps or Maybe'.
27. This is the tension that marks Alasdair MacIntyre's influential *Short History of Ethics* (2nd edn, London: Routledge, 1998). MacIntyre wants to associate a founding truth of ethics with a pre-philosophical (for example Homeric) moment at which ethical judgements were tied unproblematically with social function, and so writes a book devoted to lamenting ethics as the history of the loss of this (pre-)ethical truth. We might want to say against this that ethics only begins with the (primary) divorce between function and action, and that this is just a version of the pre-ethical opening of ethics. Ethics on this view would be bound up with its necessary *im*possibility, which could not then reasonably be the object of the sort of nostalgic pathos given to it by MacIntyre.
28. Derrida discusses Schmitt at length in *Politiques de l'amitié* (Paris: Galileé, 1994), and recalls that discussion in 'Le mot d'accueil' (p. 52, n2).
29. Here too, ethics would involve a certain experience of the impossible, which Derrida is happy to associate with deconstruction as such. This is of a piece with the sense of an obligation to be inventive or creative. For a non-deconstructive view of the link between creativity and impossibility, see Margaret Boden, *The Creative Mind* (London: Weidenfeld and Nicolson, 1990). It seems to me that Simon Critchley misconstrues the logic of decision by associating it with a 'decided' use on his own part of the language of the tradition, and by insisting in the light of *that* decision on *opposing* the factical or the contingent to what he can then only understand as Derrida's transcendentalism (*The Ethics of Deconstruction* (Oxford: Blackwell, 1992), p. 43 and Chapter 5).
30. See Derrida's developments of this theme in work on Joyce (see especially

'Ulysse gramophone' in *Ulysse gramophone, deux mots pour Joyce* (Paris: Galileé, 1987) and, in more autobiographical vein, *Le Monolinguisme de l'autre* (Paris: Galilée, 1996). This theme of the constitutive other-in-me is, naturally enough, developed in Derrida's work on Freud: see especially *Mal d'archive* (Paris: Galilée, 1995) pp. 124–5, and the untranslatable formula 'L'un se garde de l'autre'.

31. Cf. 'La guerre des noms propres', in *De la grammatologie*, pp. 157–73 [107–18], and the distinguishing there of three levels of violence. On the 'opening' of ethics, see especially p. 202 [140]: 'Archi-writing is the origin of morality and of immorality. Non-ethical opening of ethics. Violent opening.' On the para-doxical relationship of names and their bearers, see too 'L'aphorisme à con-tretemps'.

32. See my article 'Derrida' in *A Companion to Continental Philosophy*, ed. S. Critchley and W. Schroeder (Oxford: Blackwell, 1998), p. 553.

33. It is curious that Derrida has nowhere published a detailed analysis of this moment in the *Greater Logic*, which he cites, apparently with approval, in 'Violence et Métaphysique' (p. 227, n.1), but which he evokes more critically in *Positions* (Paris: Minuit, 1972), pp. 59–61 [43–4].

34. This is already the effect of the analysis of the trace in the *Grammatologie*, where the choice of that term is, interestingly enough, in part motivated by Lévinas's own usage (pp. 102–3 [70]). The trace is explicitly presented in the *Grammatologie* as opening up the areas of language, temporalization, and the relation to the other (p. 69 [47]).

35. 'War does not merely line up – as the greatest of them – among the trials that morality lives on. It renders morality derisory. The art of foreseeing and win-ning war by any means – politics – then imposes itself as the very exercise of reason. Politics is opposed to morality as philosophy is opposed to naivety' (*Totalité et infini*, p. ix).

36. See especially 'Donner la mort' in *L'Ethique du don*, ed. Jean-Michel Rabaté and Michael Wetzel (Paris: Metailié, 1992), pp. 79–108 [82–115], *Politiques de l'ami-tié*, p. 259 [232], and *Mal d'archive*, p. 123.

WORKS CITED

Bennington, Geoffrey (1991), 'Derridabase', in G. Bennington and J. Derrida, *Jacques Derrida* (Paris: Seuil) [trans. G. Bennington (University of Chicago Press, 1993)].

—— (1995), 'Lecture – de Georges Bataille', in *Georges Bataille – après tout*, ed. D. Hollier (Paris: Belin), pp. 11–34.

—— (1996), Genuine Gasché (perhaps)', *Imprimatur*, 1: 2–3, pp. 252–57.

—— (1998), 'Derrida', in S. Critchley and W. Schroeder (eds), *A Companion to Continental Philosophy* (Oxford: Blackwell), pp. 549–58.

—— 'Faire semblant' (forthcoming).

Bernasconi, Robert (1997), 'Justice without Ethics', in *Responsibilities of Deconstruction*, ed. J. Dronsfield and N. Midgley (*PLI – Warwick Journal of Philosophy*), vol. 6 (Summer 1997)), pp. 58–67.

Boden, Margaret (1990), *The Creative Mind* (London: Weidenfeld and Nicolson).

Critchley, Simon (1992), *The Ethics of Deconstruction* (Oxford: Blackwell).

—— (1997), 'The Ethics of Deconstruction: an Attempt at Self-Criticism', in *Responsibilities of Deconstruction (PLI – Warwick Journal of Philosophy)*, vol. 6 (Summer 1997) pp. 87–102.

Derrida, Jacques (1961), 'Introduction', in E. Husserl, *L'Origine de la Géométrie* (Paris: PUF) [trans. John P. Leavey, Jr (Stony Brook, NY: Nicholas Hays, 1978)].

—— (1967a), *La voix et le phénomène* (Paris: PUF) [trans. D. Allison, *Speech and Phenomena* (Evanston, IL: Northwestern University Press, 1973)].

—— (1967b), *De la grammatologie* (Paris: Minuit) [trans. Gayatri Chakravorty Spivak (Baltimore, MD: The Johns Hopkins University Press, 1976)].

—— (1967c), *L'écriture et la différence* (Paris: Seuil) [trans. Alan Bass, *Writing and Difference* (Chicago, IL: University of Chicago Press, 1978)].

—— (1967d), 'Violence et métaphysique' [1964], in *L'écriture et la différence*, pp. 117–228 [trans. Alan Bass, *Writing and Difference* (Chicago, IL: University of Chicago Press, 1978)].

—— (1967e), 'Freud et la scéne de l'écriture', in *L'écriture et la différence*, pp. 293–340 [196–231].

—— (1972), *Positions* (Paris: Minuit) [trans. Alan Bass (Chicago, IL: University of Chicago Press, 1981)].

—— (1979), 'Spéculer – sur "Freud"', in *La Carte postale de Socrate à Freud et au-delà* (Paris: Aubier-Flammarion), pp. 277–437 (pp. 303–11) [trans. Alan Bass (Chicago, IL: Chicago University Press, 1987), pp. 257–409].

—— (1980), 'En ce moment même dans cet ouvrage me voici' (1980) in *Psyché – Inventions de l'autre*, pp. 159–202 [trans. Ruben Berezdevin, in R. Bernasconi and S. Critchley (eds), *Re-reading Lévinas* (Bloomington, IN: Indiana University Press, 1991), pp. 11–48].

—— (1983), 'Mes chances: Au rendez-vous de quelques stéréophonies épicuriennes' (*Tijdschrift voor Filosophie*, **45**:1 pp. 3–40 [trans. I. Harvey and A. Ronell, in *Taking Chances: Derrida, Psychoanalysis and Literature*, ed. J. H. Smith and W. Kerrigan (Baltimore, MD: Johns Hopkins University Press 1984), pp. 1–32].

—— (1986a), 'Admiration de Nelson Mandela, ou Les lois de la réflection', in *Psyché – Inventions de l'autre*, pp. 453–75 [trans. Mary Ann Caws and Isabelle Lorenz, in *For Nelson Mandela* (New York: Seaver Books, 1987), pp. 13–42].

—— (1986b), 'L'aphorisme a contretemps' in *Psyché – Inventions de l'autre*, pp. 519–33 [trans. Nicholas Royle in *Acts of Literature*, ed. D. Attridge (London: Routledge, 1992), pp. 414–33].

—— (1987a), 'Nombre de oui' in *Psyché*, pp. 639–50 [trans. B. Holmes, 'A Number of Yes', *Qui Parle*, vol. 2, no. 2 (1988), pp. 120–33].

—— (1990a), *Limited Inc.* (Paris: Galilée) [trans. J. Mehlman and S. Weber (Evanston, IL: Northwestern University Press, 1988)].

—— (1990b), *Du droit à la philosophie* (Paris: Galilée).

—— (1991), *L'autre cap* (Paris: Minuit) [trans. M. Naas and P. A. Brault, *The Other Heading* (Bloomington, IN: Indiana University Press, 1992)].

—— (1992), 'Donner la mort', in *L'Ethique du don*, ed. J.-M. Rabaté and M. Wetzel (Paris: Métailié), pp. 11–108 [trans. David Wills, *The Gift of Death* (Chicago, IL: University of Chicago Press, 1995)].

—— (1993a), *Passions: l'offrande oblique* (Paris: Galilée) [trans. David Wood, in *Derrida: A Critical Reader*, ed. D. Wood (Oxford: Blackwell, 1992), pp. 5–35].

—— (1993b), *Spectres de Marx* (Paris: Galilée) [trans. Peggy Kamuf, *Specters of Marx* (London: Routledge, 1994)].

—— (1993c), *Apories* (Paris: Galilée) [trans. T. Dutoit, *Aporias* (Stanford: Stanford University Press, 1995)].

—— (1994a), *Force de loi* (Paris: Galilée) [trans. Mary Quaintance, 'Force of Law: the "mystical foundation" of authority', with original French text in *Cardozo Law Review*, vol. 11, nos 5–6 (1990), pp. 920–1045].

—— (1994b), *Politiques de l'amitié* (Paris: Galilée) [trans. George Collins, *Politics of Friendship* (London: Verso, 1997)].

—— (1995), *Mal d'archive: une impression freudienne* (Paris: Galilée) [trans. Eric Prenowitz, *Archive Fever: A Freudian Impression* (Chicago, IL: University of Chicago Press, 1995)].

—— (1996), *Le Monolinguisme de l'autre* (Paris: Galilée).

—— (1997), 'Le mot d'accueil' (1996), in *Adieu: à Emmanuel Lévinas* (Paris: Galilée), pp. 37–211.

—— (1987b), 'Ulysse gramophone: l'ouï-dire de Joyce' in *Ulysse gramophone, deux mots pour Joyce* (Paris: Galilée) [trans. Tina Kendall, 'Ulysses Gramophone: Hear Say Yes in Joyce', in *Acts of Literature*, ed. Derek Attridge (London: Routledge, 1992), pp. 256–309].

Derrida, Jacques and Alexander Garcia Düttmann (1997), 'Perhaps or Maybe', in *Responsibilities of Deconstruction*, ed. J. Dronsfield and N. Midgley (*PLI – Warwick Journal of Philosophy*), vol. 6 (Summer 1997)), pp. 1–18.

Gasché, R. (1994), *Inventions of Difference* (Cambridge, MA: Harvard University Press).

Kant, Immanuel (1997), *Critique of Practical Reason*, trans. Mary Gregor (Cambridge: Cambridge University Press).

Lévinas, Emmanuel (1961), *Totalité et infini: essai sur l'extériorité* (The Hague: Martinus Nijhoff) [trans. Alphonso Lingis, *Totality and Infinity* (Pittsburgh, PA: Duquesne University Press, 1969)].

—— (1972), 'La signification et le sens', in *Humanisme de l'autre homme* (Fata Morgana; rpt Le Livre de Poche, 1987) [trans. Alphonso Lingis as 'Meaning and Sense', in *Collected Philosophical Papers* (Dordrecht: Martinus Nijhoff, 1987)].

—— (1974), *Autrement qu'être, ou au-delà de l'essence* (The Hague: Martinus Nijhoff) [trans. Alphonso Lingis, *Otherwise than Being, or Beyond Essence* (The Hague: Martinus Nijhoff, 1981)].

MacIntyre, Alasdair (1998), *A Short History of Ethics*, 2nd edn (London: Routledge).

Miller, J. Hillis (1987), *The Ethics of Reading* (New York: Columbia University Press).

5

Deconstruction and Feminism

Diane Elam

Feminism. Again? There is now talk that feminism is yesterday's news, an item to be consigned to suitcases belonging to the historically inclined and the academically obsessed. Politics has moved on, passions have faded, feminism is history. Irrelevant rather than irreverent as far as new generations of women are concerned, feminism, some say, is marked as the rebel whose causes will be left behind, back in the twentieth century.

To some extent, such pronouncements are the result of feminism's success. Feminism indeed has called attention to gender inequities in both workplace and home, demanding change and gender justice. It has made women a topic of study in the academy, redressing the exclusion of work by and about women in numerous fields. It has caused a fundamental rethinking of gender and sexuality. It has provided women with opportunities they have never had before. Put like this, feminism begins to sound like the all-time political and intellectual success story, a revolution of which its participants should be justly proud. With so much to its credit, what work would feminism possibly still have to do? Feminism. Again? Been there, done that.

The same could be said of linking feminism with deconstruction. I for one have definitely been there and done that too. However, being there and doing that does not exclude the possibility that 'that' needs to be done again, again differently, differently again. If deconstruction has taught us anything, it should be a suspicion of such totalizing claims on behalf of any political programme. Feminism's success is not as complete as I have just made it sound and as others would like to believe. Just because feminism now has a history does not mean that feminism has therefore reached its end, done all that it can do, and duly exited from the political stage declaring simple triumph or defeat. Granted, feminism's early targets have largely disappeared, some may even have been more of a political and rhetorical mirage in the first place – a universally oppressive patriarchy, casting all men indifferently as automatic members, would be one example. But over the years, with first battles at least partially won, feminism's agenda has become more complex, its questions as well as its answers less easy to articulate.

The terms through which feminism now accounts for itself are increas-

83

ingly deconstructive ones. Feminism lives on through a deconstructive tension between conservation and change: preserving feminist traditions while also producing feminist differences.[1] Or to put this another way, feminism continues to be effective not because it is a codified set of rules, positions or platforms, a set of regulating devices in need of constant policing, but rather because its repetition also produces revisions, is marked by a deconstructive resistance to always conforming to itself. A repetition leading to difference. An invention that is not purely original. Feminism again differently.

And feminism again differently here as well. Rather than continue to think in such general terms, I am going to shift the focus to a case study of sorts, which provides a chance to consider more carefully both a deconstructive account of feminism and a feminist account of deconstruction. In what follows, I will be discussing the work that visual artist Jenny Holzer has produced in the last twenty years or so.

Since at least the late 1970s, Holzer has shown a keen interest in language and repetition. Her work is sometimes concerned with feminism, although not always. It often contains a deconstructive impulse, but she does not use the term herself. My choice of Holzer is not because her agenda is exclusively feminist or her art glossed with remarks about deconstruction. Indeed, Holzer's work engages a wide range of sometimes conflicting issues and, if anything, serves as a reminder that neither deconstruction nor feminism acts in isolation from a constellation of other political, ethical, epistemological and aesthetic concerns. Ultimately, what I think makes Holzer so compelling, and so necessary in the context of deconstruction and feminism, is that her aesthetic experimentations open up spaces for feminist politics and incite interest in discourses of justice. In Holzer's images, we find feminism and deconstruction at work; we see, at least in part, what they are capable of accomplishing, what they might yet have to do.

By way of a quick introduction, Holzer's art could be called language-based: she writes phrases that she then anonymously displays in various locations using different materials. While her work first appeared in the late 1970s as small flyposters on the streets of New York City, Holzer is probably best known for the slogans she places on massive LED (light-emitting diode) public signboards, spaces more frequently associated with advertisements than conceptual art. Her first electronic display appeared in 1982 in New York City's Times Square, when she programmed its 800 square foot Spectacolor board to project phrases like: 'PRIVATE PROPERTY CREATED CRIME', 'YOUR OLDEST FEARS ARE THE WORST ONES', 'OFTEN YOU SHOULD ACT SEXLESS', 'TORTURE IS BARBARIC'. Numerous other LED installations have followed, including her 1986 infiltration of the electronic sign capital of the world: Las Vegas, Nevada. Thanks to Holzer, the sign at Caesar's Palace that usually informed its clientele of the evening's lounge room entertainment now reminded its viewers that 'LACK OF CHARISMA CAN BE FATAL', while the baggage-claim area of the local airport greeted travellers with circulating Holzer messages alongside the luggage: 'MONEY CREATES TASTE' proclaimed one carousel.

Holzer has not, however, let electronic technology limit her opportunities for display, and almost every discussion of her work includes a description of the various methods she uses. Holzer repeats her phrases again and again, working in a variety of media, ranging from paper and ink to carved marble, from the virtual materials of the internet to the contours of human skin and bone. She is just as likely to display her work on mass produced t-shirts, caps and stickers, as she is to have it turn up in newspapers, screensavers, art galleries, museums, MTV clips and former monasteries. Perhaps the one thing all of these images share is Holzer's preference for them to be public property; her philosophy is 'the more people who run into them the better' (Holzer in Kämmerling, 1996, p. 121). And run into them we do. Unlike the precious paintings in front of which museum curators draw lines on the floor that the viewers are not meant to cross, Holzer's images are often designed to be touched, worn, sat on and even walked across in the case of inscribed marble floor tiles. Her art is not something we keep at a set distance so much as something we inhabit.

Domestic economies have long been on feminism's agenda, to be sure, but to make clearer what Holzer's work has to do with deconstruction and feminism, I first want to look closely at an example with a specifically feminist content from her *Truisms* series. Consisting of a series of over 250 one-line statements, *Truisms* was written between 1977 and 1979, and selections have appeared in numerous different contexts and formats, including a web-site version that allows anyone who logs on to add their own truism.[2] The particular instance I have in mind is a 1987 installation on the Sony JumboTRON scoreboard, located in Candlestick Park baseball stadium, during a game between the home team, the San Francisco Giants, and the visiting New York Mets. While the game played on and the scoreboard registered its usual array of statistics, it also flashed in huge gold letters, displayed on alternating pink and blue backgrounds, the phrase: 'RAISE BOYS AND GIRLS THE SAME WAY' (see Figure 1). Holzer had conspired with Artspace in San Francisco to place some *Truisms* on the field of America's favourite sport, but what exactly was she up to?

On the surface, this selection certainly looks like a basic feminist statement about equality, much in the tradition of Mary Wollstonecraft's writing on equal education opportunities for girls. At the same time, the two colour-coded versions call attention to the cultural inscriptions of sexual difference that begin even before birth: to be a girl is to be pink, while boys are always blue. Given this brief, shown in the context of a professional baseball game, Holzer's truism evokes an ironic commentary on

Figure 1 *Raise Boys and Girls the Same Way*, from *Truisms*, Sony JumboTRON video sign, 24 × 32 feet; installation: Candlestick Park, San Francisco (1987), organized by Artspace, San Francisco.

the state of play. Women do not play professional major league baseball; girls have trouble asserting their rights to play ball in 'little league', the organized level of the sport for youngsters. Boys and girls are clearly not being raised the same way; the cultural inscription of sexual differences does not stop with the colour-coding of baby accessories. Major League baseball take note. We might also send Holzer's statement in the corporate directions of Sony, who manufactured the sign, and Coca-Cola, who advertise their logo on the scoreboard. Do their corporate policies and practices promote sexual equality? Is raising boys and girls the same way the real thing and commensurate with the production of state of the art electronics?

Such an obligation to the effects of sexual difference has, in part, defined feminism. But this obligation is not without its complications, and the truism is also capable of generating some rather more difficult questions. What exactly would it mean to raise boys and girls the same way? How could it be brought about? What cultural differences or contexts would be needed as frames in which to generate any answer? Is it always desirable to raise boys and girls the same way? Should gender difference be done away with altogether to produce a society that is gender indifferent, or should there be gender difference that is not also a gendered hierarchy? Who takes responsibility for raising boys and girls the same way? Child rearing has often been a woman's responsibility. How and where would different forms of feminist politics intervene to insure that boys and girls are raised the same way? Do we even want to maintain the binary thinking behind the division of girls and boys? And anyway, is it always possible to distinguish between them? If medical evidence is anything to go by, gender differentiation is not necessarily as straightforward as it is commonly presumed to be.[3]

All of this might seem a long way off from what was happening on the field that night between the Giants and the Mets. The stadium did not sell its tickets to a crowd of feminism and deconstruction fans. People did not fill Candlestick Park to look at art; these were not questions listed in the official souvenir programme. But that is part of the point. Holzer's guerrilla electronic art tries to draw in a wide audience and catch it off guard with unexpected messages. The hope is that viewers will stop and think, even if only for a few seconds, about what they have just read.

Indeed, Holzer's work is all about getting people to think, to ask questions about issues that they may not have considered before. And a lot can come out of these seemingly simple soundbites; viewers can chew them over for as long as they want, following lines of inquiry like the ones I have just suggested in my own reading. Or not. For the risk that Holzer takes is that the truisms go unnoticed, merely adding to the white noise of useless information that viewers already dispose of on a daily basis. However, in an age when public discourse leans more towards confessional talk shows and tabloid journalism, this strikes me as a risk worth taking. Holzer's art is accessible and thoughtful, while at the same time not pretending to offer an over-simplified version of how language and communication work. There is an underlying deconstructive gesture here, which reveals that communication is necessary but not transparent; language has meaning but that meaning is not absolutely determinable. In effect, Holzer asks us to think about the complex nature of a speech act, the relationships between text and context, sender and receiver.[4]

Her messages appear to come from nowhere. Unsigned, unauthorized, there is no obvious single source to which a viewer can appeal for meaning or legitimation. No authoritative voice defines the immediate context. 'RAISE BOYS AND GIRLS THE SAME WAY' is not signed by an artist, a feminist, a deconstructor, or the Major League Baseball Association. Even the assumptions under which advertising slogans operate – that the company that makes the product is making the claim – fall away here; there is no obvious product, no obvious corporation behind the LED messages. In a sense, only the sign signs the work. Aporias of cognition are not checked by a signature or apparent authorial intention. Viewers are left to their own devices to develop a context in which to make sense of the message and to think about questions of legitimation and authority.

Yet Holzer's insistence on the anonymity of her work is, to some extent, itself a form of authorial intention that has important implications for feminism. Holzer reasoned that if she made her 'work sex blind and anonymous . . . it wouldn't be dismissed as the work of a woman or the work of an individual' (Holzer in Auping, 1992, p. 79).[5] In the instance of 'RAISE BOYS AND GIRLS THE SAME WAY', the effect can be productive, in so far as a potentially feminist message might be read and considered precisely because it was not signed by either a woman or a feminist. Releasing language from the constraints of the signature does not, however, automatically liberate readers from gender stereotypes. That viewers have often assumed the voice of authority behind Holzer's statements is male, that women's work is more readily dismissed, could be the undesirable results of not raising boys and girls the same way.

Anonymity is indeed not always synonymous with interpretative freedom, and it can also readily provide political cover, act as refuge from owning up to responsibility, including the action that words produce, the action that is the very utterance of the words themselves. Yet to appeal to anonymity in order to question the nature of communication, in order to deconstruct the act of communication, is not necessarily an escape from responsibility. While in some contexts a *Truisms* selection may appear to be anonymous, the *Truisms* are signed in so far as Holzer claims them as 'her work' and assumes the political responsibility that goes along with the act of the signature. It would be more precise to think that in certain contexts Holzer's signature is written in invisible ink.

And it is this potentially invisible signature that is held responsible not only for the text itself but also for its context, for its continued recontextualization. Holzer has always been keen to repeat her writings and take account of different interactions between text and context. To this extent, she signs her works through the act of selecting a particular context in which to insert her text. Viewers interpret the phrases differently in different contexts and interpret the contexts differently when the words appear in them. While Holzer's work depends on site specificity, the sites themselves are almost infinite, infinitely different. By linking repetition to alterity, she enacts what Derrida has called the iterability of writing and puts into practice one of his definitions of deconstruction: 'the effort to take this limitless context into account, to pay the sharpest and broadest attention possible to context, and thus to an incessant movement of recontextualization' (Derrida, 1988, p. 136).[6]

Holzer's phrases refuse to go away. In part, this is because it is impossible to be sure that they deliver what they say they will. There is no guarantee that the prescriptions are also performatives, that by saying 'RAISE BOYS AND GIRLS THE SAME WAY', boys and girls will then be raised the same way, or that we would even know what that would mean. Moreover, and at the risk of repeating myself, there is not even a guarantee that anyone will respond to the text at all. Viewers may not read the phrase, much less evaluate its validity or perform any action as a result of an interpretation. 'FAKE OR REAL INDIFFERENCE IS A POWERFUL PERSONAL WEAPON'. Something, including thinking, still remains to be done, and repetition is the possibility of making that something happen, happen again differently.

To return to my example, consider three contextualizations of 'RAISE BOYS AND GIRLS THE SAME WAY'. First written in the late 1970s, it then appears in the late 1980s, on a baseball scoreboard in San Francisco. In the late 1990s, it crops up again, this time as part of the *Truisms* web-site and painted on the hoods of Florence taxis.[7] Different media, different countries, different decades, and, one would hope, different moments in feminism. But the message continues to matter; the force of the text and the context are far from exhausted. Necessary repetition in the name of feminism.

Given the ephemeral nature of her media, repetition may obviously seem necessary for Holzer to keep her work visible in public places, but she is also no outsider to the art establishment, where she also continues to repeat herself. Holzer's reputation may be secured on the billboards, t-shirts and taxi cabs of the world, but that has not excluded her from museums and galleries. On the one hand, traditional art institutions might seem like a very different sort of context – the sanctioned world of high culture with its potentially more limited audience and less public engagement with feminism. On the other hand, however, Holzer uses museum and gallery spaces much like she does Times Square or the Las Vegas airport's baggage-claim area. LED displays figure prominently in both; benches used as installations in public parks are equally at home in museums. The messages on the gallery walls are the same ones that appear in baseball stadiums. Feminist texts are exposed to good lighting as well as fresh air.

Holzer's 1989–90 transformation of Frank Lloyd Wright's Solomon R. Guggenheim Museum in New York remains a remarkable example of these aspects of her practice. Treating the white parapet of Wright's spiralling central ramp as if it were a long billboard', she installed a 535 foot LED display to run a selection of all of her texts.[8] Stone benches inscribed with her *Survival* texts and placed in a circle on the rotunda floor doubled up as aesthetic artefacts and nice places to sit and watch the LED displays whirl. Another gallery upstairs contained more benches, this time inscribed with texts from the Living series and arranged in rows. Rather than treating the spaces of high art and everyday life as two separate spheres, Holzer's recontextualizations push to make them more of a continuum, more in dialogue with one another. She makes the spaces different by making them less different from one another. It is, in effect, a deconstructive move that aims to change the way we inhabit the space of the museum, as well as the baggage-claim area.

The textual material that Holzer uses in the museum and the gallery is as wide-ranging as her other public displays; some of it touches on feminist issues, some does not. Yet the implications for feminism exceed the content of the texts themselves. Women with shows in major museums and galleries are still few and far between, as The Guerrilla Girls have pointed out over the years.[9] Holzer's visibility is not just passing tokenism and marks a positive step in the direction of feminist equality politics in the art world. If the last ten years are any indication, feminism has cause to be optimistic that Holzer's work will continue to receive the attention it deserves. Shortly after her New York Guggenheim installation, in 1990 Holzer became the first woman ever to be chosen to represent the United States in the Esposizone Internationale d'Arte La Biennale di Venezia. While her work unconventionally spilled out all over Venice, much like her treatment of Las Vegas, she also walked away with the prestigious Leone d'Oro award for best pavilion.

Yet there is probably no better confirmation that Holzer has indeed arrived in the art world to stay than the decision to give her permanent space in the new Frank Gehry-designed Museo Guggenheim Bilbao. Holzer's contribution consists of a site-specific installation in a central, ground-floor gallery, along with plans for a xenon projection on the Nervión River that runs alongside the museum. Both inside and on the outside of the museum, Holzer's art becomes a part of the permanent structure, at the same time that it cannot fully be housed within its walls. It is partially an acknowledgement of the museum as a space of culture, at the same time that it questions the boundaries of that space.

The text Holzer uses in Bilbao is a variation of Arno, which she first displayed in 1996 at the 'Biennale di Firenze: il Tempo e la Moda'.[10] As you approach the interior installation from the central atrium of the museum, the text runs up and down nine vertical LED columns, which display red lettering on the front side, throwing a red reflection on the sloping sides of the building, and blue lettering on the far side, throwing a blue reflection on the sloping rear wall (Figure 2). The LED columns themselves resemble structural girders in a building that is constantly playing with form, hiding and revealing actual structural supports, adding decorative features that resemble structural supports, and even blurring the very distinction between what constitutes structure and decoration. In this respect, Gehry and Holzer are well matched, both performing deconstructive gestures on Wright's building and the institution of the museum itself.[11]

Like Gehry's building, Holzer's installation deconstructs the space of the museum, inviting viewers to interrogate the conventions they usually observe there. To read both sides of the LED display, viewers must pass between a relatively small space between the columns, which many visi-

Figure 2 From 'Arno' (1996), nine 2-sided electronic LED signs, each 1300 × 16 cm; perma-nent installation: Museo Guggenheim, Bilbao (1997). Photographed by Erika Ede.

tors hesitate to do at first.[12] The columns function like a line on the floor in front of a painting: a line you don't cross, the other side of the looking glass you can't see. But break with convention viewers often do, walking through the space between the columns. Viewers on their own frequently appear self-conscious, wondering perhaps if they have done something they really shouldn't be doing. In a crowd, the transgression turns into a bit of an adventure. Trying to read the moving text on both displays, viewers must then negotiate the other viewers trying to do the same thing, trying to pass between the narrowly spaced columns at the same time and collect in the relatively small area on the far side – a trip that can also lead to unexpected collisions with the sloping, dark rear wall of the building, which seems to spring from nowhere.

The whole affair is strangely social in a way art museums rarely are.[13] And, interestingly, the feminist concerns are not necessarily obvious here; rather, they are integrated into the piece, a part of a potential constellation of issues. The Bilbao installation can, for instance, lead to reflection on how gender becomes a factor determining how viewers are moving in the space, moving in relation to one another in the space. Who transgresses, and who does not? Who leads, and who follows? Who talks to whom? Who touches whom? Who watches whom watching? A single conclusion is not drawn in advance of the event. Performances of gender relations are repeated in this space, but it is not always the same performance.

The text displayed on the LED signs creates a similar effect. Consisting of a series of short statements, the majority of which are constructed in the first person, the text exhibits no strong narrative impulse. It is, however, possible to impose narratives to link the phrases. The results can be rather innocuous scenarios, or they can turn in decidedly more sinister directions. For instance, 'I WALK IN / I WATCH YOU / I SCAN YOU / I WAIT FOR YOU', could be the voice of a museum guard, or another viewer in the installation, or the voice of a stalker in a victim's house. 'I FORGET YOUR NAME / I DON'T THINK / I BURY MY HEAD' may narrate an experience of minor social guilt and embarrassment, but continued as it is with 'I BURY YOUR HEAD/I BURY YOU', it takes an ominous and deadly turn. Likewise, what to make of the sequence: 'I AM CRYING HARD / THERE WAS BLOOD / NO ONE TOLD ME / NO ONE KNEW / MY MOTHER KNOWS'. Is this a girl's reaction to the first onset of menses? Reflections on a brutal rape? A first sexual encounter? A scraped knee in a playground accident? And what's more, from whose perspective is this narrative told?

To think more specifically about a feminist interest in gender here, we might wonder about the fact that the only gendered reference in the sequence is to 'my mother'. What is that suggesting? To what extent do the pronouns acquire different gendered referents in any attempt to read and interpret them? Is it possible to think these phrases without attributing gender? Is it possible to build narrative links that do not have gender as a structuring component? Why would gender matter here? To whom would it matter? And what of the other categories of difference? How do they take on significance here as well? Should a reading consider race? Class? Sexual preference? Nationality? Ethnicity?

As the multiple phrases flow across the display, there is no single set of criteria that determine how the phrases should be linked. There is no assurance that the phrases can all be linked or even that they should be linked. The potential agenda here is vast, and the larger question probably is: what encourages viewers to link the phrases together in the first place? In effect, Holzer's installation reflects viewers' expectations and cultural assumptions much like the LED lights cast their own partial reflections on Gehry's curving walls.

To say this much is already to suppose a lot; for few viewers take the time – and it is considerable – to read all of Holzer's text, work out the entire sequence, and see all of the different light patterns through which the 57-phrase text is projected in three languages: English, Spanish and Euskara (Basque).[14] Moreover, the installation itself does not particularly encourage visitors to change their high-speed viewing habits. The text moves at different, sometimes disruptive speeds, none of which are slow enough to allow a viewer to easily write down the sequence of words. In the ground floor gallery, there is no place to sit except the floor; an upstairs space offers a bench with a view that only allows a small section of the columns to be seen, rendering the text even more difficult to read.

The experience of Holzer's installation is inevitably a fragmentary one: viewers experience fragments of text, and the text itself is a series of fragments that do not add up. The conclusions drawn, the questions asked, the links made, depend on the particular moment, the particular fragments, the particular agendas one has in mind. The ongoing interplay between text and context, between viewer and sender, can lead in a potentially infinite number of directions, for Holzer's deconstructive moves have an abyssal rather than a unifying effect. The more one looks the more there is to see; the more one questions, the more questions there are to ask, not least whether the particular questions asked are the right ones. What does a viewer have a responsibility to address in this space? For instance, should feminism even be a central focus?

And if feminism is the concern, which feminism should be doing the talking? Feminism does not always speak the same language or say things that are translatable across different cultural and linguistic boundaries. To do justice to women, to gender issues, in English, in Spanish and in Euskara will not necessary be to do the same things, to read the same texts or share the same spaces. Feminism has a difference within itself and also needs to be thought alongside other responsibilities.

Perhaps it is because Holzer's work consistently acknowledges this deconstructive movement of multiplicity and heterogeneity that she has been able to engage feminist issues successfully without being relegated to the special-interest section of 'feminist and women artists'. Admirably, her work has also not been compromised by her partnerships with the art establishment. She has retained her critical distance, and her work has lost none of its political or aesthetic edge. While indeed some of Holzer's strategies are familiar by now, a part of the conceptual art world and feminist politics that still bears repeating, this is not to say that she never engages feminist issues more challenging than 'RAISE BOYS AND GIRLS THE SAME WAY' nor addresses feminist issues any more specific than the way spaces are gendered.

In 1990 Holzer began to explore the relationship between mother and child. The title of this series is simplicity itself: *Mother and Child*. The text that follows is not. Here Holzer's writing is neither the stuff found on mother's day greeting cards, nor a mere recycling of familar iconographic images, whether they be secular or sacred.[15] Instead, her gritty prose works through complex emotions, ranging from guilt and desire, to love and despair; from pain and apprehension, to fear and remorse. They make for uncomfortable reading and are often filled with uncertainty, not least around the question of voice. Some phrases are clearly spoken by a mother (who of course was once a child herself): 'I AM INDIFFERENT TO MYSELF BUT NOT TO MY CHILD'. 'MY NEED TO PROTECT COMES WITH THE CHILD'. Others could be ascribed to either mother or child: 'FUCK ME AND FUCK ALL OF YOU WHO WOULD HURT HER'. 'I EXPERIMENT TO SEE IF I CAN STAND HER PAIN / I CANNOT'. 'NOW I MUST BE HERE TO WATCH HER'.[16]

Feminism has sometimes been guilty of either sentimentalizing or demonizing motherhood, and Holzer's text invites a confrontation of such stereotyping. It avoids essentialist and naturalizing discourse, without simply substituting obscure and unfamiliar language in its place. *Mother and Child* manages to be both an accessible and a contemplative work. The result has often been strong emotional reactions on the part of viewers, and this may, in part, also be attributed to the type of spaces in which it has been displayed.[17] First shown at the New York Guggenheim (1989) and installed the following year in the Venice pavilion, *Mother and Child* has been repeated mainly in museums and galleries, where it is projected on LED screens and inscribed on marble tablets and floor tiles.

Holzer has not, however, elected to reserve all of her more demanding work for the museum and gallery spaces accorded to *Mother and Child*. She remains committed to the gaze of the wider public eye and continues to be interested in giving it challenging feminist material to look at. To this effect, it is important to consider another of Holzer's repeated series. Each year the German newspaper *Süddeutsche Zeitung* devotes an issue of its Sunday magazine supplement to an individual artist, and in 1993 it chose Holzer. This took her into the new territory of print journalism, while it also marked a return to her more populist roots of the mass circulation of images. It could have been an opportunity to do a project that was effective but not risky: for instance, repeating portions of the *Truisms* series again. But Holzer did not take an easy path. Instead, she chose the *Magazin der Süddeutsche Zeitung* for the first appearance of her *Lustmord* texts, and the response was far from neutral.[18]

But what was it about this new work that upset viewers like never before? 'Lustmord' roughly translates as 'sex-murder', 'lust-killing' or 'rape-slaying'. While certainly unpleasant, the title itself did not prove controversial. The text confronted violence, violence against women and specifically the violence of war crimes against the women in Bosnia, which were going on at the time. Again, viewers took this on board without complaint. This issue of the magazine consisted of an interview with Holzer and thirty close-range photographs of German and English texts handwritten in ink on human skin (Figure 3). While this did indeed upset some viewers, it was not what led the Archbishop of Munich, for one, to respond so strongly.

What did offend the Archbishop, and a large number of other readers, was the fact that the front cover of the *Magazin* had the words 'DA WO

FRAUEN STERBEN BIN ICH HELLWACH' ('I AM AWAKE IN THE PLACE WHERE WOMEN DIE') printed in red ink coloured by human blood donated by German and Yugoslavian women for this express purpose. Seven litres of blood-ink made its way onto German news-stands; a public outcry followed. Responses in the press called Holzer's work perverse, wasteful, macabre and sensationalist. Any number of reports about violence against women, about war crimes in the Balkans, left morning readers sipping their coffee without complaint. Such issues have been notoriously difficult to mobilize public opinion and action around. But when it came to being confronted with real blood over breakfast, things changed.[19]

To some extent, one could say Holzer had been naive in not anticipating the public's reaction. And what was always going to be a sensitive issue escalated further when the appearance of the issue coincided with a scare about an HIV infection in the German blood supply. That the ink was prepared under strict medical supervision and contained only the colouring agent in blood, which did not pose any threat to public health, seemed often to go unregarded by Holzer's critics. The sensationalist response by public, press and clergy threatened to overshadow the messages about violence that Holzer set out to convey in the first place.

It is, however, important to recover these messages and look at the

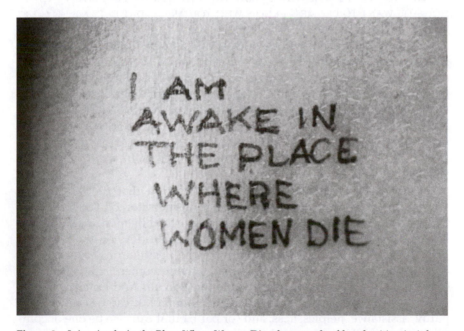

Figure 3 *I Am Awake in the Place Where Women Die*, photograph of handwriting in ink on skin (1993); reproduced in *Süddeutsche Zeitung Magazin*, 19 November 1993. Photographed by Alan Richardson.

opportunities for interrogating violence that they offer. The *Lustmord* text is composed of fifty-five sentences divided into three perspectives: 'Perpetrator' (twenty-seven sentences), 'Victim' (fifteen sentences) and 'Observer' (13 sentences). The Perpetrator's language is aggressive, active, sexual and violent, emphasizing the first person singular pronoun and a third person singular, female pronoun toward which the action is directed: 'I STEP ON HER HANDS'. 'I HOOK HER SPINE'. 'I WANT TO FUCK HER WHERE SHE HAS TOO MUCH HAIR'. And the final chilling sentence, 'THE COLOR OF HER WHERE SHE IS INSIDE OUT IS ENOUGH TO MAKE ME KILL HER'. The descriptive remarks about the female victim in this section are no less violent: 'HER SWALLOW REFLEX IS GONE'. 'HER HEAD EXPLODES IN THE FIRE'. 'SHE HAS NO TASTE LEFT TO HER AND THIS MAKES IT EASIER FOR ME'.

The language the Victim speaks directly acknowledges the violence being performed on her: 'MY BREASTS ARE SO SWOLLEN THAT I BITE THEM'. 'HAIR IS STUCK INSIDE ME'. 'MY NOSE BROKE IN THE GRASS. MY EYES ARE SORE FROM MOVING AGAINST YOUR PALM.' The Victim's remarks, although fewer than the Perpetrator's, are also generally longer and move beyond description to comment on the psychological responses she understands herself and her perpetrator to be experiencing: 'I AM AWAKE IN THE PLACE WHERE WOMEN DIE'. 'WITH YOU INSIDE ME COMES THE KNOWLEDGE OF MY DEATH'. 'YOU CONFUSE ME WITH SOMETHING THAT IS IN YOU. I WILL NOT PREDICT HOW YOU WANT TO USE ME.' 'I KNOW WHO YOU ARE AND IT DOES ME NO GOOD AT ALL'. 'I TRY TO EXCITE MYSELF SO I STAY CRAZY'.

Finally, the observer, with the fewest but also the longest remarks, has language that oscillates between descriptions of the Victim's condition and the Observer's own responses, often suggesting an intimacy between Observer and Victim not unlike that of a mother and child: 'I WANT TO LIE DOWN BESIDE HER. I HAVE NOT SINCE I WAS A CHILD. I WILL BE COVERED BY WHAT HAS COME FROM HER'. 'SHE SMILES AT ME BECAUSE SHE IMAGINES I CAN HELP HER'. 'SHE COUGHS THE MOUTH STRINGS'. 'I WANT TO SUCK ON HER TO MAKE HER RESPOND'. 'SHE IS NARROW AND FLAT IN THE BLUE SACK AND I STAND WHEN THEY LIFT HER'.

While all three perspectives offer confirmation that the Victim is a woman, none refer to the gender of the Perpetrator or the Observer. Violence against women may usually be performed by men, including the sexual violence in the Balkans to which Holzer alludes. Yet the language here does not rule out women occupying the position of Perpetrator, of committing acts of violence against other women. Likewise, the Observer's role can be taken up by men or women. And exactly of what this role consists retains a degree of undecidability. It can be one of sympathy, assistance, helplessness, and/or pain, but it can also be one of complicity. *Lustmord* keeps several possibilities open at once.

Whatever aspect of *Lustmord* one considers, the text is a difficult one to read. Holzer admitted from the start that the language she used in the *Lustmord* series is 'pornographic and precise' (Kämmerling, 1996, p. 122). The problem she was trying to confront was *how* to represent violence against women: domestic violence, the violence of rape in war that was going on in the former Yugoslavia when Holzer was writing the text. While violence spurred on by misogyny and racial hatred should be less easy to incorporate into the background noise of everyday life, to a large extent that is exactly what usually happens: the unseen, unspoken violence done to women every day, in peacetime and in war. The initial shock of Holzer's work is to make this violence visible, to represent it and to do so without using a soft focus lens or a veil of easy rhetoric.

But there is a risk in doing this, a risk that goes beyond simply having the project swallowed up by a tide of sensationalism. As Holzer stated in her accompanying interview: 'realistic representation runs the risk of being misused as pornography again. The most perverse example is documentary films about abuses in [the former] Yugoslavia which are available as pornovideos in shops – and they bring the highest prices!' (Holzer in Kämmerling, 1996, p. 122). Language can inflict its own violence, and neither a feminist deconstruction of representation nor a commitment to documentary realism are guarantees that justice will be done.[20] It would be possible for Holzer's work to be recontextualized to serve the very violence it is intended to confront.

With the *Lustmord* series, the political and ethical stakes involved in the relationships between sender/receiver and text/context are higher than in much of her other material, and they need to be considered with care. *Lustmord* constitutes an especially uneasy relationship with the viewer, for to some extent the viewer is implicated through the very act of reading, and must confront the existence of violence, of violence against women. But how should the viewer respond? What would constitute a just response, and would that change depending upon the context in which the words were read? Could feminism and deconstruction work to do justice to violence against women?

These are certainly questions that bear repeating, and bear repeating in various contextualizations of *Lustmord*, which follow in the wake of the *Magazin der Süddeutsche Zeitung* episode. A former Carthusian monastery (the current Kunstmuseum in Thurgau, Switzerland) as well as other gallery and museum installations, offer more contemplative spaces for *Lustmord*, aligning it with *Mother and Child* and marking a retreat from the sensationalism surrounding the newspaper appearance. But these repetitions are not mere capitulations to formats already familiar to Holzer; they offer their own, different challenges. By locating work in a former monastery, Holzer takes on the historical shift from sacred to secular institutions as places for reflection. She situates concerns about violence and sex in a space usually associated with peace and celibacy; she raises issues especially affecting women in a location historically given over to men with a deeply divided relationship to women.[21]

Virtual reality, 3-D LED and screensaver versions of *Lustmord* go on to suggest that new technologies may offer new forms for communication, for art and for politics, but they also can contain familiar problems of violence against women. New contexts do not simply provide an escape from old issues, although they may offer different opportunities for reflection, for action. Likewise, moving *Lustmord* into spaces with more limited access does not necessarily release it from public display. Holzer has retained a public commitment to this material, orchestrating huge laser projections of *Lustmord* on the Leipzig Battle of Nations Monument in 1996.

Holzer has also juxtaposed different spaces with different temporalities of viewing, emphasizing that there is not a proper time or a proper amount of time in which it would be possible to account completely for the violence being done to women. This is most apparent in the contrasting temporalities associated with the stone benches and the rapid LED displays. On the one hand, the benches on which the static text is inscribed offer a potentially endless amount of time to work through the meaning of a *Lustmord* selection and consider how to respond to it. Yet, like the *Arno* installation in Bilbao, to what extent can the individual phrases, the textual fragments, make sense on their own, lead to a comprehensive response to violence against women, however much time is spent thinking about them? On the other hand, the vertical LED displays are too large and move too quickly for a viewer to be able to read them carefully. Technically, the entire text is visible in a compressed time, but that does not mean that, as a result, a viewer is capable of effectively responding to the text, to facing up to the matter of violence. As Holzer explains in another context, 'The signs can destroy thought, as modern life does at times. You can't grasp all that's going on and you can't make yourself focus and act' (Holzer in Auping, 1992, p. 97).

How to read, how to respond, are questions that are constantly foregrounded in the *Lustmord* series. How indeed would it be possible to face up to the fact of violence, to acknowledge that it may be a matter of life and death? In this sense, the inescapable text and context of *Lustmord* is the body: the body marked by language and inscribed within language; the body as both word and flesh, both alive and dead, both intact and damaged; the bodies of women to which we have an obligation, bodies that should be accorded respect and all too often are not.

While the blood in the ink and the photographs of human skin in the *Magazin der Süddeutsche Zeitung* version are vivid reminders of this, so too are the human bones with inscribed silver rings around them that Holzer has used in several of the museum and gallery installations (Figure 4).[22] To read the *Lustmord* texts on the rings, the viewer has to pick up the

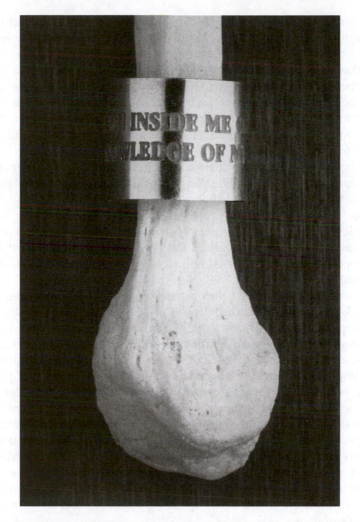

Figure 4 *With You Inside Me Comes the Knowledge of My Death: Bone Tables* (detail), human bones and engraved and etched silver; installation: Galerie Rähnitzgasse der Landeschauptstadt, Dresden (1996). Photographed by Werner Lieberknecht.

bones and be brought into contact with the physicality of the body that offers a material reminder of the death of which the text speaks. The point here is not to effect a clear division between the material and the linguistic or the living and the dead. Rather, it is a deconstructive move that calls attention to their proximity, their interdependence. It is also a way to emphasize the necessary inadequacy of any representation by asking viewers to question the extent to which words have rendered experience visible, as well as the extent to which experience is made possible through the words that have been made visible.

The result of Holzer's multiple contextualizations and textual repetitions is not finally to lift the ideological scales from our eyes to reveal THE
FEMINIST TRUTH OUT THERE – the truth of women's experiences, whether it
be motherhood or sexual violence or gender difference. This is not an *X-
Files* approach to art and politics. Holzer's work encourages us instead to
remember the divide between truism and truth: the former remains open
to question, questioning norms, questioning authorities; the later, 'truth',
has all too often been thought of as the unquestionable, foundational
ground for art and politics.

In this way, Holzer's work promotes a politics and an aesthetics of
questioning. And importantly, this is not a simple attempt to collapse aesthetics into politics. While aesthetics is always in relation to the political,
there should not be a political rule for all aesthetics, an aesthetic rule for
all politics. Feminism cannot look to deconstruction for a method to make
the distinction dissolve altogether. Rather feminism and deconstruction
work together to convey the complexity of the articulation of aesthetics
and politics.

This would be a feminist deconstruction, a deconstructive feminism,
that seeks not political truth but *political justice*. The search is unending
like the questioning that goes along with it, for the call to justice is never
fully answered and never fully calculable.[23] In deconstructive terms, feminism's ethical obligation is not that pronounced by a moral subject
upholding moral norms. It is spoken by multiple voices in multiple contexts; it is repeated over time, yet never quite the same. While not altogether an international feminism – because not solely dependent on the
borders of nation states for definition – it is potentially a global feminism,
asking for justice in different parts of the world. Politically contiguous but
not universal, deconstructive feminism, feminist deconstruction, does not
pretend to be everywhere and be everywhere the same. At the risk of
questioning, at the risk of uncertainty, feminism and deconstruction
remain responsible to the now, speaking to the future about the past.
Again. Feminism.

NOTES

1. I could, of course, also argue that deconstruction lives on through feminism.
2. The on-line version of *Truisms* has been running since 1995 and, according to
   Holzer, contains around 10,000 additions to her initial 254 (Holzer in Simon,
   1998, p. 38). It can be accessed at http://adaweb.com/cgi-bin/jfsjr/truism.
3. For an informed discussion of this topic, see Suzanne J. Kessler, 'The Medical
   Construction of Gender: Case Management of Intersexed Infants', *Signs*, **16**:1
   (1990), pp. 3–26.
4. In other words, Holzer's work does not act out an instrumentalist account of
   language, where language is simply a tool used by subjects to convey meaning to other subjects. *Truisms* does not give rise to an uninterrupted line of

communication between sender and receiver, a signifying act that looks like an illustration out of Saussure's *Course in General Linguistics*.

5. Significantly, Holzer goes on to say that part of the attraction of not signing her work also had to with the fact that her interests were not 'only what are traditionally known as 'women's issues'. By remaining anonymous, she could avoid the trap of women artists being expected always and only to address women's issues.

6. Derrida's discussion of iterability appears in 'Signature Event Context' (1988). Holzer's interest in repetition also bears comparison with pop art and minimalist predecessors. For an illuminating discussion of repetition, minimalism and pop art, see Hal Foster, *The Return of the Real: The Avant-Garde at the End of the Century* (Cambridge, MA: MIT Press, 1996), pp. 60–69.

7. The hoods of white taxis were painted with black text as part of her 1996 project 'Biennale di Firenze: il Tempo e la Moda', which also included xenon projections on the exterior of the Palazzo Bargagli next to the river Arno, hanging LED signs in the pavilion itself, and a perfume in collaboration with Helmut Lang.

8. Holzer was the first person ever to use this space. Dan Flavin and Lothar Baumgarten were later to follow her example. Flavin placed his neon installation in the central area for the Guggenheim's 1992 grand reopening, and in 1993 Baumgarten painted it with the names of indigenous societies in North and South America (*America Invention*). Holzer refers to the parapet as 'a long billboard' in Waldman (1997, p. 35).

9. For examples of what the Guerrilla Girls have produced, see the Guerrilla Girls, Confessions of the Guerrilla Girls (New York: Harper Perennial, 1995) or visit their web-site: http://www.guerillagirls.com.

10. According to Holzer, she developed the 'Arno' writing as 'text for a video directed by Mark Pellington for "Red Hot and Dance", an AIDS fund-raiser' (Holzer in Simon, 1998, p. 33).

11. While I cannot do justice in a brief note to Gehry's magnificent Museo Guggenheim Bilbao, it is worth mentioning here that Gehry interrogates the museum's relation to culture, questions how the museum could be integrated into the fabric of daily lives, by literally integrating his building into the structural composition of Bilbao. A train runs underneath one wing; a large gallery stretches under a major city bridge. Where precisely the walls of the museum itself begin is visually complicated by multiple reflections produced by a large pond surrounding the building, the river running next to the pond and the building, titanium scales placed over large portions of the building's surface, and a use of glass that produces visual uncertainty from both the interior and exterior. The materials and visual composition also take into account the industrial history of Bilbao; for instance, one side of the building has structural shapes that resemble the containers that are in the loading field next door, while from another angle the building itself looks like a ship. What's more, all of these moves are made possible by taking apart the shapes of Wright's New York Guggenheim and putting them back together again, differently.

    In their attention to the form and function of the museum itself and Wright's building in particular, both Gehry and Holzer demonstrate Derrida's claim that 'deconstruction is not simply forgetting the past'; deconstruction pays attention to tradition while also not blindly accepting it. In this sense, the Museo Guggenheim Bilbao is very much an archive of deconstructed structures, which is 'as readable as possible' (Derrida, 1989, p. 73).

12. The museum tries to encourage viewers to walk between the columns by

including in its brochure a photograph taken from the far side of the LED columns and by having staff lead their tours to the back of the installation. In effect, the museum has been cornered into participating in Holzer's deconstruction.

13. Whether a conscious feature or not, the Guggenheim Bilbao opened with two other large works that tackle similar issues: Richard Serra's site-specific installation *SNake* (1996) and Robert Morris's *Untitled, Labyrinth* (1974).

14. I have focused on the English text in my discussion, although a more detailed reading would need to take into account the linguistic variations between the texts, including the specificities of Basque, where there are fewer restrictions on word order than in either English or Spanish. The juxtaposition of these three languages is also not without its significance. Again like Gehry, Holzer takes into account the particular cultural context in which her work is viewed, calling attention to the specific cultural differences of the Basque region, its cultural and political relationships to Spain and Spanish culture, which have included separatist movements that have at times led to violence. Banned during the Franco years, Basque was considered unpatriotic, and it would have been unthinkable to include it in a public work of art between 1939 and 1975. Finally, English plays a role not only as Holzer's first language but also as the language of the Solomon R. Guggenheim Foundation and international capital. Viewers may be sharing the same space but that does not necessarily mean they also share the same cultures or speak the same languages.

15. In this respect, Holzer's series is more like Mary Kelly's *Post-Partum Document* (1974) than a Hallmark product.

16. Significantly, the pronoun that circulates throughout these sentences is always 'her' and could refer to either a mother or a daughter; the later reading is of interest to those attaching autobiographical significance to the text: Holzer wrote it shortly after giving birth to her own daughter.

17. Holzer describes reactions to *Mother and Child* in the Venice Pavilion like this: 'There were strong responses. People stood very still. Some would cry and others would turn and walk out quickly. Many would tell me stories about children they had lost' (Holzer in Simon, 1998, p. 14).

18. *Lustmord* could be compared to Holzer's earlier series, *Under a Rock* (1986), which also confronts violence, rape, pain and death.

19. Clearly one group not bothered by Holzer's choice of materials was the Art Directors Club of Europe, who later awarded the issue a Gold Medal for Title and a Gold Medal for Design. For a reflection on the controversy surrounding the appearance of *Lustmord* in *Süddeutsche Zeitung*, see Noemi Smolik, 'Geschichte Auf Frauenkörper Geschrieben'/'History Inscribed on Women's Bodies' (Ittingen: Kunstmuseum des Kantons Thurgau, 1996).

20. The violent force of language is a matter of increasing concern, especially in the United States. For informed discussions see: Judith Butler, *Excitable Speech: A Politics of the Performative* (New York and London: Routledge, 1997) and *Words that Wound: Critical Race Theory, Assaultive Speech and the First Amendment*, ed. Mari J. Matsuda et al. (Boulder, CO: Westview Press, 1993).

21. For an excellent study of medieval conceptualizations of gender, which offers useful reflections on Bernard of Clairvaux's attitudes towards women, see Caroline Walker Bynum, *Fragmentation and Redemption: Essays on Gender and the Human Body in Medieval Religion* (New York: Zone Books, 1992).

22. Even in the apparently uninhabited rooms and landscapes of the virtual reality version of *Lustmord* the body is made present through its ghostly absence in the visual imagery and its materialization in language.

23. Derrida has articulated these concerns on several occasions, including a brief

but effective summary in 'The Villanova Roundtable' (1997). In the name of feminism and deconstruction, I have also argued for ethical activism and groundless solidarity, which can be understood as ways of phrasing political action as both endless and contingent (Elam, 1994).

WORKS CITED

Butler, Judith (1997), *Excitable Speech: A Politics of the Performative* (New York and London: Routledge).
Bynum, Caroline Walker (1992), *Fragmentation and Redemption: Essays on Gender and the Human Body in Medieval Religion* (New York: Zone Books).
Derrida, Jacques (1988a), 'Afterword: Toward an Ethic of Discussion', in *Limited Inc.* (Evanston, IL: Northwestern University Press).
—— (1989), 'Jacques Derrida in Discussion with Christopher Norris', in *Deconstruction Omnibus Volume*, ed. Andreas Papadakis, Catherine Cook and Andrew Benjamin (New York: Rizzoli).
—— (1988b), 'Signature Event Context', in *Limited Inc.* (Evanston, IL: Northwestern University Press).
—— (1997), 'The Villanova Roundtable: a Conversation with Jacques Derrida', in *Deconstruction in a Nutshell*, ed. (John D. Caputo (New York: Fordham University Press).
Elam, Diane (1994), *Feminism and Deconstruction: Ms. en Abyme* (London and New York: Routledge).
Foster, Hal (1996), *The Return of the Real: The Avant-Garde at the End of the Century* (Cambridge, MA: MIT Press).
Holzer, Jenny (1997), *Lustmord*, in *Jenny Holzer*, ed. Diane Waldman (New York: Harry N. Abrams).
—— (1997), *Living*, in *Jenny Holzer*, ed. Diane Waldman (New York: Harry N. Abrams).
—— (1997), *Mother and Child*, in *Jenny Holzer*, ed. Diane Waldman (New York: Harry N. Abrams).
—— (1997), *Survival*, in *Jenny Holzer*, ed. Diane Waldman (New York: Harry N. Abrams).
—— (1997), *Truisms*, in *Jenny Holzer*, ed. Diane Waldman (New York: Harry N. Abrams).
—— (1997), *Under a Rock*, in *Jenny Holzer*, ed. Diane Waldman (New York: Harry N. Abrams).
Kämmerling, Christian (1996), 'Interview, Christian Kämmerling und Jenny Holzer', *Süddeutsche Zeitung*, 19 November 1993, *Magazin* no. 46; reprinted and translated in *Jenny Holzer: Lustmord* (Ittingen: Kunstmuseum des Kantons Thurgau).
Kessler, Suzanne J. (1990), 'The Medical Construction of Gender: Case Management of Intersexed Infants', *Signs*, **16:1** pp. 3–26.
Mari J. Matsuda *et al.* (1993), *Words that Wound: Critical Race Theory, Assaultive Speech and the First Amendment* (Boulder, CO: Westview Press).
Simon, Joan, (1998), 'Interview, Joan Simon in conversation with Jenny Holzer', in *Jenny Holzer*, ed. David Joselit, Joan Simon and Renata Saleci (London: Phaidon).
Smolik, Noemi (1996), 'Geschichte Auf Frauenkörper Geschrieben'/'History Inscribed on Women's Bodies', in *Jenny Holzer: Lustmord* (Ittingen: Kunstmuseum des Kantons Thurgau).

The Guerilla Girls (1995), *Confessions of the Guerilla Girls* (New York: Harper Perennial).
Waldman, Diane (1997), 'Interview, Jenny Holzer and Diane Waldman', in *Jenny Holzer*, ed. Diane Waldman (New York: Harry N. Abrams).

6

Deconstruction and Fiction

Derek Attridge

FICTION, TRUTH AND DECONSTRUCTION

'Now, for the poet, he nothing affirms, and therefore never lieth.' This is how Philip Sidney, writing in his *Defence of Poetry* in the late sixteenth century, carves out a space for fiction, a space in which the accusation of telling lies (which Plato, for instance, had accused poets of doing) simply does not make any sense. This distinction between two primary modes of discourse, fictional and nonfictional, has often been made since Sidney's day, and it operates strongly in much thinking about language use in our own time.

The crucial difference that is articulated by means of this distinction is between two kinds of *claim*: some sentences claim to be telling the truth, making a statement about really occurring events or existing entities, and can therefore be judged in these terms; others make no such claim, and therefore escape any such judgement. Sidney's sentence, for instance, carries with it the implication that an appeal to the criterion of truthfulness *would* be legitimate, and so does the sentence you are reading now. It is possible that these sentences are not true, that they are lies or errors; but no one would dispute that they operate within the arena of truth and its alternatives. However, the opening of James Joyce's *Ulysses* – 'Stately, plump Buck Mulligan came from the stairhead' – makes no such claim; anyone trying to assert that this sentence is untrue would be thought to be making a very odd statement indeed, perhaps one which itself was not meant to be judged true or false.

There have existed many names for discourse which makes no claim to the condition of truthfulness. Sidney calls it *poetry*, as did Chaucer (although the narrower meaning of 'composition in verse' was also common in medieval and Renaissance times); and as late as 1755 Samuel Johnson includes in the definition of *poet* in his *English Dictionary* 'an inventor, an author of fiction'. As this definition indicates, though, the term *fiction* was available by Johnson's time, providing a less slippery, less limitingly honorific name for writing that situates itself outside the true/false distinction. Originally a general term for inventing or feigning, *fiction* began to be applied to linguistic productions involving imaginary characters and events (whether in prose or verse) at the end of the six-teenth century.[1] (Neither term is coterminous with the even more prob-lematic term *literature*: at different periods in its history, this term could embrace a greater or lesser amount of nonfictional writing, and has always excluded some fictional writing, such as jokes and tall stories. We will not be concerned with literature in this essay – but see, in particular, J. Hillis Miller's contribution to this volume.)

Theoretically speaking, there seems no problem in distinguishing between the fictional and the nonfictional. The problems that arise with the distinction appear to stem largely from the pragmatic difficulties in given instances: how do we know whether a sentence or a longer text is or is not making a claim to be truthful (and hence whether or not it makes sense to judge it wrong or deceitful)? Languages, at least in their written form, don't usually include markers that indicate unambiguously the existence of such a claim; Joyce's sentence about Buck Mulligan could occur in exactly that form as a statement about a real individual. Although there are syntactic forms that are associated with narrative (such as the use of free indirect discourse – sentences like 'Tomorrow he would show them'), these may be used just as effectively in a historical narrative as in a fictional one. Since sentences don't themselves advertise their status as fictional or nonfictional, the distinction depends entirely on the context in which they appear to the reader or listener, and the context may not furnish sufficient information. The same problem arises with *irony*, which is a use of language in which the literal assertion being made by the words is modified (or even contradicted) by some feature of the context – example, circumstances which make it impossible for the state-ment to be literally true. Indeed, fiction could be considered a branch or type of irony, one in which the context informs the reader that the sen-tences are to be taken as referring to an imaginary reality.

What are the clues in the context, then, that lead us to the conclusion that a sentence or a text is fictional? The simplest answer would seem to be: features making it evident that the author of the sentence or text *meant them to be read* as fictional. This would seem to be implied in the notion of a 'claim' being made by any sentence to be true or to be outside the realm of true and false: the claim is, presumably, made by the author of the sen-tence as he or she writes it. The context that tells us this could be in the form of other sentences or words, such as a title or a blurb, or the physi-cal appearance of the publication, such as a scientific journal or a paper-back novel, or it could be the circumstances under which we encounter the text, such as recommendation by a friend or teacher. Of course, it is always possible to overlook or misread clues, and to reach the wrong con-clusion about an author's intentions; but this would seem to be an inescapable problem about the pragmatics of reading, not a theoretical problem about the distinction being made. A writer does, or does not, expect any given sentence to be read as fictional or nonfictional, ironic or literal, and it is the job of the reader to find out, by whatever means possible, which of these it is.

Alas, things are not so simple. A number of philosophical and critical traditions have shown that the writing process and the reading process are more complicated than this model suggests. One of the most powerful of these traditions is deconstruction. Jacques Derrida has examined a number of attempts to provide a philosophical grounding for the view of writing and reading I have just sketched, and found, again and again, highly instructive failures. Yet the word 'failure', like my 'Alas' at the start of this paragraph, conveys the wrong impression: deconstructive readings are not aimed at exposing inadequacies in arguments and intellectual limitations in their authors, and the fact that the simple model doesn't work is as much a cause for rejoicing as for regret. It is precisely in their forceful and meticulous engagement with these questions that a wide range of philosophers have demonstrated the complexity of such notions as 'meaning' and 'truth', and it is precisely on this complexity that we depend in all our cultural, political and economic practices.

One of the most effective ways in which Derrida has brought into focus the complicated operations of language as it is produced and received is by tracing in a number of philosophical works the role played by the notion of *writing*, and its relation to notions such as *truth* and *presence*. The pure expression of truth, if there were such a thing, would be *immediate*: it would not rely on anything external to it, since the utilization of some outside aid would always threaten to contaminate its purity. But the utterance of the truth – or of a statement making a truth-claim – is in fact always *mediated* by language, language which has its own sedimented history, structural properties and figurative potential. The truth in language is never simply present; it always has to pass through space and time, and this means that the context in which it is produced is always different from that in which it is received. But why pick on writing? Historically, it has frequently been language in the form of writing that has been identified as the troublemaker, intervening between the author's attempt to enunciate the truth and the reception of this enunciation by readers distant in space and time and thereby subject to unpredictable vagaries of transmission. Speech, on the other hand, has seemed to philosophers at least since Plato (and to many an unphilosophical language-user) to be a guarantor of authenticity, of the here-and-nowness of one person's communication with another. Irony, for example, is often signalled by a particular way of speaking which is lost when the words are written down; and if the hearer is not certain, he or she can always ask 'Are you being serious?' There are also certain inflections of the voice associated with story-telling, so any difficulties we have in distinguishing between fiction and nonfiction could be said to be the fault of writing.

However, Derrida has shown in a number of works that philosophical arguments in support of this position always fall short of their goal: speech is revealed as subject to the same mediations as writing, in spite of the illusion of immediacy and presence. The signals whereby a speaker conveys the fictionality of an utterance, for instance, are as much part of the language system as the vowels and consonants, and are just as liable to reinterpretation in new contexts. The preferring of the spoken word as the locus of truth is, in fact, one aspect of a much wider tendency in Western thought that prefers presence to absence, the immediate to the mediated, originals to copies, and nonfiction to fiction – and in so doing creates simple oppositions where there is something more complicated, and more productive, at work.

Because of the mediatedness of all utterance, the difficulties besetting the distinction between fiction and nonfiction (or between the literal and the ironic) cannot, after all, be regarded as purely pragmatic. It is not just that sometimes it is hard to tell whether a sentence is meant to be taken as an assertion of the truth or not. Pushing the argument to the limit, it is more accurate to say that it's never possible to be sure, with absolute certainty, that it is (or is not) appropriate to regard a sentence as an assertion of a truth, for the type of context that would be necessary tell us this – a totally reliable and fully ascertainable context – does not exist. Any context can always be further contextualized. Past contexts can never be wholly ascertained; future contexts cannot be wholly predicted. This condition even affects the act of writing: the writer does not have full access to the context which makes it possible – for instance, the unconscious motivations that underlie certain choices of words. Without realizing it, writers who think of their work as entirely inside the nonfictional realm often write *as* this or that character, the hard-bitten journalist, the empathetic historian, the meticulous philosopher. Perhaps writing is only possible with at least this degree of the fictional – but then the same would be true of speaking. These conditions, which may seem a check on human ability, spring from the same structural properties that make the assertion of truth possible at all: if language were not a system of mediations, if utterances were not always open to new contexts, it could not begin to function. If a statement could not always be fiction, it could never make a claim to truth.[2]

The impossibility of keeping the fictional totally at bay in writing nonfiction has graver consequences for some genres than for others. If in reading a philosophical treatise or a scientific report, for instance, one finds one cannot be certain that there are no fictional statements among the nonfictional ones, the attainment of what is thought of as philosophical or scientific truth becomes problematic. Another place where fiction is banned – but perhaps cannot be kept out – is the law. Derrida touches on all of these in his discussion of Kafka's brief story 'Before the Law'. He presents Kafka's text as a parable – a fiction – about the fictionality at the heart of the law, and shows that both Freud and Kant, scientist and philosopher, rely on something like fiction, and cannot avoid doing so. Commenting on Kant's elaboration of a categorical imperative at the heart of moral law, he states: 'Though the authority of the law seems to exclude all historicity and empirical narrativity, and this at the moment when its rationality seems alien to all fiction and imagination ... it still seems *a priori* to shelter these parasites' (Derrida, 1992, p. 190). As parasites, fiction and imagination are external to the law (and science and philosophy – all governed by rationality), but their hosts depend on them for their operation, even if that operation is not as smooth as, by their own lights, it should be.[3]

Another mode of writing where it would seem to be imperative that the reader be able to identify fictional moments is autobiography.[4] In autobiographical narrative, a narrator makes the claim: the events affirmed in these sentences happened to me. In a genuine autobiography it is possible to identify this narrator with the actual author of the sentences, and we are entitled, perhaps even encouraged, to judge each of the sentences as true or false. (In fictional autobiographies, of course, such as Defoe's *Moll Flanders* or Dickens's *Great Expectations*, we make a clear separation between the 'I' of the text and the author; the 'I' is capable of lying, but not the author.) Among autobiographies, those which stake most on this claim are those we call *confessions*: autobiographies where one is led to feel that the truth has been hidden – for good reason – until the moment of articulation in language.[5]

Here we would seem to be at the furthest remove possible from fiction. If we find in reading a confessional autobiography that we are uncertain whether we should be judging its statements on the basis of their truthfulness or enjoying it as fiction, we might as well give up all possibility of experiencing anything like confessional power. (The same is not true if we find ourselves *disbelieving* certain statements – to catch an autobiographer lying may be to register a moment of fierce internal struggle with memory and conscience, and to find the power of the confession enhanced.) Yet, as we have seen, what we think of as telling the truth is always mediated by linguistic and other systems – by the history of the genre of autobiography (including fictional autobiography), for instance – and we are only likely to experience as truth a work which successfully exploits those systems, and which is therefore to some degree a fiction, the elaboration of a believable character on existing models. For the writer, producing a convincing confession may mean the repudiation of conventional forms and fictional precedents, but this repudiation is itself thoroughly conventional. (The speaker in Philip Sidney's sonnet sequence, *Astrophil and*

Stella, who may or may not be identifiable with the author, repeatedly bases his claim to truthful utterance on his rejection of Petrarchan conventions.) Thus even the most powerful of confessional autobiographies cannot, and need not, escape fiction, and some of the most interesting confessions acknowledge this and yet manage to preserve the truth-telling power of the confession. We shall now turn to an example.

CONFESSION AS WRITING: J. M. COETZEE'S *BOYHOOD*

The South African writer J. M. Coetzee is not known for confessional self-revelation. In a series of seven novels, from *Dusklands* in 1974 to *The Master of Petersburg* in 1994, he has honed a fictional style that, whatever the mode of narration, offers no hint of a personal authorial presence. Coetzee's substantial body of critical commentary, too – which includes the books *White Writing* and *Giving Offense* as well as the articles collected in *Doubling the Point* – is not in anyway self-revelatory. His reluctance to account for his fictions in the terms provided by his own life reaches a somewhat absurd extreme in the written interview that was published in the 1994 special issue of the *South Atlantic Quarterly* devoted to Coetzee: questions that occupy some thirteen pages in all receive answers that add up to little more than a page.

It is not really as straightforward as that, of course – and Coetzee would be the first to agree. At the beginning of the series of interviews that make up part of *Doubling the Point*, he answers David Attwell's first question, which concerns just this issue of the absence of autobiographical writing from his output, as follows:

> Let me treat this as a question about telling the truth rather than as a question about autobiography. Because in a larger sense all writing is autobiography: everything that you write, including criticism and fiction, writes you as you write it.   (Coetzee, 1992, p. 17)

Autobiographical moments of a more explicit kind occur now and then, and Coetzee's conversations with Attwell in *Doubling the Point* provide a vehicle for an extended meditation on his own intellectual development. The last of the interviews in that book ends with a rather extraordinary passage in which Coetzee tells the story of his life up to the years 1981–83. Not the least remarkable feature of this passage is that Coetzee chooses to speak of himself as a boy in the third person and the present tense. Here is his description of part of his early boyhood:

> His years in rural Worcester (1948–51) as a child from an Afrikaans background attending English-medium classes, at a time of raging

Afrikaner nationalism, a time when laws were being concocted to prevent people of Afrikaans descent from bringing up their children to
speak English, provoke in him uneasy dreams of being hunted down
and accused; by the age of twelve he has a well-developed sense of
social marginality.   (Coetzee, 1992, p. 393)

It is only in recounting when, at the age of twenty-five (that is to say,
halfway through his life up to the time of the interview), he went to the
University of Texas as a graduate student that he says '*he* now begins to
feel closer to *I*: *autre*biography shades back into autobiography.'

None of this, however, could have prepared his readers for the book
that appeared in 1997. *Boyhood*, subtitled *Scenes from Provincial Life*, is a
short (and very selective) account of the young John Coetzee's life in
Worcester and a few of his experiences as a teenager in Cape Town. The
major events of the book occur when John is between the ages of ten and
thirteen (which is to say, between the years 1950 and 1953); the background (seen only through the eyes of the young boy) is that of the early
years of South Africa's Afrikaner Nationalist government and of the
Coetzee family's slide from middle-class respectability into something
approaching poverty. It is told, like the passage on his boyhood in the
Doubling the Point interview, in the third person and the present tense.

The result of this choice of presentational mode is a singular immediacy, one might almost say a depthlessness, in the recounting of events, but
not the sense of intimacy we gain from confessional autobiography of a
more orthodox sort. Here is a sample of straightforward narrative, in
which the effect of Coetzee's unusual choice of person and tense is evident:

> Once a year Boswell's Circus comes to Worcester. Everyone in his class
> goes; for a week talk is about the circus and nothing else. Even the
> Coloured children go, after a fashion: they hang around outside the tent
> for hours, listening to the band, peering in through gaps.
>   They plan to go on the Saturday afternoon, when his father is play-
> ing cricket. His mother makes it into an outing for the three of them. But
> at the ticket booth she hears with a shock the high Saturday afternoon
> prices: 2/6 for children, 5/- for adults. She does not have enough
> money with her. She buys tickets for him and his brother. 'Go in, I'll
> wait here,' she says. He is unwilling, but she insists.   (47)

This style of narration, I scarcely need to say, is unusual for autobiography. *The Education of Henry Adams* and *A Portrait of the Artist as a Young
Man*, to take two obvious precursors that narrate the childhood of a writer
with exceptional gifts, both use the third person (Joyce's work, of course,
is a deliberate mixture of fact and fiction), but are written in the past tense

– and both, as a result, can introduce an adult irony to complicate the naivety of the boy's outlook. Much of Coetzee's fiction comes closer to an autobiographical mode than *Boyhood*: most of it makes use of first-person narrators, and, of the two exceptions, one uses the past tense. Only *The Master of Petersburg* makes use of both the third person and the present tense, and it is noteworthy that this novel, the last to be written before *Boyhood*, could be regarded as the most confessional.[6]

Turning to the content of Coetzee's work, we may note that it calls to mind a number of well-known confessional autobiographies, whether genuine, fictional or semi-fictional. As with the young Augustine in the *Confessions* and the young Marcel in *À la recherche du temps perdu*, the most potent presence in young John's life is that of his mother, even when he is rebelling against her; and it is hard to escape the feeling that to admit this degree of attachment requires an intense internal struggle. As in Rousseau's *Confessions* and in many of Dostoevsky's fictional confessions, the life that is narrated is marked by fiercely-kept secrets and an acute sense of shame. The very shock of autobiographical explicitness after so many years of tight-lipped resistance is suggestive of the confessional mode. The question I want to address is whether confession is *possible* in the third person and in the present tense.

Coetzee himself is the author of an acute analysis of confession that will throw light on this question, a lengthy essay entitled 'Confession and Double Thoughts' first published in 1985 and reprinted in *Doubling the Point*. (It is the composition of this very essay in 1982–83 that Coetzee, in the final interview of the volume, sees as the pivotal moment in his twenty-year writing career, the moment beyond which he finds he cannot narrativize his life in the third person.) In discussing Tolstoy's *Kreutzer Sonata*, Rousseau's *Confessions*, and Dostoevsky's *Notes from Underground, The Idiot*, and *The Possessed*, Coetzee demonstrates the structural interminability of confession in a secular context. Every act of confession is subject to self-reflexive scrutiny: its motivation can be questioned, and its impurity (or the inevitable falsehood of its claim to purity) confessed, and the motivation for this further questioning questioned and its imperfection confessed, and so on without end. (In the larger scheme of Coetzee's writings one might perhaps see the essay on confession as itself an instance of this sceptical self-reflexivity on the part of the person attempting to confess.) Only confession in the sacramental context, an act of faith confirmed by the operation of grace, can have a conclusion that is not arbitrary.

In *Boyhood*, it is primarily Coetzee's choice of person and tense that prevents the interminable spiralling of confession by short-circuiting it before it even gets going. The use of the third person implicitly dissociates the narrative voice from the narrated consciousness, telling us that this was another person, that we are reading, to use Coetzee's term, an *autre-*

biography, not an autobiography. The use of the present tense both heightens the immediacy of the narrated events and denies the text any retrospection, any place from which the writer can reflect on and express regret about (or approval of) the acts and attitudes described. In other words, Coetzee achieves the same effect that we find in his works of fiction: the reader is refused the comfort of a meta-narrative level or perspective from which authorial judgements (here, judgements on his earlier self) could be made. If anyone is to take responsibility for judgements on the boy of *Boyhood*, it is the *reader*, and the reader is thus implicated in the ethical web spun by the work.

In his essay on confession, Coetzee lays particular emphasis on the connection between confession and truth. Focusing his attention on secular confession, he proposes the following distinction:

> We can demarcate a mode of autobiographical writing that we can call the *confession*, as distinct from the *memoir* and the *apology*, on the basis of an underlying motive to tell an essential truth about the self. (Coetzee, 1992, p. 252)

This 'essential truth' is not a matter of historical or factual truth, which is the domain of the *memoir*, nor is it a matter of explaining or excusing the construction or deformation of the self, which is the function of apology.[7] Here we would seem to be far from the insights of deconstruction. But in his first interview with Attwell in *Doubling the Point*, Coetzee makes it clear that the 'essential truth' of confession is not to be thought of as a 'higher' or 'deeper' truth to which the confession, if it is made in good faith and with sufficient courage, may penetrate. He describes the process of attaining to the truth of autobiography (he doesn't use the term *confession* here, but the connection is clear) as a process of writing, and *writing* understood in a particular way:

> It is naive to think that writing is a simple two-stage process: first you decide what you want to say, then you say it. On the contrary, as all of us know, you write because you do not know what you want to say'. . . . Writing, then, involves an interplay between the push into the future that takes you to the blank page in the first place, and a resistance. Part of that resistance is psychic, but part is also an automatism built into language: the tendency of words to call up other words, to fall into patterns that keep propagating themselves. Out of that interplay there emerges, if you are lucky, what you recognize or hope to recognize as the true.   (p. 18)

And he adds:

I don't see that 'straight' autobiographical writing is any different *in kind* from what I have been describing. Truth is something that comes in the process of writing, or comes from the process of writing.   (p. 18)

The 'essential truth about the self' that is the goal of confession, then, is not just the revelation of what has been known all along by the author but kept secret for reasons of guilt and shame; rather, it is something that emerges in the telling, if it emerges at all. Nor can it be 'read off' by the reader, as a series of facts hitherto unrevealed; it can be experienced only *in the reading*, or in a certain kind of reading. The text does not *refer* to the truth; it produces it. Confession, that is to say, is not separable from fiction.

Now, as Coetzee points out in his essay, confession is usually thought of as one element in a series: transgression, confession, penitence and absolution. But, in discussing Augustine's story of the stealing of pears from a neighbour's garden, he argues that 'transgression is not a fundamental component' (p. 252). What Augustine is searching for is a truth about himself that would *account* for the theft, a 'source within the self for that-which-is-wrong'. For Augustine, he will not find this source before he is admitted to God's grace: discovery of the truth will be, at the same time, absolution. But in the realm of secular confession, such absolution is not possible; even self-forgiveness, Coetzee demonstrates in his discussion of *The Possessed*, is subject to further self-doubt. 'The end of confession', states Coetzee near the end of his essay, 'is to tell the truth to and for oneself' (p. 291).

At first sight, this may seem a surprising statement: is confession not premised upon telling the truth to another, or the other, a making public of what has hitherto remained secret? This would seem to be the basis of Rousseau's *Confessions*, and of many confessional works that have followed in its powerful wake. But Coetzee's assertion is of a piece with his understanding of truth as something arrived at in the process of articulation, not a hidden fact finally revealed. If the struggle to articulate that which is not yet known by the writer is complicated by the consciousness of an audience, by the need to convince another party, it will be weakened, turned aside from its goal. Earlier in the essay, Coetzee has said, following Tolstoy, that 'the condition of truthfulness is not perfect self-knowledge but truth-directedness' (p. 261), and this overriding concern with the truth can only be deflected and dissipated by a concern with an interlocutor.[8]

One does not need to read Bakhtin or Derrida to be aware that the attempt to write only for oneself is doomed to failure; articulated language is always already premised on the existence of an interlocutor or potential interlocutor, and the 'self' for which one writes is not some hermetically-sealed space but a site of constant traffic with that which is not the self. Confession is, inescapably, public, because language is. But the impossibility of the project of telling the truth to and for oneself is not a reason for its not being desirable; on the contrary, desire is at its most powerful in the face of the impossible. The impossibility of this project is, however, one more reason for the interminability of confession.

If the articulation of the truth of oneself to oneself is the goal of secular confession, it is evident that the next in the series of traditional components, repentance, is not an essential accompaniment. To feel and express regret for what it is that one has discovered (or produced) in one's articulation will add nothing to the truthfulness, or truth-directedness, of the confession; and it will provoke a further round of self-interrogation as the subject doubts the genuineness of his or her emotion. (This will hold true all the more if the confession is being made to another or to others, when there is everything to gain from an appearance of remorse.) It may be that repentance – or what is of value in repentance – only repeats what is already implicit in confession in the fullest sense. For if to confess is to discover in language a truth of the self that had eluded one, that one did not know, and did not know one did not know, it would seem to involve a kind of *taking responsibility* for that truth. It is *my* truth I confess, and mine alone. In giving it form, and thus bringing it into being as truth, I acknowledge it as true and as mine. If the most appropriate form for this taking of responsibility is fiction – and this is not something that can be known in advance, as Coetzee stresses – then fiction is more truthful than the 'truth' would have been.[9]

Now let us return to *Boyhood*. Although it lacks the trappings of a conventional confessional work – notably, as we've seen, in its use of the third person and the present tense – the book exemplifies the project of confession as presented by Coetzee in the essay we've been discussing and in the interviews of *Doubling the Point*. Of course, that project cannot be judged by the reader, in so far as the goal of confession is 'to tell the truth to and for oneself'; but the reader can testify to what we might call, in imitation of Roland Barthes on realism (see Barthes, 1986), a *confession effect* – the *experience*, in the reading, of a truth-directed articulation of an author's past life. This is not to say that the work reads as artless; on the contrary, every sentence seems to have been sculpted into maximal effectiveness. Here is an example that occurs not in the present-tense narrative but as a memory while John and his younger brother are playing with a book press in their Aunt Annie's storeroom. The two boys, visiting a farm, had come upon a machine for grinding maize:

> He persuaded his brother to put his hand down the funnel where the mealie-pits were thrown in; then he turned the handle. For an instant, before he stopped, he could feel the fine bones of the fingers being crushed. His brother stood with his hand trapped in the machine, ashen with pain, a puzzled, inquiring look on his face.

Their hosts rushed them all to the hospital, where a doctor ampu-
tated half the middle finger of his brother's left hand . . .

He has never apologized to his brother, nor has he ever been
reproached for what he did. Nevertheless, the memory lies like a
weight upon him, the memory of the soft resistance of flesh and bone,
and then the grinding.   (p. 119)

The chiselling of language that the reader senses here is part of the experience of a struggle to shape (and hence discover) the truth, an element of
that interplay between 'the push into the future' and the resistance of the
psyche and of the medium that Coetzee himself describes. That there is no
attempt to explain or excuse the horrifying action described does not
diminish its truth-directedness. And the use of the third person and the
present tense is part of this attempt to be true: we have seen that in narrating this period of his life in an interview Coetzee falls into just this
mode.

Confession and truth are inseparable from articulated language, as
Augustine pointed out in an early instance of deconstructive thinking.
Derrida, reading Augustine's statement to God that he is making the truth
'in my heart, before Thee in confession; and in my writing, before many
witnesses' (*Confessions* X, I, 1), raises the question of whether the act of
writing itself is a crime that demands confession (1993, pp. 46–8). This
suggestion finds echoes in two other authors who might be called deconstructive. De Man, in his essay on Rousseau's *Confessions*, finds Rousseau
threatened by language's machine-like functioning, which drives a wedge
'between the meaning and the performance of any text' (1979, p. 298).
And Coetzee, in *The Master of Petersburg*, invents a character who confesses – to himself – that he experiences writing as an entry into evil. The
character is only partly fictional: his name is Fyodor Dostoevsky, and he
is on the point of embarking on a new novel, *The Possessed*, in which confession plays a crucial role. He is also, of course, J. M. Coetzee, confessing
the truth by making a fiction.

NOTES

1. There are other types of utterance besides fictional ones that do not make truth-
   claims; for instance, performative utterances make things happen (or attempt
   to do so). 'I name this child Catriona' does what it says (if the conditions are
   right); it doesn't assert a truth about something. However, performative utterances also occur in fiction, which can be troublesome for philosophical analysis – see Derrida's essay 'Signature Event Context' in Derrida (1988), pp. 1–23.
2. In response to John Searle's assertion that the relation between fiction and nonfiction is one of 'logical dependency', Derrida comments: 'The real question, or
   at any rate in my eyes the indispensable question, would then become: what is
   "nonfiction standard discourse", what must it be and what does this name

evoke, once its fictionality or its fictionalization . . . is always possible (and moreover by virtue of the very same words, the same phrases, the same grammar, etc.)?' (Derrida, 1988, pp. 102, 133). He goes on to point out that the very rules or conventions governing the distinction between fiction and nonfiction partake of the fictional, as they are symbolic inventions, not 'things found in nature' (pp. 133–4).

3. Derrida notes that writing has always been treated as a 'parasite' by the philosophical tradition (Derrida, 1988, p. 102). See also Miller (1979).

4. For a discussion of the necessarily fictional nature of autobiography, see de Man (1984).

5. Interestingly, Derrida has associated both his own intellectual development and the institution of literature with the notion of confession. In an interview he talks of an adolescent desire to capture the memory of what happens – 'something like a lyrical movement toward confidences and confessions' (Derrida, 1992, p. 34) – and remarks that among the first texts he became interested in were confessions, notably the confessional writings of Rousseau and Gide. He then identifies literature as an institution (albeit a fictional institution) which in principle allows one to 'say everything' (*tout dire*), both in the sense of a total representation and also in the sense of speaking without constraints.

6. For a discussion of this novel that addresses its confessional force, see Attridge (1996).

7. To offer an excuse would seem to be to undermine a confession, since it involves an avoidance of the guilt on whose acknowledgement confession depends. But the relation is somewhat more complicated, as Paul de Man argues in his discussion of confessional moments in Rousseau (1979, pp. 278–301). For de Man, 'Excuses generate the very guilt they exonerate, though always in excess or by default' (p. 299).

8. Confession is, structurally, similar to the gift, as analysed by Derrida; if a true act of giving ever occurs, it must be without any consciousness of the possible response of the other. See Derrida (1991).

9. Derrida, in *his* most confessional work, *Circumfession* (another work deeply concerned with the relationship with the mother), expresses his fascination with Augustine's phrase *veritatem facere*, to make the truth, a truth 'that I'm not sure comes under any religion, for reason of literature, nor under any literature, for reason of religion' (Derrida, 1993, p. 48).

WORKS CITED

Attridge, Derek (1996), 'Expecting the Unexpected in Coetzee's *Master of Petersburg* and Derrida's Recent Writings', in *Applying: to Derrida*, ed. John Brannigan, Ruth Robbins and Julian Wolfreys (London: Macmillan), pp. 21–40.

Barthes, Roland (1986), 'The Reality Effect', in *The Rustle of Language*, trans. Richard Howard (Oxford: Blackwell), pp. 141–8.

Coetzee, J. M. (1992), *Doubling the Point: Essays and Interviews*, ed. David Attwell (Cambridge, MA: Harvard University Press).

—— (1994), *The Master of Petersburg* (London: Secker and Warburg).

—— (1997), *Boyhood: Scenes from Provincial Life* (New York: Viking).

de Man, Paul (1979), *Allegories of Reading: Figural Language in Rousseau, Nietzsche, Rilke, and Proust* (New Haven, CT: Yale University Press).

—— (1984), 'Autobiography as De-Facement', *The Rhetoric of Romanticism* (New York: Columbia University Press), pp. 67–81.

Derrida, Jacques (1988), *Limited Inc.*, ed. Gerald Graff (Evanston, IL: Northwestern University Press).
—— (1991), *Given Time: I. Counterfeit Money*, trans. Peggy Kamuf (Chicago, IL: University of Chicago Press).
—— (1992), *Acts of Literature*, ed. Derek Attridge (New York: Routledge).
—— (1993), *Circumfession*, in Geoffrey Bennington and Jacques Derrida, *Jacques Derrida*, trans. Geoffrey Bennington (Chicago, IL: University of Chicago Press).
Miller, J. Hillis (1979), 'The Critic as Host', in Harold Bloom *et al.*, *Deconstruction and Criticism* (New York: Seabury Press), pp. 217–53.

7
Deconstruction and Film

Robert Smith

PREQUEL

So then. 'Deconstruction and Film'. Not much to go on here.

True, Derrida has published with Bernard Stiegler a book about television (Derrida and Stiegler, 1996); he occasionally makes reference in seminars to films;[1] he even made an appearance in the film *Ghost Dance* (McMullen, 1983); and he claims to watch a lot of movies (Brunette and Wills, 1994, p. 9) – but in contrast to his voluminous contributions in other areas, Derrida's 'work on film' remains to my knowledge minimal. He has published varying amounts of work in adjacent areas like photography, dialogue, music, painting and narrative,[2] but almost nothing about film – even though, one could argue, film comprises a combination of some or all of those adjacent areas. All that has been published are a few remarks in a general interview concerning the spatial arts (remarks we shall certainly look at). Some may be surprised and possibly disappointed by Derrida's reluctance to engage in the topic, given that (a) he *has* written about those adjacent areas, (b) his work is *so* wide-ranging that to overlook film can make it seem a blind spot, (c) there are substantial philosophical texts dealing with film that warrant serious critical attention (not to mention the abundance of demanding and provocative films), and (d) Derrida's background in phenomenology – a discipline which deals so intensively with sound and image in time – equips him splendidly for the task. On the other hand, to complain of Jacques Derrida's lack of productivity (a glance at his list of publications will be bracing for those unacquainted with it) is to be churlish. Derrida's comparative silence has not, in any case, deterred scholars in film studies from writing deconstructively *about* film or writing *about* deconstruction *and* film (nor has it deterred Woody Allen from making a film called *Deconstructing Harry*). There is a book, for example, called *Screen/Play: Derrida and Film Theory*, which maps the field usefully (Brunette and Wills, 1989). There is also more broadly 'post-structuralist' work on film, constellating, according to one perspective, around Stephen Heath in the United Kingdom and Gilles Deleuze in France, which is not unrelated to the work of deconstruction. The present essay stays close to Derrida, employing the words 'Derrida' and 'deconstruction' virtually synonymously – not an uncontentious practice, it should be acknowledged.[3]

PRESENCE AND THE FRAME

Ideally we would need to know what deconstruction is, and then what film is, before grappling with what links them. However, the question 'what is deconstruction?' forms an intrinsic, troubling part of deconstruction, so that asking it makes for a rather complicated gesture; not to mention deconstruction's resistance to definition even when one ignores this problem and tries to answer the question from a more straightforward point of view. As a 'what is?' type of question, 'what is deconstruction?' also perpetuates a long-established and pervasive style of thinking classifiable as 'essentialist', which assumes that things have essences and that these may be deduced with due philosophic rigour; whereas deconstruction, while just as rigorous, challenges indefatigably and diverges from the essentialist approach. I shall stay at a more local level, choosing themes Derrida has developed that are applicable to the study of film, rather than assuming that the weight of a unified project named Deconstruction can be leveraged with or against it.

If this proviso about deconstruction implies that by contrast film presents a tidy object of study, it shouldn't. Even in the (let us call it) essentialist domain, controversy crowds around the definition of film. We have already taken sides by entitling our essay 'Deconstruction and Film' rather than 'Deconstruction and Cinema' – or 'Deconstruction and the Movies', for that matter. Each phrase carries its own bias. 'Cinema' indicates the industry and the social activity rather than the aesthetically purer artefact indicated by 'Film', yet 'Deconstruction and Cinema' remains more high-brow than the demotic 'Deconstruction and the Movies'. Academics tend to write about 'film'; journalists about 'the movies'. One could analyse such things at length: the choice of terms opens out into vast cultural, political and economic questions. Playing behind all three terms, for example, is a struggle between Europe and America over which is the authentic home of film/cinema/the movies (though India from its centre in 'Bollywood' actually produces of all nations the largest number of films per year). When I come to discuss *Jurassic Park* I'll be going further and suggesting that despite the breadth of these terms – film, cinema, movies – none spans even in combination with the others the range of phenomena involved today in the experience of, well . . . what do we call it?

Where to draw the border around film in general or a film in particular would itself be a characteristic issue for deconstruction to address, and we shall look at an example in a moment. But first let's step back and try posing the essentialist question, 'What *is* film?' – and hope to answer it in a less essentialist, more 'deconstructive' manner.

Regardless of its content or style, a film of any kind (from home movie to cineplex blockbuster) is, at least, a record. It records what is present, what will have been present, in front of a camera.[4] Even in the case of a 'live recording' as it is paradoxically known, a film has the capacity to be viewed again at a later date, after the present moment is gone. Even though live, it already exists in principle as a record. It can thus prolong what would otherwise be lost. Film 'guards against the misery of things', in the words of German director Wim Wenders, 'namely their disappearance' (quoted in Beicken and Kolker, 1993, p. 4).

Early viewers of film were amazed and moved by this miraculous gift dispensed by film, that of reanimating what had gone. The visual form of film superseded sound recordings in the capacity to simulate the experience of presence. Like Christ calling Lazarus, film seemed to bring back to life what had been irrevocably lost; it blurred uncannily the distinction between life and death. Debatably the most seminal text in film studies, Siegfried Kracauer's *Theory of Film*, isolates this essential trait and emphasizes its importance when, with similarly Christian connotations, it takes for its subtitle *The Redemption of Physical Reality* (Kracauer, 1960). The restoration of lost presence, with all the pathos, religious or secular, implicit in it, appears to define the essential function, and thus the nature, of film.

But are we certain that film has so simple a compensatory structure? Or rather, are we certain that *presence*, the value film trades in, buying it back from the past to sell it in the future, can be lost and won so symmetrically? A consideration of what Derrida has to say about presence should give us pause.

With various qualifications, one could describe Derrida as a philosopher of the transcendental tradition – 'of' in both senses: belonging to that tradition but also philosophical about, critical of, it. Typical of this tradition would be a line of questioning that asks not 'What is it?', in the essentialist mode, but 'How is it possible?' Applying this type of question to film – where film is understood as a recording of presence – we might ask, 'How is it possible for presence to *be* recorded? What is it about presence that is recordable? If presence can be recorded, repeated, reproduced, quoted, and so, on, what does this say about presence?'

So let us try to answer the question. A first observation would be that presence is indeed recordable. This being the case, presence hearkens towards the future, so to speak, since a recording of presence is in principle designed to be reactivated *after* the recorded event that was present; it would be impossible to view a recording of something before that something had happened, by definition. The present already enjoys an implicit rapport with the future: this we can deduce from its recordability. To be more precise, this rapport with the future designates the present's rapport *with itself* in the future, not just with some vague future in general, because we are talking about the possibility of a *recording*, and thus necessarily a recording of *it*. In so far as it is recordable, the present relates to its (recorded) self in the future.

The implications of a 'transcendental' and incipiently deconstructive deduction such as this are more far-reaching than might be guessed from its dry tone. Two such implications concern time in general and film in particular. Regarding time we can infer that the future is, as the saying goes, not what it used to be. If a part of the present (in the form of a recordability embodied in this case by film) already relates to itself in the future, the future in a sense already exists, and thus fails to qualify as perfectly 'futural'. The recordability of the present suggests that the future baulks at being shunted forward and away from the present. The future interferes with the present before the future has happened. Such a proposition threatens to play havoc with the received idea of time as a consecutive series of 'nows', an idea that forms the basis of so much thinking not only in metaphysics but in everyday life.

So what is a camera recording when it is recording something supposedly present? Indeed, whether the present gets recorded or not, its recordability belongs to it, a state of affairs which puts the present into relation with itself in the 'future'. This can only mean that the present is divided from itself: in order to relate to itself over 'time' or whatever this strange new medium is, there must be a break, division, space, time, fissure for the present to relate to itself across. The so-called 'present' fails to be entirely present to itself; it is both deferred from itself and divided from itself into a 'future'. Derrida famously invents the term *différance* to capture the double movement of a present both differing from and dividing itself, deferring itself, across time (Derrida, 1972a). This crisis in its status stems from the present's recordability, a condition akin to what Derrida refers to as 'iterability' (Derrida, 1972c).

By this logic we are brought to recognize that the definition of film as a recording of presence will not do. The present recorded by film not only is not present, that is not fully present to itself, *but becomes recordable only if it isn't* . . . The present has to be something other than itself for film to be possible; film depends upon the non-identity of the present with itself. The film may think it is recording presence, as it were, but there would be no such thing as film if the present were indeed simply and only present. The essentialist question 'What is film?' has led to the transcendental question asking how film is possible, which has led in turn into a deconstructive vortex where something becomes possible only if it's impossible. What kind of rationalism is that? The logic is hard to fault, so perhaps we are dealing with a logic that is rational without being rational*ist*. Are there forms of reason outside rationalism?

The notion of presence reveals one of the richest areas of overlap between deconstruction and film. It suggests, for example, a much more strange and counter-intuitive version of the 'return of the dead' associated with film's power to revive figures from the past: if those figures already fell short of their own self-identity, were they already ghosts? What sort of multiple haunting must then be at play in the experience of the screen?

Let us move on. Another area where deconstruction and film engage each other from within, concerns the 'frame' or 'border'. A border is probably as indispensable to a film as the possibility of recording: after all, what would a film without a (physical and temporal) border be? Derrida elaborates the notion of the artwork's border or frame most extensively in *The Truth in Painting* (Derrida, 1978), but I have another essay in mind, 'To Speculate – on "Freud"' (Derrida, 1980). Of the myriad issues it raises, that of the tension between internal and external forces in a given piece of work serves our purposes best. In this case the piece of work is Freud's notorious *Beyond the Pleasure Principle*. Derrida's essay constitutes a tenaciously close reading of Freud's text.

In the course of *Beyond the Pleasure Principle* Freud begins to talk about a boy (actually his grandson), Ernst, and Ernst's relation to his mother (actually Sigmund's daughter, Anna). In Freud's view, Ernst's perception of the relationship is symbolized in a game Ernst plays. The little boy takes a bobbin or spool and keeps throwing it out and pulling it back towards him. 'Away!', he exclaims, when the thing is thrown out; 'Here!', each time he retrieves it. Freud argues the toy symbolizes the mother, and the boy is staging her leaving and returning to him. It is a moot point and a great deal of psychoanalytical argument has been expended on it.

Rather that stepping into the psychoanalytical debate per se, Derrida notices and elects to investigate something apparently peripheral to the game (like a good psychoanalyst, ironically). He notices that throughout the text Freud keeps vacillating over the main hypothesis of his paper, namely that the pleasure principle amounts to an instinct for death. Freud makes courageous steps in the direction of this hypothesis but then timidly withdraws, in a recurring pattern. Derrida speculates as to whether Freud is playing his own bobbin game, rejecting the hypothesis and then avowing it . . .

If this is the case, the relation between the two scenes, grandfather writing and grandson playing, is tacitly autobiographical, and not only because Freud chooses to write about his own grandson in what is otherwise a purportedly 'scientific' or disinterested account; nor autobiographical only in a psychological kind of way; but also because Sigmund and Ernst are caught in the same pattern of rejection and retrieval: the text moves in this pattern and the 'autobiography' occurs at a structural (textual) rather than psychological level. The relation between the inside and the outside of the text, the question of its border, suddenly transforms. For example, is Freud the author of this text or is there a more powerful machine manipulating him? What of this relationship between content (the story of the boy's game) and form (the to-ing and fro-ing of Freud's argument, if indeed this counts as form), where we cannot say the content *reflects* the form since it is a part of it and thus cannot mirror it back? Or if it can be said to reflect it, does this not lead to a *mise en abyme*, that is an infinite mirroring (as for example when a device on a shield portrays the shield it decorates), which would preclude in principle a closure of the text by a secure border? And if the content contains the form by reproducing it, doesn't the paradigm form/content stop making sense? The questions begin to multiply.

Just as we moved from transcendental to deconstructive thinking, we now move from a broadly 'structuralist' to 'post-structuralist' approach. Derrida notices and analyses how a text is structured, its rhythmic and conceptual patterns, and at all levels. Because those structures criss-cross the text's borders, it cannot be decided ultimately what level or structure confronts us. The various structures share a formal identity, creating a synergetic excess that makes it impossible to settle the status of the work as a whole.

Mindful of such 'logic', let us turn to a film. I have already mentioned Wim Wenders, and his film *Paris, Texas* offers a workable example. It turns out that rather as in *Beyond the Pleasure Principle* in Derrida's reading of it, bizarre doublings shuttle between the production of, and the narrative told by, *Paris, Texas*.

The film's story relates among other things the search by its hero, Travis, for his place of origin. It emerges that he was conceived in the incongruously-named Texan town of Paris, and this is where he is headed at the beginning of the film, as he stumbles through the desert from his self-imposed exile in Mexico across the border into the United States. This apparently innocuous, free-standing story of a man's search for a place of beginning actually duplicates, however, and gets snarled up in, the film's own search for where to start.

A written text by Wenders, 'Like Flying Blind without Instruments: on the Turning Point in *Paris, Texas*' (Wenders, 1991), records this search. In the opening sentence, Wenders dutifully relates that '[t]he story's about a man who turns up somewhere in the desert out of nowhere and returns to civilization.' He then says that 'prior to filming we drove the entire length of the US–Mexican border'. That time 'prior to filming' doubles the prehistory of the film's own narrative, namely Travis's wandering exile around that border in the time before the narrative proper begins. The story of the director's recce and that of the film's leading character interfuse. Another case of *mise en abyme*, the film's origins get shuffled into the story it narrates. The 'frame' of the film, its production history, collapses into the 'frame' of the narrative, making any fixing of the frame look arbitrary. A structure, more dominant than either story, imbues and over-brims both.

Somewhat like Freud's *Beyond the Pleasure Principle*, Wenders's film obeys a law of autobiographical confusion that cracks the frame of the work, causing a leakage between levels. The autobiography relates not so much to a personal psyche as to an imperious force with something machine-like or automatic about it. Where does the force of *Paris, Texas* lie? Neither quite in the film, nor quite in the production. In 'To Speculate – on "Freud"' Derrida speaks of 'autobiography of the writing': might we be justified in speaking here of 'autobiography of the film'?

DERRIDA IN HIS OWN WORDS

So far I have concentrated, because of the paucity of work on film by him, on extrapolating work published in other areas by Derrida in order to apply it to film. There is, however, the interview on the spatial arts, and this deserves close attention. Asked about the spread of deconstruction into at first sight remote areas such as cinema, Derrida responds:

> I am . . . a little surprised by the extent to which deconstructive schemas can be put into play or invested in problematics that are foreign to me, whether we are speaking about architecture, cinema, or legal theory. But my surprise is only a half-surprise, because at the same time the program as I perceived or conceived it made that necessary. If someone had asked me twenty years ago [the interview takes place in 1990] whether I thought deconstruction should interest people in domains that were foreign to me, as a matter of principle my response would have been yes, it is absolutely indispensable, but at the same time I never would have believed it could happen. (Brunette and Wills, 1994, p. 11)

Because deconstruction thematizes the necessity of dissemination, the *a priori* possibility of confusion and grafting among all sorts of taxonomies, it is not surprising that deconstruction itself should not remain confined to the analysis of philosophical texts. This is the 'matter of principle' to which Derrida refers. The fact that 'deconstructive film studies' exists only proves the point. So much for the status of deconstruction in relation to film: their combining was in a sense inevitable.

The interviewers, Peter Brunette and David Wills, then go on to more specific questions. They want to hear Derrida's thoughts on the silent 'thereness' of the visual object. Peter Brunette asks:

Is there some kind of phenomenological presence that words don't
have, that has to be dealt with in the visual object? Is film perhaps an
intermediate area because it is sort of present like a visual object, yet it
has to be read through like words?   (p. 12)

Derrida's answer gives a lot a food for thought. He says there are two
ways to interpret the fact that a spatial work of art doesn't speak. On the
one hand 'there exists, on the side of such a mute work of art, a place, a
real place from the perspective of which, and in which, words find their
limit.' But on the other hand we can always receive, read or interpret such
works as potential discourse:

That is to say, these silent works are in fact already talkative, full of virtual discourses, and from that point of view the silent work becomes an
even more authoritarian discourse – it becomes the very place of a word
that is all the more powerful because it is silent, and that carries within
it, as does an aphorism, a discursive virtuality that is infinitely authoritarian, in a sense theologically authoritarian.   (p. 13)

Consequently, 'one is always between the two' interpretations, silence
and (potential) discourse. But what about film? Where does film fit in?
    Film, as Peter Brunette has suggested, makes for an intermediate case.
Derrida concurs. His answer in full runs as follows, and I have numbered
certain points for commentary:

Now, film is a very particular case: first, [1] because the effect of presence is complicated by the fact of movement, of mobility, of sequential-
ity, of temporality; second, [2] because the relation to discourse is very
complicated, without even speaking about the difference between
silent and sound film, for even in silent film the relation to the word is
very complicated. [3] Obviously, if there is a specificity to the cinematic
medium, it is foreign to the word. That is to say even the most talkative
cinema supposes a reinscription of the word within a specific cinematic
element not governed by the word. If there is something specific in cinema or in video – without speaking of the differences between video
and television – it is the form in which discourse is put into play,
inscribed or situated, without in principle governing the work. So from
that point of view we can find in film the means to rethink or refound
all the relations between the word and silent art, such as they came to
be stabilized before the appearance of cinema. Before the advent of cinema there was painting, architecture, sculpture, and within them one
could find structures that had institutionalized the relation between
discourse and nondiscourse in art. If the advent of cinema allowed for
something completely new, it was the possibility of another way of

playing with the hierarchies. [4] Now here I am not speaking of cinema in general, for I would say that there are cinematic practices that reconstitute the authority of the discourse, while others try to do things more closely resembling photography or painting – still others that play differently with the relations among discourse, discursivity, and nondiscursivity. I would hesitate to speak of any art, but in particular of cinema, from that point of view. I think that there is probably more difference among different works, different styles of cinematic work, than there is between cinema and photography. In that case it is probable that we are dealing with many different arts within the same technological medium – [5] if we define cinema on the basis of its technical apparatus – and thus perhaps there is no unity in the cinematic art. I don't know what you think, but a given cinematic method may be closer to a certain type of literature than to another cinematic method. And thus we need to ask whether or not identifying an art – presuming we can speak of cinema as though we knew what art was – proceeds from the technical medium, that is to say, whether it proceeds from an apparatus such as a camera that is able to do things that can't be done by writing or painting. Does that suffice to identify art, or in fact does the specificity of a given film depend in the end less on the technical medium and more on its affinity with a given literary work, rather than with another film? I don't know. These are, for me, questions that have no answers. But at the same time I feel strongly that one should not reduce the importance of the film apparatus. (pp. 13–14)

Let's take the points in order:

(1) We have already talked about presence: its recordability implied its non-self-identity. Thus, if I take a portrait-style photograph of my sister, her presence that I record in fact already splits off ahead. What if I were filming her and she were moving? Added to the play of *différance* in her presence that infinitely multiplies and divides her, her body moves and from one instant to the next she is already 'reproducing' herself in a certain sense. Each new instant marks a 'repetition' of her. At the same time each repetition, as an instant in its own right, is itself divided and deferred. The substantial presence of a human body flickers, alters, not fully present – rather like, in fact, an image on the silver screen.

(2) There is an obvious difference between sound film and silent film in relation to discourse: one speaks and the other doesn't. But the silent film may be full of the 'potential discourse' identified by Derrida a moment before. Not only do characters mouth words that are not all transcribed in captions but each scenic situation may be redolent with potential discourse, gestures, meaningful looks, and so on. In turn

there exists a level of interpretation on which what is not said in the film may be made explicit by a viewer, a rule applying equally, of course, to sound film. The cinema oscillates between and perhaps surpasses the poles of discourse (actual and potential discourse) and non-discourse (the word reaching its limit and approaching a mutism akin to that of sculpture or architecture).

(3) The 'specificity' of the cinematic medium remains 'foreign to the word'. Discourse does not govern the medium. If it did, the medium would change. It would become essentially discursive, word-governed, and cease to be cinematic – for the cinematic necessarily includes moving images which prevent discourse from taking over. If discourse governed to the extent of excluding the moving image, we would not be talking about cinema. Hence 'discourse is put into play, inscribed or situated, without in principle governing the work'. So cinema offers a new way of construing the 'hierarchies' within art, vis-à-vis the authority of discourse.

(4) Nonetheless some cinemas will be more traditional, more complicit with that authority than others. An example of such 'cinema' might be films with a lot of narrative voice-over, or documentaries. These may have more in common with discursive non-cinematic works than with non-discursive cinematic ones.

(5) The final point concerns the legitimacy of defining an artwork according to its technical medium: in the case of film, the camera. Derrida both doubts this legitimacy and also 'feel[s] strongly that one should not reduce the importance of the film apparatus'. The previous point itself gives grounds for doubt: if certain films share more with non-cinematic art forms than with other films, then defining cinema on the basis of the camera becomes immediately untenable. Equally, if one were to define other art forms in this way – writing, for example – things would soon get out of hand: does one define writing according to the use of a pen or a laptop computer or a dictaphone? Another problem with defining cinema in this way is that the advent of digital technology has made it possible to bypass the use of a camera by generating films out of other films or images (see note 4). On the other hand, the camera will have been there – even in the case of digital technology there will have been a camera to record the original image. That Derrida wants to insist on its importance resonates with his emphasis that purportedly ideal concepts must yet go by way of writing, of the graphic inscription. For example, the 'concept' *différance* has to be referred to its written form in order for the idea to work, such that one cannot simply separate or oppose the conceptual/ideal and the concrete/material (Derrida, 1972a).

The interview proceeds and the discussion turns to the role of the creator in an artwork. Both the body and the signature of the creator are involved. The example comes from painting – Vincent Van Gogh. Derrida talks fascinatingly about the quality of bodily presence that affects a Van Gogh canvas, but right at the end of his answer he raises a question about the applicability of his comments to film. He says that '[f]or Van Gogh we can say that he was an individual with his brush, but in the case of film, what is the equivalent, where is the body in that case?' (p. 16). There is no single creator, no single body, that creates a film, for all the talk in film studies about the 'auteur'. Highly polymorphous and fragmentary, the creative body in film fails to stabilize our experience of it.

Nevertheless the origin of a film will be marked in a certain way that Derrida chooses to discuss in terms of the signature. This does not refer to a signature conventionally understood, but rather to the conditions of an artwork's 'thereness' again, the possibility of its being there and being recognized and received. Here's what he says:

> [T]he signature is not to be confused either with the name of the author, with the patronym of the author, or with the type of work, for it is nothing other than the event of the work in itself, inasmuch as it attests in a certain way . . . to the fact that someone did that, and that's what it remains. The author is dead – we don't even know who he or she is – but it remains. Nevertheless, and here the entire politicoinstitutional problem is involved, it cannot be countersigned, that is to say, attested to as signature, unless there is an institutional space in which it can be received, legitimized, and so on. There needs to be a social 'community' that says this thing has been done – we don't even know by whom, we don't know what it means – however, we are going to put it in a museum or in some archive; we are going to consider it as a work of art. Without that political and social countersignature it would not be a work of art: there wouldn't be a signature. In my opinion, the signature doesn't exist before the countersignature, which relies on society, conventions, institutions, processes of legitimization. Thus, there is no signed work before the countersignature . . .   (p. 18)

Though Derrida's remarks point to 'art' of a more established type than film, they still apply. Though the creative 'body' of a film be diffuse, there the film exists as an 'event'. The fact of its thereness constitutes a kind of signature – *there it is*. Nobody says or writes this: it is implicit in its being done. But the 'thereness' cannot exist in a vacuum. The silent declaration of thereness calls out to be attested to, precisely because it is declarative in a certain sense. The signature-mark which says of the artwork 'there it is' requires or implies recognition by something else. Hence the need for 'countersignature', an implicit response from the political, social and institutional space around the artwork and in which it exists. The 'there it

is' of the artwork calls for a 'yes, there it is' from this space. And in so far
as the artwork requires this recognition, in so far as the recognition is
already inscribed in the artwork's declaration of its own thereness, the
recognition can be said, as paradoxical as it may seem, to precede or pre-
date the work's own signature. The institutional space occupied by the
artwork already addresses it with a 'yes, you are there' before the artwork
itself declares 'I am here'.

JURASSIC PARK

To mobilize some of the above I want to consider a particular film in more
detail, though I shan't limit myself to expanding on those arguments
already sketched out. For the sake of accessibility I have chosen a famous
film 'by' a famous director: Steven Spielberg's *Jurassic Park* (Spielberg,
1993).

If film involves a reanimation of lost presence, *Jurassic Park*, with its
dinosaurs revivified by cloning, looks strikingly like an allegory of film in
general – and thereby creates a *mise en abyme* effect into the bargain. There
is a complex 'history' here. Dinosaurs once lived and became extinct,
unbeknownst to humans. Then millions of years later humans discovered
their bones and began reconstructing the (true) history of the dinosaur.
Now we switch into fiction. In 1993, Steven Spielberg makes a fictional
account in film of a man who clones dinosaurs 'successfully'. *Jurassic Park*
tells the story of a man who brings creatures back to life, and therein lies
an allegory of film, perhaps, a film allegorizing film, thus producing a
mise en abyme, an infinite regress. The film itself, on the other hand, that is
the film's conception rather than the story it narrates, constitutes an exercise in imagination, not itself capable of bringing dinosaurs to life.
However, the quality of the special effects may lull us into forgetting this
fact and suspending our disbelief, especially as cloning no longer strikes
us as far-fetched (could film more generally be described as two-dimen-
sional cloning?). After all, the story is not just about the man, it is about
the dinosaurs, which we see. We're watching a film about reconstruction
which shows us what has been reconstructed, thus achieving in its own
terms an evidentiary authority, so to speak, the dummy of science and yet
not inferior perhaps to scientific efforts in its skill at reconstruction (what
'science' could have reconstructed the dinosaur better than Spielberg's
film?). There is a kind of hyperbolic reconstruction effect, with the fiction
crossing back over into a kind of veracity even as it retains its generic status as film/fiction. And this hyperbolic effect points to a difficulty in the
course of the history I have just told, with its orthodox movement from a
factual origin (actual living dinosaurs) to a fictional supervention (digital
cloned ones within a movie). What if it were only starting from the possi-

bility of the fictional – the cinematic, the filmic – that the factual ever came to be? So that the two were not at odds? So that the factual were a modality of the fictional, as is perhaps the case in *Jurassic Park*?

But were they ever really there? True, we know dinosaurs 'existed' and that they died out. But were they ever present? Present in the full and proper sense?

Now, cameras may have been invented quite a time after the Jurassic era but this does not mean dinosaurs were not in theory recordable even then (and thus reproducible, and so forth). Had a camera been trained on them they could and would have been recorded. And if this hypothesis be granted then the logic we used above, concerning presence, may be invoked. That is to say, the recordability of dinosaurs implies they were *never* fully present. Yes, they 'existed' in a certain sense, but in a certain sense that gives no reassurance as to their presence. If they were recordable they were non-self-identical and already divided from themselves, deferring themselves anachronistically across time. In a sense they were already cloned. For all its innovativeness *Jurassic Park* merely tells a story instantiating what was already true. Anachronism belonged to the dinosaur in its own time – just as it belongs to every 'present' thing.

But perhaps *Jurassic Park* should take credit for imagining (or 'imagineering') that 'deconstructive' possibility into existence in the form of a story. From this point of view *Jurassic Park* also bears out Derrida's suggestions regarding the 'specificity of the cinematic medium'. Recall that 'the word' does not govern the latter: a film such as *Jurassic Park* and Spielberg films more generally with their emphasis on the visual, the marvellous, the prodigious, the wondrous, seem particularly 'filmic' in this regard. Ostensibly, Spielberg films are 'talkies' (characters in them speak aloud) and the very fact of my writing this essay about *Jurassic Park* and making it say what it does not explicitly state, attests to its 'potential discourse', yet the movie privileges a mute beholding of the moving image in all its miraculousness. As in other Spielberg movies (*Saving Private Ryan, Close Encounters. . .*), there is a determined bringing of the almost-inconceivable into the realm of the emphatically visible, as if trading in some risky, unassuring reassurance. We watch the characters played by Jeff Goldblum, Laura Dern and Sam Neill, dumbfounded upon their arrival at the Park by the spectacle of a herd of grazing brontosaurus, and we in turn are struck dumb. We watch the watchers watching and their reaction guides us as we watch along with them: at both levels the voice bows before this feast for the eyes (there is an interesting role played by the background music here: as it swells, the watchers fall silent, as if the music contains a force of paralysis). Which means perhaps that we are viewing the cinematic medium express itself as such, as the vision of the moving image swallows up the tongue. *Jurassic Park* marks itself as 'cinema' in an especially intense way.

Yet let us not forget Derrida's reservations concerning the definition of cinema. *Jurassic Park* may be highly filmic for effectively disabling the governance of the word, but this quality that makes it so cinematic serves equally to set it apart from a host of other cinematic works. *Jurassic Park* arguably has more in common with Madame Tussaud's waxwork museum or Disneyland than with so many other films (think of *Secrets and Lies* or *American Graffiti* or *Belle de Jour* or *High Noon* or *Manhattan* or *The Big Sleep*, and so on and so forth). Should that not deter us from latching onto *Jurassic Park* as so definitive of cinema, or in trusting cinema to let itself be so acquiescingly defined? If *Jurassic Park* is so cinematic, does it mean *The Godfather* isn't? Should *Jurassic Park* be catalogued with works of virtual reality or computer art, rather than with films?

We can approach *Jurassic Park* also in the terms of Derrida's 'To Speculate – on "Freud"' essay – in the terms, that is, of a kind of autobiographical border crisis. Attenborough and Spielberg begin to merge – or are they clones? They function almost identically, for the dinosaur-reviving achieved by Richard Attenborough's character as park director matches that achieved by Steven Spielberg as film director . . . somewhat as Freud's grandson, Ernst, unwittingly replicates his grandfather, or vice versa. The extra-filmic and the intra-filmic projects coalesce. That causes the border between inside and outside to dislimn, giving the appearance of an autobiographical link between director and character, but a link that may go beyond mere psychology and express the machinations of an impersonal force reigning over the superstructure of the project as a whole. Another *mise en abyme* opens up, Richard Attenborough portraying not only his character but also his director (who in turn would be creating or realizing Richard Attenborough's character, and so on). The 'outside' gets sucked into the 'inside'. Where do we situate the film in this case? Where is it? How do we draw its border?

The border also opens out along the notion of 'capital'. The Attenborough–Spielberg twin machine doesn't recreate dinosaurs merely for the sake of imagination: it also wants to make money. In this respect, too, the film spills over its borders. What we denote today by 'film' does not stop at the artefact on the screen. To begin with, there has for a long time been a cult of the star, supporting the movie from 'outside'. In parallel the movie supports the star, so that the two exist in a mutually parasitic relationship. Then there is the hype that surrounds a given movie. Does the experience of a movie begin with the trailer? Factors such as these have for just as long been fraying the film's border. But in the era of *Jurassic Park* (so to speak) a new, or at least augmented, kind of dissemination has emerged, in the form of merchandising. A 'film' today, particularly at the Spielberg end of the market, operates more like a large business venture than an exclusively aesthetic enterprise (though film, as allegedly the most 'popular' art form, has traditionally occupied a middle ground between the two), concerned to maximize its profits by using the power of its 'brand'. The *Jurassic Park* emblem is branded on lunchboxes, underwear, bedding, key chains, toys, backpacks, stationery, and so forth, not to mention the profit opportunity represented by a sequel. What does the name '*Jurassic Park*' refer to if not this phantasmagoria of products, among which the film may be only one? At least, if the film does hold fast as the indispensable object of reference, it *also* functions as the brand origin from which that merchandise derives. '*Jurassic Park*' indicates capital, in other words, a money-potential which will always seek to expand its limits, thus instantiating the near-irresistible dissemination of capital beyond its borders.

Jurassic Park presents perhaps a hyperbolic case of capital-proliferation, because the latter provides one of the story's principal themes. Some may see this as hypocritical, in that the movie chastises Richard Attenborough's character for profiteering ('We're going to make a fortune with this place!'), while doing exactly the same thing at a safe distance: it uses Attenborough as a 'screen' in every sense. The movie also 'discusses' merchandising. Does this mean it contains its own critique? That it deserves to be considered liberal, ironic, politically aware? Jeff Goldblum's character, for example, voices doubts about the Park project in terms of both its evolutionary viability and its monetary goals; and his scepticism is vindicated. But it makes no difference. So maybe the movie is deeply conservative – the critique gets absorbed. Is that a sign of the times? Is capital now capable of, even comfortable with, producing self-critique, because it knows itself impregnable to it? Is it pre-empting critique from other quarters? Does its acquisitiveness stretch to consuming even its own negative?

The question of the border, through merchandising, relates also to the notion of the counter-signature. *Jurassic Park* opens with a shot of the helmet worn by one of the workers at the park. On it appears the emblem of *Jurassic Park* just as it appears on all those lunchboxes – red and black with a fearsome raptor baring its fangs. The emblem, that is to say, the ready image of the *Jurassic Park* 'brand', crosses over into the social space around the movie. One could argue it illustrates the tension of signature and counter-signature (with the qualification that Derrida's remarks on this subject clearly derive from a register that does not translate unproblematically into such illustrations). The helmet emblem 'in' the movie pertains to the park in the story, but it also labels the movie, referring to the movie as the movie that it is, confirming the fact of its being there. In this respect the emblem could be seen to work as 'signature'. All the while the emblem gestures to the movie's consumption in the marketplace, in the social 'institution' that provides its context. It labels the movie from within while offering to detach itself simultaneously and give itself to the audience as the means with which the audience will recognize and acknowledge the film. This demand for recognition upon which the movie's own relation to itself is based, could perhaps constitute its 'counter-signature', the means by which it is recognized, as it were, even before it is, even before it is 'there'. On the other hand, because the *Jurassic Park* emblem is so emphatically directed towards the manipulation of its audience, of capital, it could be doing precisely the opposite, namely attempting to efface the possibility of recognition, acknowledgement or apostrophe, subordinating this as it were ethical relation to a purely commercial one.

SEQUEL

It would be possible to develop these ideas at much greater length – they are certainly fecund enough. With regard to anachronism, for example, one could elaborate the issues raised by the fact that one of the dinosaurs in *Jurassic Park* catches a cold from a human (we see it sneeze). What about the anachronism of disease? If anachronism affects all 'present' things, does this mean an *a priori* infection menaces us, that we are sick from the future, as it were? It would also be possible to draw on other areas of Derrida's vast output to finesse our notion of film and films. With respect to *Jurassic Park* one might adapt Derrida's analysis of the 'Logique du Vivante' or 'Logic of the Living Feminine' for a consideration of the feminine in Spielberg's movie (only female dinosaurs are bred at the Park; Jeff Goldblum's character quips, 'Dinosaurs eat men. Woman inherits the earth'). Derrida talks precisely about a law of female survival (Derrida, 1984).

To the sceptic it might seem *Jurassic Park* accommodates a deconstructive approach with suspicious facility. No doubt 'deconstruction' would have a harder time dealing with other movies, but then again since deconstruction also insists on its own lack of mastery over various works, perhaps the failure would be an instructive one. This does not mean that deconstruction or Derrida do not promote the highest standards of scholarship and rigour, and that insights are not gained, but that its rigour and courage often lead to more questions than answers, leaving the deconstructive author with a well-thought-through but still baffling object of study. It is only for lack of space that I have not considered more films in detail, particularly more 'resistant' ones. After all it is precisely a work's resistance to philosophical control of it that stirs deconstruction into motion. I had planned, for instance, a reading of Hitchcock's *Vertigo* both as a foil to *Jurassic Park* and as a peculiarly enigmatic or resistant work in itself. I would have spoken about the vertigo of mimesis in Hitchcock's movie, where James Stewart's character, Scottie, having retired from police work on account of his condition (he suffers from vertigo) is hired as a detective by a friend to watch over the friend's wife – Stewart's character is already reprising a role, in other words, and as such participates in a giddy profusion of imitations and reprises. He pursues Kim Novak, who plays a girl called Judy who has been hired (by the same friend) to play the friend's wife, Madeleine. While in this double-role, Novak/Judy/Madeleine further imitates a woman (Carlotta Valdes) – and not even from life, but rather from a painting of Carlotta, creating another level of imitation. Meanwhile, Scottie's female friend, Midge, played by Barbara Bel Geddes, jealous of Scottie's growing interest in Novak/Judy/Madeleine/Carlotta/Carlotta's portrait, decides to paint a painting of herself, thus replicating herself – a painting, moreover, that is a copy of the painting of Carlotta, with the difference that Midge paints her own face in the painting rather than Carlotta's. . . . The 'original' in all this, the real wife of the friend, the real Madeleine, is killed off and never seen as such. Mimesis without origin, this vertiginous schema corresponds to another which Derrida has analysed in reference to Mallarmé (Derrida, 1972b), where the derivative relation of a simulacrum to an original comes undone.

I offer no conclusion as such, but perhaps the notions of presence, anachronism, the border, the specificity of the cinematic medium, the signature and counter-signature, and so on, can help in giving film studies the breadth and depth it will need in order to address the increasingly complex world of the film. Without a rigorous understanding of concepts of time and of recording, of the subjugation of the discursive, of revival and survival, concepts which are fundamental to film, how can we begin to get the measure of it? And where can we go for such an understanding if not to the texts of Jacques Derrida? No matter where else we may turn, are these not indispensable?

NOTES

1. For instance, I have heard informally that Antonioni's *Blow Up* was discussed in Derrida's Paris seminar a few years ago.
2. See respectively 'Lecture de "Droit de Regards"' (*Feu la Cendre*), 'Ce qui Reste à Force de Musique' (*La Vérité en Peinture*) and 'Survivre' in the list of written works cited.
3. Readers may wish to consult also my 'Short Cuts to Derrida', an essay on Robert Altman's film *Short Cuts* in relation to Derrida's notion of 'degenerescence' (Smith, 1996).
4. The advent of digital technology complicates this scenario in that it allows for creating a moving image out of other moving images, thus breaking the link to presence. But the link is not necessarily broken, merely attenuated.

WRITTEN WORKS CITED

Beicken, Peter and Kolken, Robert (1993), *The Films of Wim Wenders: Cinema as Vision and Desire* (Cambridge: Cambridge University Press).

Brunette, Peter and Wills, David (1994), *Deconstruction and the Visual Arts: Art, Media, Architecture* (Cambridge: Cambridge University Press).

—— (1989), *Screen/Play: Derrida and Film Theory* (Princeton, NJ: Princeton University Press).

Derrida, Jacques (1972a), 'La Différance', in *Marges – de la Philosophie* (Paris: Minuit).

—— (1972b), 'La Double Séance', in *La Dissémination* (Paris: Seuil).

—— (1972c) 'Signature Événement Contexte', in *Marges – de la Philosophie* (Paris: Minuit).

—— (1978), *La Vérité en Peinture* (Paris: Flammarion).

—— (1980), 'Spéculer – sur "Freud"', in *La Carte Postale: de Socrate à Freud et au-delà* (Paris: Aubier-Flammarion).

—— (1984), 'Logique du Vivante', in *Otobiographies: L'enseignement de Nietzsche et la Politique du Nom Propre* (Paris: Galilée).

—— (1985),'Lecture de "Droit de Regards"', in M.-F. Plissart, *Droit de Regards* (Paris: Minuit).

—— (1986), 'Survivre', in *Parages* (Paris: Galilée).

—— (1987a), 'Ce Qui Reste à Force De Musique', in *Psyché: Inventions de L'Autre* (Paris: Galilée).

—— (1987b), *Feu la Cendre* (Paris: Des Femmes).

Derrida, Jacques and Stiegler, Bemard (1996), *Échographies – de la Télévision* (Paris: Galilée).

Kracauer, Siegfried (1960), *Theory of Film: The Redemption of Physical Reality* (New York: Oxford University Press).

Smith, Robert (1996), 'Short Cuts to Derrida', *Oxford Literary Review*, vol. 18 (1996), pp. 135–44.

Wenders, Wim (1991), 'Like Flying Blind without Instruments: On the Turning Point in *Paris, Texas*', in Wim Wenders, *The Logic of Images*, trans. Michael Hofmann (London: Faber and Faber).

FILM WORKS CITED

Allen, Woody, *Deconstructing Harry* (1997).

—— *Manhattan* (1979).

Antonioni, Michelangelo, *Blow Up* (1969).

Buñuel, Luis, *Belle de Jour* (1967).

Coppola, Francis Ford, *The Godfather* (1972).

Hawks, Howard, *The Big Sleep* (1946).

Hitchcock, Alfred, *Vertigo* (1958).

Leigh, Mike, *Secrets and Lies* (1996).

Lucas, George, *American Graffiti* (1972).

McMullen, Ken, *Ghost Dance* (1983).

Spielberg, Steven, *Jurassic Park* (1993).

Wenders, Wim, *Paris, Texas* (1983).

Zinnemann, Fred, *High Noon* (1952).

8

Deconstruction and Hermeneutics

Rodolphe Gasché

Of the contentious debates that deconstruction has touched off, the one concerning its relation to hermeneutics has drawn special attention. As Pöggeler has noted, one can already create a small library from the pertinent writings about this subject (Pöggeler, 1994, p. 481). In any event, what distinguishes the debate is a seemingly uncompromising confrontation with no end in sight. Derrida's critique of hermeneutics' postulation of a master sense, a sole and true meaning of texts, has triggered the verdict by hermeneutic philosophers, including Gadamer, that deconstruction celebrates the end of the philosophies of meaning in a Nietzschean feast of, and free play on, words. However, it is worth remarking that Derrida only rarely, and merely in passing, takes on the various positions in the institutionalized discipline of hermeneutics. Certainly, at times, Derrida's statements about hermeneutics read like a critique of Ricoeur's hermeneutic philosophy. But, except for Derrida's response to Gadamer's intervention during their meeting in Paris in 1981, references to Gadamer's philosophical hermeneutics are absent from his examination of hermeneutics. Still, what about the occasional presence of the name of Schleiermacher in Derrida's writings? Does it not at least suggest a concerted and focused debate with the historical forms of the art of interpretation, and the hermeneutic tradition? Given the slim evidence to sustain such a view, it must be assumed that the target of Derrida's critique is not primarily the discipline of hermeneutics and its various proponents. Its proper domain must lie elsewhere. Yet, the fact that in almost all instances where Derrida explicitly brings up the question of hermeneutics, his overall concern is with the possibility of assuming a fixed, self-identical and self-present meaning-content of discourses, or texts, capable of being recovered in full, provides a clear hint as to where this domain might be.

As Jean Greisch has persuasively argued, the original context of his critique of hermeneutics, although no direct reference to 'hermeneutics' is found there, is Derrida's discussion in *Speech and Phenomena* of the distinction, in Husserl's *Logical Investigations*, between indication and expression, and of Husserl's subsequent attempt to secure in the soul's soliloquy an expression free of all signs – a self-present and self-evident meaning which is capable of being fully intuited and which is to serve as the foundation of phenomenology. Indeed, after having shown in *Speech and Phenomena* that for Husserl presence enjoys a special privilege, and is an intrinsic characteristic of the phenomenological conception of meaning, Derrida goes on to demonstrate that the perception constitutive of live consciousness is never pure, but presupposes indication (hence re-presentation), and concludes that, therefore, not only the Husserlian distinction between indication and expression becomes questionable, but that self-consciousness, presence and, finally, meaning must cohabit with a certain nonpresence, nonidentity and lack of intention. This critique of the phenomenological weighing of presence, and of the concomitant concept of meaning, is further played out in Derrida's discussions of Heidegger's hermeneutical phenomenology and its guiding question concerning the meaning of Being. However, if the prime thrust of Derrida's debate with hermeneutics concerns phenomenology's founding distinctions and asserted privileges, deconstruction and hermeneutics have also a point of contact, Greisch concludes. Greisch highlights this issue in order to argue not only that the idea of deconstruction is phenomenological through and through, but also that it stands in no way in a relation of opposition to hermeneutics. To bear out this point, he traces deconstruction back to Heidegger's conception of destruction, and recalls that, from the conception of a hermeneutics of facticity to the problematic of *Being and Time*, the successful completion of the task of hermeneutic requires destruction (Greisch, 1996, pp. 353–86). But if it is true that in Heideggerian phenomenology, hermeneutics and destruction are intimately interconnected, how does Derrida's querying phenomenology affect that intimate relation?

At this point we need to remind ourselves of the fact that the two main trends in contemporary hermeneutics, Ricoeur's hermeneutic philosophy and Gadamer's philosophical hermeneutics, are strongly anchored in phenomenological thought. As Ricoeur notes, 'phenomenology remains the unsurpassable presupposition of hermeneutics', adding that since interpretation is required to fulfil phenomenology's philosophical task, phenomenology cannot correspondingly 'constitute itself without a hermeneutical presupposition' (Ricoeur, 1981, p. 101). But notwithstanding this mutual belonging, hermeneutics also needs to criticize phenomenology if it is to further its philosophical agenda, Ricoeur contends. However, it is a criticism that does not concern, as with Derrida, the founding assumptions and distinctions of phenomenology. Rather, it is limited to a critique of what Ricoeur calls Husserl's idealism and Heidegger's obsession with foundations (Ricoeur, 1981, pp. 102, 59). Similarly Gadamer has stressed time and again that his philosophical hermeneutics is tributary to Heidegger's thought. But such lineage does not exclude criticism of what he characterizes as Heidegger's 'adventurous journey into error', for instance, his belief in being able to reach a beyond of metaphysics, by way of asking the question concerning Being 'outside' metaphysics' determination of Being (Gadamer, 1989, p. 104). What Gadamer retains of Heidegger's phenomenological philosophy is the early conception of a hermeneutics of facticity. Here too, the critique of phenomenology is limited, and takes place in view of a furthering of hermeneutics. Yet, if phenomenology and hermeneutics mutually belong to each other, one can easily see that a deconstruction of the founding concepts of phenomenology poses a major threat to the philosophical foundations of hermeneutics.

The most vehement objections to deconstruction from a hermeneutical viewpoint originate in the work of Gadamer and some of his followers. It is certainly significant that although these objections betray gross misinterpretations of Derrida's thought – as when, for example, Gadamer holds that Derrida's conception of presence is modelled after Heidegger's notion of *Vorhandenheit* (Gadamer, 1993, p. 15), or when Grondin characterizes Derrida's discussion of indication in the *Logical Investigation* as based on a 'semiotic physicalism (*Physikalismus des Zeichenhaften*)' (Grondin, 1994, p. 138) – they are mostly misrepresentations of those instances where structural limits concerning the fundamental distinctions of phenomenology and its hermeneutical presuppositions are worked out. Even though these objections are intent on severing all ties of hermeneutics to deconstruction, Greisch's argument of a point of contact between both signals an imbrication that foregrounds all the disputes. However, the question remains of what happens to this mutual belonging, to the intimate link between hermeneutics and deconstruction, once the deconstruction of phenomenology not only touches upon the latter's founding assumptions, but also implies a radical questioning of the hermeneutical presuppositions on which phenomenology rests.

As I said before, Derrida has only tangentially taken on (some of) the existing forms of hermeneutics. But if the originary realm in which deconstruction impacts upon the possibility of hermeneutics is, indeed, the debate with phenomenology, one must suspect these insights to weigh with the entirety of all hermeneutics whatever their shade. However, as we shall see, if deconstruction affects hermeneutics, it is not because deconstruction would say the opposite of hermeneutics. Contrary to the hermeneuticians' fears, hermeneutics is not simply broken up by deconstruction. If it is not the reverse of hermeneutics, deconstruction does not simply disqualify the latter to the point of making it illusory, or merely irrelevant. But neither does it, therefore, continue in some subtle way to further the task of hermeneutics, as Greisch's thesis of a point of contact seems to suggest. To sketch out an answer, however schematic, as to how to conceive the relation in question, I turn to Derrida's discussion of the project of hermeneutics in *Spurs: Nietzsche's Styles* (1979). This essay on Nietzsche, apart, perhaps, from 'Shibboleth: For Paul Celan', is the place where Derrida's most elaborate and differentiated confrontation with hermeneutics is to be found.

First, a note of caution may be warranted. *Spurs* is not to be tagged 'Nietzschean'. In no way does Derrida assume here any determinable Nietzschean position. The essay's frame is made up by a caustic critique of contemporary French Nietzsche interpretations that lay claim to so-called Nietzschean positions, the truth of Nietzsche, or of Nietzsche's text. Targeted at those interpretations, especially at Deleuze's effort to appropriate Nietzsche for a reversal of Platonism; and aimed as well at those readers of Heidegger's *Nietzsche* who retained of Heidegger's work only the thesis that Nietzsche's gesture is restricted to overthrowing Platonism, the multilayered and heavily encoded text of *Spurs* seeks to show that there is no such thing as a unique and fixable meaning of 'Nietzsche' (nor, for that matter, of 'Heidegger', or 'Derrida' himself). By reclaiming Nietzsche against Heidegger's alleged reduction of Nietzsche to being the last metaphysician, the Nietzsche interpreters Derrida criticizes proceed on the basis of a postulation of a fixed meaning of Nietzsche writings, and pretend that they know what his *oeuvre* means. They have decided what the meaning of his work is, having distinguished it from, and in opposition to, Heidegger's so-called reduction. Their approach is hermeneutic through and through.

Spurs broaches hermeneutics from a variety of angles – as a component of traditional philology (including psychoanalysis) and the rules it prescribes for the interpretation of texts; as tributary to metaphysics, and informing the philosophical question *ti esti*; in relation to fundamental ontology, and hence to the question of Being and so forth. But in every case the issue of a 'master sense, a sole sense, . . . free of all grafts' (Derrida, 1979, p. 98) dominates the discussion. The fact that Derrida's most exhaustive discussion of hermeneutics takes place with regard to Nietzsche, and the hermeneutic underpinnings of the interpretations his work has undergone, does not by itself change Derrida's 'take' on hermeneutics. At its centre is still the same question addressed to phenomenology.

Spurs opens up the question of hermeneutics through an investigation of what at first sight has all the appearances of a subject or a theme – 'woman' in Nietzsche. Considering Nietzsche's disparate statements on woman, ranging from the vehemently gynophobic to the progressively feminist, is it possible to derive from them woman's proper nature, her essence, or truth? Given that, traditionally, and to some degree in Nietzsche as well, she has been an allegorical figure of truth, the impossibility of showing her to be a determinable entity in his text, would also affect Nietzsche's truth concept, and ultimately the truth of his texts. Although, as Derrida argues, the subject 'woman', in Nietzsche, is indissoluble from other subjects such as style, art and truth, I limit myself, in discussing her purported identity, to evoking her relation to truth. On the one hand, Nietzsche evokes the representation of truth as woman, or the veiling movement of female modesty, which he attributes to the credulous dogmatic philosopher who also courts woman (and truth) just as if she were an easy woman to be won, or possessed. On the other hand, Nietzsche holds the credulous philosopher up for ridicule for having understood nothing of woman, or truth. As Derrida writes: 'For, indeed, if woman *is* truth, *she* knows that there is no truth, that truth has no place and that one has no truth. She is woman in so far as she does not believe in truth, hence in what she is, in the truth she is believed to be, and what, therefore, she is not' (p. 52). These statements underscore that 'woman (truth) does not allow herself be taken' (p. 54). But although both types of propositions, because opposite, could possibly suggest a unified meaning of 'woman', there is a third class of propositions which, according to Derrida, marks a turn in Nietzsche's conception of woman and truth, and thoroughly undercuts this possibility. This third class concerns that which of the woman, and of truth (itself), cannot be lifted, and won, to pin woman down. These, then, are the statements in which woman herself is shown to separate, swerve away, to distanciate herself from herself (*écarte et s'écarte d'elle-même*), and thus to lift herself from herself (*s'enlève d'elle-même*), thus thwarting in advance all attempts to take possession of her. What Nietzsche calls 'woman' in this context is not only an entity that has no essence, but also, more importantly, what in itself is 'nothing but' a movement of de-essentializing and de-identifying. Derrida calls it 'the feminine' or, more precisely, in order to demarcate it from such essentializing fetishes as a woman's femininity or female sexuality, 'the feminine operation' (p. 56).

The groundwork for this conclusion is laid in Derrida's discussion of the section from *The Gay Science* entitled 'Women and Their Action at a Distance' (Book 2, section 60), Nietzsche's analysis of distance as an 'attribute' of the woman. If this distance is required both to protect against the beguiling force of women, and to become seduced by them in the first place, is it not, Derrida asks, because this distance that characterizes women and their *actio in distans*, hence woman herself, lacks 'the determinable identity of a figure which announces itself in distance, in distance from something else from which one could retreat or to which one could come close?' (p. 48). Rather than being an entity distinguishable from, or with respect to, another entity (man, for instance) that would be its opposite, woman is perhaps 'the distancing of the distance' that is required for an identifying determination via opposites, in short, 'the engulfing (*abîme*) of distance, the distancing of distance, the sectioning of spacing, distance itself, if one could still say so (which is impossible), distance *itself*' (p. 48). To further conceptualize this distancing of distance, and hence 'woman' in Nietzsche's aphorism, Derrida has recourse to Heidegger's concept of *Entfernung*. This is the first instance, in *Spurs*, in which a Heideggerian concept (rather than being reductive of Nietzsche's insights) is shown to name the 'same' as in Nietzsche. As Derrida argues, the distancing of distance, which seems to underlie woman's *actio in distans*, operates in the same way as the distantiation at work in *Entfernung*, as a 'parting and withdrawing opening . . . which gives rise to truth, and [in which] woman separates herself from herself'. It follows then that 'if there is no essence of woman it is because she separates and separates from herself. Endlessly, and without foundation, she engulfs and distorts at bottom all essentiality, all identity, all propriety' (p. 50). And Derrida concludes: 'There is no truth of woman [not because she is lie, or error, but] because this abyssal swerving of truth, this non-truth is "truth". Woman is one of the names of this non-truth of truth' (p. 50). In Nietzsche, of course.

Woman, or rather the 'feminine operation', is this operation through which woman distanciates herself from herself, and puts herself – her essence and identity – into brackets, as it were. Not only is the 'feminine operation' made to foreground the traditional, and opposite, views on woman, according to which she is either truth or lie, but 'it writes (itself). The style belongs to it' (p. 56), Derrida remarks. Since the pointed object of the style has apotropaic *and* aggressive power – it can *both* serve to protect oneself against some threat, and to viciously attack – the question of style, as broached in *Spurs*, apart from its own polyvalence (one that makes it difficult to know *what* style itself *is*), concerns a medium that is anterior to all difference in so far as the latter has the form of opposition. The reference later in *Spurs* to the hymen's graphic and the pharmakon further stresses this point. (We will come back to these again, in due course.) Now, by arguing that Nietzsche's style and Nietzsche's woman are interlinked, and offering the aphorism from the *Gay Science* as evidence, the feminine operation to which the style is said to belong is thus the operation constitutive of that medium in advance of all opposition (including the one between the determined sexes). Also called 'writing' – in a sense that precedes its determination by its opposite, speech – the feminine stylate operation by which Nietzsche's woman (and truth) separates and separates herself, is the operation by way of which woman or 'truth becomes *inscribed*, and, as a rigorously necessary consequence, inscribed in general'. Evoking Nietzsche's style which 'like the prow, for example, of a ship rigged with sails [the vessel in the aphorism in question], its *rostrum*, the projection of the ship, surges ahead to meet the sea's attack by cleaving its hostile surface', Derrida concludes that the style can also use its spur 'as a means of protection against the terrifying, blinding and mortal threat (of what) *presents* itself, or obstinately thrusts itself into view: namely, presence, consequently, the content, the thing itself, meaning, truth' (p. 38). It follows that style, and by extension the feminine operation, by separating and separating from itself, guards against everything that hermeneutics valorizes. But as should already be clear, the stylate operation does not simply jettison what it pierces with a pointed object, since such piercing amounts to an inscription, an inscription in general, one in which content, meaning, truth are shown to be embedded in a network of referrals that strip them of their presence, and that inhibit them from throwing *themselves* into view. To conclude this analysis of the first move of *Spurs* which concerns the hermeneutic conception of subject, or theme, I underscore the outcome of this analysis of Nietzsche's woman: not only does Nietzsche's woman appear to be inextricably linked to truth and style, hence not susceptible of isolated thematization, or even identification, of what she most properly is, she also thwarts identification in so far as she escapes determination via an opposite. Not endowed with a meaning and identity of her own, Nietzsche's woman is not to be pinned down. As the medium in which identifying decisions can be made, she is the undecidable space of inscription anterior to all determined property.

In a second move, *Spurs* instigates a discussion of another of the exigencies of hermeneutics, namely the demand for systematicity, for a unity of meaning of a theme, work or *oeuvre*. Derrida opens up this question by asking what kind of 'congruence' or logic exists between the very diverse statements on woman and truth that range from the apparently feminist to Nietzsche's inveterately anti-feminist ones. 'As truth woman is skepticism and veiling dissimulation. This is what one ought to be able to think', Derrida writes (p. 56). Such thinking requires an exhaustive codification of the different types of statements before moving upstream to a principle prior to them, in view of the formal rule or law that governs them. I underline that, although it will be followed by a reflection on 'the essential limit of such a codification' (p. 94), the formalization in question, and the assembling of the diverse statements on woman and truth into a unity of congruence, is 'rigorously necessary' (p. 56) from the viewpoint of what is to be thought.

Mapping first Nietzsche's statements on woman, Derrida distinguishes three types of fundamental proposition which amount to three different positions of value, each deriving from three different situations. According to the first type, woman finds herself debased in the name of truth and dogmatic metaphysics as a figure or potentate of falsehood. In the second type, woman is condemned in the name of art as a figure, or potentate, of truth, in short, as a philosophical being, either because she identifies with truth, or because, at a distance from truth, she plays with it, without believing in it, to her own advantage. Distinct from these two propositions that negate woman, and that relate to one another in a mode of inversion, there are, finally, those propositions in which woman is recognized and affirmed as an affirmative, dissimulating and artistic power. It is an affirmation that does not originate in man; woman here 'affirms herself, within herself and in man' (p. 96). Now,

> for these three types of statements to form an exhaustive code, and to make possible the reconstruction of their systematic unity, it would be necessary that the parodying heterogeneity of the style, the styles, be masterable and reducible to the content of a thesis. In addition, it would be necessary . . . that each one of the values that is implicated in the three schemata be *decidable* within an oppositional couple as if each term had its counter term.   (p. 98)

Only under these conditions is it possible to meet the hermeneutic demand for a meaningful unity of the entirety of Nietzsche's propositions about woman and truth. But, however pertinent the hermeneutic and systematic questions are, an irreducible limit prevents mastering Nietzsche's heterogeneous statements by subsuming them under one single thesis or theme. According to Derrida, Nietzsche himself, 'did not clearly, or in one single glance, understand what he was up to (*n'y voyait pas trés clair ni d'un seul clin d'oeil*) . . . Nietzsche is a little lost here' (p. 100). Even though the different styles in Nietzsche's texts which yield the three positions on woman, call upon understanding, and are formalizable up to a point – Derrida warns against 'passively taking sides with heterogeneity and parody' as reductive of heterogeneity and parody (p. 98) – the 'presence' and effects of the medium of oppositional bifurcation in Nietzsche's text inhibit all totalizing comprehension in an authorial intention, or in that of an interpreter. 'The hymen's graphic, and that of the pharmakon . . . which is everywhere at work, particularly in Nietzsche's text, limits without appeal [this possibility, and with it] the pertinence of these hermeneutic and systematic questions. This graphic always hides a margin from the control of meaning, or the code' (p. 98). As seen, style itself, in Nietzsche, names the undecidable graphic that harbours the possibility (and limits) of decision.

Given the ultimate impossibility of accounting hermeneutically for the heterogeneity of Nietzsche's text, and also that the surrender of all attempts at mastery, as found in some of the contemporary, French interpretations, amounts to 'nothing more than a glamorous declaration of the antithesis' (p. 94), which remains prisoner of the logic of opposition, Derrida will sketch out another operation, one that does not stand in opposition to hermeneutics. This is similar to Nietzsche, of whom Heidegger states that he '"seeks something else"' than merely inverting Platonism (p. 78), and to Heidegger too, who, in addition to his onto-hermeneutic reading of Nietzsche, practises wherever the problematic of propriation is brought to bear on the question of Being another reading, other to the point that it does not actually undo the first (p. 114). Derrida performs a reading that, rather than countering hermeneutics, recasts the way hermeneutics relates to its limits.

Following the attempted codification of Nietzsche's heterogeneous statements about woman and truth, Derrida seeks to get a handle on the law to which they submit. I recall that the credulous philosopher believes a woman (and truth) can be won like a wench. But woman is also portrayed as merely playing with truth, as self-adornment or as a veil, to secure her mastery over man. Finally, there are those statements in which woman affirms herself ('free' of the viewpoint of man), not as a dissimulating power, but as playing 'at dissimulation, ornamentation, deceit, artifice, and at an artist's philosophy' (p. 66). A first hint at the kind of logic that governs these three positions emerges from Nietzsche's discussion of woman's '"delight in dissimulation"', histrionics and play-acting. In *The Gay Science*, Nietzsche observes '"that they 'give themselves for', even when they – give themselves"' (p. 68). 'This play on "to give", "to give oneself" and "to give oneself for"' (p. 70) is, as Derrida will show, operative in the three types of statements. It constitutes what Derrida calls their 'formalized law' (p. 108). According to this law,

> sometimes woman is woman in giving, *in giving herself*, while man takes, possesses, takes possession. At other times, woman by giving herself *gives herself for*, simulates, and thus assures possessive mastery for herself. The *for* in the 'to-give-oneself-for', whatever its value, whether it deceives by giving only an appearance of, or whether it introduces some destination, finality, or wily calculation, some return, redemption or gain, into the loss of property (*le propre*), this *for* retains the gift of a reserve. Henceforth all the signs of sexual opposition are changed.   (pp. 108–10)

If woman gives-herself-for when giving herself to man, whose sexual distinction is to take possession, sexual distinction rooted in the opposition of the give/take becomes perturbed. First, because in giving herself for, it is woman who occupies the place of man. But the reserve which restrains the gift, and by way of which Derrida deepens his analysis of the 'feminine operation', perturbs the process by which each sex becomes what he or she properly is, on a still more fundamental level, one not limited to a mere reversal, because the 'for' in giving-herself-for remains undecidable. The marker 'for' can yield structurally several possible values. It follows from this that the self-affirmation of woman by way of the gift of the reserve that restrains her giving herself coincides with the name for the medium in which 'man and woman change place, and infinitely exchange their masks' (p. 110). Because of her reserve, woman appears as the medium in which the opposite distinctions of the sexes are carved out, and which therefore have no existence in themselves. Derrida likens them to what Kant called transcendental illusions when he writes: 'If the opposition of *give* and *take*, of *possess* and *possessed*, is nothing more than a transcendental take-in (*leurre*) which is produced by the graphic of the hymen, the process of propriation escapes all dialectic as well as all ontological decidability' (p. 110).

What is called 'the process of propriation' is the 'principle' on the basis of which Derrida establishes the impossibility of a deciding by dint of a thesis or theme about the entirety of Nietzsche's statements about woman and truth. Yet, as the principle, or the formalized law, for the codified statements in question, 'the process of propriation' also assembles them into some sort of unity, and thus accounts for their heterogeneity. Distinct from a thesis or theme, 'the process of propriation' that characterizes the 'feminine operation' does not assemble the diversity of positions of truth into one all-embracing meaningful position. Rather, it accounts for the plurality of the positions by working out their syntax, so to speak. Further, unlike a thesis or theme, which is of the order of the fundamental, 'the process of propriation', by which nothing ever comes properly and forever into its own, but in which that which something properly is passes indefinitely into its other, is 'a non-fundamental structure, at once superficial and bottomless' (p. 116). At this point it needs to be remarked that 'the process of propriation' which, according to Derrida, describes the feminine operation in Nietzsche, and its manipulation of the style, corresponds to the Heideggerian notion of *Ereignis*. As Heidegger has shown, the coming into its own of something, and hence its becoming what it properly is, entails a disappropriation with the effect that it is what it is only in terms of something else. The reserve Derrida distinguishes in the 'for' of the giving-oneself-for, describes an analogous process. In analyses too lengthy to sum up here, Derrida, in *Spurs*, valorizes this Heideggerian notion of *Ereignis* in order to argue that the latter's interpretation of Nietzsche not only is much less simple than what many of his French commentators have retained from it, namely that Nietzsche merely inverts metaphysics, and hence remains strapped within it, but that it is a most exacting reading, aware of the fact that Nietzsche sought to exceed metaphysics and Platonism, not merely through a reversal of a given hierarchy, but by transforming the hierarchical structure itself. Still, according to Derrida, Heidegger follows up on this operation of Nietzsche in terms, and on the basis of presuppositions, that Nietzsche's operation should have unsettled; he addresses what Nietzsche does by way of a form of question that belongs to hermeneutics – for instance, when asking whether Nietzsche succeeds in achieving the projected overthrow of Platonism, a project defined as what Nietzsche most intimately intended. Yet even though, for the most part, Heidegger's reading remains within an onto-hermeneutical horizon, it also opens up to another kind of reading, one that it cannot encompass or enclose within itself, Derrida contends. This happens each time Heidegger refers the question of Being to the question of propriation. Yet since the question 'what is (the meaning of) Being' is the onto-hermeneutical question *par excellence*, and as such posits in advance a property, identity, meaning, and truth of Being, the 'more powerful' (p. 110) question of propriation – more powerful because it refers to the undecidable process, or operation, by which things only come into their own with the caveat of a reserve, before collapsing into decidable possibilities – is bound to unsettle 'the onto-hermeneutic form of interrogation' in general (p. 112). More precisely, with this question concerning the undecidable process of propriation, the onto-hermeneutic interrogation encounters its limits. Indeed, given that the onto-hermeneutic question only lets itself be posed after the decision has been made that there is property (*propre*), in short after the undecidable process of propriation in which properties pass into one another, and change places, has been arrested and collapsed simultaneously into definite, opposite and hierarchized values, the onto-phenomenological or semantico-hermeneutic mode of questioning cannot answer the question concerning property itself. 'The question of meaning, or of the truth of Being, is not *capable* of posing the question of property, of the undecidable exchange of more into less, of the give-take, give-keep, give-harm, the *coup de don*. It is incapable of this because inscribed in it' (pp. 110–12). Derrida holds that the whole problematic of propriation which reveals a limit of Being itself, not only impacts on Heidegger's onto-hermeneutic phenomenology, it also affects his interpretation of Nietzsche. Even though it explicitly avoids the question of woman in Nietzsche, and hence the feminine operation, the problem of the *Ereignis* brings to bear a question on Heidegger's mainly onto-hermeneutic interpretation whose effects are not unlike those that woman and style have for truth in Nietzsche's text. When Derrida asks 'whether truth's abyss as non-truth, propriation as appropriation/a-propriation . . . is what Nietzsche is calling the form of the style and the no-place of woman', he clearly suggests that Heidegger has not missed what is at stake in Nietzsche (pp. 118–20). If this is so, it is because Heidegger in his reading of Nietzsche has, with the more powerful question of propriation, exceeded not only the metaphysical horizon of the question of the meaning of Being, but of all hermeneutics as well.

This, then, is also the point at which the question needs to be addressed of how an other, no longer hermeneutic, reading, relates to one that remains within the limits of onto-hermeneutic questions. As Derrida emphasizes with respect to Heidegger's reading of Nietzsche, another reading opens up within Heidegger's text, in addition to the one that proceeds on hermeneutical grounds, and 'opens up, without undoing it [the hermeneutic reading], by a certain dehiscence' – gaping open, or opening by divergence of parts, as in a natural process. Yet, it does not 'in return have a critical or destructive effect' on the first reading (p. 114). It does not stand in opposition to the hermeneutic inquiry, any more than does the reading that Derrida attempted with respect to Heidegger's reading of Nietzsche. As becomes obvious at this juncture, the reason for this is that with the question of propriation, not only a limit of hermeneutics has been revealed, but a medial or processual structure of passage of one property into an other, that is anterior to differential opposition. It follows that with propriation one touches also on the limit of the opposition itself between metaphysics (hermeneutics) and non-metaphysics, that is, on the limit of 'the form of opposition. If the form of opposition, the oppositional structure, is itself metaphysical, then the relation of metaphysics to its other can no longer be of the order of an opposition' (pp. 116–18). How, then, are we to conceive of the relation between the two readings? If onto-hermeneutics cannot pose the question of propriation itself, since this question is presupposed by the form of its questions, the reading concerned with propriation (or, for that matter, with woman and style in Nietzsche) cannot become enclosed within it. What happens, instead, is that the reading around the question of propriation 'reinscribes the hermeneutic gesture' (p. 114) in so far as all the values of hermeneutics (Being, meaning, truth, etc.) appear as the result of decisions that collapse the state, or matrix, of propriation into definite (and opposite) properties. Such reinscription, however, is anything but a critical destruction. Rather, it consists in bringing to bear on the hermeneutic question those questions that its very constitution prevents it from asking.

In its turn, the hermeneutic question does not become obsolete because of readings that bring to light its intrinsic limits. The question of what something properly is, is an inevitable, and as we will see in a moment, a necessary question. When, after having shown that in Nietzsche's text, the feminine operation triggers the passage of properties into one another, Derrida asks 'what precisely is it that I am here doing at this moment', this question is labelled 'a question that remains' (p. 56). Undoubtedly, this is a question that does not allow for any satisfactory answer, precisely because the feminine operation unsettles the hermeneutic question of what something properly is. But at the same time, the 'question that remains' is also a question that does not go away. Let me also mention that, according to *Spurs*, despite the fact that the question '"What is woman?"' becomes suspended because indissociable from the questions of art, style and truth, and that consequently 'one can no longer seek woman, any more than one can search for woman's femininity or female sexuality', it remains the case that 'it is impossible to resist looking for her' (p. 70). Whence this impossibility, one may ask? If woman is understood as giving herself, and to give-herself-for – *as* being or meaning something – the very nature of this gift is an invitation to look for her. More generally, since all statements, texts and *oeuvres*, have the structure of the trace, the latter implying an address, they demand a response. Since it is structurally impossible to establish once and for all the context of a trace, these statements, texts and *oeuvres*, which *can* always lack definite meaning, 'simulate a hidden truth in their folds' (p. 132) which one cannot but seek to find.

In the third part of *Spurs* Derrida cites Nietzsche's proposition, ' "I have forgotten my umbrella" ', as an instance of an utterance whose context it is impossible to reconstruct, and whose meaning thus remains enigmatic, even though the statement is intelligible through and through. In this way he suggests that Nietzsche's whole *oeuvre*, as well as Derrida's own text, could possibly be of the same order as that statement. At the same time, however, he stresses the necessity – in spite not merely of the factual, but especially structural, limits that make it forever impossible to securely know what Nietzsche meant with this perfectly legible sentence – of continuing to seek to try to establish its meaning. Its very readability amounts to an obligation to seek to understand it. Derrida argues that to conclude that because of the structural impossibility to ever know the meaning of the sentence, one could abandon the search altogether, is 'still an aestheticizing and obscurantist reaction of the *hermeneuein*'. 'On the contrary, in order to take into account as rigorously as possible, this structural limit . . . it is necessary to push deciphering as far as possible' (p. 132).

Commenting on the editors' note of justification for including in their edition of *The Gay Science* the fragment 'I have forgotten my umbrella', Derrida terms it 'a monument to hermeneutic somnambulism, every word of which covers over in blithest complacency a seething mass of critical questions' (p. 124). Inquiring into the possibility of fixing unequivocally what something properly is, an inquiry that weighs on all hermeneutic founding concepts, deconstruction confronts hermeneutics with questions that it does not, and cannot, ask. Undoubtedly, Ricoeur's and Gadamer's hermeneutics no longer assume that texts have one sole meaning which lies concealed behind them, and which needs only to be uncovered. But this in no way exempts them from these critical questions. Gadamer's conception of the *Sache* [the subject matter] at the heart of all traditional texts, which historical understanding makes meaningful in innovative fashion in any given present, as well as Ricoeur's conception, in his later works, of a 'world of the text' in front of which the subject discovers his or her ownmost possibilities, which is thus enabled to reform his or her subjectivity, presuppose nothing less than the unbreached identity of the *Sache* and world of the text, respectively. However violent it may be to submit hermeneutics to the questions that it not only does not, but also cannot, ask itself – a submission necessary notwithstanding the violence, since it concerns the undecidable matrix within which hermeneutics carves out its leading oppositions – the confrontation does not diminish hermeneutics' legitimate inquiries. Yet, one may wish to ask whether a reinscribed hermeneutics, one that has awakened to the critical questions, can still be a hermeneutics as we know it? Does such a hermeneutics still deserve its title? Vice versa, one cannot but also wonder what it is that deconstruction is doing by asking these critical questions. Although incessantly querying the congealing of the graphic of the hymen, or pharmakon, into a figure of knowledge, can one resist the temptation of figuring it as a 'hermeneutics' of some sort? An inevitable temptation, entirely illegitimate? In any case, these questions remain.

WORKS CITED

Derrida, Jacques (1979), *Spurs: Nietzsche's Styles/Éperons: Les styles de Nietzsche* (Chicago, IL: University of Chicago Press). (Page numbers in the text refer to this edition. All translations from this work are mine – RG.)

Gadamer, Hans-Georg (1989), 'Destruction *and* Deconstruction', *Dialogue and Deconstruction: The Gadamer–Derrida Encounter*, ed. D. P. Michelfelder and R. E. Palmer (Albany, NY: SUNY Press), pp. 102–13.

—— (1993), *Gesammelte Werke*, vol. 2: *Hermeneutik II. Wahrheit und Methode. Ergänzungen Register* (Tübingen: J. C. B. Mohr).

Greisch, Jean (1996), 'Déconstruction et/ou Herméneutique', *La théologie en postmodernité, Lieux Théologiques*, vol. 29, ed. P. Gisel and P. Evrard (Geneva: Labor et Fides), pp. 353–86.

Grondin, Jean (1994), *Introduction to Philosophical Hermeneutics*, trans. J. Weinsheimer (New Haven, CT: Yale University Press).

Nietzsche, Friedrich (1974), *The Gay Science*, trans. Walter Kaufmann (New York: Vintage).

Pöggeler, Otto (1994), 'Hermeneutik und Dekonstruktion', *Schritte zu einer hermeneutischen Philosophie* (Munich: Karl Alber), pp. 479–98.

Ricoeur, Paul (1981), *Hermeneutics and the Human Sciences* (Cambridge: Cambridge University Press).

9

Deconstruction and Love

Peggy Kamuf

*Can one speak of loving without declaring love, without declaring war,
beyond all possible neutrality? Without confessing, be it the unspeakable?*

Jacques Derrida, *Politics of Friendship*

The conjunction of deconstruction and love will seem an unexpected one
to some. It is not an association authorized by the widely circulated image
of deconstruction as an essentially negative operation, as if the term were
really a synonym of 'destruction' and the additional syllable simply
superfluous. This persistent reduction has come about only after many
repetitions, performed most often so as to give someone a pretext for
denunciation. Deconstruction has had bad press almost since it first
appeared in Derrida's writings. Things got quickly worse when others
began to pick up the term, perhaps because this could be taken as a signal that something larger was afoot and would have to be dealt with more
severely. Thus it is that, after several decades of such severity, one cannot
approach an essay on deconstruction and love without anticipating a
resistance fed by the rumour that deconstruction is essentially destructive
and even that it destroys everything we, as members of civilized societies,
ought to work to preserve from destruction, which is to say, everything
we love, as well as everything we are told we ought to love. Beginning
with love itself. At its core, this resistance would be working to protect
love itself from destruction. And what could be more natural than that?
The nature of this resistance would thus be that of the tautology assumed
between acts of loving and acts of preserving or protecting from destruction. As such, it is likely to be activated by very powerful forces indeed.

The task of this essay cannot be to overcome this powerful resistance,
assuming that such a thing were even possible. It cannot be our aim, in
other words, simply to dismantle the resistant idea that love essentially
seeks to preserve from destruction and is therefore what must, above all,
be preserved. Rather, we will try to make apparent how a loving movement is the indispensable key to what deconstruction does. In the process
– and this would be the ultimate stakes of the undertaking – we will have

151

to approach the idea that even if it is essentially preservative, love (and therefore deconstruction) is nevertheless no stranger to destruction, to loss, and to ruin. To put it less litotically, in other words, to avoid that figure of speech whereby an affirmation is expressed by the negative of the contrary, we will be approaching the figure of love as affirmation that deconstructs the opposition between preservation and destruction, love, therefore, as that which, like deconstruction, takes place along the divided, ruined border of this alternative.

We can begin by citing just one of the many occasions on which Derrida has sought to arrest the assimilation of deconstruction to a negative operation, to a destruction. It is from the transcription of a discussion he had with some colleagues in Montreal in 1979. Derrida (who is thus not the only signatory of this text) is explaining that he initially never intended to attach any privilege to 'deconstruction', which he began using in a chain with many other terms. This privilege got assigned when the term began to be repeated as the principal designation for what he, and soon many others, were interested in doing. But in so far as the term carried connotations, as he puts it, 'of a technical operation used to dismantle systems', he has never much liked it (Derrida, 1985, p. 85). The technical reference, he explains, tends to screen out the more important association for him: that the deconstructive gesture be, we quote, 'accompanied, or can be accompanied (in any case, I would hope to accompany it), by an affirmation. It is not negative, it is not destructive'. He goes on to recount that, once it became clear how 'deconstruction' was being singled out by others, he tried 'to determine this concept', as he writes, 'in my own manner, that is, according to what I thought was the right manner, which I did by insisting on the fact that it was not a question of a negative operation' (p. 87). And then, so as to make his insistence on the non-negative, affirmative concept of deconstruction clearer still, Derrida speaks of love:

> I don't feel that I'm in a position to *choose* between an operation that we'll call negative or nihilist, an operation that would set about furiously dismantling systems, and the other operation. I love very much everything that I deconstruct in my own manner; the texts I want to read from the deconstructive point of view are. texts I love, with that impulse of identification which is indispensable for reading. They are texts whose future, I think, will not be exhausted for a long time. . . . [M]y relation to these texts is characterized by loving jealousy and not at all by nihilistic fury (one can't read anything in the latter condition) . . . (Ibid.)

Before underscoring a few points about these remarks, we might ask: Is it certain that this is the most auspicious place to begin a discussion of deconstruction and love? When one says that one loves a *text*, when the object of the transitive verb 'love' is such a thing, then is there not a very large distance taken at the outset from the heart of the love relation, which has to be (does it not?) either interpersonal or at least a relation formed between animate, living beings? In other words, by setting out from a remark about love for something like texts, are we not going off in a wrong direction, which has to lead wide of the animate heart of love? Worse still, beginning in this fashion might risk confirming yet another facet of deconstruction's negative association in many people's minds, all those for whom, for example, Derrida's famous assertion 'there is no out-side-the-text' is heard only as an intellectual's negation of all activity other than writing and reading. To even seem to imply that the love in question in deconstruction is *first of all* the love of texts appears designed to discourage at the outset anyone who might harbour this misguided notion from giving it up.[1]

That is always possible. Yet, if these risks seem worth taking, it could well be for a reason not unlike the one that leads Derrida, in the above passage, to insist to the extent he does that, contrary to a common per-ception, his own practice of deconstruction proceeds out of love rather than under the sway of a destructive impulse: that reason is to add the force of *affirmation* to what otherwise appears destined to have only the negative force of its technical, dismantling operation. Likewise, if we begin by speaking of the love of texts with some faith that we will thereby be led to the heart of the matter, then it must be because we have already begun to affirm something about love's heart: it is that which would be able to hold together in an essential relation the movement towards the animate as well as towards the inanimate, towards life as well as non-life, or death, and therefore towards that which can be preserved in life as well as that which has never had or no longer has any life as such to be pre-served. At the heart of love, all of these apparent oppositions would be suspended, no longer or not yet in force, or already ruined, in ruins.[2]

But this is indeed to anticipate where our opening quotation may lead us. To consider these remarks less precipitously, we should recall that they were improvised for a specific occasion and in response to another's question; as such, they are perhaps less guarded, less policed than they might otherwise be for publication under an author's sole signature. Which is not to say, of course, that they are unsigned or unattributable, but merely that they bear a particular relation to the movement whereby one signs something. Indeed, Derrida had been invited on this occasion to air thoughts about that movement itself, to characterize his own gesture when he signed other texts elsewhere, to offer reflections from a certain remove about what put them and his signature in motion.[3] As remarks about the relation one may have to the writing and reading one does (or to which one submits), they would attempt to configure those activities (or those passions) from somewhere exterior to them, at some distance before or beyond what is being described. And since what is being described or characterized is the relation, passion or impulse called love, then the external vantage point aimed for here would itself have to stand outside that love relation, in a position of 'objective neutrality', as it is called, which would be the position of the would-be scientist or scholar. But is this attempt in fact a success? Is there, in other words, an objectively neutral, scholarly position that can be identified there?

That is very doubtful, for reasons we may quickly see. As already pointed out, the remarks we have cited from *The Ear of the Other* summarize how Derrida had to work to counter a prevalent understanding of the deconstructive gesture as negative or destructive. They give a condensed account of his efforts to resituate this concept 'according to what [he] thought was the right manner', which was the manner of an affirmation. Notice, however, that at a certain point, the point at which the quoted extract begins, the speaker is no longer giving simply an account of what he has done, of other texts he has signed; the mode or manner of his remarks also shifts to that of affirmation. And it is at this point that he invokes love: 'I love very much everything that I deconstruct in my own manner; the texts I want to read from a deconstructive point of view are texts I love . . .'. Such phrases, and those that surround them, can no longer be heard as merely descriptive – or constative, as speech acts theorists would say; in other words, they do not only describe a state of affairs, which led someone to do something, and then what that something was ('to determine this concept in my own manner'. and so on). Without drama, but with indisputable emphasis, these phrases also do something: they *declare love*, and as such they perform the affirmation by which, as Derrida had earlier observed, the deconstructive gesture 'is accompanied, or can be accompanied (in any case, I would hope to accompany it)'. In doing so, in declaring love, they affirm the accompanying affirmation in the present of their performance, at the scene of discussion with some colleagues in Montreal 1979, but also, of course, at every other scene at which these remarks can be and have been repeated, including this one. Each repetition differs in force, but with each quotation or repetition, the affirmative declaration remains, as it were, in excess over the descriptive value of these sentences. In excess, or rather let us say that the affirmative force of the declaration is that which conditions the description as more, less or simply other than the description that it also is, but that it is only by virtue of having been declared. In other words, when Derrida (or anyone else) says or writes: 'I love X very much', he is describing a certain relation, but he can describe it only by affirming (again) that he loves X very much. Because an affirmative accompaniment puts in place the description, which it thereby precedes and conditions, objective neutrality is not to be found outside this structure, but only already within it, which is to say, within a structure conditioned by the non-objective, non-neutral, affirmative declaration: 'I love . . .'.[4]

This suggests that, without much apparent calculation (for that is the character of improvisation), the remarks we've quoted would have performed once again the accompanying affirmation that Derrida finds to be missing whenever deconstruction is construed as a merely technical operation of dismantling, whenever its gesture is taken up and repeated as technique or mere method, whenever an external, objectively neutral position is assumed as the place from which to deconstruct whatever by whomever, and by anyone at all like everyone else. The affirmation by which Derrida would wish to accompany the deconstructive gesture cannot be neutral,[5] it is, rather, of the nature of love, that is, of that whose non-neutrality must be thought of in at least two different ways.

On the one hand, when one loves something or someone, one is partial to it, to him, or to her; one even has a passion, as we say, for that thing or that person or that creature. That is why, for example, in allegories of love (e.g., Cupid), love's passion will often be represented as some kind of blindness. But its impaired vision or visibility is precisely not the blindness we believe to be required of justice, which is conceived of or allegorized as a blindness in the interest of dispensing a neutral, or just, justice. The blindness of love, in its partiality, is assumed to prevent, overturn, or at least make improbable the blind, impartial neutrality of justice.[6] *On the other hand*, love is not neutral in the sense that he or she who loves is not just anyone, no matter who; he loves as the one he is and no other, and she loves as she does because it is she. Each has, in other words, his or her idiom of love, but this idiom is less something one *has* or *knows* than something one *does*. (We will return to this notion of idiom below.)

Now, these two faces or figures of love's non-neutrality might be called objective and subjective if it were not that such a distinction is suspended by or from the *passion* of love, in other words, by or from that which one experiences in a certain passivity under the influence or the pull of another whom one loves, that is, the other to whom one's feeling of love becomes addressed and by whom it is therefore determined as address. Determined by the other, the address of love is never issued by a pre-existent subject in the direction of an object, its object, or destination. As Jean-Luc Nancy has put it:

> Love re-presents the 'I' to itself as broken . . . To the 'I' it presents this: that it, this subject, has been touched, breached, in its subjectivity, and from now on, it *is*, for the time of love, broken or cracked, however slightly. It *is* so, which means that the break or the wound is neither an accident nor a property that the subject could make its own. Since it is a break of its property as subject, it is, essentially, an interruption in the process of relating to oneself outside oneself . . . . For as long as it lasts, love does not cease to come from without and to remain, not outside

but this outside itself, each time singular, a blade plunged into me and
that I cannot rejoin because it disjoins me . . .   (Nancy, 1990, pp. 247–8)

One could say, in somewhat simple terms, that the position of subject, the
subject position, the positionality of subject/object are, as such, incapable
of the experience of love's passion or even that they are *opposed* to that
experience in so far as it knows no subject, no 'I' who loves 'X', outside or
before the passion of the subject's address of love. In other words, love is
not a matter of position, whether of subject or object, and therefore of
opposition, but of an address that does not originate from any home, as it
were. An address without home, without the property of a subject from
which it is sent and to which it returns, love always brushes up against
the uncanny, the *unheimlich*, the un-homelike. Love brings with it the un-
homelike because it is the experience of the sudden or not-so-sudden
arrival of the other who *expropriates* address, which is to say *appropriates*
it, *exappropriates* it: When I say 'I love . . . ', it is always the declaration of
the other at my address.

There is at least one more thing to notice about the improvised character of the remarks that led Derrida to make his declaration of love. The
repetition of a phrase, 'à ma maniére' ('in my own manner'), scans the
declaration in a manner that, had this been a more calculated, written text,
would probably have either provoked the style censor or else prompted a
reflection about that idiomatic phrase. As it is, however, the phrase
repeats of itself and insists – idiomatically, mechanically, or manneristi-
cally – on doing what one does in one's own manner. 'I tried to determine
this concept in my own manner, that is, according to what I thought was
the right manner . . .; I love very much everything I deconstruct in my
own manner . . .'. The modest adverbial modifier can in fact be read as a
key to the affirmative tenor of the passage, which culminates in the declaration of love's conjunction with deconstruction. The affirmation that
would accompany the deconstructive gesture, at least when that gesture
is performed by the one who signs here in his own manner, would always
proceed in some manner or another, according to this person's idiom. It is
thus, as well, an affirmation of the idiom in the idiom. This is to underscore once again that deconstruction in the 'right manner', deconstruction
accompanied by affirmation rather than confined to a negative or technical operation, has never been performed by just anyone at all and no one
in particular, for example, by *the* philosopher of pure reason, an ideal subject, or from some position of objective neutrality. The accompanying
affirmation, which makes for all the difference from the idea of philosophy or from the notion of a pure technique, is carried, as it were, in an
idiom, by which one does not mean only a particular language, but everything that can inform and deform anyone's use of a common, so-called
natural language: the domain of personal and family history, of conscious

experience and unconscious desire, of civil, public identity and private identifications. In other words, all that is implied whenever anyone says 'I love . . .'. The affirmation, carried by the idiom, will be an affirmation of all that, all that is in play whenever anyone, this one in particular, says, declares, affirms: 'I love . . .', 'j'aime . . .', 'yo quiero . . . .', 'ich liebe . . .', in whatever idiom.[7]

We have, it seems, let ourselves be tempted to read these few phrases of an impromptu exchange as if they supplied all the coordinates needed to plot the conjunction of deconstruction with love. As yet, however, we have said little about what is most striking, perhaps, about these lines, the fact that they declare a love of texts. We may recall our initial question about the risks this kind of declaration might present for our task, the risk of being led astray from the heart of the matter of love. We nevertheless wagered at the beginning that, by keeping to this course, we would be able to affirm something about love's heart, as that which can accommodate, in a relation of love, the animate and the inanimate, the living and the dead, persons and texts. It is time now to renew the wager.

——Before you take that step, remember the lines placed in epigraph: 'Can one speak of loving without declaring love, without declaring war, beyond all possible neutrality? Without confessing, be it the unspeakable?'[8]
——Are those rhetorical questions? If so, they are themselves a declaration, a non-neutral act.
——Indeed. So, do you think an essay titled 'Deconstruction and Love' escapes the necessity to risk confessing the unspeakable? Somewhere you have begun to answer the question: whom or what do you love?
——If that is not another rhetorical question, then it sounds like a question for the police.
——How could it be a rhetorical question?
——Perhaps not in the usual sense, a question that *forces* a response and only one response. But if rhetorical or poetic force can indeed be other than police force, then it must somewhere be allied with whatever permits the response of *more than one, other than one, other than just one*. Rhetoric allows also allegory, and an allegory is always some kind of text.
——So you would declare you love a text?
——Yes, if that is possible.

How is it possible to love a text? That is, how is it possible to say one loves a text, of any and every sort, without that declaration being simply an abuse of the language, a stretching of the proper sense of love to the point of breaking? Or even an abasement of the highest sense, which should be reserved for the love of one's fellow human beings, if not, indeed, for the love of God, for God's love?[9] To be sure, the idea of a loving God is preserved in texts, which are themselves revered as sacred by the 'religions of the book'. But, for those religions or those cultures, this consecration is precisely what sets these texts apart from texts of any and every sort, from the non-sacred texts that one cannot say one loves without improperly invoking the very notion of sacrality. In other words, as soon as one declares love for a text classified as, for example, fiction or poetry or philosophy,[10] then a whole theologically buttressed doctrine of love is at stake. It is, therefore, no small matter when someone says such a thing, provided he or she means to declare more than just a passing appreciation. It is especially no small matter if it can be shown not only that such a declaration does not abuse or abase love in the proper or highest sense, but also and more affirmatively, that from the possibility of this declaration is suspended whatever anyone can mean in the most proper or highest sense of love, the most sacred address of 'I love you' for him or her – love, therefore, in all its mysteriously infinite singularity. This means, in a terrifyingly simple sense, that if we ceased, for some barely imaginable reason, to be able to *declare* a love of texts, to renew and preserve the force of that declaration, then we would also have ceased being able to love anything or anyone at all. So, yes, indeed, much is at stake; perhaps everything.

Which is why one should not take lightly the fact that, for such a declaration to be possible, we cannot know ultimately either to whom it will have been declared or who is the *object*, as we say, of such a declaration. Suppose I want to declare I love something of this sort, a novel, a work of poetry, or even a critical essay. To whom can I say such a thing so that it may have the performative force of a declaration? If I announce it just to anyone within earshot, it may indeed provoke various interpretations about my state of mind, my taste in literature, or perhaps even my 'race-classgender' coefficient, but all such interpretations would take my statement as having solely constative value, that is, as a statement concerning some fact. True, it is a strange kind of fact because no neutral observer can verify it or falsify it, but fact it remains for this 'neutral observer' nonetheless, that is, for whoever can hear such a statement without taking it as a *declaration* of love made to him or to her and to which he or she can and even *must* respond (walking away or pretending one has not heard the declaration would also be responses to it). It is, then, this address with the possibility and even the necessity of response that makes the difference between the constative statement and the performative declaration. So the question we were asking becomes the following: To whom, to which addressee, does one address a love of texts? For whom can such an address have the force of declaration, or the force of love, without which all such statements circulate as merely unverifiable, neutral and finally indifferent facts?

Suppose the novel, poem or essay I love was written by a still-living author. I might therefore declare my love to him or to her, as if there were finally no difference between author and text, signatory and that which he or she signs. This happens everywhere, every day, which for many is no doubt a sufficiently gratifying reason to write or to make any kind of work that another can love. If one dares to be lucid about this situation, however, then one knows that such tributes carry with them the recognition that one's name, one's signature is, as Shakespeare's Juliet analyses it, 'no part of thee'.[11] Because the name, the signature is not the bearer of the name, it is also always the mark of the definitive detachment that others must experience upon the death of the name's bearer, when the name will cease to be a possible form of address to someone else living and will commence functioning, as it were, independently of any individual bearer. But this functioning *simply is* the general possibility of naming, of language, or more generally still, of *iterability*, to use the term Derrida has made available.[12] Which means, of course, that it does not await anyone's individual, punctual death to begin to accompany every use we make of his or her proper name, including its most proper use: to call one to respond to a declaration of love. Here, then, is something no one likes to think about too much, even as it always accompanies every thought we ever have of love for another; here is an unbearable thing that must be borne, which is also to say carried and renewed beyond any single one's ability to bear it: the names we give to love when we declare it are the names of mortals. Whenever we declare love to another by addressing him or her by name, we address it also to his or her mortality.[13]

We call 'text', however, that which bears its name not as the mark of mortality but rather as the very possibility of its living on and continuing to be called by its name. I can thus say 'I love Emily Dickinson' without much risk that my meaning will be mistaken: I love a text, the text that is now, seemingly, *inseparable* from the name it bears but the name that it also just *is*, its name *as* text. But if I *can* say such a thing, and if I can say it not just as some kind of fact but affirm or declare the love I say I bear, if, in other words, I can *address* love to another with these words, then the name 'Emily Dickinson' will also have to be able to name, *still*, this other who would be addressed and the other to whom I am already responding. The other, who? Emily Dickinson herself? No, of course not, but rather 'someone' to whom I give that name, all the same, within myself, a site of and for another within me. When one declares love to a text, one declares it *necessarily* to another within oneself. Is this, then, a distinction that has to be made between this act and the act of addressing love to another who is *also* other than oneself, a now living person, that is, one who is not only an other within?

Yes and no. Yes, because the independent exteriority of the other is the condition of my being able to address love or anything else to him or her, as well as the condition for any such declaration to receive from another a response that is not already determined by the address. That the other exists independently from the subject of the declaration is simply, we could say, the condition of love as other than self-love, other than a love whose object is oneself or any part of oneself. However, the distinction cannot be made in these terms, because a declaration of love is also a declaration that some internalization of the other has begun; the subject of the declaration is already not just itself, and that is what it declares. It declares that between itself alone and the self that shelters another within, no line can be drawn separating the two as simply exterior to each other. There is at once a division, an other within the self who is not the self, and no division, the other internalized by the self as the self. But if both these conditions are necessary, if both the other's exteriority and internalization are the conditions of love, this means, doesn't it, that no difference can ever be laid down with certainty between, on the one hand, what is called, most often reprovingly, self-love and, on the other hand, its other, the other love that is love for the other, addressed to another.

If this is so – and it is so – then who could ever affirm love for another, to another, without at the same time addressing love to himself or to herself? And therefore without also appropriating what is meant for the other? Perhaps indeed this is always what happens, one way or the other; perhaps there has never been a declaration of love that did not keep for itself what it wanted the other to have or to feel.[14] The very least we can say is that we cannot know that there has ever been *in fact* a declaration of love that did not appropriate the address to itself, because every such address will have been conditioned by the possibility of its cancellation as address to another outside the self. We have already remarked this condition when we said, a moment ago, that love is declared to mortals, by mortals, that is, beings who internalize and are internalized in the face of the impossibility, inevitable one day, of an external address to those whom they love. Yet, is this inevitable impossibility also a reason to question that there has ever been or could ever be a declaration of love for another, a truly other other? Do we question that such a thing has happened and can happen? Doubtless no, we do *not* question this possibility so long as we can still *think* a love that does not address only itself, that does not appropriate the address of love for itself. So long as we do have this thought, it is even what we think love *must be*: the love of another. It is what we think must be given or received in the name of love, without, nevertheless, being able to affirm in absolute certainty that we have ever given or received such a thing. We can and do think this; moreover, we can cite examples, which is to say, texts.

For example, Henry James's *The Aspern Papers*, a love story in which the only love that is finally declared is for a text, and even for *this* text here, the one we are reading. Because the title designates both this text and the text in this text, it embeds, at the outset, a figure for itself, a set of 'papers' that will be the object of blinding love. (In a moment, we will consider what this figure of the self-loving text may be doing here.) These papers are presumed to be letters from the great American poet Jeffrey Aspern, dead for many years when the novel opens, and, if they exist, they may still be in the possession of the woman to whom they were originally addressed, the now-ancient Miss Juliana Bordereau. Miss Bordereau lives, a virtual recluse, in her Venetian villa, which is why, the narrator reasons, she has been able to keep the papers secret for so long. That secrecy is about to end, if the narrator succeeds in doing what he has come to Venice to do: he wants the papers more than anything in the world and will try to get them away somehow from their owner. The first-person narrator, who never mentions his name, is one of the two foremost editors of Aspern's works; he shares with his co-editor the responsibility for preserving the poet's name, which had been somewhat forgotten in the world of letters before their edition. In other words, Aspern's now-celebrated greatness (if, at least, we can believe the narrator) is at least partially owed to the narrator's own labours. We note this circumstance because it alone would be sufficient to cast doubt on the claim that, as the narrator confides, he is doing what he does for 'Jeffrey Aspern's sake', for the sake, then, of this other whom he loves.[15] This is doubtful not just because the name of the dead poet can only be the name of some other in himself, but because, as a name, it is *bound up* with the narrator's own, in the edition that both will have signed. For 'Jeffrey Aspern's sake' is also always for his own sake or the sake of his own name.

The novel, then, is narrated from the position of one who can never know whether he acts for his own sake or for the sake of the other, for the sake of his name or in the name of the other. As such, the text of *The Aspern Papers* evinces a considerable lucidity about love. In its lucidity, this text would declare: love just *is* that impossible knowledge, the impossibility of discerning for whose sake, in whose name, one acts. Now, if this sounds like a contradiction, or worse yet, an obfuscation, that is probably because we too readily locate lucidity in a subject, and in just one subject. It is clearly not, however, the narrator himself who is lucid about what he is doing; he declares – or wants to declare – that he is acting out of love for another, rather than in view of an appropriation for himself of the papers and all they represent for him. We believe we can see through the narrator's conscious self-justifications ('it is all for Jeffrey Aspern's sake'), which can only have the force of *self*-justifications because they invoke justice done to the other. Because this discourse holds up the other's name in self-defence, it creates the window through which to see through it – to the other other, the other who is expropriated when a subject would claim *to know* that whatever he does, no matter how deceitful, duplicitous, or even murderous, he does for love of another and not for himself. So, the 'lucidity' we alluded to above is not to be found in the narrator's conscious discourse, and this is true despite the fact that every single word of the text (with the possible exception of its title) belongs to that discourse, is re-cited and narrated by the narrator. Despite that, there is an excess to be accounted for because, as we said, beyond the blinded *discourse*, there is a *text* that can evince lucidity about love, which the narrator seems unable to see for himself. If such a text can be 'lucid', it is because it figures somehow *in itself* this border between everything it contains, all the words constituting the text, and what is *at the same time* an excess of text over all the words it contains. A border is thereby traced or re-marked, setting off an outside within.

Notice, however, that to call this re-marking of textuality 'lucid' and lucid about love (but is there anything else to be lucid about?) is already to begin to *configure* it once again as a subject, a *seeing* subject, that is, as what we have just said it is not. Configuration like this is inevitable because it is the very movement by which we are able to read, as figures and faces, what has in itself nothing of a face.[16] If, then, a text re-marks itself in excess over any subject, any one subject, and therefore any one subject's discourse, it also does so by figuring within itself the viewpoint of subjects. (And there must necessarily be always more than one of these if a text evinces lucidity about love.) In *The Aspern Papers*, the figure of lucidity, as opposed to the narrating figure of blindness, is Juliana Bordereau, the other other who stands to be expropriated by the narrator if ever he succeeds in justifying to himself the theft he has come to perpetrate. Hers, then, is perhaps the lucidity about love that, as we said, the narrator cannot see for himself.

There is much in the novel to suggest that this is so. In particular, there is a device that holds in place the structure of a blindness that is not just opposed to lucidity, face to face, as it were, but *pierced* by it. This device is the strange, disfiguring apparatus that Juliana Bordereau wears over her eyes. It is the focus of all the narrator's thoughts when he sees her for the first time, without, however, being able to come face to face with her:

> it almost exceeded my courage (much as I longed for the event) to be left alone with such a terrible relic as [Juliana Bordereau]. She was too strange, too literally resurgent. Then came a check, with the perception that we were not really face to face, inasmuch as she had over her eyes a horrible green shade which for her, served almost as a mask. I believed for the instant that she had put it on expressly, so that from underneath it she might scrutinize me without being scrutinized her-

self. At the same time it increased the presumption that there was a ghastly death's-head lurking behind it. The divine Juliana as a grinning skull – the vision hung there until it passed. Then it came to me that she *was* tremendously old – so old that death might take her at any moment, before I had time to get what I wanted from her. The next thought was a correction to that; it lighted up the situation. She would die next week, she would die to-morrow – then I could seize her papers.

(pp. 229–30)

That he sees himself seen without seeing, scrutinized without scrutinizing in return, has the curious effect here of bringing the narrator as close as he can come to confessing the event he most longs to see: the death of the other who sits before him. It suggests that he does not need to say as much to her; she sees all. Hers is the point of view of that most powerful spectator, the one who can pierce the plane of deceptive appearance because her own faculty of vision is not implicated in the scene she sees. She is a purely seeing subject who cannot become an object in the other's sight. Hence it can seem that she sees what he vainly attempts to hide from her and even that she foresees, from the first, the terrible scene that is going to unfold close to the end of the novel, after months of proximity to her deadly enemy, the narrator.

One evening as Miss Bordereau lies close to death (or so he believes) in an adjacent room, the narrator slips into the salon and approaches the secretary where he is convinced the letters lie concealed. As he is about to test the lock by touching its button, protesting as he does that it was not his intention to steal the papers ('I did not propose to do anything, not even – not in the least – to let down the lid; I only wanted to test my theory, to see if the cover *would* move'),[17] he happens to look over his shoulder and sees there Miss Bordereau herself, as if risen from the dead; she no longer wears the shade over her eyes, with the result that he beheld 'for the first, the last, and the only time . . . her extraordinary eyes. They glared at me, they made me horribly ashamed.' As he turns to look into those eyes, for the first and last time, 'she hissed out passionately, furiously: "Ah you publishing scoundrel!"', before she falls back 'with a quick spasm, as if death had descended on her . . .' (p. 286). The next day, the shamed narrator quits Venice for a week of distracted tourism, leaving others to bury the consequences of his failed theft and successful murder.

To be sure, the novel does not telescope (as we have just done) these two scenes, the first and last meetings between the adversaries who are locked in a death struggle over the possession of the letters. By juxtaposing them, we have sought only to bring out the pattern that opposes the narrator's love, which makes him blind, to Juliana's love, which makes her lucid. Can she, however, be lucid about what opposes her to the 'publishing scoundrel'? That is, about the love whose object is the papers? In other words, can the love she bears for them be simply opposed to the thieving narrator's? We assume that it can by virtue of the letters' address: her own name on the letters is what makes them precious to her. She loves above all their *singular* address, and that is what she wants to preserve from the destruction of publication, which would send the letters to innumerable addresses. What she hates is the idea of repetition or reproduction of her name when she is not there to respond to it as addressed to her alone. This is also what she shows through the act of veiling or shrouding her eyes: no other may ever gaze into them, that is, no other may read there Jeffrey Aspern's address to her. We might even go so far as to say that Juliana Bordereau hates the *letter* of the address, which will always make the papers she holds readable and repeatable for another. In all of this, she is apparently opposed to the narrator, who loves not the singular address on the letters (and especially not their addressee, whom he would rather see dead) but precisely their reproducibility. He indeed wants to publish them, and under his own name. As we have already noticed, the narrator can never be certain that he is not acting out of love for his own name; his efforts to appropriate the letters, in that case, would be driven above all by the wish to appropriate their address to himself. If Juliana Bordereau is indeed able to see through to this wish expressed in each of his acts (or so we may imagine), it is because she has the same wish: to appropriate the address of the letters. But aren't the letters already addressed to her? Yes, but only because they *can* be addressed to anyone at all, only because they are repeatable. Since they are repeatable, which is the condition of their arriving at an address, they also do not arrive once and for all, if ever.[18] Doubtless Juliana Bordereau, for all her lucidity, does not see this; but more important, it is what she, unlike the narrator perhaps, does not love.

In the charged space between the narrator and Miss Bordereau, there is, then, love for a text as that which can be *both* repeated because addressed, *and* addressed because repeated. This struggle thereby spaces out and opposes what the iterability of the name does not and cannot dissociate. Neither of them can love the letters without wanting to destroy them, either by publishing them, and therefore destroying their unique address, or by assuring that they can never be published, and therefore destroying any chance of repetition. That Miss Bordereau may think to destroy the letters is the narrator's greatest fear:

> 'But why should she not destroy her papers?'
> 'Oh, she loves them too much.'
> 'Even now, when she may be near her end?'
> 'Perhaps when she's sure of that she will.'   (p. 264)

When it is said, 'she loves them too much', we understand first: she loves them too much to destroy them. And we understand this simply enough because, like the characters in dialogue here, we can easily assume love is simply that which would not destroy what it loves. However, we may also overhear this exchange as reflecting someone's judgement that Juliana loves the letters *too much*, she is wrong to love them as much as she does, to the exclusion perhaps of anyone or anything else. But who can make such a judgement?

This is not the narrator speaking, but the third principal character in the narrative, or rather, we should say the fourth since the great Jeffrey Aspern is already the third party to a triangle. The speaker is another Miss Bordereau, the middle-aged niece of Juliana, and her constant companion for an untold number of years. Miss Tita, as she is called, plies the middle ground between the other two. She ministers to the love each of them bears towards the letters, apparently promising *both of them* that she will prevent the destruction of what they love. Her compliance, her pliability with one and the other (the narrator repeatedly qualifies her by this pliability) makes her the site or the shuttling vehicle between the poles placed in deadly opposition to one another: *both* her aunt and the narrator want *both* to preserve and destroy the letters, either to destroy them *by* preserving them or to preserve them *by* destroying them. Between the poles of this reversal, Tita Bordereau *complies without contradiction* with one and the other, with the other and with the other of the other. The mortal combat in which these two are locked is at the same time unlocked by her capacity to fold the opposition of the other two into a non-opposition. It is as if, with her name, she redivided the *border* across which they stand opposed. She would thus figure that oddly bordered space in which each of them is interiorized by the other but within her. As such a figure, she is the heart or at the heart of this text because she is the *possibility of love* between these two mortal enemies.

At the end of his narrative, when he has returned to the villa after Juliana Bordereau's death and funeral, the narrator has two further interviews with the niece of his nemesis. In the first, she lets him know that, if he wishes it, the letters could be his. 'I would give you everything – and she would understand, where she is – she would forgive me'. This offer is made in the conditional but the condition is never stated, never declared by either of the interlocutors.[19] The narrator has no doubt, however, that she is inviting him to propose marriage to her. In reply to this non-declaration, he can only stammer and make 'a wild, vague movement, in consequence of which I found myself at the door. . . . The next thing I remember I was downstairs and out of the house' (p. 296). He continues to run in the other direction until he wakes the next morning with a start and only one question in his calculating heart: 'Was I still in time to save my goods? That question was in my heart . . .' (p. 299). He goes to the final interview and there, through some strange 'optical trick', he has a startling vision:

> Now I perceived it; I can scarcely tell how it startled me. She stood in the middle of the room with a face of mildness bent upon me, and her look of forgiveness, of absolution made her angelic. It beautified her; she was younger; she was not a ridiculous old woman. This optical trick gave her a sort of phantasmagoric brightness . . . . (p. 300)

It is a vision that might have lasted if Tita Bordereau had not had the 'force of soul', as he calls it (and the idea of the compliant 'Miss Tita with force of soul was a new conception'), to tell him the 'great thing' she has done.

> 'I have done the great thing. I have destroyed the papers.'
> 'Destroyed them?' I faltered.
> 'Yes; what was I to keep them for? I burnt them last night, one by one, in the kitchen.'
> 'One by one?' I repeated, mechanically.
> 'It took a long time – there were so many.' The room seemed to go round me as she said this and a real darkness for a moment descended upon my eyes. When it passed Miss Tita was there still, but the transfiguration was over and she had changed back to a plain, dingy, elderly person.   (p. 301)[20]

When Miss Tita declares that she has burnt the papers and in that she has done 'the great thing', she affirms something in two apparently different senses: on the one hand, she declares something to be the case, a fact, an event, a truth. 'I burnt them last night, one by one, in the kitchen', This affirmation of fact is preceded, on the other hand, by a different and seemingly tautological affirmation. With 'I have done the great thing', she says in effect: I myself affirm that I have done this affirmatively, with a greatness of love for the great thing I was doing, performing, bringing into the world, and here I repeat all this to you, in my truthful declaration or confession to you of what I have done. Unlike the confession of a fact, this other affirmation does not merely confirm a state of affairs, an event or a fact that pre-exists the statement. It affirms also that it affirms its own act. It says, yes, yes, I sign this event. I *love* it. I myself love what I have done.

But still, can we know what the 'great thing' is that she has done? Is it an act of destruction? An act of preservation? Of revenge? Of memory? Of forgetting? Of forgiveness? Or, if indeed it is *great*, then wouldn't that have to be the *possibility* of any one and all of those things, a possibility that can only be *declared* or *opened* by some kind of affirmation? Here, then, with this double affirmation or double declaration, *The Aspern Papers* addresses the possibility of love beyond what any subject can want to mean by it. 'I have done the great thing' it says. The text constitutes itself as text, in excess of any subject's discourse, with this affirmation that can never be mistaken for a statement of fact or mere opinion. This is because the distinguishing border between the two kinds of affirmation depends *in fact* on a fiction, on the fiction according to which Tita Bordereau can be believed when she says she has burned the papers, or even when she says that they ever existed. If we *can* believe her, if that possibility exists, it exists only in fiction, that is, *as and in a fictional text.* As such a text, then, it would suspend the difference between the affirmative declaration of 'greatness' and the affirmation of the truth of fact, of 'what really happened'. In 'reality', what has 'burned' is but a *figure* in the text for itself. The self-affirmation of the self-loving greatness of the text for what it has done, for the text it is and for the text that is signed. This is the seal burned into the text, turned into a text. The allegorizing figure of self-love has to let itself burn up and to love the growing pile of ashes. Only then has it done a great thing, affirmed nothing but the affirmation itself, so that it may repeat: yes, yes.

Yes, yes, they burned, one by one, each one, each singular one. And already, yes, one by one, they begin to repeat mechanically: ' "One by one?", I repeated, mechanically'. If this is the heart of the text, it is also an artificial or mechanical heart.

But this cannot surprise us altogether because 'the great thing' is done *in* a text and *by* a text, the artifice, fiction or allegory we have been reading, one by one. Or rather, *not* one by one but all shoved together into a bundle behind the scrutinizing mask of critical commentary, as if there were only one pair of eyes able to take in the whole complex scene. Can such coldly analytic, selective, reductive, *non-singularizing* commentary ever declare love to the text it takes as its object? That seems very unlikely, which is why we will not risk any more of it here. We have already said that we love this text, *too much.*

——To whom or to what do you think you have said it?
——Look there: on the shelf, its pages yellow around the borders, their acid beginning to consume them, a cheap (i.e., non-scholarly) volume titled *Great Short Works of Henry James.* Who ever came up with such a great title? Who could have authored such a thing?
——If you really want to know, write to the publisher.
——Oh, you scoundrel you!

NOTES

1. For instance, the ethical philosopher Martha C. Nussbaum has evinced how much she clings to this notion. Quoting Zarathustra's model, 'Of all that is written, I love only what a man has written with his blood', she characterizes her reaction to, in her terms, 'Derrida's perceptive and witty analysis of Nietzsche's style' in *Eperons*: 'After reading Derrida and not Derrida alone, I feel a certain hunger for blood; for, that is, writing about literature that talks of human lives and choices as if they matter to us all' (Nussbaum, 1990, p. 171). In other words: too much attention to textuality leads to bloodlessness. But is that a good or a bad thing? Says who?

2. 'How to love anything other than the possibility of ruin? Than an impossible totality)?' Nicholas Royle quotes these lines from Derrida's *Memoirs of the Blind* before advancing his own affirmation of the phrase he once heard Derrida pronounce, at another improvised discussion: 'Deconstruction is love'. Royle writes: 'Deconstruction is love. That would be the final aphorism here, but only on condition that it could never be mine – or Jacques Derrida's either' (Royle, 1995, pp. 139–40).

3. The discussion from which these remarks are taken followed a lecture by Derrida on Nietzsche's signature: 'Otobiographies: The Teaching of Nietzsche and the Politics of the Proper Name', trans. Avital Ronell, in Derrida (1985).

4. For Bill Martin, the limits of a 'fully predictive science' appear with the example of love. He writes: 'For example, if all of the physical, and even chemical determinants of a loving relationship could be specified, and if such a relationship could be fully contextualized in terms of economic, political, and other material factors, would we have really described even one instance of love?' (Martin, 1995, p. 17). Martin appears to suggest, however, that his 'example' is just one among many he might have chosen.

5. In both the original French and the English translation, the phrasing can be construed as meaning it is he himself who accompanies this gesture, he accompanies it by and as affirmation; deconstruction, therefore, is not just something he *does* but something he accompanies affirmatively. And therefore something that accompanies him. If this were an essay, necessarily interminable, on 'love' in the writings of Jacques Derrida, then among all the other texts one would have to invoke and attempt to read is *Politics of Friendship* and in particular a chapter titled, with echoes of Blanchot, 'The one who accompanies me'. See Derrida (1997).

6. Does the distinction between the partiality of love and impartial justice hold up or is it also deconstructible? That question may be addressed in Derrida's essay on justice, which evokes the idea of undeconstructible justice, the justice deconstruction is mad about, perhaps even madly in love with. 'This "idea of justice" seems to me to be irreducible in its affirmative character, in its demand of gift without exchange, without circulation, without recognition or gratitude, without economic circularity, without calculation and without rules, without reason and without rationality. And so we can recognize in it, indeed accuse, identify a madness. . . . And deconstruction is mad about this kind of justice. Mad about this desire for justice' (Derrida, 1990, p. 965).

7. We should note, however, that as an affirmation of love, in all its infinite manners, the marking force of the idiom bears little resemblance to what in common psychological parlance is called 'self-affirmation'. Indeed, if that popular pedagogical or pop-psychological slogan means, as it very often appears to, the self's triumphal movement out from under the sway of others, then the affirmation of love's idiom admits, and affirms, a contrary movement.

8. Derrida, 1997, p. 228.
9. The order of acceptation in the OED records first this 'proper',.sense, the most widely understood sense: 'That disposition or state of feeling *with regard to a person* which (arising from recognition of attractive qualities, from instincts of natural relationship, or from sympathy) manifests itself in solicitude for the welfare of the object, and usually also in delight in his or her presence and desire for his or her approval; warm affection, attachment'. Emphases added to the key or determining phrase here: 'with regard to a person'. Consider, however, the first sense in the French *Robert*, which prefers 'humanized entity' to 'person': 'Disposition à vouloir le bien d'une entité humanisée (Dieu, le prochain, l'humanité, la patrie) et à se dévouer à elle'.
10. But also – whyever not? – soap operas, fanzines, rave music, whatever.
11. For an unflinching, even a *cruel* (i.e., bloody) analysis of *Romeo and Juliet*, see Derrida (1992).
12. In particular, in Derrida (1973).
13. Deconstructive thought does not deny this condition of iterability but affirms it, because iterability is also the possibility of addressing love to another. This is doubtless the principal reason such thinking has been excoriated as 'negative'.
14. In the chapter 'The One Who Accompanies Me' in *Politics of Friendship*, Derrida characterizes what is 'most beautiful and most inevitable about the most impossible declaration of love', one which would declare love by *prescribing* that the other be free not to respond, 'for', he writes, 'I need his or her freedom in order to address myself to the other as other, in desire as well as in renunciation'. But since the prescription in advance cancels the freedom it prescribes, this declaration of love remains the most impossible. For a brief discussion of this passage, see Kamuf (1996, p. 199).
15. 'I can arrive at the papers only by putting her off her guard, and I can put her off her guard only by diplomatic practices. Hypocrisy, duplicity are my only chance. I am sorry for it, but for Jeffrey Aspern's sake, I tackle the main job' (James, 1996, p. 222).
16. Such figures, in other words, provoke 'that impulse of identification which is indispensable for reading' that Derrida mentions in the passage we quoted at the beginning of this essay.
17. This detail of the 'button' is alone enough to justify comparing this text's secret or not-so-secret economy to that of Poe's 'Purloined Letter' in which a 'trumpery filigree card-rack of pasteboard . . . hung dangling by a dirty blue ribbon, from a little brass knob just beneath the middle of the mantle-piece'. Rather than holding a 'trumpery filigree card-rack', rather, that is, than this dangling apparatus in which Lacan, at least, identifies the phallus of the woman, James's text places the button on a secretary, a piece of furniture but also someone, most often a woman, who, like Miss Tita with her aunt, accompanies another, writes another's letters, and keeps another's secrets. Whereas Poe's narrative needs someone like Dupin to put his hands on the hidden letter, James's has the force, 'the force of soul' perhaps, to depict the inviolable secret of the secretary.
18. Because, as was suggested in the previous note, James's novel shares many features with Poe's 'The Purloined Letter', central elements of Derrida's famous analysis of the latter can be carried over to the former. In particular, there would be much more to say in a longer reading of *The Aspern Papers* with regard to this structure of the non-arrival of a letter even when it has apparently arrived at its destination. See Derrida (1986).
19. A less rapid discussion of this text could bring out that such a state of non-dec-

laration, specifically, the withheld or secret declaration of love, informs all the interactions among the three characters.
20. This fading of the erotic hallucination could call to mind the sort of deconstruction of sense certainty that Paul de Man has elaborated through an attention to textual figurality. He writes, for example, in his essay on Rousseau's *Nouvelle Héloïse*: 'Like "man" "love" is a figure that disfigures, a metaphor that confers the illusion of proper meaning to a suspended, open semantic structure. In the naïvely referential language of the affections, this makes love into the forever-repeated chimera, the monster of its own aberration, always oriented toward the future of its repetition, since the undoing of the illusion only sharpens the uncertainty that created the illusion in the first place' (de Man, 1979, p. 198); and in a note to an essay on Michael Riffaterre's notion of hypogram, 'Rather than being a heightened version of sense experience, the erotic is a figure that makes such experience possible. We do not see what we love but we love in the hope of confirming the illusion that we are indeed seeing anything at all' (de Man, 1986, p. 53; my thanks to Nicholas Royle, for reminding me of this note).

WORKS CITED

de Man, Paul (1979), *Allegories of Reading: Figural Language in Rousseau, Nietzsche, Rilke, and Proust* (New Haven, CT: Yale University Press).
—— (1986), 'Hypogram and Inscription', in *The Resistance to Theory* (Minneapolis, MN: University of Minnesota Press).
Derrida, Jacques (1973), *Speech and Phenomena*, trans. David B. Allison (Evanston, IL: Northwestern University Press).
—— (1985), *The Ear of the Other: Otobiography, Transference, Translation*, trans. Peggy Kamuf (New York: Schocken Books).
—— (1986), 'Le Facteur de la Vérité', in *The Post Card: From Socrates to Freud and Beyond*, trans. Alan Bass (Chicago, IL: University of Chicago Press).
—— (1990), 'Force of Law: The "Mystical Foundation of Authority"', trans. Mary Quaintance, *Cardozo Law Review*, vol. 11, nos 5–6 (July/Aug.)
—— (1992), 'Aphorism Countertime', trans. Nicholas Royle, in *Acts of Literature*, ed. Derek Attridge (New York and London: Routledge).
—— (1997), *Politics of Friendship*, trans. George Collins, (London: Verso).
James, Henry (1996), *Great Short Works of Henry James* (New York: Harper and Row).
Kamuf, Peggy (1996), 'Derrida on Television', in *Applying: To Derrida*, ed. John Brannigan *et al.* (London: Macmillan Press).
Martin, Bill (1995), *Humanism and Its Aftermath: The Shared Fate of Deconstruction and Politics* (Atlantic Highlands, NJ: Humanities Press).
Nancy, Jean-Luc (1990), 'L'amour en éclats', in *Une pensée finie* (Paris: Galilée).
Nussbaum, Martha C. (1990), *Love's Knowledge: Essays on Philosophy and Literature* (New York and Oxford: Oxford University Press).
Royle, Nicholas (1995), *After Derrida* (Manchester: Manchester University Press).

10

Deconstruction and a Poem

J. Hillis Miller

Le poème échoit, bénédiction, venue de l'autre. [The poem falls, benediction, come from the other, the coming of the other.]
Jacques Derrida, 'Che cos'è la poesia?'

A poem comes by fate or by chance. lt 'befalls' the one who receives it, like a benediction, that is, like words that confer a blessing or that invoke a blessing. Benediction means, literally, speaking well, usually of some person, not of some thing. A benediction invokes what comes from the other or is the coming of the other, subjective and objective genitive at once. The 'other' in question here is that wholly other about which Derrida writes, tautologically, in *The Gift of Death*: 'tout autre est tout autre'. This means, among other possibilities, 'every other is wholly other' (see Derrida, 1992a, pp. 79–108; Derrida, 1995a, pp. 82–115). We usually think of the 'other' as just somewhat different, for example someone from a different culture. For Derrida the other in question in a poem's benediction is entirely different, 'wholly other'. The consequences of accepting such a notion are not trivial. Something wholly other is frighteningly alien, unassimilable. Nevertheless, Derrida argues that a poem comes from such a wholly other and speaks for it. Just what that might mean this essay will try to show.

My title says 'deconstruction and a poem' rather than 'deconstruction and poetry' for several reasons. I shall be responding to the benediction of a single poem, W. B. Yeats's 'The Cold Heaven'. Moreover, a feature of so-called 'deconstruction' is that, for the most part, it takes its poems one at a time rather than making pronouncements about 'poetry'. In addition, the words 'poetry', 'poésie' (French), 'poesia' (both Italian and Spanish), 'Dichtung' (German) are notoriously equivocal. Aristotle used the Greek equivalent, 'poiesis', making, to name the whole field of what today, and for only a little more than two hundred years, we in the West have called 'literature', 'littérature', 'letteratura', 'literatura', 'Literatur'. 'Poetry' is still sometimes used in this extended sense to name in general any special use of language that involves 'literarity', whatever *that* is. I take it my learned friend Nicholas Royle, in charging me to write about 'deconstruction and poetry', means primarily if not exclusively lyric poetry. He means those conglomerations of words marked by rhythmic, semantic and sonorous repetitions (rhyme, assonance, alliteration, etc.) and printed in odd or conventional ways, line by line, with blank spaces around. You can tell a poem when you see one, on the page, even if it is an abstract from a newspaper or from a telephone book arranged 'poetically', as a 'found poem':

> Blue Angels Youth Ski and Snowboard Program;
> Blue Auto Glass;
> Blue B;
> Blue Beet Café The;
> Blue Bell Foundation for Cats;
> Blue Bell Pools;
> Blue Betty PhD;
> Blue Bird Motel & Cafe.[1]

That such a fortuitous set of words can be 'taken as a poem' indicates that 'poetry', in the narrow sense, is both an intrinsic feature of certain words taken together and at the same time the product of a complex set of historical determinations. It is not the case that I am free to take anything I like as poetry. Rather, a large overdetermined set of collective conventions and rules acts through me to lead me to take a given group of words as a poem and treat it as such. These rules and conventions are historically situated, for example in relation to certain technological regimes. They change from time to time, from country to country, and from language to language. Poetry is a subset of what we have meant by 'literature' in the West since the eighteenth century. As such, it is associated, as Jacques Derrida has cogently argued, with democracy and with freedom of speech (Derrida, 1992b, pp. 36–39; Derrida, 1993a, pp. 63–71, 89–91; Derrida, 1995c, pp. 27–31; pp.142–44). Freedom of speech would include the privilege, never of course perfectly realized, to say anything, to put anything in question, and not to be held responsible for it, to disclaim responsibility in the name of another responsibility or a responsibility to the other. I can always say, 'That was not me speaking. That was an imaginary or fictive voice speaking in my poem. I wrote out of an obligation to the wholly other'. This excuse, I hasten to add, would not exonerate someone hailed before one or another of the censoring powers that exist even now in democratic countries. Nevertheless, if Derrida is right in historicizing literature this way, it would follow that poetry in 'our' sense did not exist prior to the development of Western-style democracies. Poetry in the modem Western sense, contrary to received opinion, did not exist, for example, in classical Greece or in medieval Europe, nor does it exist now in all non-Western parts of the world. What looks like poetry in those cases had or has different constraints and functions. Poetry could cease to exist and civilization would not come to an end. In so far as what we mean by poetry belongs to the post-Cartesian epoch of print culture in the West, that is, the period of a particular subject/object dichotomy strongly reinforced or even generated by the technology of the printed book, what we call 'poetry' may now be coming to an end. This is happening as print technology is replaced by television, cinema, VCRs, computers and the Internet, in short by the new regime of telecommunications.

Within print culture, poetry as a subcategory of literature depends on the possibility of suspending in a given case the 'transcendental' or referential force that all language has and attending to the words in themselves, as a benediction from the other, the coming of the wholly other. My telephone-book poem exemplifies that. In the real world one might urgently need to order something from the Blue Beet Café, or to make a contribution (or send a cat) to the Blue Bell Foundation for Cats, or enlist the services of Dr Betty Blue. In that case the accuracy of the telephone numbers listed with each entry would be crucial. As Paul de Man observes, an 'irresistible motion . . . forces any text beyond its limits and projects it towards an exterior referent' (de Man, 1979, p. 70). We use the telephone book to make telephone calls. When the extract I have cited (omitting the numbers) is taken as a poem, however, those pragmatic uses are not so much abolished (that cannot be) as short-circuited. A poem is like an extract from a fictional telephone book or, rather, like an extract from a telephone book whose truth or fictionality does not determine its literary function or lack of it. As a poem my citation would work just as well even if there were no such thing as the Blue Bell Foundation for Cats or the Blue Beet Café. The power of Henry James's *The Wings of the Dove* does not depend on whether or not Kate Croy, Merton Densher and Milly Theale were 'based on' real people, nor does the power of Yeats's 'The Cold Heaven' depend on whether or not the 'experience' 'recorded' in the poem 'really happened' to Yeats, though much criticism in both cases and in most other such cases mistakenly assumes that it does.

These assertions must not be misunderstood. 'The Cold Heaven', *The Wings of the Dove* and my telephone-book 'poem' are all deeply embedded in history, surrounded by complex, overdetermined historical contexts. As I have said, the possibility of taking them as literary works depends on specific historical conditions and expectations. The inalienable referential or mimetic dimension of language, however, is in literature turned or troped to become what I call performative catachreses for that 'wholly other' Derrida names. A catachresis is a name taken from its ordinary referential use and transposed to name something that has no literal name, as when we say 'face of a mountain' or 'headland' or 'chair arm'. The catachreses in literature are performative in two senses. They are speech acts in response to the demand made on the poet by the 'tout autre'. They give names to a wholly other that does not have any given names. The poem or novel whenever it is read then re-enters history, intervening not just to mirror history but to alter it performatively, in however minuscule a way. What we call history is generated by innumerable such small performative speech acts.

I shall return later by way of my example from Yeats to the question of what implications this transformation of the referential force of language might have. Now I must stress the important role poetry in the narrow sense has played in the work of the chief writers who represent so-called deconstruction. I shall take Paul de Man and Jacques Derrida to 'stand for' deconstruction. If any writers represent deconstruction – indeed more than simply 'represent' it by synecdoche, part for whole – they do. One strange but widespread canard is the notion that neither de Man nor Derrida is interested in literature, and neither therefore *a fortiori* is interested in poetry. They are, we are told, philosophers or theorists, never literary critics. They use literature to make philosophical or theoretical points (Gasché, 1979; 1986, pp. 2–3; Loesberg, 1991). The effect of this allows those who study or read poetry to breathe a sigh of relief and say, 'Thank heaven. I don't need to read all that difficult stuff. It belongs to a different discipline'. The truth is otherwise. It is easy to demonstrate that 'close readings' of poems, acts not of theory but of literary exegesis, have played a crucial role in the work of both de Man and Derrida, not to speak of work by associates such as Barbara Johnson, Andrzej Warminski, Cynthia Chase or myself, such as it is (Johnson, 1979; Warminski, 1987; Chase, 1986; Miller, 1985), along with work by many others influenced by so-called deconstruction. De Man produced 'readings' of poems by Yeats, Mallarmé, Rilke, Wordsworth, Hölderlin, Hugo and Baudelaire. Derrida has done the same for poems by Mallarmé, Baudelaire, Ponge, Angelus Silesius and Celan. (Selections from all of these but the Silesius are conveniently collected in English translations in Derek Attridge's anthology, *Acts of Literature* [Derrida, 1992b]. For Angelus Silesius see Derrida (1995b), 'Sauf le nom', trans. John P. Leavey, Jr., in *On the Name*, pp. 33–85; Derrida, (1993b), *Sauf le nom*.) These readings look like literary criticism to me, not philosophy or theory. To say this assumes we can make clear distinctions among these, which of course we cannot, except arbitrarily and with a certain violence. What we call philosophy and theory always enter into any reading of a poem, even into readings that are the least philosophical or theoretical in appearance.

What can be said of these acts of criticism that take poems as their objects? Four features stand out. First: both de Man and Derrida respect the idiosyncrasy, the idiomatic singularity, of the poems they read. Whatever generalizations they make are based on this respect. Such respect might be defined by saying it springs from a belief that each poem takes the reader to a certain place that can be reached in no other way.

Secondly: it follows from this respect that each critic pays the closest

attention to details of the poems read, to nuances of semantic, etymolog-
ical and figural implication, to apparently trivial words like 'and' or 'for'.
One example is de Man's comment on 'thing', 'now', and 'she' in
Wordsworth's 'A Slumber Did My Spirit Seal' (de Man, 1983, pp. 224–5).
Another example is Derrida's elaborate unfolding of various meanings in
the word 'für (for)' as used in a poem by Celan: ' "Für", c'est donc le mot
à la fois le plus décisif et le plus indécidable du poème'. (' "Für", this is
therefore at once the most decisive and the most undecidable word in the
poem') (ms, p. 25). The idiosyncratic is exemplified in the idiomatic, in the
special way each poem has with words. The procedures of these critics
might be described as a hyperbolic exploitation of traditions of New
Critical close reading, or, rather, it might be better to say, since both are
Europeans, these critics exploit hyperbolically the European or specifically French tradition of 'explication du texte'. One reason de Man and
Derrida choose poems is that they are short enough to read in detail.

Thirdly: each critic tends to involve the poem chosen in a certain problematic that the poem itself generates: the problematic of signature, for
example, in Derrida's discussion of Ponge, or the relation of dates to the
poetic event and its iterability in his book on Celan, or the relation of allegory to temporality in de Man's reading of Wordsworth's 'A Slumber Did
My Spirit Seal' in 'The Rhetoric of Temporality', or the figure of
prosopopoeia and its implications in two poems by Baudelaire in de
Man's 'Anthropomorphism and Trope in the Lyric' (Derrida, 1984, 1986;
de Man, 1983, pp. 223–25; de Man, 1984, pp. 239–62).

Fourth feature: both critics appropriate speech act theory and twist that
from its conventional definitions in what they say about poems. Each, in
different ways, sees poems not just as constative or descriptive but also as
performative. A poem is a speech act of a peculiar kind. It makes something happen, perhaps something irreversible, for the reader who reads it
seriously, responsibly, with his or her whole heart, as they say. Doing so
has its dangers, however, and most people, perhaps wisely, guard themselves from taking poems too seriously. De Man and Derrida do not so
guard themselves. They expose themselves to the power of the poem as
speech act, bearing witness to that power and passing the poem's benediction on to the reader in their criticism as another demand for respon-
sive, responsible reading.

Acts of reading by both de Man and Derrida are crucial to the
encounter of what is for each writer an enigmatic pivot around which all
their work turns. I say 'enigmatic', because for both critics this pivot is all-
important and at the same time difficult to grasp, perhaps even impossi-
ible to understand, perhaps not amenable to rational comprehension.
Writing readings of poems is a way for de Man and Derrida to respond to
a kind of black hole of unintelligibility or non-knowledge at the motivat-
ing centre of their work. Around that absent or non-phenomenal centre

the work of each critic rotates, strongly attracted by it but at the same time called or invoked by it to write what is outside it, what stands in the light or emits light, elucidation, that is, the reading. The reading leads to formulas that are twisted or invaded by a darkness that is generating the light. In the case of de Man, this black hole is what he calls 'the prosaic materiality of the letter', as he encounters it, for example, in the way Victor Hugo's poem, 'Écrit sur la vitre d'une fenêtre flamande', is, literally, inscribed, scratched on a windowglass (de Man, 1986, pp. 50–1). In the case of Derrida, the black hole is what he calls the coming of the wholly other, that occurs as the happening of the impossible, for example in the reading of Ponge's short poem, 'Fable', in 'Psyche: Invention of the Other' (Derrida, 1987, pp. 17–61). 'Fable' is a strange speech act that works to 'laisser venir l'aventure ou l'événement du tout autre (to let the adventure or the event of the wholly other come)' (ibid., p. 61). This event is 'impossible' in the sense that it is the occurrence of something unforeseen and unforeseeable, something that cannot be predicted or programmed beforehand. This means it cannot be assimilated into what is already known. For both de Man and Derrida, though in different ways, the benediction of the poem culminates in a non-knowledge.

What I have given so far is an account of what happens when two critics who 'represent' deconstruction, if anyone does, encounter poems. I turn now to attempt a reading as further exemplification of what is always to some degree sui generis, an example only of itself, a poem as read. I choose W. B. Yeats's 'The Cold Heaven'. It comes from his 1914 volume, *Responsibilities*. Here is the poem:

The Cold Heaven

Suddenly I saw the cold and rook-delighting heaven
That seemed as though ice burned and was but the more ice,
And thereupon imagination and heart were driven
So wild that every casual thought of that and this
Vanished, and left but memories, that should be out of season
With the hot blood of youth, of love crossed long ago;
And I took the blame out of all sense and reason,
Until I cried and trembled and rocked to and fro,
Riddled with light. Ah! when the ghost begins to quicken,
Confusion of the death-bed over, is it sent
Out naked on the roads, as the books say, and stricken
By the injustice of the skies for punishment?

                                              (Yeats, 1977, p. 316)

This poem is characteristic not only of Yeats, but of the Romantic lyric tradition he inherited. Yeats's work is, according to Pater's formula in

'Aesthetic Poetry', a 'strange second flowering after date' of that tradition (Pater, 1889, p. 213). The poem presents itself as the record in the past tense of a powerful subjective event that happened at some indeterminate time in the past. This event was generated by the confrontation of something in nature, the winter sky.[2] The poem is not so much emotion recollected in tranquillity, as Wordsworth said a poem should be, as it is emotion recollected in agitation. Memory, for Yeats, and its expression in words, repeat the emotion, renew it. The speaker is agitated even at the beginning of the poem, not just at its end. 'Suddenly', it seems, may name the now of the speaker's speech, or the writer's writing, as well as the moment in the past when he suddenly saw the cold and rook-delighting heaven. Six times intersect or are superimposed in 'suddenly': the moment of the original event commemorated in the poem, the earlier time, 'of love crossed long ago' that was remembered and renewed in that event, the now of the putative speaker's speech, the now of the writing of the poem, the anticipated moment of death, and the reader's repetition of all these in their overlapping when the poem is read or recited. The last of the six is indicated, it may be, in the perpetual present of the title. The poem asks how all these are related, after a sudden insight that they *are* related.

'Suddenly' and 'sudden' are recurrent words in Yeats's poetry. They are used to name the moment of poetic vision, as in the first words of 'Leda and the Swan': 'A sudden blow' (Yeats, 1977, p. 441), or as in climactic lines in 'Vacillation': 'While on the shop and street I gazed/My body of a sudden blazed' (Yeats, 1977, p. 501). Like Wordsworth, Yeats focuses on a moment of visionary interruption and breakthrough. In that moment ordinary indifference to one's surroundings is for some reason shattered. Suddenly one *sees*. In Wordsworth this often happens at the moment of breakdown of an expected reciprocity between self and its surroundings, as in 'The Boy of Winander' or as in De Quincey's report of Wordsworth listening with his ear to the ground for the expected mail cart and not hearing it (De Quincey, 1970, p. 160). In a more exalted form, the crossing of the Simplon Pass in *The Prelude* is such an abrupt interruption and breakthrough. It is when the expected does not happen that the sudden visionary insight occurs. Paradoxically, you see what is there or you see through what is there when the subject/object mirroring breaks down. Rather than making nature a mirror in which you see your own excited face, to alter a figure Yeats uses in 'The Symbolism of Poetry' (Yeats, 1961, p. 163), nature now enters into a subjectivity that has been emptied out. Or the naked power of that subjectivity appears when nature no longer reflects and supports it. Consciousness becomes mirror of the non-personified, deathly impersonality of nature. This nature, called in this poem the 'cold heaven', may delight the rooks but it delights not the normal 'I' that can easily and unselfconsciously appropriate nature, for example by personifying it. In reporting this afterwards you can or must say, 'Suddenly I saw'. Wordsworth's personification of nature: 'And then my heart with pleasure fills/And dances with the daffodils' (Wordsworth, 1966, p. 149) is by comparison a relatively tame reciprocity.

'The Cold Heaven' figures the injustice of the skies in the combination of contradictories, ice and fire, that brings visionary insight ('Suddenly I saw') if one takes the blame out of all sense and reason. This recalls the catharsis of tragedy, for example in those dramas of *Oedipus the King* and *Oedipus at Colonus* that Yeats adapted for modern stage performances. In Sophoclean tragedy the protagonist retains or regains his freedom by taking the blame and punishment for something he has been fated to do, but has done without meaning to do it, without knowing he did it, has done without doing it. Oedipus did not mean to kill his father and marry his mother. Nevertheless Jocasta hangs herself and Oedipus blinds himself as self-punishment for crimes they did not knowingly or intentionally commit. The 'love crossed long ago' was not Yeats's fault, but he takes the blame, out of all sense and reason.

A slightly closer look at 'The Cold Heaven' shows that the little word 'and', the copula, occurs an amazing number of times – eleven, to be exact – whereas, for example, in the poem just previous in *Responsibilities*, 'Friends', the word occurs only twice, though that poem is longer: 'The cold and rook-delighting heaven'; 'as though ice burned and was but the more ice'; 'And thereupon imagination and heart were driven'; 'every casual thought of that and this'; 'Vanished, and left but memories'; 'And I took the blame'; 'out of all sense and reason.' The 'ands' rise to a climax with 'Until I cried and trembled and rocked to and fro', three ands in a single line. After the 'Ah!' that comes next, only one more 'and' appears ['and stricken'] – as though the need for 'and' had exhausted itself for some reason in that 'Ah!'

Why all these 'ands'? Are they the sign of narrative progression or perhaps of non-progressive metonymic side-by-sideness or contingency? First this and then that. This and that and that and that, one after the other. It might seem so from lines three, five and seven: 'And thereupon'; 'and left but memories'; 'And I took the blame'. Or perhaps these ands indicate a causal progression. Suddenly he saw the cold and rook-delighting heaven 'and thereupon' something happened that was a result of the seeing. Or are the 'ands' not rather, in several cases at any rate, the sign of an alternation, a vacillation between what look like extremes, opposites: 'this and that'; 'to and fro'. Does the 'and' not join in a copula what only appear to be opposites, so that 'x and y' expresses an unfolded or elaborated oxymoron? This heaven is 'cold', inhospitable, detached, inhuman, unsympathetic. At the same time it delights the rooks. The cold heaven is the rooks' element. It seems warm to them. The heaven is 'cold and rook-delighting'. The second line unfolds the implicit oxymoron 'fiery ice' in 'seemed as though ice burned and was but the more ice'. This is no natural heaven. It seems icy cold and at the same time fiery hot. Other nouns paired by the copula, 'and', seem, however, perhaps mere poetic redundancies. In any case they are not obviously opposites, so the reader's mind puzzles over them. Fire and ice are clearly opposites, but what is the difference between 'imagination' and 'heart', or between 'sense' and 'reason'? The first eight lines of the poem seem to exploit all these different uses of 'and', alternating from one to another. The 'and' of alternation ultimately dominates, as casual thoughts of that and this were transformed, when he took the blame out of all sense and reason, into an oscillation so rapid that it became an incandescent blur that almost reduced all language to 'and, and, and, and', as he 'cried and trembled and rocked to and fro/Riddled with light'. At that moment of taking fire, 'and' has been heard so often that it is becoming empty of sense. The word has been taken out of all sense and reason and approaches pure sound. 'And' then is transformed into the senseless violence of an involuntary exclamation: 'Ah!', the first phoneme of 'And' without the second differentiating one that makes it an articulate word: 'Say Ah!' 'Ah!' is said with 'bouche ouverte', an open mouth to modulate as little as possible the sound of expelled breath from low in the throat. *The American Heritage Dictionary* defines 'Ah' as an interjection 'used to express various emotions, such as surprise, delight, pain, satisfaction, or dislike'. 'Ah!' is a double or antithetical word, combining opposites. It can be the expression of extreme physical pleasure but also marks the moment of expiration when the ghost is exhaled at the instant of death. You die a little death every time you say, or are forced to say, 'Ah!' All the merely sequential elements in the poem, all the causal followings (this and thereupon that), all the opposites both outside (fire and ice) and inside (imagination and heart), come together in the nonsense of that 'Ah!' 'Ah!' is the register of a visionary insight beyond all sense and reason. 'And' returns like a secret refrain, beneath the overt prosody, punctuating the poem rhythmically in counterpoint until its incandescent transformation into visionary insight happens in a moment of radical caesura or halt in the rhythm, dividing before from after and leading to the proleptic question: 'And . . . and . . . and . . . and . . . Ah! Is the soul . . . ?' That 'Ah!' marks the moment of a tense shift from past to present, to the present now of the speaker who asks his urgent question about the future moment of death.

'Visionary insight' into what? Just how is the insight achieved or how does it come about? The title names the scene, 'The Cold Heaven'. In early printings of the poem, 'Heaven' was capitalized within the poem, but in most late printings not. It seems as if Yeats had to have his heaven both ways and could not quite decide between the two. He alternated to and fro between them. 'Heaven' is of course a double word, as it was conspicuously for Wordsworth, as in 'The Boy of Winander'. 'Cold Heaven' names the actual natural sky on a wintry day. It also names a place of supernatural power and judgement. The word 'H/heaven' itself is a place of ambiguous alternation.

That folding of incompatibles in a single word mimes in miniature the way the poem concentrates entire regions from Yeats's life and thought. Each is squeezed in by synecdoche to make an explosive mixture. This is a regular feature of Yeats's work, one of the ways he gets concentration and power, even self-deconstructing violence, in his poems. In 'The Cold Heaven' the phrase 'love crossed long ago' contains in miniature, it may be (though the poem does not explicitly say so), the long story of Yeats's failed courtship of Maud Gonne, to whom he formally proposed marriage over and over again, only to be rejected again and again. 'Sent out naked on the roads' is a part standing for the whole of Yeats's esoteric ideas about the soul's adventures after death, with 'roads' containing all Yeats's ideas about the circling gyres, the trajectory or journey of the soul, as well as a possible covert allusion to the Sphinx's riddle, and to the place where three roads intersect, the crossroads where Oedipus killed Laius. One section of Yeats's *Autobiographies* is called 'Hodos Camelion-tos', the road of the chameleon. All this 'context' is buried in that one word 'roads'. The poem exploits these concentrating powers of the synec-dochic in enacting a to and fro that builds up to a moment that takes fire 'suddenly' when contradictory elements are brought together and fused, like fire and ice, guiltlessness and guilt, freedom and necessity, responsi-bility and passive suffering, this-worldly experience of a certain weather on a certain day in Ireland and other-worldly experiences of the soul after death.

The poem ends then with an urgent, unanswered and perhaps unan-swerable question. Is the newly quickened ghost 'sent/Out naked on the roads, as the books say, and stricken/By the injustice of the skies for pun-ishment?' This is not a rhetorical question, as Harold Bloom avers (Bloom, 1970, p. 175). It is a real question, and a lot hangs on the answer. The poet would like to know. The reader would like to know too. In this climactic question 'skies' substitutes for 'heaven'. If the answer is an affirmative one, then 'skies' or 'heaven' becomes the emblem of a supernatural unjust judging power. On the other hand, a certain notion of the supernatural, what those old esoteric books Yeats read told him, is expressed in a strik-ing natural image. The ghost, confusion of the deathbed over, 'quickens' as an embryo is said to 'quicken' when it becomes viable, or as a seed quickens when it sprouts. The deathbed becomes figuratively a birthbed, perhaps even a bed of lovemaking leading to conception. The quickened ghost is then, in a powerfully naturalistic image, 'sent out naked on the roads', as if it were a naked person. There this quasi-person is stricken by the injustice of the skies for punishment, as every mother's son or daughter is born naked into a cold world, or as a naked living person outcast outside the safe enclosure of home might wander homeless on the roads and suffer cruelly from being out in the open, on the roads, in bad weather.

Another way to ask the question that ends the poem would be to ask which takes precedence here, natural image or supernatural emblem (to borrow the terms that organize de Man's reading of Yeats in 'Image and Emblem in Yeats' [de Man, 1984, pp. 145–238]). Is the human, natural scene, Yeats looking at a cold sky and imagining what it would be like to wander naked on the roads under such a cold heaven, an emblem of the experience by the 'ghost' after death of 'the injustice of the skies', or is it the other way around? If 'things below are copies' (Yeats, 1977, p. 556), nevertheless things above can only be named by human beings with the names of things below. 'Heaven' is at first the natural sky's name and then by transfer the name of a supernatural place. Which is the literal, which the figurative, heaven or Heaven? There is no way to know, and so the concluding question hovers interminably and unanswerably in the air. How could we know the answer until we are dead?

Dead men, however, tell no tales. The meaning of 'The Cold Heaven' is this undecidability, the impossibility of knowing whether the most extreme experiences, triggered by earthly memories, such as the experience this poem may possibly be thought to record of Yeats's memories of love crossed long ago, are copies of things above, immemorial memories, proleptic foretastes of the soul's experience after death, or whether there are certain purely human, bodily, experiences that make one tremble and rock to and fro, experiences so extreme that the only adequate expression in language for them is what the old books say, perhaps meretriciously, about what happens to the soul after death.

This uncertainty about which H(h)eaven is the emblem of which, is expressed in concentrated form in the marvellous climactic phrase, just before the 'Ah!': 'riddled with light'. The poem reaches that climax by a series of precisely and succinctly enumerated steps, each the necessary presupposition, so it seems, of the next. It is not entirely clear, however, just why the sudden seeing of the cold heaven should make the poet remember love crossed long ago, unless the sky's coldness and indifference is the emblem of the woman's repudiation, nor why that memory should lead him to take the blame out of all sense and reason. The sequence of events, nevertheless, could not happen in any other order. Each has to happen before the next can happen. Like the sequence of events in a Greek tragedy, *Oedipus the King* or *Oedipus at Colonus*, the series is fortuitous and necessary at once. The poet sees the cold sky that combines ice with fire, burning ice that is all the colder for burning. This drives his imagination and heart, that is, both his mental power of forming images, of imagining things, and his heart, his power of feeling, including sexual feeling, emotions that tie him to the earth, so 'wild' that 'every casual thought of that and this' 'vanishes' and all his powers of thinking, imagining and feeling are focused on memories of love crossed long ago. These memories are out of season in the sense that they are appropriate not for an ageing man but for the hot blood of youth. Those memories lead him to a decision, to an act, to a silent and therefore anomalous speech act. Though the 'crossing' of his love was not unambiguously his fault, any more than it was Oedipus's fault that he killed his father, married his mother and begat children who were his own brothers and sisters, nevertheless the poet 'took the blame out of all sense and reason', just as Oedipus took the blame on himself for the parricide and incest he did not mean to do and did not know he was doing. Implicitly the poet in 'The Cold Heaven' says: 'I did it, and I accept responsibility', though he does not, apparently, speak aloud, and though no witness attests to his speech act, except you and I as readers of the poem. This taking the blame is an odd and anomalous speech act. It is private and mute, unless the 'Ah!' can be taken as its speaking out. The poem itself articulates for us as readers the taking of blame. The poem records a singular and private experience. Turning it into poetry, however, makes it infinitely repeatable. The poem may be printed and reprinted, read over and over by thousands of different people all over the world. Does the speech act not reoccur every time the poem is read, happen again not as 'mention' but as 'use', in the endless iterability of the poem as benediction? The speech act is then transferred to the reader. It becomes through the recitation of the poem the reader's speech act, no longer Yeats's private one.

If it is such a speech act, what does it do? How is the poem when I read it a way of doing things with words? Only when the speaker takes the blame does what might be called the apotheosis occur: 'Until I cried and trembled and rocked to and fro/Riddled with light. Ah! . . .' The reader must repeat through reading this taking of blame if the poem is to work as benediction, the coming of the wholly other, a riddling of the reader with light. He or she must, like the speaker of the poem, take the blame out of the realm of sense and reason into the realm of unanswerable enigma, in another possible meaning of the phrase.

I call it an apotheosis because the poet is filled with light, penetrated by it, perforated by it, riddled by it, as in a moment of mystic illumination. It is an apotheosis in the sense of being filled by a god, though in this case an exceedingly dark and ominous god, an impersonal god of injustice, insoluble riddle and death. The *American Heritage Dictionary* gives three meanings for the first form of 'riddle' as a verb: 1. To pierce with numerous holes; perforate, as in *riddle with bullets*; 2. To put through a coarse sieve. (A riddle is a coarse sieve for separating or grading materials such as gravel and the like, as in *potato riddle*, a meaning quite likely known to Yeats); 3. To find or show weakness in; disprove or damage. Though

Yeats probably did not know it, the root is *skeri* meaning cut, separate, sift, also the root of words like crime and discriminate, discern, scribble and script, not to speak of crisis and critic, all words naming some act of sifting in the sense of dividing this from that, the sheep from the goats. To be riddled with light means not only to be penetrated, perforated, and filled with light, but also to be judged by it, as the speaker imagines the ghost after death stricken by the injustice of the skies as punishment for a crime he did not commit. To be riddled with light also no doubt invokes the other, etymologically unrelated, form of 'riddle' as 'a question or statement requiring thought to answer or understand; a conundrum. Something perplexing; an enigma', for example the Sphinx's riddle: 'What walks on four feet in the morning, two feet at noon, and three feet at the end of the day?' As a verb this second form of 'riddle' means either 'to solve or propound riddles' or 'to speak in riddles'. To be riddled with light is to have a perhaps unsolvable riddle propounded on one's body, to be riddled with a riddle. All good riddles obscurely or openly involve death, or are deadly to answer, as in the angry question posed by that goddess of crossroads, Hecate, to the three witches in *Macbeth* III,v: 'How did you dare / To trade and traffic with Macbeth / In riddles and affairs of death?' or in the way Oedipus in answering 'man' to the Sphinx's riddle was also unwittingly anticipating his own fate, to wander on the roads, self-blinded as a result of seeing too much, feeling his way with a stick, therefore walking on three legs, making his way on a journey leading ultimately to his death and apotheosis at Colonus. What the deadly riddle in 'The Cold Heaven' is, the reader knows. It is propounded in the question of the final lines: 'Is the ghost after death sent out naked on the roads, as the books say, and smitten by the injustice of the skies for punishment?' Well, is it, or is it not? The poet and the reader need urgently to know. No answer to the riddle is given, just as no answers are given to the riddles that end 'Among School Children' and 'Leda and the Swan'. The reader is left at his or her peril to hazard an answer, though to answer may be deadly.

What is that light that riddles the poet? What is its source? Far from illuminating the poet, this light puts him, it may be, in a permanent state of unseeing perplexity. It is a blinding light. The climactic cry of 'Ah!' that responds to being riddled with light is a strange kind of asemantic oxymoron. The light that riddles the poet is the diffused figure of that sun the wasteful virtues earn.[3] Among the wasteful virtues are being secret and taking defeat out of every brazen throat ('To a Friend whose Work has come to Nothing'), the desire to destroy the half-imagined, the half-written page and, in this poem, taking the blame out of all sense and reason. *Responsibilities* sets those reckless, spendthrift ancestors Yeats praises in several poems, or the reckless patriotism of Daniel O'Leary and other heroes of the long Irish fight against England, or Major Robert Gregory's sacrifice of his life as an Irish airman fighting for the English in the First World War, that is, fighting for a cause in which he did not believe, against the bourgeois shopkeepers (mostly Catholic) whom Yeats so detested for 'fumbling in a greasy till', for 'toiling to grow rich'. To say only the wasteful virtues earn the sun looks like saying you gain by throwing away, by spending as a spendthrift. In fact you gain, as poem after poem makes clear, nothing but death and the injustice of the cold heaven. This is affirmed overtly in the next poem after 'The Cold Heaven', 'That the Night Come', as well as, for example, in 'An Irish Airman Foresees His Death'. To put this in the terms of 'The Cold Heaven', you gain through taking the blame out of all sense and reason not the sun as gold, as the greatest value, as measure, logos, ratio, ruler, dispenser of justice, but rather the absent sun as absolute loss, as injustice, the injustice of the cold heaven. The sky in Yeats's poem is empty. The sun is nowhere overtly mentioned in the poem, though it must somehow be the source of the light that riddles the poet. The absent sun is present only in dispersed figure, as burning ice, or as the 'light' with which the poet is 'riddled'. Instead of earning the sun as a positive recompense through the wasteful virtue of taking the blame out of all sense and reason, the poet earns the injustice of the empty skies for punishment. The injustice of the skies is the absence of the sun, a measureless lack of just measure. Yeats's absent sun is a figure for something like Derrida's wholly other, what the latter calls, at the very end of 'Aphorism Countertime', 'a true sun, the other' (Derrida, 1992b, p. 433).

'The Cold Heaven' itself is a mirroring example of the earning of the injustice of the skies the poem names. Rather than achieving the plenitude of accomplished organic form and powerfully expressed meaning, as we have been taught to believe all good lyric poems should do, 'The Cold Heaven' violently empties itself out. It wastes itself, spends itself, cancels itself out in that final question and in the impossibility of deciding whether natural image or supernatural emblem takes precedence as the literal referent of which the other is the figure. This self-cancelling leaves the reader empty-handed, riddled with light, driven out of all sense and reason by an effort of reading. Reading is conventionally defined as an accounting for the text that brings it back to sense and reason, finds out its sense, in the sense of meaning, and its reason, in the sense of its underlying ground or reason for being, according to the Leibnizian 'principle of reason' (*Satz vom Grund*) that says everything has its reason, can have its reason rendered back to it. The research university exists as the place that accounts for everything, renders everything reasonable, including poems and other literary works. Literary history, philology, biography, *Literaturwissenschaft* in general, have this latter task as their charge. Poetry, however, or 'the poetic' in language, if there is such a thing, is what cannot be rendered reasonable. It takes the reader out of all sense and reason. The reader will note that my reading of a poem, like those of de Man and Derrida, has differed from a New Critical 'close reading', which it might seem superficially to resemble in its attention to detail and to figurative language, in three fundamental ways: (1) it overtly uses speech act theory; (2) it encounters the limits of the assumption that a good poem must be an 'organic unity'; (3) it also encounters, within the poem, invoked by the poem, something unintelligible, something 'wholly other'. The most extreme efforts to preserve sense and reason, those saving virtues of literary studies, must be made, however, as I have sought to make them in this reading, before the reader meets at the border of the intelligible (for example in 'The Cold Heaven') the black hole of what is beyond all sense and reason.

NOTES

1. From an Orange County Pacific Bell phonebook, with telephone numbers omitted.
2. The poem does not say it is winter, but Yeats told Maud Gonne, who asked the meaning of the poem, 'that it was an attempt to describe the feelings aroused in him by the cold detached sky in winter' (Jeffares, 1968, p. 146).
3. Yeats puts it this way in an enigmatic aphorism in the 'Introductory Rhymes' of 'Responsibilities': 'Only the wasteful virtues earn the sun' (Yeats, 1977, p. 270).

WORKS CITED

Bloom, Harold (1970), *Yeats* (New York: Oxford University Press).

Chase, Cynthia (1986, *Decomposing Figures: Rhetorical Readings in the Romantic Tradition* (Baltimore, MD: Johns Hopkins University Press).

de Man, Paul (1979), 'Reading (Proust)', *Allegories of Reading* (New Haven, CT: Yale University Press).

—— (1983), *Blindness and Insight: Essays in the Rhetoric of Contemporary Criticism*, 2nd edn (Minneapolis, MN: University of Minnesota Press).

—— (1984), *The Rhetoric of Romanticism* (New York: Columbia University Press).

De Quincey, Thomas (1970), *Recollections of the Lakes and the Lake Poets* (Harmondsworth: Penguin).

Derrida, Jacques (1984), *Signéponge/Signsponge*, trans. Richard Rand (New York: Columbia University Press).

—— (1986), *Schibboleth: pour Paul Celan* (Paris: Galilée).

—— (1987), *Psyché: Inventions de l'autre* (Paris: Galilée).

—— (1991), 'Che cos'è la poesia', Bilingual in French and English. Eng. trans. Peggy Kamuf, *A Derrida Reader: Between the Blinds*, ed. Peggy Kamuf (New York: Columbia University Press), pp. 221–37.

—— (1992a), 'Donner la mort', in *L'éthique du don: Jacques Derrida et la pensée du don*, ed. Jean-Michel Rabaté and Michael Wetzel (Paris: Métailié-Transition) pp. 11–108.

—— (1992b), *Acts of Literature*, ed. Derek Attridge (New York/London: Routledge).

—— (1993a), *Passions* (Paris: Galilée).

—— (1993b), *Sauf le nom* (Paris: Galilée).

—— (1995a), *The Gift of Death*, trans. David Wills (Chicago, IL: University of Chicago Press).

—— (1995b), 'Sauf le nom', trans. John P. Leavey, Jr, in *On the Name*, ed. Thomas Dutoit (Stanford, CA: Stanford University Press), pp. 33–85.

—— (1995c), 'Passions', trans. David Wood, in *On the Name*, ed. Thomas Dutoit (Stanford, CA: Stanford University Press), pp. 1–31.

Gasché, Rodolphe (1979), 'Deconstruction as Criticism', *Glyph* **6**.

—— (1986), *The Tain of the Mirror: Derrida and the Philosophy of Reflection* (Cambridge, MA: Harvard University Press).

James, Henry (1976), *The Wings of the Dove: The Novels and Tales of Henry James* (New York Edition), Scribner Reprint Edition, vols 19–20 (Fairfield, NJ: Augustus M. Kelley).

Jeffares, A. Norman (1968), *A Commentary on the Collected Poems of W. B. Yeats* (Stanford, CA: Stanford University Press).

Johnson, Barbara (1979), *Défigurations du langage poétique* (Paris: Flammarion).

Loesberg, Jonathan (1991), *Aestheticism and Deconstruction: Pater, Derrida, and de Man* (Princeton, NJ: Princeton University Press).

Miller, J. Hillis (1985), *The Linguistic Moment* (Princeton, NJ: Princeton University Press).

Pater, Walter (1889), *Appreciations* (London: Macmillan).

Warminski, Andrzej (1987), *Readings in Interpretation: Hölderlin, Hegel, Heidegger* (Minneapolis, MN: University of Minnesota Press).

Wordsworth, William (1966), *Poetical Works*, ed. Thomas Hutchinson and Ernest de Selincourt (London: Oxford University Press).

Yeats, William Butler (1961), *Essays and Introductions* (London: Macmillan).

—— (1977), *The Variorum Edition of the Poems*, ed. Peter Allt and Russell K. Alspach (New York: Macmillan).

11

Deconstruction and the Postcolonial

Robert J. C. Young

When Mahmoud Wad Ahmed was brought in shackles to Kitchener after his defeat at the battle of Atbara, Kitchener said to him, 'Why have you come to my country to lay waste and plunder?' It was the intruder who said this to the person whose land it was, and the owner of the land bowed his head and said nothing. So let it be with me. . . . The ships at first sailed down the Nile carrying guns not bread, and the railways were originally set up to transport troops; the schools were started so as to teach us how to say 'Yes' in their language. They imported to us the germ of the greatest European violence, as seen on the Somme and at Verdun, the like of which the world had never previously known, the germ of a deadly disease that struck them more than a thousand years ago.

Salih, 1969, pp. 94–5

I

'I do not believe that anyone can detect by *reading*, if I do not myself declare it, that I am a "French Algerian"' (Derrida, 1998, p. 46). True, for when I wrote *White Mythologies*, I knew that you had been born in Algeria, in the very year that had witnessed the celebrations of the centenary of the French invasion. (Something for Algerians to celebrate indeed.) You had once guardedly spoken of your childhood memories, your 'nostalgeria', far more briefly though than Cixous had recalled her 'Algeriance' (Derrida, 1985; Cixous, 1998). That was, however, my only lead, apart from when I had first seen you in 1979 and understood immediately that you were no 'français de souche'. What a relief. No blockhead, at least. All the same, even before that moment I already knew that something serious was going on. It was as plain as punch even if I found it impossible then to identify where it was coming from. What was certain was that it was

somewhere else, and that it was producing a strong effect of disorientation (for which read 'disoccidentation'). When you visited Oxford that
time, the first question we put to you was about your use of the terms 'the
West' and 'Western metaphysics': 'The category of the "West" and the
continuity of philosophical discourse from Plato to the present remains
unexplicated and unjustified in your work', we complained. You
answered that there was nothing 'which would be considered the essence
of the West in Western philosophy', that you didn't believe in the
continuity of the philosophy of the West, that the unity of 'Western
philosophy' was an illusion, the product of the effects of a representation,
a dogma, and that in your work you were always insisting on splits,
fissures, discontinuities in the corpus. 'It's a contradictory, conflictual
structure which has to repress forms trying to disrupt this unity from
inside and out' (Derrida, 1979). Twenty years later you would still have
to make the same protest (Derrida, 1998, p. 70). In Oxford that day, you
didn't comment further on 'the West' as such, but the link was easy to
find:

> Metaphysics – the white mythology which reassembles and reflects the
> culture of the West: the white man takes his own mythology, Indo-
> European mythology, his own *logos*, that is, the *mythos* of his reason, for
> the universal form of that he must still wish to call Reason. Which does
> not go uncontested. . . . White mythology – metaphysics has erased
> within itself the fabulous scene that has produced it, the scene that nev-
> ertheless remains active and stirring, inscribed in white ink, an invisi-
> ble design covered over in the palimpsest.   (Derrida, 1982, p. 213)

Years later, when I sent you a copy of *White Mythologies*, you wrote and
thanked me with great courtesy, and remarked that I had indeed detected
'a thread' that ran through your writings. That 'thread' which I followed,
with such labour, has finally become the explicit subject of some of your
recent work. I knew it all along, for you showed it to me in your writings
from the first: whereas other philosophers would write of 'philosophy',
for you it was always 'Western philosophy'. Whiteness, otherness; margins, decentring: it was obvious to me what you were up to, what possibilities you were striving towards, what presuppositions you were
seeking to dislodge. And this was why I gave my book a title alluding to
your essay, which I have since often seen referred to as 'White
Mythologies'. Permit me to recall the opening of that book:

> If so-called 'so-called poststructuralism' is the product of a single his-
> torical moment, then that moment is probably not May 1968 but rather
> the Algerian War of Independence – no doubt itself both a symptom
> and a product. In this respect, it is significant that Sartre, Althusser,

Derrida and Lyotard, among others, were all either born in Algeria or personally involved with the events of the war.　(Young, 1990, p. 1)

'Poststructuralism', if I may reinvoke that once startling term, as a form of epistemic violence, has always represented one echo of the violence of Algeria playing itself out in an insurrection against the calm philosophical and political certainties of the metropolis, a revolution initiated, as you argued, just 'at the moment when the fundamental conceptual system produced by the Greco-European adventure is in the process of taking over all of humanity' and achieving 'worldwide dominance'. An imposition, as you now put it, of 'a sovereignty whose essence is always colonial' (Derrida, 1978, pp. 82, 297; 1998, 39–40, 59). From the first, then, your target was, as we would say these days, Western globalization, conceptual in form but material in its effects, and the Eurocentrism of Western culture – 'nothing but the most original and powerful ethnocentrism in the process of imposing itself upon the world' (Derrida, 1976, p. 3). I knew all along, as I say, that was what you were doing, and that book of mine sought to retranslate what had been predominantly regarded up to that point as deconstruction's philosophical or literary strategies into the more painful framework of colonial and postcolonial history. How to rewrite history when the very model of history was so much a product of the history that I wanted to rewrite? Your problematic exactly. It was your critique of the philosophy and concept of history, starting with Husserl, that indicated the first possibilities to me, offering 'a system of critiques' for *'shaking the entirety* of Occidental history'; your strategy of postcolonial retaliation, of overturning – you who when at school in Algeria in typical colonial pedagogic fashion had been taught 'History' as the history of France: 'an incredible discipline, a fable and bible, yet a doctrine of indoctrination almost uneffaceable for children of my generation' (Derrida, 1978, p. 235; 1998, p. 44).

Or as Aijaz Ahmad has described it:

Robert Young, who had until a decade ago devoted himself almost entirely to propagating French poststructuralism in the British Isles, with hardly a thought to spare for the erstwhile colonies, suddenly emerged as a leading theorist of what got called 'postcolonial criticism': even though he hardly uses the term in his *White Mythologies*, the book signifies his first major awakening to the fact of imperialism, but in a world already populated by poststructuralist thought. . . .

(Ahmad, 1996, pp. 281–82)

Ahmad's characteristic method here of reductive *ad hominen* and *ad feminam* critique betrays his accompanying claim to Marxist objectivity – for indeed he knows as little of my thoughts in 'the British Isles' before writing *White Mythologies*, as I know of his thoughts in the USA before writing *In Theory*, where, for all the world knew, he had 'devoted himself almost entirely to propagating' translations of Urdu poetry in North America (and why not?) (Ahmad, 1992, 1969). Behind this endearing personalism, Ahmad's critique is predicated on the assumption that 'French poststructuralism' has nothing to do with 'the erstwhile colonies', and that when I 'awoke' to the fact of imperialism, it was, as it were, too late, for the world had already been populated by dreaming, idealist poststructuralists. Ahmad here engages in a common anti-postcolonial trope, the form of which repeats the assumption of cultural inferiority so searchingly analysed by Fanon: anything that has come to be regarded as being of intellectual or political significance in the West could have nothing to do with the (so-called) third world, even when it is itself a critique of the West from the position of the third world. Postcolonial theory 'must' be European, if it has made such an impact on the West. It is Derrida that, as Bart Moore-Gilbert observes, 'is usually the chief bogeyman in attacks on postcolonial theory's reliance on European methodological models' (Moore-Gilbert, 1997, p. 163, citing Ahmad, 1992, and Tiffin and Slemon, 1989). Those who reject contemporary postcolonial theory in the name of the 'third world' on the grounds of it being Western, however, are themselves negating the very input of the third world, starting with Derrida, disvowing therefore the very non-European work which their critique professes to advocate at the moment when they espouse it. While European Marxism is always somehow excluded from the terms of this critique, outside the ideology of India's BJP and RSS at least, a related argument often sets up an opposition between Western theory and the particularity of third-world experience. This assumes either patronizingly or deferentially that theory is itself completely western, while the only thing that the third world can be allowed is experience, never anything so conceptually or politically effective as its own theory or philosophy. Such an argument unconsciously perpetuates the relation of adult to child that was at the heart of colonial ideology.

Any interrogation of this notion must also call into question the presupposition that the 'third world' is the only domain that has sought to challenge the dominance of the West. Though structuralism and poststructuralism were taken up and developed in Europe, both were alien: anti-Western and of non-European origin. In fact structuralism itself was developed by the Prague school as a self-conscious anti-Western strategy, directed against the imperialist and hierarchical cultural and racial assumptions of European thought. It was for this reason that it was seized upon by French intellectuals such as Claude Lévi-Strauss and Roland Barthes who were disenchanted with, and trying to challenge, the universalist assumptions of French culture in the wake of the violence and mass slaughter that preceded the defeat of the French in Indochina and Algeria. In this respect it is entirely fitting that many of those who developed the theoretical positions known collectively as poststructuralism came from Algeria or had been involved in the war of independence. None of them, it is true, were Algerians proper, in the sense of coming from the indigenous Arab, Berber, Kabyle, Chaouia or Mzabite peoples that make up the population of modem independent Algeria (Bourdieu, 1958). They were, so to speak, Algerians improper, those who did not belong easily to either side – a condition that the subsequent history of Algeria has shown is in its own way characteristically Algerian, for the many different kinds of Algerians 'proper' do not belong easily to the Algerian state either. Some of them, such as Althusser, were *pieds-noirs*, as was Camus, coming from the mixed communities of poor whites who had migrated from the most impoverished areas of the Mediterranean basin; Althusser's family had been deported to Algeria, along with thousands of others, as a consequence of the Franco-Prussian war, and the annexation of Alsace-Lorraine by Germany in 1871. Others, such as Derrida and Cixous, came from the so-called indigenous Jewish community originally expelled with the Moors from Spain by Ferdinand and Isabella in the fifteenth century (Laloum and Allouche, 1992; Wood, 1998). Memmi, another Maghrebian Jew, was born in Tunis and then studied at the University of Algiers and then the Sorbonne. Others, such as Fanon or Lyotard, went to Algeria to work or on military service and became actively involved with the revolution (Pierre Bourdieu was also in Algeria in the fifties doing anthropological sociological research (Bourdieu, 1958, 1963, 1964, 1979) and saw Derrida frequently while he was on military service there). The poststructuralism associated with these names could even be characterized therefore as Franco-Maghrebian theory; its theoretical interventions have been actively concerned with the task of undoing the ideological heritage of French colonialism and with rethinking the premises, assumptions and protocols of European imperial culture.

'For all its potentially useful insights, post-structuralist philosophy remains the handmaiden of repression', declares Helen Tiffin, 'and, if I may mix metaphors, serves as District Commissioner of the 1980s, his book title now changed from *The Pacification of the Primitive Tribes of the Lower Niger* to *Enjoying the Other: or Difference Domesticated* (cited in Moore-Gilbert, 1997, p. 21). The assumption here is that 'post-structuralist philosophy' is just another white mythology of Europe, Tiffin never apparently imagining that 'the Other' could now be writing the book him or herself. As Spivak observes of a similar critique of her own work, 'When Benita Parry takes us [Spivak, Bhabha, JanMohammed] to task for not being able to listen to the natives, or to let the natives speak, she forgets that the three of us, postcolonials, are "native" too. . . . The resistant post-colonial has become a scandal' (Spivak, 1993, p. 60). Tiffin's comment only requires an apparently unthinkable, scandalous reversal of subject position: poststructuralism, in fact, was produced by repression, for it developed in large part out of the experience of colonialism. The structure to which it is post is the colonial apparatus, the imperial machine. Its deconstruction of the idea of totality was borne out of the experience of and forms of resistance to, the totalizing regimes of the late colonial state, particularly French Algeria. That machine operated like no other, often being later redeployed, as liberals always feared it would, in the metropolis. Fascism, as Césaire pointed out, was simply colonialism, colonial totalitarianism, brought home to Europe. Totalitarianism is always colonial – externally or internally. After imperialism, after fascism, after Stalinism, it was time to challenge the notion of totality on which ideas of the state and the party had been based, and which problematically Lukács had also argued was the means by which to challenge capitalism. Sartre tried hard to reformulate a Marxist theory of history which, while amounting to totality and a totalization of historical processes, would also allow for the active interventions of the agents of history. Having himself fought the Nazis as a member of the French resistance, he must have known that this theory was working against the grain, and cannot have been altogether surprised when he failed to complete its philosophical argument. His key move, which only complicated things further, and which appears at the end of the first volume of the *Critique of Dialectical Reason* as the opening that would never allow that work to be closed, was to produce the first Marxist philosophy of history in which colonialism, and the endemic violence of the colonial regime, was a central component: 'Violence, as bourgeois *exis*, exists in the exploitation of the proletariat as an inherited relation of the dominant class to the dominated class . . . and violence, as the *praxis* of this bourgeois generation, lay in colonization' (Sartre, 1976, p. 719; 1991; Young, 1990, 28–47). Sartre's emphasis on the role of violence marked the direct influence of Frantz Fanon, Algeria's most famous adopted son, who had argued that 'colonialism is not a thinking machine, nor a body endowed with reasoning faculties. It is violence in its natural state, and it will only yield when confronted with greater violence' (Fanon, 1967, p. 48).

After 1962, more *colons*, *pieds-noirs* and exiles from Algeria arrived in Paris: few 'poststructuralists' have been 'françaises de souche'. Althusser made the first move. Like Lyotard, he had experienced the 'relative autonomy' of the colonial apparatus in Algeria, its determination by Paris only in the last instance, and this suggested that the postcolonial state, far from existing in a passive position as an identical effect of capitalism, might share in the freeing up of the economism assumed to operate in the metropolis through the separate spheres of core, semiperiphery and periphery (Meynier, 1981; Prochaska, 1990). Derrida went further, redeploying Sartre's worried observation that 'the totalisation is never

achieved and that the totality exists at best only in the form of a detotal-
ized totality' (Sartre, 1963, p. 78). Totalitization, Derrida argued, was in
fact impossible not only empirically, but also conceptually: 'that is to say,
because instead of being an inexhaustible field, as in the classical hypothesis, instead of being too large, there is something missing from it: a centre which arrests and grounds the play of substitutions' (Derrida, 1978, p.
289). The centre cannot hold, as Yeats observed on the eve of Irish independence. Colonialism and the operation of the colonial apparatus,
Derrida recognized, typically produced politically and conceptually
ungoverned effects. These could then be redeployed against it. So
Derrida, neither French nor Algerian, always anti-nationalist and cos-
mopolitan, critical of Western ethnocentrism from *Of Grammatology*'s very
first page, preoccupied with justice and injustice, developed deconstruction as a procedure for intellectual and cultural decolonization within the
metropolis to which he had sailed on the *Ville d'Alger* in 1949, and to
which he had returned after doing military service in Algeria from 1957–9
in the name of a France that expected no ambivalence despite having itself
rejected and disowned him and then readmitted him to citizenship. The
surgical operation of deconstruction was always directed at the identity
of the ontological violence that sustains the Western metaphysical and
ideological systems with the force and actual violence that has sustained
the Western nations in their colonial and imperial policies, a structural
relation of power that had to be teased apart if it was ever to be over-
turned. This preoccupation with the encounter with force and violence
and their effects on history, politics, ethics and language, has always been
fundamental to Derrida's work from the early volumes, *Of Grammatology*
(1967), *Writing and Difference* (1967), and *Margins of Philosophy* (1972)
onwards.

II MAKE THE OLD SHELL CRACK

> The phenomena which interest me are precisely those that blur the
> boundaries, cross them, and make their historical artifice appear,
> also their violence, meaning the relations of force that are concen-
> trated there and actually capitalize themselves there interminably.
> Those who are sensitive to all the stakes of 'creolization'. . . assess
> this better than others.   (Derrida, 1998, p. 9)

Derrida himself came from the margins, from El-Biar, itself located in the
margins of the city of Algiers, to Paris, the metropolitan centre. In the
political geography of colonial dislocation, whereas British colonialism
was nothing if not eccentric, French colonialism always operated according to what Ferdinand de Saussure's brother Léopold, who became a 'nat-

uralized' Frenchman after serving as an officer in the French Navy in Indo-China, characterized as 'excessive centralization' (de Saussure, 1899, p. 16). French culture, he argued, has

> a tendency towards uniformity, simplicity, and symmetry. An antipathy for all that is disparate, complex, unsymmetrical. . . . It has engendered the extreme centralization of the administration. . . .
>
> (de Saussure, 1899, p. 307)

'Try, sir, I ask you', wrote de Tocqueville in 1841, just eleven years after the first French invasion of Algeria, 'to imagine these agile and indomitable children of the desert entwined in the milieu of the thousand formalities of our bureaucracy and forced to submit to the dilatoriness, the regularity, to the documents (*écritures*) and minutiae of our centralisation' (de Tocqueville, 1988, pp. 40–1). The French invaders destroyed the local administrative system and replaced it with a centralized administration, based on the production of *écriture*. Writing and imperialism, the violence of the letter: a topic that Angel Rama has already elaborated so effectively in his account of what he has called 'the lettered city' in the case of Spanish colonial America (Rama, 1996). Derrida's way in, infiltration, and act of liberation would be through reconceptualizing the relation of writing to centralization, a theme that he would treat on a philosophical rather than an historical level, but without ever leaving history free from its strictures. The deconstruction of the many forms of centrism, logo, phallo or structural, only makes sense fully in the context of the extreme centralization of the French administrative system. Four years after the French withdrawal from Algeria, Derrida was to propose, by means of his notion of *écriture*, the idea of a structure without a centre, or, if that was unthinkable, the problematic way in which, in the human sciences, structures are always organized around centres, origins, points of presence and power, while their boundaries remain impermeable and open. Open to people like him. Between the centre and the margin, Derrida finds a leeway, the lateral deviant drift and meandering movement of a dislocated economy, from a resistance built into the attempted uniformity of the system, and locates its breakdown at the point at which it tries to draw its own limits. In any system of force there will always be sites of force that are, precisely, forced, and therefore allow for pressure and intervention. Force and its traces in language from which there must be emancipation or which at the very least must be subject to resistance, madness as the excluded other of the operation of reason, inside/outside structures, the same and the other, the reign of violence in the difference between the same and the other, the ethical relationship to the Other, alterity, difference, differences in identity, identity that is different from itself, translation, displacement, the destabilizing encroachment of the marginal, the subversive subaltern, the constitutive dependency of the centre on the marginal or the excluded, dissemination and the concept of a diaspora without the end point of a final return, and above all history as violence, ontological, ethical and conceptual violence, all these formed the subjects of Derrida's early books. The concept of erasure echoes and denies the violent *Razzias* with which General Bugeaud first attempted to subdue the Algerian interior. Derrida, who was to attend the grotesquely named *Lycée Bugeaud*, constitutes the trace of that incursion that has now come home to roost in its own system.

All these concepts offered the possibility of redefining subaltern positions both within and outside Western cultural norms, but were predominantly predicated on a fifth-column politics, 'the necessity of lodging oneself within traditional conceptuality in order to destroy it' (Derrida, 1978, p. 111). Derrida recognized the belatedness of the postcolonial, that the postcolonial system operates according to what Partha Chatterjee has called 'a derivative discourse', namely that the legacy of colonialism was that the postcolonial states were left inscribed with the political concepts of the West (Chatterjee, 1986). As Spivak puts it, the situation of the postcolonial subject is that she or he has to inhabit the conceptual, cultural and ideological legacy of colonialism inherent in the very structures and institutions that formed the condition of decolonization, a situation which Spivak describes under the rhetorical trope of *catachresis* – a space that the postcolonial does not want to, but has no option to, inhabit (Spivak, 1993). Deconstruction was founded on the 'problem of the status of a discourse which borrows from a heritage the resources necessary for the deconstruction of that heritage itself' (Derrida, 1978, p. 282); it represents a strategic alternative to the passivity of dependency theory or the nationalism of the return-to-the-authentic-tradition-untrammelled-by-the-West of fundamentalist parties that respond to the present by seeking to deny the past.

Along with the power structures of centralization and totality, and the violence fundamental to their strategic operation, Derrida was also concerned to strike at the heart of the other component in the Western mix: rationality and the logic of reason. Not that he was ever in favour of the substitution of irrationality, as is sometimes assumed. No, his move was altogether more subtle and difficult to guard against. His argument was rather that rationality depends on a series of logical decisions, each one of which constitutes an interpretation. The deconstruction of a text consists of the undoing of that narrative of interpretation, and in showing how it could be interpreted in a different logical sequence that would be incompatible with the first. So, for example, he writes of Hegel:

No more than any other, the Hegelian text is not made of a piece. While respecting its faultless coherence, one can decompose its strata and

show that it *interprets itself*: each proposition is an interpretation sub-
mitted to an interpretive decision. The necessity of *logical* continuity is
the decision or interpretive milieu of all Hegelian interpretations. In
interpreting negativity as labour, in betting for discourse, meaning, history, etc., Hegel has bet against play, against chance.

Since no logic governs, henceforth, the meaning of interpretation,
because logic is an interpretation, Hegel's own interpretation can be
reinterpreted – against him. . . . Reinterpretation is a simulated repetition of Hegelian discourse. In the course of this repetition a barely per-
ceptible displacement disjoints all the articulations and penetrates the
points welded together by the imitated discourse. A trembling spreads
out which then makes the entire old shell crack.   (Derrida, 1978, p. 260)

Here, Derrida comes as close as he ever gets to defining deconstruction as
an analytic method – if the accompanying footnote on a 'method' derived
from Bataille does not put it even more clearly:

Each proposition, which is already interpretive in nature, can be interpreted by another proposition. Therefore, if we proceed prudently and
all the while remain in Bataille's text, we can detach an interpretation
from its reinterpretation and submit it to another interpretation bound
to other propositions of the system.   (Derrida, 1978, p. 338)

Deconstruction consists of this reinterpretation through a simulated repetition: postcolonial history uses this technique against the historical narrative of colonialism that has hitherto been presented. Postcolonial
politics use these forms of redeployment against systems that sustain the
status quo of the many vested interests of the *polis*.

III   STRUCTURALISM, 'PRIMITIVE' RATIONALITY AND DECONSTRUCTION

When Derrida came to Paris, all the parties on the left, including the
socialist and communist parties, were committed to the endurance of a
French Algeria. Lyotard's tiny ultra-left 'Socialisme ou Barbarie' group
was to be one of the few honourable exceptions to this rule; Sartre's commitment to the independence struggles was a major reason for his refusal
to join the Communist Party (Lyotard, 1993; Lamouchi, 1996). This put all
Algerians and Franco-Maghrebians in an ambivalent position towards
French Marxism, which at that time was the dominant ideology among
French intellectuals (Derrida, 1980, p. 22). Derrida, a colonized subject
bearing the effects and affects of the complex recent history of French
colonial Algeria, was immediately placed in a marginal position to the

still imperial social and cultural politics of metropolitan Paris. He was to recognize very quickly, however, that the appearance of structuralism from 1945 onwards initiated at a theoretical level a postwar process of cultural decolonization, by turning the critical ethnography that had been developed for the analysis of non-Western cultures onto the culture of the West itself. Claude Lévi-Strauss in particular, in the tradition of the first anti-racist anthropologist Franz Boas who had been an inspiration for the original structuralists of the Prague School, and in the post-1945 ambience of UNESCO statements on racial equality, was concerned to show that the same structure of mind was common to all humans, universal in its capacities rather than made up of a hierarchy of inequality. Despite the postmodern prohibitions on universalism, universalism must always be deployed in the fight against racism. As its detractors always pointed out, structuralism as a method made no value distinction between different cultures (West or non-West) or even between different forms of culture ('high' and 'low') within the West: it was, therefore, essentially democratic, egalitarian, deliberately unconcerned with the aesthetics of value, evaluation, discrimination and taste, that have always been deployed in the West to shore up claims of cultural superiority. In the same way, Lévi-Strauss disputed the noxious effects of the division, central to Western notions of culture, between the civilized and the primitive, by demonstrating that 'primitive' logic was as valid, and as controlled in its method, as that of Western rationalism itself (Lévi-Strauss, 1968). The direction of his whole work was anti-Eurocentric, directed against the assumption of civilized superiority, of Western difference.

Derrida's so-called 'critique' of structuralism – which has been said to have initiated the whole movement of poststructuralism – analysed Lévi-Strauss so as to demonstrate that these two logical possibilities were already at work within his own argument. Derrida showed that Lévi-Strauss's texts themselves operate by different forms of multiple logics: his heuristic method, which was to become central to the strategy of deconstruction, is to employ the very concepts that he wants to undo, a double intention 'to preserve as an instrument something whose truth value he criticizes'. In other words, he separates the instruments of method from the truth that that method envisages:

. . . conserving all those old concepts within the domain of empirical discovery while here and there denouncing their limits, treating them as tools which can still be used. No longer is any truth value attributed to them; there is a readiness to abandon them if necessary, should other instruments appear more useful. In the meantime, their relative efficacy is exploited, and they are employed to destroy the old machinery to which they belong and of which they themselves are pieces. (Derrida, 1978, p. 284)

Against Western ethnocentric assumptions, Lévi-Strauss argues that 'primitive thought' is, in its own way, as rational as that of the West. Derrida points out that in order to prove this in *The Savage Mind*, Lévi-Strauss himself moves into a form of contradictory logic that incorporates both. So, on the one hand, the anthropologist continues to use the nature/culture opposition whose truth his own work has exploded, while on the other hand, he presents a discourse on his own method: he opposes the scientist or engineer, the technician who formulates an abstract idea, a plan, a model, a technical drawing, and then constructs the actual object accordingly, whose structures will be systematic and functionally true, to his own method as *bricolage*. The *bricoleur* is the handy man, the jack of all trades:

> The 'bricoleur' is adept at performing a large number of diverse tasks; but, unlike the engineer, he does not subordinate each of them to the availability of raw materials and tools conceived and procured for the purpose of the project. . . . the rules of his game are always to make do with 'whatever is at hand', that is to say, with a set of tools and materials which is always finite and is also heterogeneous because what it contains bears no relation to the current project, or indeed to any particular project, but is the contingent result of all the times there have been to renew his stock, or to maintain it with the remains of previous constructions or destructions (*les résidus de constructions et de destructions antérieures*). The set of the 'bricoleur's' means . . . is to be defined only by its potential use or, putting this another way and in the language of the 'bricoleur' himself, because the elements are always collected or retained on the principle that 'they may always come in handy'. (Lévi-Strauss, 1966, pp. 17–18)

'To maintain it with the remains of previous constructions or destructions': *bricolage* is never about the application of a pre-formulated theory or method; pragmatically it uses remainders, whatever material is to hand from previous deconstructions in an interactive, critical way. Derrida's strategy is to see this *bricolage* as a description of critical language itself. For the engineer, who is his own absolute origin, is essentially a myth: 'If one calls *bricolage* the necessity of borrowing one's concepts from the text of a heritage which is more or less coherent or ruined, it must be said that every discourse is *bricoleur*'. Derrida goes on to argue that Lévi-Strauss' double intention, producing texts that are simultaneously scientific and mythopoetic, forms essentially the model for how discourses work, producing meanings 'which are absolutely irreconcilable even if we live them simultaneously and reconcile them in an obscure economy' (Derrida, 1978, pp. 285, 293). He then takes it one stage further to show how such multiple, differential logics operated not only in non-Western mythology, or in the method of Lévi-Strauss's argument, but even in the most exalted expressions of Western thought and rationalism in its philosophical traditions. Indeed, as we have seen, Western philosophy, through which the West in part defines itself, operates by exactly this kind of double logic which conflates a myth with a universal truth, the myth of reason for Reason.

> Metaphysics – the white mythology which reassembles and reflects the culture of the West: the white man takes his own mythology, Indo-European mythology, his own *logos*, that is, the *mythos* of his reason, for the universal form of that [which] he must still wish to call Reason. Which does not go uncontested.   (Derrida, 1982, p. 213)

Deconstruction, we might say, therefore, has itself been a form of cultural and intellectual decolonization, exposing the double intention separating the rational method from its truth.

IV   IDENTITY AS DIFFERENCE

It is hardly coincidental that so many of the concepts developed by Derrida were so quickly extended to the social and political experience of minority groups. For that was where they came from. The problematic was certainly a different one from that of the dialectics of the national liberation movements, the opposition of colonizer and colonized, largely because the latter opposition could only be constituted by bringing together all those who were structured as being different into one identity that was founded on their opposition to the same, that is, the colonizer.

In the postcolonial period, for those outside the West, and for those minorities within it, the opposition of sameness and difference, and its relation to identity, has been fundamental. Since Derrida, identity has come to mean not sameness, but difference. *The Concise Oxford Dictionary* defines the word 'identity' as the relation expressed in mathematics and logic by the equals sign (=), as absolute sameness, individuality, the condition of being a specified person who is the same in all situations and circumstances, through time (who, one might ask, is this person?). Yet, if identity is sameness it is also specified by being different – paradoxically it can only be defined by difference from others. As a concept, identity has thus the unusual characteristic of necessarily immediately summoning up its opposite, difference. Identity is primarily asserted by distinguishing that person or thing from someone or something else. Rather like the structure of metaphor, in which, as Aristotle pointed out, you can only say what something is by saying what it is not, so in order to say who you are you have to say who you are not. At the same time, identity politics also declares a form of sameness between two or more persons. Identity politics can only work by asserting these simultaneously: the individual asserts him- or herself as a part of a group, but the group identifies itself by being different from the dominant group. Therefore, you assert your difference (from the dominant group) by declaring an identity with another group that defines itself differentially.

From the viewpoint of the dominant group, this division has often been conceptualized, particularly via Hegel, Sartre, Lévinas and Lacan, as that of the same and the other. The same is taken to represent the dominant group, whose identity is normative and assumed. This apparently comfortable identity is sustained, however, only through the constitution of an other against whom it is defined. In terms of nationalisms and ethnicities, this will take the form of a nearby community (English vs. French), while often being simultaneously sustained by an internal differentiation (English vs. Celt or Jew, the latter more or less swapping places in the nineteenth century). The same principle operates for gender identities – men as against women, heterosexuals as against homosexuals, etc. One of the main arguments of identity politics is directed not only against the power structure implicit in this hierarchy, but also the fact that in this same–other relation, the identity of the other is only defined in relation to that of the same. It is only a negative image of the identity of the dominant group; so, for example, in the case of women, while men defined themselves as active, intellectual, participating in the realm of culture, so women were characterized as passive, bodily, belonging to the realm of nature. The 'other' is a unitary category, applicable to any minority group, who are all characterized without any specificity, only in as much as they are 'others'.

Ethnicity is defined in very similar, often feminized terms in relation to the dominant, implicitly male group. He is ethnic because he is other. She is other because she is ethnic. This kind of characterization of ethnicity as otherness conforms to the basic model that Edward Said established in *Orientalism* (Said, 1978). The oriental other's only identity comes from its relation to the West, and not surprisingly turns out to be nothing more than a mirror in which the West sees the rejected and disavowed parts of itself. The actuality of what is really there never affects the identity of the other as other. For the same reason, Said argues, the Orient as such does not exist. There is no 'real' Orient because the Orient was a Western construction in the first place. The Orient is a part not of the East but of the identity of the West. The Orient is like Dorian Gray's mirror – its image is made up of everything disavowed by the West. In the same way, patriarchal male identity needs a submissive female identity as a part of itself in order to be itself. The one cannot exist in isolation without the other. So, in order to define itself, any majority must 'simultaneously set itself apart from what it is not' and yet remain 'ineluctably haunted by what it seeks to exclude' (Weber, 1982, p. 33). Take a specific historical example: think of the way in which Nazi Germany pursued the ideal of the purity of the Aryan race, to the extent that it not only persecuted its minorities but attempted to erase them altogether. Yet today it is impossible to disassociate Nazi identity from its relationship to the Jews: they are inescapably bound up together. Nothing defines the Nazis more centrally than the place of the Jews in Nazi ideology and practice (Hutton, 1999). Contrary to the somewhat simplistic precepts of the Nazis, if an other is defined in this way, it means in a profound sense it is not really other at all, because the other has become part of the same. If the other must be a part of the identity of the same for the same to be itself at all, then the same is riven with an alterity which opens it up to the difference of the other, effecting an inner dispersal. Identity becomes decentred. This also means that identity is not self-sufficient, not defined only in terms of intrinsic qualities, but, rather as with Saussure's account of how words achieve meaning diacritically, it must be differentially defined as a non-essentialist, negative identity. The significance of this, as in Saussure, is that it means that meaning is not fixed: if your identity is differential in this way, it is open to change. It can constantly be being remade in relation to all through which it is negatively defined. Identity turns into a form of process: 'No, an identity is never given, received, or attained; only the interminable and indefinitely phantasmatic process of identification endures' (Derrida, 1998, p. 28).

However, it is not quite as easy as in Saussure's model, because his account of difference involves no structural power relation. For Derrida, by contrast, difference always involves the violence of a hierarchy, a forced inequality (Derrida, 1981, p. 41). This is why Hegel's analysis of master and slave is more useful to him. In the *Phenomenology*, Hegel posits that the master is dependent on the recognition of the slave for his position of mastery, in which case the power structure begins to reverse: he is only master because of the slave, and without that recognition, he would be nothing: 'the truth of the master is in the slave' (Derrida, 1978, p. 255). In terms of the realities of power, this may be little consolation for the slave, beyond giving him or her a sense of the metaphysical fragility of the master's power. However, in terms of identity, it makes a significant difference. What Hegel shows is that mastery is a dialectical concept which is partly made up of its opposite. Mastery has to include slavery within itself in order to be itself As Fanon shows again, via Kojève, this power structure is always reversible (Fanon, 1967, p. 66).

The terms of the Hegelian master–slave structure had always hitherto been repeated as those of the same and the other. As Lévinas put it succinctly, 'the same is a violent totality' (Derrida, 1978, p. 119). In the *Murder of the Other*, Cixous was to elaborate the same thought from her own experience:

I come, biographically, from a rebellion, from a violent and anguished
direct refusal to accept what is happening on the stage on whose edge
I find I am placed. . . . I learned to read, to write, to scream, and to
vomit in Algeria. Today I know from experience that one cannot imagine what an Algerian French girl was: you have to have been it, to have
gone through it. To have seen 'Frenchmen' at the 'height' of imperialist
blindness, behaving in a country that was inhabited by humans as if it
were peopled by nonbeings, born-slaves. I learned everything from this
first spectacle: I saw how the white (French), superior, plutocratic, civilized world founded its power on the repression of populations who
had suddenly become 'invisible', like proletarians, immigrant workers,
minorities who are not the right 'colour'. Women. Invisible as humans.
But, of course, perceived as tools – dirty, stupid, lazy, underhanded,
etc. Thanks to some annihilating dialectical magic. I saw that the great,
noble, 'advanced' countries established themselves by expelling what
was 'strange'; excluding it but not dismissing it; enslaving it. A commonplace gesture of History: there have to be two races – the masters
and the slaves.   (Cixous and Clément, 1986, p. 10)

The Russian exile Alexandre Kojève had taught how Hegel's
master–slave dichotomy could be politicized into a violent revolutionary
philosophy, but it is only more recently that the reversal of the dichotomy
of same and other has been exploited for its full philosophical and ethical
as well as its political implications. In his long meditation on the relation
between violence and metaphysics, Derrida starts with the fundamental
problematic of Lévinas, how the same–other relation can involve a non-
violent, ethical relationship. The problem with Lévinas's approach, he
suggests, is that he retains the notion of a distinct division between the
two. One of the major arguments of Derrida's work that enabled him to
take this further was his challenge to a principle fundamental to Anglo-
American philosophy, namely the identity principle, according to which
A cannot be both A and not A at the same time. Deconstruction is all
about how one can be both the same and diffierent simultaneously, about
how one can even be different from oneself, arguing that it is possible for
people as well as texts to contain in an economy of difference, incompatible entities that are going on at the same time without cancelling each
other out. This opens up the possibility of multiple and even mobile identities. The best way of thinking through the idea of something being different from itself is by distinguishing the notion of difference between
things – the classical definition of identity – from a concept of a difference
within – the Saussurian and Derridean models. In the object world things
are separable and distinct entities, a brick is not a potato, but in language,
and therefore culture, it does not work so discretely – linguistically, a
brick can also be a friend. Its difference is within. The uniqueness of lan-

guage lies in 'its difference to itself: in difference *with itself* [*avec soi*] rather than difference *from itself* [*d'avec soi*]' (Derrida, 1998, p. 68).

The same and the other works according to a comparable logic. Though they are generally thought of as opposed, a binary opposition, the same versus the other, the same cannot be the same on its own, it has to be defined against the other in order to be the same, in order to have any meaning as the same. It is only the other in fact which makes the same the same. But then, the same can't be the same, except by being also the other for the other, while 'the other cannot be the other – of the same – except by being the same (as itself: ego), and the same cannot be the same (as itself: ego) except by being the other's other: alter ego' (Derrida, 1978, p. 128). The difference between them is therefore rather within them: for the same and the other to be the same and the other, they must differ from themselves. In short, difference is itself a relative concept, not an absolute or essential quality. Derrida, in his well-known neologism, calls this differance with an 'a'. He does this to suggest a sameness that is not identical. Heard, the word differance (with an a) is the same as difference (with an e), but written, it is different. This may seem scholastically trivial, but it has significant consequences for all kinds of difference, including ethnic and gender difference, which is why feminists were quick to make use of Derrida's work. Its significance is that it perfectly describes the political condition of a minority group: a minority wants to make a claim that according to the classical account of identity is impossible, namely that it is the same and different.

The deconstructive positing of difference to 'within' has important political implications because it allows both individuals and groups to claim this necessary contradiction. As feminism has discovered in its long history since Wollstonecraft, there are problems for any minority in claiming simply that it is the same, or, that it is different. If any group claims that it is the same, then it loses its own specificity, but if it claims that it is different then it is vulnerable to the response that that is what the majority thought all along, and which therefore justifies a relation of inequality. Only by claiming that it is first the same, with the same rights, can it then equitably make the second claim, that it is different.

This could be described as representing a strategic reworking for group politics of the old humanist ethics which always denied forms of collective identity. Humanism suggests that we are all human, and therefore humanity is one, but we are also all different, because we are all individuals. There is no place here, however, for the group. Derrida's logic enables a new compatibility between the individual and the group, and between smaller and larger groups. It is for this reason that Laclau and Mouffe have recognized that deconstructive logic can enable new forms of counter-hegemony, or, to put it more simply, a new theory of class that enables solidarity between diverse social groups (Laclau and Mouffe, 1985).

V   PILLAR OF SALT

> I love words too much because I have no language of my own, only
> false *escarres*, false foci (eskhara).
>
> (Bennington and Derrida, 1993, pp. 92–3)

However much your work may have been 'postcolonial', and formed the
basis of so much postcolonial theory, yours was no ordinary experience of
colonialism. Algeria, to begin with, was no ordinary colony, though it was
for France the archetypal colony in the same way as India was for Britain.
Algeria's history is in fact quite extraordinary: first invaded in 1830 as a
deliberate strategy of metropolitan imperialism, never effectively sub-
dued in one hundred and thirty years – no need for clever critics to read
against the grain, searching for subtle strategies of resistance, in the case
of Algeria – a settler colony that was already more than full with settled,
farming indigenous inhabitants, the most violent history from the first
day to this, it was, finally, the inspiration and basis for Fanon's *The
Wretched of the Earth* (1961). You could neither repeat his sublime injunc-
tions for revolution, nor simplify the situation and the peoples in the
name of revolutionary action. With Memmi you were in a category all of
its own, coming from 'a disintegrated "community"'. Your identity was
not fixed on one side or the other, but amounted rather to a 'disorder
[*trouble*] of identity', the result of a too rapid assimilation of the indigenous Jews of Algeria within two generations after the Crémieux decree of
1870 that granted French citizenship to Algerian Jews, a reclassification
suddenly revoked in 1940 (Derrida, 1998, p. 55, 14). The acculturation and
embourgeoisification of the Jews after 1870 left them cut off, strangers to
their own culture and even to cultural memory, strangers to Arab or
Berber culture, and yet strangers also to the French culture and language
which they acquired: 'Such, in any event', you comment, 'would have
been the radical lack of culture [*inculture*] from which I undoubtedly
never completely emerged' (Derrida, 1998, p. 53). Pillar of salt: to succeed
in a colonial culture one must reject the identities of Jew, Arab or African.
The Jews of Algeria were, as Memmi put it, 'eternally hesitant candidates
refusing assimilation' while they were being refused it anyway, the very
pattern of undecidability:

> Their constant and very justifiable ambition is to escape from their col-
> onized condition. . . . To that end, they endeavour to resemble the col-
> onizer in the frank hope that he may cease to consider them different
> from him. Hence their efforts to forget the past, to change collective
> habits, and their enthusiastic adoption of Western language, culture
> and customs. But if the colonizer does not always openly discourage
> these candidates to develop that resemblance, he never permits them to

attain it either. Thus, they live in constant and painful ambiguity.
(Memmi 1967, p. 15)

The Jews live in the most acute ambivalence of hybrid states, an in-between limbo world in which on the one hand they identify with the colonizer with whom they can never be fully assimilated, but whose life they try to live in abject mimicry, while at the same time they remain always condemned to live the life of the colonized. Or as you put it, 'certain people, myself included, have experienced colonial cruelty from two sides' (Derrida, 1998, p. 14, 39). And, of course, colonial opportunity: you, like Memmi, like Fanon, like so many of those who led the independence movements, travelled to the imperial capital for your education.

Memmi was the first to protest against the strict dichotomy between colonizer and colonized laid down by Sartre and Fanon, arguing for an understanding of the mutual mental relations between colonizer and colonized, producing, as he puts it, 'portraits of the two protagonists of the colonial drama and the relationship which binds them', while at the same time undoing the dialectic by emphasizing the spectral presence of all those liminal figures who slipped between these two categories (Memmi, 1967; Derrida, 1998, p. 62). That exploration of the relationship that binds colonizer with colonized ended in the necessity of deconstruction. The scenario began with the imposition of the French language by the colonial regime so that Arabic became an alien, foreign language in its own home, the first stage of what Calvet calls *glottophagie*, the colonizer's attempt to devour indigenous languages by devaluing them (Calvet, 1974; Fabian, 1986). As you have now revealed, you spoke French without it ever being your mother tongue, which remained unknown to you, French possessing you rather than being possessed by you, so that you were always existing on the shores of a French that was both yours and, to you, the language of the other: 'you see, never will this language be mine. And truth to tell, it never was' (Derrida, 1998, p. 2). You did not have the comparative luxury of choosing to write in your native tongue, or succumbing to the necessity of the language of the international market place. Deprived of all language, inhabiting only foreign languages – 'French, English, German, Greek, Latin, the philosophic, the metaphilosophic, the Christian, etc.' – you were thrown into 'absolute translation, a translation without a pole of reference, without an originary language, and without a source language' (Derrida, 1987a, p. 562n; 1998, p. 61). Your speech was encrypted inside a stranger's language that was not your own, making you a stranger to yourself: 'it exists asymmetrically, always *for the other*, from the other, kept by the other. Coming from the other, remaining with the other, and returning to the other'. Your writings represent an exploration of the experience of French as a colonial discourse that was also your discourse: doubtless it is for this reason that Joyce, writing in an

English that was also not his mother tongue, represents so significant a figure for yourself and Cixous: '*Yes, I only have one language, yet it is not mine*'. You write, therefore, not in order to produce the rules of colonial discourse, as Foucault demanded, but from the experience of inhabiting it, of being its subject of enunciation put into a perpetual process of translation. Small wonder, then, that you wished to free up the monolingualism of its pellucid prose, to locate some of the heterogeneity of the alterity that remains both yours and alien to you, 'to make something happen to this language'. The language of the master, the colonist, was also yours, yours to dispossess him of, to expropriate from him inappropriately. 'Charlatan!' An incomprehensible, univited guest harbouring in the host language, the language of the masters, 'a new-comer without assignable origin, [who] would make the said language come to him, forcing the language then to speak itself by itself, in another way, in his language. To speak by itself. But for him, and on his terms . . .' (Derrida, 1998, pp. 40, 51). But for you, and on your terms.

VI THE MARRANO: 'A LITTLE BLACK AND VERY ARAB JEW WHO UNDERSTOOD NOTHING ABOUT IT'

> What is Franco-Maghrebian? . . . The silence of that hyphen does not pacify or appease anything, not a single torment, not a single torture. It will never silence that memory. It could even worsen the terror, the lesions, and the wounds. A hyphen is never enough to conceal protests, cries of anger or, suffering, the noise of weapons, airplanes, and bombs.   (Derrida, 1998, p. 11)

So now you have said it up-front, and aligned deconstruction with your 'Judeo-Franco-Mahgrebian genealogy':

> Certainly, everything that has, say, interested me for a long time – on account of writing, the trace, the deconstruction of phallogocentrism and 'the' Western metaphysics . . . all of that could *not* not proceed from the strange reference to an 'elsewhere' of which the place and the language were unknown and prohibited even to myself, as if I were trying to *translate* into the only language and the only French Western culture that I have at my disposal, the culture into which I was thrown at birth, a possibility that is inaccessible to myself. . . .   (Derrida, 1998, pp. 70–1)

Clearly too, for you have repeated it several times to my knowledge at least, in *Le Nouvel Observateur* in 1983, in *La Carte postale* in 1980, in *Psyché: Inventions de l'autre* in 1987, in *L'autre cap* in 1991, and in *Le Monolingualisme de l'autre* in 1996, while its experience haunts your

'Circumfession' in *Jacques Derrida* (1991) and so many other texts: that moment of literal 'degradation' in 1940, when the Vichy-aligned French state in unoccupied Algeria revoked the Crémieux decree of 1870 and took away your French citizenship, producing in you 'on the one hand . . . the theme of a necessary or rather fatal degradation, as the very form of progress; on the other hand, nostalgia for what preceded this degradation, an affective impulse towards islets of resistance. . . .' (Derrida, 1976, p. 134). The immediate effect of this degradation for you was that on the first day of the new school year you were told to leave the *lycée* and to return home because the percentage of Jews allowed in the school (the *Numerus Clausus* law) had just been lowered by the Rector from 14 to 7 per cent. That moment exists like a precarious primal scene of *ressentiment* in your writing, the moment of not belonging, of being both inside and outside: 'It's an experience which leaves nothing intact, something you can never again cease to feel' (Derrida, 1985, p. 113). Refusing to go to the school that had been set up by some Jewish teachers who had also been expelled from the school system, you then existed in a state of truant limbo for a year. You felt doubly displaced:

J.D.   A paradoxical effect, perhaps, of this bludgeoning, was the desire to be integrated into the non-Jewish community, a fascinated but painful and distrustful desire, one with a nervous vigilance, a painstaking attitude to discern signs of racism in its most discreet formations or in its loudest denials. Symmetrically, oftentimes, I have felt an impatient distance with regard to various Jewish communities, when I have the impression that they close in upon themselves. . . . From all of which comes a feeling of non-belonging that I have doubtless transposed.
Interviewer – in Philosophy?
J.D.   Everywhere.   (Derrida, 1985 p. 114)

This 'difficulty with belonging', as Geoffrey Bennington puts it, started with this moment and has affected all of your writing (Bennington and Derrida, 1993, pp. 326–27). You have turned that resented degradation back and deployed it upon the culture's institutions, inveigling and ensnaring them with deconstruction's fragile language of the degraded, the subaltern, the dispossessed, the forcibly converted, the crypto-Jew. You call yourself a Marrano, one of the Iberian Jews who were forced to convert and eat pork, but continued to practise their faith in secret – but even then, you are not a proper Marrano: 'If I am a sort of *marrane* of French Catholic culture . . . I am one of those *marranes* who no longer say they are Jews even in the secret of their own hearts, not so as to be authenticated *marranes* on both sides of the public frontier, but because they doubt everything' (Bennington and Derrida, 1993, pp. 170–1).

208 *Deconstructions*

The official degradation and regradation of your citizenship only institutionalized and formalized your status as a cultural and political marrano. You were already that, born into marranic colonial lack. 'Marranos that we are, marranos in any case, whether we want to be or not, whether we know it or not' (Derrida, 1993, p. 81). Your boundaries were always blurred – history had seen to that for you. You have always, as Bhabha puts it, survived 'the after life of translation' with an 'act of living on borderlines' (Bhabha, 1994, pp. 226–7). The internalized violence and historical artifice of the colonial power's cultural and political systems were already apparent to you. When you spoke of these things, you were dismissed as a 'charlatan', a pretentious imposter. How, indeed, could this marranized crypto-Jew, coming from Algeria, dare to challenge the canonical traditions of the West, or the privileged traditions of the elites of the East or the South? Yours were the ideas that were said to be non-philosophical, non-political, that were dismissed because they did not conform to recognized philosophical or left-political categories or, worse, because they challenged the basis on which such categories were constructed. The very idea! What, then, came the cry, were the politics of deconstruction? Just another idealism! Yet yours were the ideas that, against all apparent odds, against all patronizing assumptions that only the simplest language and ideas could ever inspire people to self-assertion and struggle towards social and political transformation, were taken up by many minorities, migrant and immigrant groups, because they felt that it was your ideas that were relevant to them and to their own cultural and political situations (and let no one assume that minorities, migrants and immigrants are exclusive to the West). They sensed that you spoke with them from their subject positions on the margins, that you had reconceptualized the world from their perspective and asserted the power of the marginalized in the heartlands of Western institutions. You enabled new political constituencies to articulate their identity and to develop their own politics. Not, indeed, a politics to cover everything for everyone in every situation, to be sure (an impossible demand), but a politics that up to then had had no homeland, no language, no vocabulary, no concepts with which to assert the claims and objectives of the earth's possessed and dispossessed, its marooned and migrant marranos, literal and metaphorical, against the ever-increasing and more fully realized power of dominating white mythologies.

WORKS CITED

Ahmad, Aijaz (1969), *Poems by Ghalib*, trans. Aijaz Ahmad *et al.*, with a Forenote by Aijaz Ahmad (New York: Hudson Review).
—— (1992), *In Theory: Classes, Nations, Literatures* (London: Verso).

—— (1996), 'The Politics of Literary Postcoloniality', in *Contemporary Postcolonial Theory: A Reader*, ed. Padmini Mongia (London: Edward Arnold), pp. 276–93.

Bennington, Geoffrey and Derrida, Jacques (1993), *Jacques Derrida* [1991] (Chicago, IL: University of Chicago Press).

Bhabha, Homi K. (1994), *The Location of Culture* (London: Routledge).

Bourdieu, Pierre (1958), *Sociologie de l'Algérie* (Paris: Presses universitaires de France

—— and Darbel, Alain (1963), *Travail et travailleurs en Algérie* (Paris: Mouton).

—— and Sayad, Abdelmalek (1964), *Le déracinement: la crise de l'agriculture traditionnelle en Algérie* (Paris: Editions de Minuit).

—— and Nice, Richard (1979), *Algeria 1960: Essays* (Cambridge: Cambridge University Press).

Calvet, Pierre (1974), *Linguistique et colonialisme: petit traité de glottophagie* (Paris, Payot).

Chatterjee, Partha (1986), *Nationalist Thought and the Colonial World: A Derivative Discourse* (London: Zed Press).

Cixous, Hélène (1998), 'My Algeriance, in Other Words: to Depart Not to Arrive from Algeria', in *Stigmata: Escaping Texts* (London: Routledge), pp. 153–72.

—— and Clément, Catherine (1986), *The Newly Born Woman*, trans. Betsy Wing (Manchester: Manchester University Press).

Derrida, Jacques (1976), *Of Grammatology* [1967], trans. Gayatri Chakravorty Spivak (Baltimore, MD: Johns Hopkins University Press).

—— (1978), *Writing and Difference* [1967] (London: Routledge).

—— (1979), Seminar with the *Oxford Literary Review*, unpublished transcript.

—— (1980), 'An Interview with Jacques Derrida', with J. Kearns and K. Newton, *The Literary Review*, no. 14, 18 April–1 May 1.

—— (1981), *Positions* [1972], trans. Alan Bass (Chicago, IL: University of Chicago Press).

—— (1982), *Margins of Philosophy* [1972], trans. Alan Bass (Chicago, IL: University of Chicago Press).

—— (1985), 'An Interview with Derrida' ['Derrida l'insoumis', 1983], in *Derrida and Difference*, ed. David Wood and R. Bernasconi (Warwick: Parousia Press), pp. 107–27.

—— (1987a), *Psyché Inventions de 1'autre* (Paris: Galilée).

—— (1987b), *The Post Card* [1980], trans. Alan Bass (Chicago, IL: University of Chicago Press).

—— (1992), *The Other Heading: Reflections on Today's Europe* [1991] (Bloomington, IN: Indiana University Press).

—— (1993), *Aporias*, trans. Thomas Dutoit (Stanford, CA: Stanford University Press).

——(1998), *Monolingualism of the Other, or the Prosthesis of Origin* [1996], trans. Patrick Mensah (Stanford, CA: Stanford University Press).

de Saussure, Léopold (1899), *Psychologie de la colonisation française dans ses rapports avec les sociétés indigènes* (Paris: Félix Alcan).

de Tocqueville, Alexis (1988), *De la colonie en Algérie*, présentation de Tzvetan Todorov (Bruxelles: Éditions Complexe).

Fabian, Johannes (1986), *Language and Colonial Power: The Appropriation of Swahili in the Former Belgian Congo, 1880–1938* (Berkeley, CA: University of California Press).

Fanon, Franz (1967), *The Wretched of the Earth* [1961], trans. Constance Farrington (Harmondsworth: Penguin).

Hutton, Christopher M. (1999), *Linguistics and the Third Reich: Mother-Tongue Fascism, Race and the Science of Language* (London: Routledge).

Laclau, Ernesto and Mouffe, Chantal (1985), *Hegemony and Socialist Strategy: Towards a Democratic Politics*, trans. Winston Moore and Paul Cammack (London: Verso).

Laloum, Jean and Allouche, Jean Luce (1992), *Les juifs d'Algérie: Images et textes* (Paris: Éditions du Scribe).

Lamouchi, Noureddine (1996), *Jean-Paul Sartre et le tiers monde. Rhétorique d'un discours anticolonialiste* (Paris: L'Harmattan).

Lévi-Strauss, Claude (1966), *The Savage Mind* [1962], trans. anon. (London: Weidenfeld and Nicolson).

—— (1968), *Structural Anthropology*, vol. I, trans. Claire Jacobson and Brooke Grundfest Schoepf (London: Allen Lane).

Lyotard, Jean-François (1993), *Political Writings*, trans. Bill Readings and Kevin Paul Geiman (London: UCL Press).

Memmi, Albert (1967), *The Coloniser and the Colonised* [1957], with an Introduction by Jean-Paul Sartre (Boston, MA: Beacon Press).

Meynier, Gilbert (1981), *L'Algérie révélée: La guerre de 1914–1918 et le premier quart du XXᵉ siècle* (Genève: Droz).

Prochaska, David (1990), *Making Algeria French: Colonialism in Bône, 1870–1920* (Cambridge: Cambridge University Press).

Rama, Angel (1996), *The Lettered City*, trans. and ed. John Charles Chasteen (Durham, NC: Duke University Press).

Said, Edward (1978), *Orientalism: Western Representations of the Orient* (London: Routledge).

Salih, Tayeb (1969), *Season of Migration to the North*, trans. Denys Johnson-Davies (Oxford: Heinemann).

Sartre, Jean-Paul (1976), *Critique of Dialectical Reason: Theory of Practical Ensembles* [1960], vol. 1, trans. Alan Sheridan- Smith (London: Verso).

—— (1978), *The Problem of Method* [1960], trans. Hazel E. Barnes (London: Methuen).

—— (1991), *Critique of Dialectial Reason: The Intelligibility of History* [1985], vol. 2, ed. Arlette Elkaïm Sartre, trans. Quintin Hoare (London: Verso).

Spivak, Gayatri Chakravorty (1993), *Outside in the Teaching Machine* (London: Routledge).

Tiffin, Helen and Slemon, Stephen (1989), *After Europe: Critical Theory and Post-colonial Writing* (Sydney: Dangaroo Press).

Weber, Samuel (1982), *The Legend of Freud* (Minneapolis, MN: Minnesota University Press).

Wood, Nancy (1998), 'Remembering the Jews of Algeria', in *Translating 'Algeria'*, *Parallax* 7, pp. 169–84.

Young, Robert (1990), *White Mythologies: Writing History and the West* (London: Routledge).

12

Deconstruction and Psychoanalysis

Maud Ellmann

Addressing a group of psychoanalysts in 1981, Jacques Derrida characterized himself as a 'foreign body' in the institution of psychoanalysis (Derrida, 1991, pp. 202–3).[1] A foreign body infiltrates the body of its host but can be neither rejected nor assimilated; its effects may be beneficent, like the bacteria that aid digestion, or baneful, like the virus that destroys the vital functions. As a foreign body in the corpus of psychoanalysis, deconstruction performs the role that Derrida, in 'Plato's Pharmacy', attributes to the pharmakon – both poison and remedy – that heals what it harms, revitalizes what it violates. For deconstruction, by its own admission, is parasitic on the works of Freud and other thinkers, and yet it seems to reinvigorate the works it vampirizes.

In his earlier writings, Derrida tends to underplay his own dependency on Freud, while stressing Freud's dependency on metaphysics. All Freudian concepts, 'without exception', he declares, 'belong to the history of metaphysics, that is, to the system of logocentric repression' (Derrida, 1978, p. 197). Logocentrism (to recapitulate a now-familiar argument) is the repression of writing in favour of speech, a repression that Derrida regards as the founding subterfuge of metaphysics. Writing, he contends, has always been perceived as dangerous because it betokens absence in the same way that speech betokens presence. In speech the speaker must be present to the interlocutor; in writing, the writer may be absent from the reader; speech is associated with the breath of life, writing with the waste of death, the corpse of words. Writing consists of material traces deracinated from their source and working their effects regardless of authorial intention. Thus the writer (to paraphrase James Joyce) is necessarily 'a ghost by absence' or 'a ghost by death' from the moment that the written word embarks upon its independent odyssey (Joyce, 1993, p.181). This condemnation of writing is as old as Western philosophy: in the *Phaedrus* Plato condemns writing as a bastardized copy of speech, liable to give rise to misunderstanding because the writer is not present to explain his meanings (Plato, 1973, pp. 95–99; 140–41). Written signs may be quoted, or misquoted, anywhere, by anyone, irrespective of the author's purposes.

Derrida deconstructs this age-old opposition between speech and writing, not by reversing its terms, or by claiming on behalf of writing the priority traditionally accorded to the spoken word, but by showing that the menace attributed to writing is equally imputable to speech. This menace lies in the repeatability of writing, its quotability or 'iterability'; for this capacity to be repeated anywhere implies its defection from its point of origin and, by extension, its perfidy to all beginnings, to the very concepts of primacy, originality, authority. Yet this dangerous quotability, Derrida demonstrates, is also the precondition of speech: the spoken word must be used repeatedly by others in order to acquire social meaning, or else it would revert into an unintelligible (albeit originary) grunt. In the beginning was the quotation – or so Derrida's argument implies. Speech, like writing, is composed of reiterable marks destined to desert the speaker and to stray, promiscuously, from voice to voice and ear to ear, in a process that Derrida has termed 'dissemination'. Thus speech – supposedly pure, present, primary, immediate – is fraught with the effects of writing: effects of absence (the author is no longer there); mediation (the conventional mark intervenes between the thought and its articulation); materiality (the transparency of thought is converted into sounds or traces); difference (the trace gains significance only through its negative or differential relation to other traces, so that its meaning is a warding-off of other meanings rather than a positive endowment); death (the trace implies the extinction, whether past or future, of its author).

If Western metaphysics is indeed based on the repression of writing, this means that philosophical discourse must conceal from itself its own writtenness, the excremental traces of its abstract musings, the tomb of print in which its insights are interred. Yet this repression invariably fails – and the symptom of this failure, Derrida argues, is the metaphor of writing that haunts philosophical discourse as the reminder of all it tries to forget (Derrida, 1978, p. 196). In accusing psychoanalysis, however, of perpetuating this repression, Derrida is not so much refuting as out-Freuding Freud: the terms 'repression' and 'return of the repressed' are of course derived from Freud himself, although for Derrida the threat to be repressed is writing rather than incestuous desire. In view of Derrida's appropriation of Freudian terms and Freudian stratagems, it is tempting to describe deconstruction as the application of psychoanalysis to the history of philosophy, and to dismiss Derrida's protests to the contrary as a repression, on his own part, of the influence of Freud (Melville, 1986, p. 84). In his early essay on psychoanalysis, 'Freud and the Scene of Writing' (1966), Derrida insists that 'despite appearances, the deconstruction of logocentrism is not a psychoanalysis of philosophy' (Derrida, 1978, p. 196). In psychoanalytic terms, this declaration looks suspiciously like a 'disavowal' that admits what it ostensibly denies. It belongs, however, to an early phase of deconstruction, which Samuel Weber has termed the 'classical' phase, when Derrida was still attempting to remain untainted by the texts that he interpreted. A more recent form renounces this delusion of aloofness to become instead 'an example of that of which it speaks or writes' (Weber, 1984, p. 44). It is in this latter phase that deconstruction assumes its fate as foreign body in the quick of Western thought, entrammelled in the problems that it brings to light.

'The interest deconstruction takes in psychoanalysis is permanent and complex', Stephen Melville has observed; 'the continuing rediscovery of this interest is of a piece with its continuing rediscovery of itself and its project of radical self-criticism' (Melville, 1986, p. 84). It is also of a piece, I shall argue, with the interest that deconstruction takes in literature. In 'Freud and the Scene of Writing', Derrida insists that there has not yet emerged 'a psychoanalysis of literature respectful of the *originality of the literary signifier*. . . . Until now, only the analysis of literary *signifieds*, that is, *nonliterary* signified meanings, has been undertaken' (Derrida, 1978, p. 197). The opposition between signifier and signified, assumed in this early formulation, is one that Derrida would now eschew. Yet the statement indicates that his intention is (or was) to bring the literary signifier to the fore – the written or acoustic texture of the word, as opposed to its semantic content – particularly in texts that disavow their 'literariness', including most philosophical writings. In these texts the literary qualities of style, tone and rhetoric tend to be regarded at best as decoration, at worst as encumbrances befuddling the purity of thought. Deconstruction, by contrast, insists that the meaning of these texts cannot be abstracted from the rhetorical ploys by which they both elicit and frustrate the wish for meaning.

Although Derrida would deny that deconstruction is a formalism, his concern with the specificity of the literary signifier links him to a tradition that reaches back through the Russian Formalists to the French Symbolists, and the repeated efforts of these thinkers to determine the uniqueness of the literary artefact. The Russian Formalists defined 'literariness' as the primacy of the aesthetic over the communicational function of language. In practical communication, where words are used as vehicles of information, their specific weight and shape and sound and density can only interfere with the message they convey. In the words of the poet Paul Valéry: 'the form – that is, the physical, the concrete part, the very act of speech – does not last; it does not outlive understanding; it dissolves in the light; it has acted; it has done its work; it has brought about understanding; it has lived' (Valéry, 1972, p. 257). In poetry, by contrast, the message cannot be abstracted from the medium; referential meaning is suspended, and the word is swept instead into the 'incessant play of meaning upon meaning' (Jakobson, 1988, pp. 31–57). Where ambiguity in practical communication is merely an annoyance to be crushed, in poetry it is a resource to be plundered to the full.

When Derrida argues that psychoanalytic criticism fails to attend to the originality of the literary signifier, he means that it ignores the form in an obsession with the content of the literary text. Characteristically the psychoanalytic critic overlooks the verbal surface of the text in order to expose the Freudian motifs – e.g. the Oedipus complex – supposedly encrypted in its depths. In his famous dispute with Lacan over Poe's detective story 'The Purloined Letter' (discussed in more detail below), Derrida argues that Lacan disregards the story's literary properties in his eagerness to loot its psychoanalytic 'truth' (Derrida, 1988, pp. 173–212). Derrida insists that literature eludes this avarice for truth: like the purloined letter itself, the meaning of the literary text can never be pinned down. Not that the meaning is ineffable (Derrida would abhor the imputation of aesthetic mysticism), but that it circulates among the readers of the tale, much as the letter does among Poe's characters, slipping out of their covetous grasp. Nor is this errancy of meaning restricted to texts conventionally classified as literary: Derrida's readings of Freud chart the ways in which the writerly features of Freud's work – the play of metaphor, the ruses of narrative, the reminiscences of myth, the idiosyncrasies of style – open forth a range of implications that exceed the limits of his logocentric premises.

Derrida's writings on psychoanalysis may be divided into three large groups: those concerned with Freud and the metaphysical tradition; those belonging to the controversy with Lacan; and those promulgating the work of Nicolas Abraham and Maria Torok. These divisions are to some extent arbitrary, since the texts thus parcelled out continually overlap, conversing with each other and with briefer references to psychoanalysis bestrewn throughout Derrida's work; yet they provide useful signposts to the route the foreign body of deconstruction has pursued through the sprawling corpus of psychoanalysis. Underlying all these encounters runs a continuous debate with Freud, in which Derrida's one-upmanship gradually gives way to admiration for the deconstructive potency of the Freudian *oeuvre*, its uncanny foreshadowings of Derrida's own methods. As opposed to the Oedipal son, dismantling the teachings of the father, Derrida increasingly adopts the role of 'hypocrite lecteur' (the famous apostrophe that T. S. Eliot, in *The Waste Land* (1922), borrows from Baudelaire) – becoming brother, intimate, accomplice, even double of the theories that he deconstructs ('You! hypocrite lecteur! – mon semblable – mon frère!'). By acknowledging the affinities between his enterprise and Freud's, Derrida comes to recognize that all readers are hypocrites, particularly those who claim to fathom meanings and motives of which the text is unaware. Freudian critics are notoriously prone to such pretensions. Yet psychoanalysis can also foster humility by showing that the reader necessarily conspires in the text's imaginings; that the act of read-ing is a process of mutual seduction in which the reader and the read arouse each other's fantasies, expose each other's dreams (Forrester, 1990, pp. 264–65). As we shall see, the story of Derrida's relationship to Freud is the story of his changing attitude to reading, his progress from 'boa-deconstructor' (in Geoffrey Hartman's words) to foreign body embedded in the systems that he takes apart (Davis, 1988, p. 144).

The following pages trace the vicissitudes of Derrida's relationship to psychoanalysis, proceeding in roughly chronological order through his early work on Freud, his contretemps with Lacan, his reading of Freud's *Beyond the Pleasure Principle* (1920) in *The Post Card* (1980), and his com-mentaries on the work of Nicolas Abraham and Maria Torok. This tour – brief as it must be – indicates how Derrida progressively insinuates his work in Freud's (and in a chosen few of Freud's successors') until the psy-choanalytic and the deconstructive enterprises often seem to coincide. Does this mean that Derrida is a plagiarist? No – for the very concept of plagiarism relies on a belief in the plenitude of origins that Derrida (fol-lowing Nietzsche) holds to be self-contradictory (Culler, 1994, pp. 86–8). What the likeness between Freud and Derrida reveals is not a simple pat-tern of priority but a web of intertextuality in which forerunner and late-comer are equally enmeshed. Within this web the rules of sequence and causality no longer hold: another temporality emerges, fraught with strange prolepses, deferrals, premonitions, survivals, reversions, advances, and arrears, in which the future may anticipate the past, the precursor hark back to the successor.[2] Coined by Julia Kristeva, the term 'intertextuality' means that texts are tissues of quotation, shaped by the repetition and transformation of other textual structures. A text (in Derrida's words) can no longer be conceived of as 'a finished corpus of writing, some content enclosed in a book or its margins, but a differential network, a fabric of traces referring endlessly to something other than itself, to other differential traces' (Frow, 1990, p. 49). The concept of inter-textuality therefore implies that creditors and debtors, proprietors and thieves, originators and imitators belong to vast concatenations of indebt-edness extending far beyond the reach of legislation.

Referring to James Joyce, Derrida complains, 'He's read us all, and pil-laged us, that guy'; the same might be said of Freud, who shares this knack of echoing the works that his descendants have not yet composed (Derrida, 1984a, p. 151).[3] When Derrida resembles Freud it is rarely because he is directly raiding him but because both writers' works are echo chambers reverberating with the voices of the philosophical tradi-tion. Both rely on binary oppositions inherited from that tradition, such as mind and body, self and other, consciousness and mechanism, while exposing the osmosis that erodes those separations. Rather than tallying up Derrida's debts to Freud – an impossible audit in any case – the present essay takes the humbler task of probing Derrida's ambivalence towards psychoanalysis. For Derrida alternately rejects and reincorporates the psychoanalytic enterprise within his own, like the child with his bobbin in *Beyond the Pleasure Principle*.

FREUD AND THE MYSTIC WRITING-PAD

Derrida's earliest essay on psychoanalysis, 'Freud and the Scene of Writing', explores Freud's lifelong quest to devise a thermodynamic model of the workings of the mind, a quest that began with the *Project for a Scientific Psychology* (1895) and culminated in the short 'A Note upon the "Mystic-Writing Pad"' (1925). According to Derrida, Freud's attempts in these and other works to explain the operations of memory after the manner of the natural sciences repeatedly give way to an uncanny vision of the psyche as a writing-machine. Freud's problem is to understand how the psyche can retain permanent memory traces and, at the same time, offer 'an unlimited receptive capacity' to new impressions (Freud, 1925, p. 227). In the unfinished *Project for a Scientific Psychology*, Freud invents a 'neurological fable' of startling complexity to account for this double functioning. To summarize (and inevitably to simplify), Freud envisages the psyche as a field of forces competing with resistances embodied in the form of mental neurones. He postulates that such experiences as pain forge pathways through these neurones, leaving 'a map of breaches', 'a topography of traces' etched into the psychic apparatus. The degree of force exerted on the neurones, and the level of resistance they oppose to it, determines the itinerary of the memory-trace. What fascinates Derrida about this model (and reveals his structuralist inclinations) is that it constitutes a system of differences without positive terms: 'It is the difference between breaches which is the true origin of memory, and thus of the psyche. . . . Trace as memory is not a pure breaching that might be reappropriated at any time as simple presence: it is rather the ungraspable and invisible difference between breaches'. Since each trace presupposes previous traces, 'the very idea of a *first time* . . . becomes enigmatic'; and indeed in *The Interpretation of Dreams* Freud dismisses the idea of primariness as a 'theoretical fiction'. As opposed to a first time, a primary inscription, Freud's model of the mind implies originary repetition: in the beginning was *re*-tracing.

Derrida believes that Freud's insistent metaphors of scratching, breaching, engraving, and imprinting open forth a vista of the psyche as a 'landscape of writing', a 'forest of script'. But writing, in this context, can no longer be understood in the ordinary sense as a transcription of pre-existent speech – 'a stony echo of muted words' – but must be re-imagined as 'a lithography before words', a (re)tracing prior and even recalcitrant to meaning (Derrida, 1978, pp. 199–207). To claim, as Lacan notoriously does, that the unconscious is 'structured like a language' is to attribute too much substance to these contentless inscriptions that canalize the psychic apparatus (Lacan, 1977, p. 234). Since logocentrism is based on the repression of writing, Derrida argues that Freud's metaphors of writing represent a return of the repressed: they are instances in which Freud's speculations overshoot the 'logocentric closure' of his mode of thought. Never content with his paradigms, moreover, Freud produces metaphor after metaphor, 'obstinately substituting trace for trace and machine for machine', in a 'dreamlike renewal of mechanical models' – as if his own prose were a machine for mass-producing writing-machines (Derrida, 1978, pp.198, 229).

The last – and best – of these machines is the 'Mystic Writing-Pad', a child's toy consisting of three surfaces: a wax slab, covered by a thin translucent sheet of waxed paper, overlaid by a transparent piece of celluloid. To write on this pad, Freud tells us, is to revert to the ancient method of writing on tablets of clay or wax: a pointed stylus is used to scratch the celluloid, producing the hollows or depressions in the lower strata that constitute the writing. To erase what has been inscribed, the two covering sheets are lifted up, and the traces, though preserved in the wax slab, disappear from view, leaving the surface clear of writing and ready to receive fresh imprints (Freud, 1925, pp. 228–9). According to Derrida, this model of the psyche does away with the 'punctual simplicity' of the classical subject (Derrida, 1978, p. 226). For Freud's metaphors of psychic writing exclude the possibility that the ego could be master of its mansion, or that the subject could command the contents of the mind. The memory trace, a furrow driven through a field of force, is not a 'thing' that ever was or could be present; nor is it a possession that a subject could remember – or forget. The subject of the mystic writing-pad is several rather than unitary, dilatory rather than 'punctual', its existence a flicker between surfaces: between the outer film that registers impressions, the inner sheet on which they are transcribed, and the lower surface, inaccessible to consciousness, where traces are preserved in perpetuity.

Samuel Weber has argued that 'Freud and the Scene of Writing', with its enthusiastic programme of purifying psychoanalysis of its naive reiteration of philosophy, belongs to the classical or triumphalist phase of deconstruction, when Derrida was still trying to preserve his distance from the texts he scrutinized (Weber, 1984, pp. 41–4). Yet even in this early essay Derrida adopts Freudian terminology, most notably the 'trace', thus anticipating later works where he allows himself to be ventriloquized by that which he interprets, miming the figures and rhythms of the texts he reads. Another set of metaphors that Derrida derives (at least in part) from Freud is that of pellicular surfaces – the skins, membranes, films, crusts, veils, folds, envelopes, tympanums, parchments, phylacteries and hymens that weave through the rhetoric of deconstruction. In particular, the foreskin – or more precisely its dismemberment – looms over both Derrida's work and Freud's. For Freud, the Jewish ritual of circumcision symbolized castration and thus explained the violence of anti-Semitism. For Derrida, circumcision represents an archive imprinted on the skin, a prosthetic memory borne upon the body yet radically inaccessible to consciousness: 'that singular and immemorial archive called *circumcision* . . . which, though never leaving you . . . is no less exterior, *exterior right on* your body proper' (Derrida, 1996, p. 26).[4] Other cutaneous images in Derrida betoken the porosity of boundaries: the 'hymen' for example, implies both merger (marriage) and separation (virginity). One source for these epidermal figures is the mystic writing-pad itself, which consists of three skins subjected to a constant process of tattooing and erasure. Moreover, Freud describes the ego as a psychic skin – a 'projection of the surface' of the body – that contains mental life much as skin contains the entrails (Freud, 1923, p. 26). There is some biological evidence for this analogy between the epidermis and the mind: the cortex of the brain is formed *in utero* by the introversion and reticulation of the surface of the embryo, in a folding-up process technically known as 'invagination' – another term that Derrida makes central to his work, partly to counter the psychoanalytic preference for penile metaphors (Anzieu, 1989, p. 9).

As terms like 'trace', and concepts like skin, infiltrate Derrida's rhetoric and methods, it becomes increasingly difficult to tell if he is using them to diagnose or to simulate the symptoms of the Freudian mind. Is it Freud or Derrida who is preoccupied with skin, with breaching, with inscription? Even in his early work (contrary to Weber's argument) Derrida seems to be allowing Freud's obsessions to interpenetrate his own, revealing that 'impulse of identification' which he later welcomes as essential to the enterprise of reading:

> I love very much everything that I deconstruct in my own manner; the texts I want to read from the deconstructive point of view are texts I love, with that impulse of identification which is indispensable for reading.   (Derrida, 1985, p. 87)

LACAN AND THE PURLOINED LETTER

It is not identification, however, but hostility that characterizes Derrida's reading of Lacan in 'The Purveyor of Truth' (1975), a critique of Lacan's Seminar on 'The Purloined Letter' (1955). Derrida's essay sparked off a debate that repeatedly erupts long after the original opponents have laid down their arms: Muller and Richardson's 1988 collection *The Purloined Poe* assembles many but by no means all the recent repercussions. Like the purloined letter itself, Poe's story continues to change hands, placing everyone who seizes it at risk of being duped and dispossessed.

Lacan's Seminar on 'The Purloined Letter' (itself a critique of Marie Bonaparte's 1933 psychoanalytic study of Poe[5]) condenses the story into two tableaux. In the first, which Lacan calls 'the primal scene', the Queen, interrupted by the King in her perusal of a letter, hastily places it face-down, while the attendant Minister, sensing her embarrassment, snatches it before her eyes and substitutes a simulacrum. The Queen, unable to intervene for fear of attracting the attention of her royal spouse, employs the Prefect of Police to search the Minister's apartments, which are duly ransacked every night to no avail. In the second scene, the detective Dupin pays a visit to the Minister and immediately spots the letter, some-what crumpled and thrust with apparent nonchalance into a card rack dangling from the centre of the mantelpiece. The police, who had scoured every inch of the apartment, even dismantling the furniture in the hope of discovering a secret cache, overlooked the prize because of their convic-tion, born of a 'realist's imbecility', that something missing must be hid-den (Lacan, 1988, pp. 29, 40). The next day Dupin reverses the original sleight-of-hand: he visits the Minister again, armed with a counterfeit let-ter that he substitutes for the original when his opponent's back is turned. The symmetry is subtly skewed, however, when Dupin inscribes his forgery with a tantalizing quotation from Crébillon – 'un dessein si funeste/S'il n'est digne d'Atrée est digne de Thyeste'.[6]

Lacan seizes on this story to exemplify his theory that the subject is con-stituted by the signifier. The signifier, not the signified – for the contents of the stolen letter are never revealed. It is not what the letter says or means which matters, but the way it circulates between the parties to the drama and determines their respective roles. The letter's displacements, Lacan claims, reveal 'the decisive orientation which the subject receives from the itinerary of a signifier' (Lacan, 1988, p. 29). Thus the Minister is feminized by his abduction of the letter, placed in the same position as the Queen and exposed to the same threat of ravishment (Lacan, 1988, pp. 22–45). From hints like these, Derrida comes to the conclusion that Lacan identifies the letter with the phallus – that is, with the penis that the mother (the Queen) does not have – although Lacan never draws this inference explicitly. According to Derrida, Lacan recognizes that the meaning of the letter is lacking, but then transforms this lack itself into the meaning and identifies this lack as the 'truth' of castration (Derrida, 1988a, pp. 184–92).

What clinches this manoeuvre, to Derrida's mind, is Lacan's insistence that 'a letter always arrives at its destination'. Since it is unlikely that Lacan is praising the efficiency of the postal service, Derrida assumes him to imply that meaning will always be delivered, whole and indivisible

(Lacan, 1988, p. 53; Johnson, 1988, p. 225). Thus Lacan's 'phallogocentrism' – his blind devotion to castration-as-truth – leads him to discount the possibility of error, accident, fragmentation, irrecoverable waste and loss; the possibility of everything, in short, that Derrida condenses in the term 'dissemination'. Determined to apotheosize the phallus, Lacan rewrites Poe's story in terms of Oedipal triangles, in which each subject is defined in contradistinction to the others by having or not having the letter-phallus. In this way Lacan blinds himself to the role of the narrator, whose intervention (Derrida insists) transforms each threesome into a foursome, each triangle into a rectangle.

It is true that Lacan's division of the story into a double scene conceals the oddity that Poe's story actually takes place within a single room: the cosy bachelor pad, described by Poe as a 'little back library, or book-closet', where Dupin and the narrator, like secret sharers, enjoy the luxuries of meditation and a meerschaum in the dark (Poe, 1988, p. 6). Only the clumsy intrusion of the Prefect of Police creates a triangle within this world of doubles; yet Dupin's closet still remains a male preserve, unruffled by the drama of gender that unfolds offstage. To underrate the impact of the narrator, moreover, is to overlook the story's literariness, and to reduce Poe's ingenious satire of interpretation to the status of a psychoanalytic 'case'. It is not that Derrida wishes to save literature from the clutches of psychoanalysis (quite the contrary, he protests), but that the story pre-empts its own interpretation, placing those who presume to penetrate its secrets in the same ridiculous position as the Prefect of Police. As Derrida writes in a footnote to *Positions*: 'certain "literary" texts have an "analytic" and deconstructive capacity greater than certain psychoanalytic discourses which *apply* their theoretical apparatus to these texts . . .' (Derrida, 1981, p. 112). Lacan underrates the text's capacity to analyse its analyst, to snatch away its meaning from underneath his nose.

If Lacan had explicitly equated the purloined letter with the phallus, Derrida's censure would be justified. Although he hints at it, however, Lacan never quite commits this gaucherie. Instead he respects the letter's emptiness, its dearth of meaning, which is precisely what enables it to gather innuendoes as it roves. Only after the Seminar was published did Lacan introduce the term castration, as if to reclaim an inadvertent insight – although the word he uses (twice) is 'châtré', which is not the technical psychoanalytic term.[7] While one could argue (as Derrida does) that to identify the letter as the phallus is to pin it down, one could also counterargue (as Barbara Johnson does) that to identify the phallus as the letter is to unpin both from any fixed position or signification. In Johnson's reading of Lacan, the letter/phallus performs much the same function that Derrida assigns to 'différance' (a portmanteau word combining difference and deferral): for the circulating missive has no intrinsic meaning; the revelation of its contents is endlessly deferred; its function is merely to distinguish those who hold it from those who don't, as it seizes them in its implacable trajectory.

It is worth examining such correspondences more closely to determine whether Derrida and Lacan are really saying the same thing, in which case Lacan, as the predecessor, must have said it first (see Staten, 1991, pp. 98–109). Both theorists belong to the structuralist tradition, and both make difference – specifically the differential nature of the linguistic sign – the cornerstone of their convictions. Lacan believes the self to be constituted in and by language, which differentiates the 'I' from the 'not I'. The new-born infant has no self because it is oblivious to difference, adrift among sensations, appetites, phantasmagoria. Its accession to language entails a loss of this ineffable experience of being, giving rise to an insatiable desire for a complement to fill the lack within the self: insatiable because no object could alleviate the longing for undifferentiated being, for the 'oceanic feeling' that Freud attributed to speechless infancy (Freud, 1930, pp. 64–5, 72). Henceforth all the subject's satisfactions will be incomplete, for desire is condemned to seek symbolic substitutes to fill in or figleaf over this fundamental lack of being (*manque à être*/want-to-be).

Put this way, Lacan's account of desire – as the drive to fill the unfillable lack – prefigures Derrida's conception of the logic of the 'supplement' and even seems to steal the latter's thunder. Derrida borrows the term 'supplement' from Rousseau, who conceives of writing as a secondary supplement to full originary speech, culture as a supplement to nature, masturbation as a supplement to coitus, and so forth. In each case Rousseau insists on the completeness of the origin, which can only be corrupted by supplementation; but Derrida points out that the very presence of a supplement implies a deficiency within the origin to be alleviated. Thus the supplement resembles Lacanian desire in that both originate in lack, and both proliferate symbolic substitutes for a lost plenitude. The difference, however, is that Derrida never grants the supplement the independence that Lacan attributes to desire: the supplement remains an intertextual construction, bound to the tradition which engendered it, circumscribed within quotation marks (tacit though these often are). Lacan, on the contrary, rarely pauses to consider how his own discourse is determined by the 'signifying chain' of his intellectual precursors. As Henry Staten has pointed out, '[Lacan] never notices that his picture of the subject-who-is-constituted-as-signifier is itself a textual construct, something woven out of the texts of Freud, Saussure, Lévi-Strauss, and others' (Staten, 1991, p. 108). Instead Lacan uses these thinkers as lenses through which to glimpse the truth of language, desire, the subject, the symbolic order, as if these were transcendent entities rather than historical constructions. While debunking the humanist conception of the subject,

Lacan seems to elevate himself into a super-subject, unencumbered by his philosophical inheritance.

This reluctance to interrogate his own procedures allows him to be duped by Freud. For instance, by according pre-eminence to language in the constitution of the subject, where Freud had granted pre-eminence to sexuality, Lacan unwittingly corroborates Freud's view that sexuality is subject to repression. The result is a sanitized version of psychoanalysis in which the phallus (the symbolic version of its fleshly counterpart) becomes a kind of civil servant, conscripting the subject into language and desire with little of the *Sturm und Drang* that Freud attributes to castration fantasies.[8] Derrida, by contrast, recognises that 'language' can be just as imperious as 'sexuality' if the genealogy of either concept goes disregarded, and if the structure of pre-eminence remains intact. Unlike Lacan, Derrida constantly reminds himself and his readers that his procedures are embroiled in those he deconstructs. If the resulting circularity of his analyses can be frustrating (there is no way out of logocentrism even though its modes of reasoning are self-defeating), Derrida at least renounces the pretensions to omniscience that make Lacan at times – quite bluntly – look the fool.

But is this foolishness itself a stratagem more daring than Derrida's tireless (and sometimes tiresome) self-scrutiny? The axiom Lacan draws from his reading of 'The Purloined Letter' is 'les non-dupes errent'; that is, the non-fools err (which is perhaps the converse of Blake's maxim that the fool who persisted in his folly would become wise).[9] In Poe's story, the first of these non-fools, the Minister, dupes the Prefect of Police only to be duped by Dupin, whose name implies that he is also duped by his attempt to dupe, ensnared in the circuit of exchange that he is trying to manipulate. (In Dupin's quotation from Crébillon, who is Thyeste and who Atrée, who the perpetrator and who the victim in this wilderness of mirrors?) 'Les non-dupes errent' is also a pun on 'le nom-du-père', the name-of-the-father which 'from the dawn of history' (Lacan proclaims with typical portentousness) has served as the 'support of the symbolic function' and the law (Lacan, 1977, p. 67). Without attempting to elucidate Lacan's theory of the paternal function, which has defeated many an intrepid commentator, it is worth noting how his use of paradox undercuts his legalistic formulations. While he attributes to the 'nom-du-père' the function of stabilizing language, he conceals the phrase within a pun which has the opposite effect, unleashing ambiguities beyond control (le non-du-pére, the no-of-the-father – the prohibition of the father – is another nifty alternative). What is more, the edict that the non-dupes err (implying that the dupes do not) is a recipe for lawlessness disguised in the sententiousness of law. Similarly, when Lacan declares elsewhere that 'there is no metalanguage', the very structure of the axiom shows that there is no escape from metalanguage either, from the dream of an idiom of knowledge purified of the delusions it interrogates (Felman, 1988, p. 152).[10]

In Lacan's defence, then, one could argue that his riddling, serpentine, allusive style subverts his dogmatism, rendering his oracular pronouncements pervious to other voices and unintended meanings. If Lacan is doing the police in different voices he is still, however, doing the police, attempting to enforce his own interpretation of the Freudian legacy. In an uncanny way, the themes of Poe's story – theft, rivalry, revenge – repeat themselves in the critical debate inspired by it. Derrida has accused Lacan of 'aggression in the form of, or with the aim of, reappropriation' – that is, of purloining Derrida's ideas; but Derrida himself could be said to have purloined his rival's slippery interpretation of the letter by reducing it to the theory of castration (Derrida, 1981, p. 107). As Johnson has pointed out, 'Derrida's own reading of Lacan's text repeats the crimes of which he accuses it'; that is, by boiling it down into a single meaning (Johnson, 1988, p. 218). Nor has Derrida relented: even in his recent essay, improbably entitled 'For the Love of Lacan' (1998 [1990]), he re-enumerates the flaws he had detected in Lacan's famous Seminar so many years before, with scarcely a nod to subsequent critiques (Derrida, 1998, pp. 57–9). For a thinker so preoccupied with alterity, and so mercurial in many of his attitudes, Derrida's verdict on Lacan is remarkably inflexible.

Curiously, Bonaparte, Lacan and Derrida triangulate themselves around the *story* of 'The Purloined Letter' much as the Queen, the Minister and Dupin triangulate themselves around the eponymous letter itself. And the story's readers, like its dramatis personae, lose the trophy at the very moment that they grasp it. Just as the Minister turns the letter blank side out, inadvertently exposing it to Dupin's depredations, each reader of Poe's tale unfolds a further underside of ambiguity for the next reader to purloin and reinscribe.[11] Thus the letter – defined either as the *billet doux* or as the literary features of the tale itself – provokes a compulsion to repeat whereby each reader, in the very effort to control its meaning and curtail its movement, is ensnared in its irrepressible automatism.

FREUD AND THE PLEASURE PRINCIPLE

The compulsion to repeat is the subject of Derrida's remarkable analysis, in 'To Speculate – on "Freud"', of Freud's even more remarkable *Beyond the Pleasure Principle* (1920). It is in *Beyond the Pleasure Principle* that Freud introduces his theory of the death drive (otherwise known as the principle of Thanatos), which several leading commentators have dismissed as an attack of mysticism, alien to the authentic core of Freudian thought. Lacan, however, takes *Beyond the Pleasure Principle* seriously. But Derrida accuses him of taking it too seriously, by mystifying the death drive and ignoring the dynamics of the argument in which it is proposed (Derrida, 1987, p. 377). What fascinates Derrida in *Beyond the Pleasure Principle* is the idea of repetition, which he detects in both its content and its idiolect; and he returns to *Beyond the Pleasure Principle* throughout his work as inexorably as Freud's death drive returns to 'an earlier state of things'.

Derrida's title plays on the term 'speculation' with which Freud opens the fourth chapter of *Beyond the Pleasure Principle*: 'What follows is speculation, often far-fetched speculation . . .' Here the primary meaning of speculation is hypothesis, but secondary innuendoes of betting, risking, gambling, as well as those of watching or spectatorship, also play their part in Freud's scenario. All these meanings coincide in the famous 'fort/da' game, in which a little boy (Freud's grandson Ernst), witnessed by his mother and his grandfather, flings a cotton reel into his curtained cot, emitting a sadistic 'oooo', and then retrieves it with an 'aaaa' of satisfaction. Freud interprets these two phonemes as rudiments of the German words *fort* [gone] and *da* [here], and argues that the child is attempting to master the anxiety of separation from his mother by 'staging' her departures and returns. According to Freud, this game performs a function similar to that of tragic drama, which inflicts upon the audience the painful experience of loss while wresting pleasure out of the aesthetic mastery of that experience. Freud observes, however, that his grandson stages the painful first act, that of departure, much more often than the second act, that of return, although the restoration of the object is supposedly more pleasurable than its forfeiture (Freud, 1920, pp. 24, 14–17). According to Freud, this addictive gambling with loss reveals a 'daemonic' element in the compulsion to repeat that ultimately overrides the pleasure principle. On this basis he posits the existence of another 'power in mental life which we call the instinct of aggression or of destruction according to its aims, and which we trace back to the original death instinct of living matter' (Freud, 1937, p. 243). The later chapters of *Beyond the Pleasure Principle* assert (with a speculative recklessness comparable to Ernst's) that '"*the aim of all life is death*"', and that the instincts are the urges '*inherent in organic life to restore an earlier state of things*', the earliest of which is nonexistence (Freud, 1920, pp. 36–8). Thus the pleasure principle, which aims for 'constancy' or equilibrium within the organism, is hijacked by the instincts of destruction, which crave the final constancy of death, the chill repose of inorganic matter.[12]

According to Derrida, the logic of the death drive is re-enacted in *Beyond the Pleasure Principle* itself, when Freud, as gambler or 'speculator', plays fort–da with everything that jeopardizes the supremacy of the pleasure principle. 'What repeats itself . . . is the speculator's indefatigable motion in order to reject, to set aside, to make disappear, to distance (*fort*), to defer everything that appears to put the PP in question' (Derrida, 1987, p. 295). Here the PP, an abbreviation for the pleasure principle, and student-slang for 'Professeur Principal', also stands for the *pépé*: Ernst's papa, first of all, whom the child also tries to throw away ('go to the fwont!' [*Geh in K(r)ieg!*] he shouts at his toys, when his father returns from the Great War); and Freud himself, the papa of psychoanalysis, and the papa of Ernst's mother Sophie, who died in 1920 when Freud was completing *Beyond the Pleasure Principle*. Ernst, by playing fort–da, is also 'going peepee' with his toys: he sends his peepee away, sends his penis away (the penis is forever going *fort* and *da* in psychoanalysis), and even sends himself away, when in a later instalment of the game he discovers how to make his own mirror-image disappear: 'Baby oooo!' [baby gone], he chortles on behalf of *Thanatos* (Freud, 1920, pp. 16, 15n.). For Derrida, the multiple meanings of PP correspond to the multiple positions Freud assumes within this text: grandfather, father, elder brother (Freud, like Ernst, was roused to violent jealousy by the birth of a younger brother who, like Ernst's brother Heinerle, died in infancy), witness, narrator, speculator, spokesman for the pleasure principle, detective of the death drive, and father of the 'science' that bears his name.

In Derrida's analysis the PP also stands for the postal principle, the principle of sending forth with no assurance of return delivery. When Freud, in his discussion of the death drive, sends the pleasure principle away, with the speculator's hope that the profit will exceed the loss, he unleashes all the forces implied by the term 'post' – postponement, delegation, distance, errancy, dissemination – which deflect the message from its destination. In his recent book *Archive Fever* (1996), Derrida points out that psychoanalysis itself, exceptionally in the history of scientific projects, is founded on a postal correspondence, the letters to Fliess in which Freud undertakes his self-analysis. Thus the deferral intrinsic to the post ('a handwritten letter takes so many days to arrive in another European city, and nothing is ever independent of this delay') is built into the Freudian legacy (Derrida, 1996, p. 17). This deferral is also enshrined in *Beyond the Pleasure Principle* itself, where 'life' is envisaged as a vast detour (*Umweg*) through which death posts itself to itself, like a letter that returns to sender.[13] The 'organism wishes to die only in its own fashion', Freud declares; it is only external influences that create the tension forcing living substance to 'diverge ever more widely from its original course of life and to make ever more complicated *détours* before reaching its aim of death' (Freud, 1920, pp. 38–9). This argument suggests to Derrida that the drive to self-identity, the drive to overcome the division implicit in the postal principle and to be re-united with one's unadulterated origin, is stronger than either the life drive or the death drive. Yet Freud's own speculations, digressive and meandering, forever losing sight of their apparent goal, re-stage that 'interminable detour' by which the postal principle waylays the death drive, preventing either arguments or organisms from achieving self-coincidence (Derrida, 1987, p. 284).

One of Derrida's most startling insights into the motivations of *Beyond the Pleasure Principle* arises from a stray remark of Freud's about the fort–da game. Freud wonders why the little boy insists on throwing the cotton reel into his bed instead of dragging it behind him like a train. Derrida observes that Freud

> seems surprised, adding to this surprise a [certain] regret that the good little boy never seemed to have the idea of pulling the spool behind him and playing at its being a carriage: or rather at its being a wagon (*Wagen*), a train. It is as if one could wager (*wagen* again) that the speculator (whose contrary preference, that is, railway phobia, *Eisenbahn*, is well enough known to put us on the track) would himself have played choo-choo with one of these 'small objects' (*kleinen Gegenstände*). . . . If he had been playing in his grandson's place (and therefore playing with his daughter [Sophie], since the spool replaces her . . . or at least, following its/his thread, is but a trait or train leading to her, in order to come just to depart from her again), the (grand)father would have played carriage . . . but the idea never occurred to Ernst. Instead of playing on the floor (*am Boden*), he insisted on putting the bed into the game . . . [translation modified]

This maze of puns and parentheses requires some unravelling. Why is Freud perplexed that the child doesn't think of playing *Wagen* with the cotton reel? Is it because the reel, which stands for Freud's daughter and Ernst's mother, has been thrust suggestively into the bed? Commentators often overlook the fact that Ernst is not in bed himself when he throws away the spool: the bed, therefore, is *fort*, 'but perhaps not *fort* enough for the (grand)father who might have wished that Ernst had played more seriously on the floor (*am Boden*) without bothering himself with the bed' (Derrida, 1987, pp. 314–15). Phobic about rail travel, Freud also had more urgent reasons at the time of writing to be preoccupied with trains. On 25 January 1920 Sophie died; but the railroads were shut down, and her parents could not go to her. Freud writes:

> We had been worried about her for two days, but were still hopeful [will she come back?]. From a distance it is so difficult to judge. The distance still remains. We could not, as we wished to, go to her at once when the first alarming news came, because there were no trains, not even a children's train. The undisguised brutality of our times weighs heavily on us. Our poor Sunday child is to be cremated tomorrow.

Sophie, then, is *fort* – 'as if she had never been' – yet her father denies that 'the monstrous fact of children dying before their parents' has anything to do with his book about the death drive. Had he been analysing someone else, he admits to his biographer, 'I certainly would have stressed the con-nection between the death of the daughter and the Concepts of the *Jenseits* [*Beyond the Pleasure Principle*]. Yet still it is wrong'. There is no such con-nection, no such train of thought involved. 'The *Jenseits* was written in 1919, when my daughter was young and blooming, she died in 1920', Freud insists. Elsewhere, however, he intimates that the work was only 'half finished' when Sophie died, and that the term 'death drive' appeared shortly after the deaths of his friend Anton von Freund and Sophie (Derrida, 1987, pp. 331, 328–9). Is there not some 'inner denial', Ernest Jones demands, in Freud's unruffled conscience about *Beyond the Pleasure Principle*, the writing of which continued without interruption for a single day of mourning? 'The death, painful as it is, does not affect my attitude toward life', Freud declares, in a letter to Ferenczi written less than two weeks after Sophie's cremation.

Whether or not the theory of the death drive emerged in response to Sophie's death, Freud's hunch that his biographers would jump to this conclusion, and his strenuous attempts to fend it off, arouse Derrida's curiosity. What is Freud trying to hide? Is it the uncanny way that Sophie's death is anticipated in the seven chapters of *Beyond the Pleasure Principle*, the number standing for the 'Sunday child' who, born on the seventh day, died in a week after seven years of marriage? The loss (*fort!*) that Freud has yet to suffer thus repeats itself demonically throughout his text (*da!*), in such symptoms as the number seven; or the spool that should have been a train; or the death drive which itself goes *fort* and *da*, appears and disappears 'while telling many stories and making many scenes'. (There is 'dead silence about death', Derrida points out, through almost half of *Beyond the Pleasure Principle* [Derrida, 1987, pp. 329, 262, 353].)

This ingenious – and deeply moving – reading of *Beyond the Pleasure Principle* employs much the same procedures as a psychobiographical analysis, though Derrida would baulk at the comparison. Indeed he deplores the 'crushing psychobiographical style' by which Freud's chron-iclers (such as Ernest Jones and Max Schur) have written off *Beyond the Pleasure Principle* as a reactive episode (Derrida, 1987, pp. 328–9) . Derrida, by contrast, discounts the empirical connection between the death of Sophie and the birth of the death drive: in deference to Freud, he argues that the dates don't correspond. But Derrida's own interpretation is more startling, not less, than those of Freud's biographers: he proposes that the death of Sophie is prefigured, rather than remembered, in Freud's text. Is this an attack of mysticism – or numerology – on Derrida's part? Or is he imputing to Freud's text the temporal inversions of *Nachträglichkeit* (deferred action), whereby the psyche strives to master trauma after the event by generating the anxiety that should have been aroused before the unforeseen catastrophe? Or is he tracking down the deadly work of the compulsion to repeat, which overrides the boundaries between life and text, before and after, cause and effect, disseminating symptoms that refer to nothing prior to their own proliferation? If so, Sophie's death, rather than precipitating this compulsion, is swept into its maelstrom, rolled round in its inexorable revolutions.

These questions could be debated at length; suffice it to say that Derrida's methods of interpretation scarcely differ from those of the psychobiographers whom he attacks, even if he sees Freud's text as the 'uncanny harbinger', rather than the memorial or 'myrmidon' of Sophie's death.[14] He deploys Freud's private letters, for example, much as Freud himself made use of his patients' free associations in determining the meaning of their dreams. With important reservations, Derrida accepts the old-fashioned notion that authors' lives inform their writings: reports of the death of the author, he would argue, have been greatly exaggerated (see Derrida, 1984b, p. 22). Indeed he insists on the autobiographical dimension not just of *Beyond the Pleasure Principle* but of philosophical writings in general, whose aspirations to universality are always undercut by stubborn traces of their historicity. For Derrida, the 'autobiographical' refers not to the fullness of a human presence, nor to the intentions of the author, but to the intrusion of the accidents of writing into the abstractions of pure reason. The autobiographical makes itself felt (in Robert Smith's words) in 'the dehiscence [or gaping] of the literary into the philosophical'; in the means by which the style of an argument inflects its sense (Smith, 1995, p. 4). Hegel insisted that the 'sole aim of philosophical enquiry is to eliminate the contingent'; Derrida, by contrast, insists that the author's name, the author's body, the author's position in space and time are obstinate contingencies that philosophy can never exorcise (see Smith, 1995, p. 13).

Derrida's distrust of psychobiography emerges in his earlier work *Of Grammatalogy* (1976 [1967]), where he demonstrates how Rousseau's view of masturbation as a 'dangerous supplement' to sexual intercourse is implicated in his view of writing as a dangerous supplement to speech. 'In spite of certain appearances, the locating of the word supplement is here not at all psychoanalytical, if by that we understand an interpretation that takes us outside of the writing toward a biographical signified', Derrida protests (Derrida, 1976, p. 159). This disclaimer, relying as it does on a questionable caveat (does psychoanalysis necessarily entail this flight from writing?), scarcely proves Derrida's innocence of psychoanalytic methods. Yet the fallacy of psychobiography, as he perceives it, is to subordinate the writing to the writer, to treat 'the work' as merely the representation of 'the life'. The very concept of representation relies on the 'violent hierarchies' that structure logocentric thought, privileging origin over derivative, signified over signifier, presence over re-presentation.[15] Psychobiography colludes in this violence when it construes unconscious motives as the prior cause of which the text is the delayed effect. This is

Socrates what it is that makes the true and proper statesman so true and proper, so exemplary, is by means of an example:

> [W]hat example is there on a really small scale which we can take and set beside kingship, and which, because it comprises an activity common to it and kingship can be of real help to us in finding what we are looking for? By heaven, Socrates, I believe I know one. Do you agree that, if there is no other example ready to hand, it would be quite in order for us to select the art of weaving for the purpose? Would you be prepared for us to choose weaving – if there is nothing else obviously suitable?   (Plato, 1961, 279b)

Having been asked so charmingly, it would be churlish, most unreasonable, of Young Socrates not to agree. Frankly, he has no option: he is *bound* to agree, as if magically obliged to do so. If he were not to agree, then either the example of weaving would have to be dropped (which would be the ruin of the argument as explication), or the Stranger would have to insist, against any objection, on the example of weaving – thus behaving like a dictator (and this would be the ruin of the argument as performative mimesis, as an example of itself both as regards the ideal of good – non-tyrannical – leadership and as regards the pedagogical ideal, the setting of an open-minded, non-dogmatic precedent).

In the above excerpt, the Stranger seems careful to present himself most agreeably, which means that by making much of a certain nonchalance, a certain 'what you will', he might have us nodding along to what he says without the least sense of being coerced. If this strikes us as a fine piece of acting, it would disconcert the Stranger who has set himself up against the Sophists, despising them as cross-species hybrids, shape-shifters and 'impersonators' (291*b–c*). The statesman, true king, is explicitly set up in opposition to both the (too, say, limp) Sophist, on the one hand, and the (unbending) tyrant, on the other hand, the one who proceeds without consent. Let us, if we have any choice, briefly go along with this example of weaving. The Stranger proceeds by sifting to distinguish weaving from other textile skills such as carding (the art that produces the stiff warp thread) and spinning (the art that produces the soft woof thread), for the speciality of weaving consists of the interlacing, *sumplokē*, of the threads thus produced. The ideal statesman is then given to us as a weaver because (having rejected the bad material within a society, presumably that which fails to meet the requisite standard or cannot be standardized) he weaves the good and serviceable threads together to produce the unified, harmonious social fabric. The serviceable threads are of two kinds: the gentle or moderate and the brave and vigorous. It is said: 'Those in whom courage predominates will be treated by the statesman as having the firm warplike [*stēmōn*, 'warp', masculine] character ... The others will be used by him for what we might likewise call the supple, soft, wooflike [*krokē*, 'woof', feminine] strands of the web. He then sets about . . . weaving together these two groups exhibiting their mutually opposed characters' (309*b*). He serves thus to marry or harmonize the virtuous masculine and feminine elements of society without losing the opposition between them, and moreover, the opposition can be said to be one of the same (a coupling of complementaries, according to a measure or standard that produces them as such, rather than a mixing of species, that being much disapproved of in the text).

Returning now to the point in the argument when the insertion of the example of weaving is first deemed necessary to it, we see that the elaboration of weaving occurs as a response to a conclusion arrived at too quickly.

> *Stranger*:   Tendance of human herds by violent control is the tyrant's art, tendance freely accepted by herds of free bipeds we call statesmanship. Shall we now declare that he who possesses this latter art and practises this tendance is the true king and the true statesman?
> *Young Socrates*:   Yes, and I should think, sir, that at this point we have really completed our definition of the statesman.   (276*e*–277)

But not. Not so fast. While the Stranger feels that the definition is incomplete because it is incomplete ('an outline sketch'), I would add that it needs to be taken further because the question remains as to what *compels* the human herd to *agree* to the control/tendance of the statesman and thus be bound by him. This is a question of what we might call 'group psychology' and with this mention we might tie in Freud's *Group Psychology and the Analysis of the Ego*. Here Freud suggests that the herd agrees to submit to the leader because the leader constitutes an 'ego ideal' for each member of the group. Furthermore, the mutuality of the ego ideal is what binds the individual members to each other. With regard to the question of how the statesman achieves social unity, posed in the concluding moments of the dialogue, Plato offers a similar answer in terms of the requisite dynamics:

> He first unites that element in their [the group's] souls which is supernatural by a divine bond since that element in them is akin to the divine. After this supernatural link [the bond between individuals and the godlike ego ideal] will come the natural bond, human ties to supplement the divine ones [insofar as they all share the same godlike ego ideal].   (309*c*)

The statesman, royal weaver, could be said to combine in himself all the best qualities in a virgin marriage. Married to himself, he could be said to be a double-bachelor or 'spinster'-bachelor or a Father-'mother'. Writing of the *pharmakon*, a term that can signify both 'remedy' and 'poison', Derrida states: 'This "medicine" is not a simple thing. But neither is it a composite . . . it is rather the prior medium in which differentiation in general is produced' (Derrida, 1981, p. 126). He goes on to cite from the *Statesman*, as follows, although I abbreviate: 'This is the talisman (*pharmakon*) appointed for them [those of leadership potential] by design of pure intelligence. This most godlike bond alone can unite the elements of virtue . . . which would else be opposing in tendency' (310*a*). So, really, the statesman would be what we might call a genius, or possessed of genius, and genius is often said to be *sui generis* (unique, of its own kind, say, of a unique kind, that would issue in an auto-hetero-generation). It is said that the true statesman 'alone is able . . . to forge [the bond of true conviction] by his wondrous inspiration of the kingly art' (309*d*). No art of weaving then, beyond him or outside of him, from which he could stand to learn? In Plato, as Derrida shows and explores at length, writing is treated as a *pharmakon*. Briefly, the statesman is a weaver who would weave without weaving, and would write without writing.

When the Stranger suggests weaving as an example for the exemplary king, he is forced to admit that: 'Example, my good friend, has been found to require an example' (277*d*). And, in order to explain this – the requirement of examples – he takes writing as an example and, in particular, gives us the example of children being taught to read. Letters are used as examples as children are taught to identify them through having recognizable letters and unfamiliar letters juxtaposed, and the teacher will have achieved his aim once the pupil has 'identified each letter with itself and distinguished it from all others' (278*c*). Writing is thus appealed to in order to explain, as Derrida says with reference to the *Sophist*, 'the interlacing that weaves together the system of differences (solidarity-exclusion), of kinds and forms, the *sumplokē ton eidon* to which "any discourse we can have owes its existence" . . . (259*e*)' (Derrida, 1981, p. 165). So writing is not a casual example but crucial, and besides this more than an example – an insight of deconstruction not confined to this instance. In a limited reading, it can be said that Plato down-plays his writing example by confining it to schoolchildren, an infantilizing move whereby we are encouraged to think of it in terms of 'baby-steps', early learning. This infantilization could then serve to mask the problematic dependency on writing, signalled in terms of the dependence on examples that the Stranger admits to, in what may be heard as a tone of some embarrassment or coyness. Interestingly, given Plato's general use of the (staged) presence of the teacher in the dialogues, what is not considered is that once the children have learnt to read and write they would be freed of a necessary dependence on their teacher, able to explore the world of learning and knowledge on their own by means of written texts.[1]

In the *Statesman*, it is not the case that writing is directly compared with weaving; rather, the example of weaving is to be explained by the example of learning to read and write. That is, the point of the analogy here is that both the skill of weaving and basic literary skills are merely elementary starting-points from which we are to progress to greater and higher understanding. It is later emphasized that the statesman is not to be bound by, dependent on, any written laws, written prescriptions, written precedents. He is thus to transcend any inscribed examples (precedents, guidelines) and the preliminary example of the acquisition of literacy, for he would be beyond learning.

What is striking about the writing of the *Statesman*, however, is that it is itself throughout a weaving operation, this operation being inseparable from the advancement of the advanced concept of statesmanship. In a sense, it could be proposed that the text does little else than colour in its original conclusion, the inspiration of the inspirational ruler: *The Statesman*! *The Statesman*. Plato's Stranger explicitly comes up with 'weaving' as a means of painting in what would otherwise be an outline sketch (and as Derrida shows more widely, the term *pharmakon* also designates pigments or pictorial colour). At the same time, the Stranger explains that written words constitute a means of portrayal that is preferable to that of visible images or illustrations, although the latter may be resorted to in the case of those who find the definition difficult to follow. And I think it might help to try out a possible visual image at this point. We could take a look at Remedios Varo's silently telling, ghostly painting: *Embroidering Earth's Mantle* (see Figure 5). In the painting, the tower may be seen as an elevated conning tower (the structure in which the ship's Captain is ensheathed and to which Plato refers) in which women work at weaving the world. A veiled figure, alchemist or pharmacist, oversees the weaving operation (the statesman, we are told, is an 'overseer' and the painting shows this). Moreover, this tower is also a fortress and the fortress, according to Lacan, symbolises the self-defensive ideal ego, originary narcissistic structure, while beyond this fortification, still according to Lacan, lie the city's refuse dumps (of, say, detritus and remains).[2] Varo's painting shows, too, a captivation of women or an imprisonment of a female labour force within this defensive, capitalizing structure. Furthermore, the painting is said to refer to Varo's experience of Catholic convent life, and one of the women in the painting wittily weaves her escape with her lover into the world-fabric that she produces.[3] Thomas Pynchon writes about this painting in *The Crying of Lot 49* (1979) when his heroine, Oedipa, encounters it in a gallery, and offers this as her response to it: 'What did she so desire to escape from? Such a captive maiden, having plenty of time to think, soon realizes that her tower, its height and architecture, are like her ego only incidental: and what really keeps her where she is is magic, anonymous and malignant, visited on her from out-

Figure 5 *Embroidering Earth's Mantle* by Remedios Varo, 1961. Reproduced by kind permission of Walter Gruen.

side and for no reason at all' (p. 13). She would seem to be spellbound by substanceless emanations, intimidations, ingratiations, from a pharmaceutical source.

However, weaving in the *Statesman* is not envisioned or exposed in quite this way, while the text can nonetheless be seen to weave. In this respect, it is a text loosely comparable to Freud's *Beyond the Pleasure Principle* (1955). Freud's text takes as its starting point, for the sake of an illustration of a compulsion to repeat, an autobiographical anecdote, that of his grandson's game with a bobbin and thread in which the bobbin is repeatedly made to disappear (*fort*, gone), and then return (*da*, there). Derrida, in his reading of this text, shows how its own movement (both as argument and performance) mimes the grandson's exemplary game, even as it would surpass it in advancing the theory of the death drive (also characterized by a compulsion to repeat). It is impossible to summarize Derrida's closely attentive reading here, one which patiently traces the vacillating rhythms of Freud's text, and so I will leave it to be read while I will try to pick up on or transfer some of its skills or lessons.

The *Statesman* is a text that weaves. It is not straightforward but keeps digressing, following false leads, backtracking and recapitulating earlier stages of itself. It wants to conclude in its own fashion – as Freud suggests 'we', organisms, all do – and this is a matter of not going too fast, concluding too quickly, whilst not slowing down to a standstill, getting nowhere. In this text about political economy, there is a continual regulation of its own expenditure, a management of its energies, combining, possibly, self-pleasing pleasure and profitable work. Not only this, there is a continual textual carding going on, that is, the Stranger (or whatever it is of the text that goes by that name) keeps sifting the good threads of the argument from the detritus, the material that cannot be serviceably used to make good the concepts being worked towards, and then, through further explication, these threads are strengthened and with that we have the firm warp of text. At the same time, for harmony, for pulling together, it has to spin its pliant woof threads – well, is that not so?

Young Socrates: Woof! Woof!

It is Young Socrates' role to agree with the agreeable Stranger (although he is energetic in his compliant agreements while the Stranger is gentle, non-coercive, in his firm leads). In this they weave together very well, are well-connected, and it is a perfectly consensual arrangement in which they complement and continually compliment each other. Together they combine the best of the Sophist – shape-shifting as flexibility, stretchability, elasticity – and the best of tyranny – hardness, stiffness. And that is how they double-band and stand erect.

The example of weaving thus undergoes, goes under, a transformation, an elevation. Before this elevation, the Stranger expresses a certain discomfort or disdain:'I cannot think that any reasonable person would want to trace down the definition of the art of weaving just for its own sake' (285*e*). So: that would be just too banausic, for how could any person of reason, or any intellectual, find anything of interest or inspiration in weaving itself? In this way any indebtedness to the art of weaving is disavowed, as something of weaving is taken over, transferred and transformed; this is the work of the metaphor and metaphoricity. What is carried across by means of analogy, in which the figurative is separated from the literal, is furthermore idealized, conceptualized, capitalized upon. While weaving itself is rendered a mindless operation, having no idea of itself, the idea of it would seem to be solely that of the Stranger or Plato. Uniquely owned, indebted only to itself, the idea, inspiration, ideal of weaving accrues enormous value whilst actual weaving is de-valued or dis-acknowledged. But the ideal has to show that it works, can be put to the test, can really be believed in. In fact, in the text much is made of the fact that 'the statesman' cannot be dreamt up on the spot but must be reached through the hard work of true philosophy (as opposed to, say, flighty poetic inspiration), that is, conceptual labour. But this work is the very busy text-work of discarding, carding, spinning, shuttling back and forth, interlacing: the text weaving itself. The statesman is re(s)-erected from this weaving operation, whereby the text would then be 'only' the skin 'he' (as the ideal) moults or sloughs (while you can yet re-cycle it).

It should be said that the *Statesman* is a text that delivers itself: it pulls itself off, it delivers the goods, wins its cup. This is one thing that makes it both slightly like and yet so different from Freud's *Beyond the Pleasure Principle*, which ends lamely, avowing its own limpness. (And, perhaps, the death drive, offered in opposition to the pleasure principle, is necessarily impotent or incapable of erection.) While Freud's text possibly cannot help its perplexed vacillations, at least in the reference offered here, Plato's text has a certain sureness about itself. The character trait that Plato gives the Stranger, also in the *Sophist*, is one of a sort of dilly-dallying, but when this is confessed by the Stranger it is arguably in tones of coyness or embarrassment, perhaps because it is not quite an honest avowal. It could be said that the *Statesman* only pretends to doubt itself, faking its false moves or steps (dissimulates its simulation), inasmuch as the Stranger seems to know exactly where he is going, never really losing it or what it is he wants to rejoin. It could be added in order to refine this, that the paralysis of Freud's text (considered at length in Derrida's reading of it) is perhaps due to the faking of its moves as opposed to false moves: that is, it seems compelled to renounce its own creative drive whilst Plato's text appropriates and makes use of, rather than wards off, a creativity that it affects not to have. In *The Clouds* (1973), Aristophanes comically has his Socrates offer the following advice to a would-be disciple: 'Don't keep your thought penned up inside you all the time. Let it out into the air for a bit, keeping it under control, of course, like a yo-yo' (p. 144). In this string-and-bobbin game, thoughts (think of them as children or puppies) would be allowed a strictly controlled play, in which they would not wander off, go astray, thanks to the thread or the tie. Indeed, they would bounce back and this would testify to the powers of their fathers to recall them or give reassurance of their remembrance of their masters or owners. The allowance of a little licence would be for the sake of a repeatedly enacted or proven fidelity. It is how people play with dogs – a stick or ball is thrown and the dog retrieves it, again and again, 'woof-woof': dogs understand this.

In French, *'fils'* signifies both 'son' and 'thread', as Derrida has often observed and drawn out further. In 'Plato's Pharmacy', he shows that in Plato's thought there is both a writing that is approved of and a writing that is disapproved of. These two types of writing could be characterized in terms of the good son, loyal to the father, and the bad son, who is cut off from the father, a pitiable orphan or an irreverent bastard – one who does not bounce back and who cannot be prevented from straying. These '*fils*', the achievements of one and the waywardness of the other, keep appearing in Derrida's work, as if part of an on-going saga. In *Glas* (1986), which we are about to come to, they serve to format the text: a column for the father-son and one for the wayward one, the mother-son. Well, what of the mother? It could be said that the mother is one who weaves the child in her womb, or that the child weaves itself in her, or that there is a weaving of both but without a subject as such. In raising this, I am not trying to suggest, in place of the father, an idealized maternal origin – for that would be to imagine a maternal omnipotence, as but a reversal of the omnipotent paternal logos. The reason that I refer to a maternal weaving here is for the sake of speculating over the possible affects and responses provoked by the imagined self-sufficiency of a maternal source, imagined as such from a position of vulnerability in relation to it. This could, amongst other possible configurations, take the form of a jealousy as regards the mother, an envy of her loom.

Where did Plato get the idea of weaving from? It could be that he 'borrowed', jealously stole or secretly copied it from his rival–friend, the poet, Aristophanes (while they both could be drawing on common cultural funds or heirlooms). In *Lysistrata* (1973), Aristophanes has the magistrate ask the women for advice on how to restore peace and harmony in the state and between states and Lysistrata suggests an example of weaving from her own experience: 'it might not be so idiotic as you think to run the whole City entirely on the model of the way we deal with wool' (p. 204). And she elaborates on this, but with no mention of an ideal leader. In the *Statesman*, the very necessity to think 'statesmanship' arises because, according to the Stranger, the Greeks have entered a phase of history in which men are no longer 'earth-born', chthonic peoples, and no longer under the tendance of a nurturing shepherd-god. Men thus are produced from themselves (not earth-born) and need to become self-reliant: self-fathering? Let us speculate on the invention of the technique of weaving. The word '*histos*' means 'anything set upright' and designates: mast; beam of loom; loom; web; woven cloth, piece of canvas (see 'Plato's Pharmacy', p. 65). The science of histology is the science of organic tissue (its histogenic production, its breakdown, its diseases, its regeneration). I should add that Ferenczi suggests that an interest in etymology, word origins, is a sublimated form of the question: where do children come from?[4]

Does this yet remain too close to the weave, too close-up to the mesh of the threads for something of a pattern of through-threads and gaps to be seen? I should perhaps over-say what I am saying. Amongst weaving's other names we could find 'creative labour' and 'the inventions of women'. Freud believed weaving and plaiting to be the only technique ever invented by women (no small invention if it leads to computers) and that women invented it to hide their genital deficiency.[5] While invention may well begin with lack or loss, we could interpret as follows: the exceptional immodesty of a female inventiveness requires the placation of the thought that this immodesty is actually a true feminine modesty, an acknowledgement on the part of women that they naturally lack the means to invent, that is, in lacking the original organ/tool of invention. Freud's idea of the origins of weaving can be juxtaposed with Woolf's observation, in *A Room of One's Own* (1929), that women have often needed to hide their creative work from view: Jane Austens hiding their novels in progress under blotting paper or, we could add, under their needlework (Woolf, 1929, p. 100). Here, weaving could be seen in terms of a protective need for privacy in the 'secretion' and maturation of the work. This is to begin to approach 'A Silkworm of One's Own', with its aptly translated title, while it yet remains necessary to allow for its timings as regards a tradition of thought from Plato onwards.

Plato's erection of the weaver is effected by separating the weaver from weaving so that the weaver can be precisely the sole and transcendental subject of weaving. Although the weaver is derived from the text, the weaver retrospectively becomes the origin and the text serves then to testify to this origin, confirming it as such – which is to renounce its, the text's, own fabricative originality. The work that goes into making the text, the work of thinking and writing, could thus be said to be idealized in the royal weaver ideal. Now this idealized leader, this king, who is not really there in the first place, ought rather to be thought of as a ghost, as Derrida considers in another context in *Specters of Marx*. Without tracing this,[6] would a ghost-weaver yet have a sex?

IMMACULATE CONCEPTION

At the outset of *Glas*, Derrida writes: 'In order to work on/in Hegel's name, in order to erect it . . . I have chosen to draw on one thread. It is going to seem too fine, strange and fragile. It is the law of the family: of Hegel's family, of the family in Hegel, of the family concept according to Hegel' (Derrida, 1986, 4a; trans. mod.). While Derrida pays attention to the question of what may be dispensable in Hegel's text (the examples that will not serve, the detritus, the remains), there is a point at which what may be conversely 'indispensable' for Hegel's thought is announced by Derrida. This occurs in a consideration of the transition from Absolute Religion (the vulnerability of which, as regards the ideal of pure conceptuality, is its reliance on pictorial thinking) to Absolute Knowledge. Derrida suggests that it is 'Immaculate Conception' that is: 'Indispensable to the Hegelian argumentation, to speculative dialectics, to absolute idealism' (233a). The conception of Immaculate Conception depends on and occurs in the absolute divorce of the father (that is, 'knowledge') from the mother who is situated in and as worldly immediacy. The father, 'the real author, subject of the conception . . . does without the woman', while the mother 'makes the child without knowledge' (223a). The father is the real author or sole author or only true parent, while the difference of the mother constitutes no difference in that it is posited in terms of her opposition. Conceptuality is thus a same-sexed, say, 'auto-generation' (in which the son, *fils*, serves to confirm the paternal origin), for which Derrida uses the term 'homosexual': 'And if the sexual difference as opposition relieves difference, conceptuality is homosexual' (223a).

Now, while this is being elaborated on the left-hand side of *Glas*, you cannot help noticing with a sideways glance or two, with a double-take, that a flagrant display of actual homosexuality is manifesting itself, Derrida citing or glossing Genet, on the other side of the page(s). This suggests to me that while conceptuality in Hegel may be 'homosexual', it is a repressed, sublimed and unavowable homosexuality – what has become known as Platonic love (perhaps misleadingly, since Plato confesses the homosexual sublimation). Homosexuality as such cannot appear in the Hegel column, in Hegel's text, for it would be the repressed or unconscious of the concept. Nonetheless, this homosexuality would be *requisite* as that which must be repressed-sublimed, where this would differ from the tragic and necessary utter dispensability represented, in Derrida's reading of Hegel, by Antigone, the *impossible* sister-daughter.

Immaculate Conception could be said to defy picturing: it is that which cannot be pictured. *Glas* itself keeps the gap between the column of a homosexuality that is but conceptual (one that would no doubt be homophobically denied or disavowed) and the column of an irreverently avowed homosexuality. However, there is one word, a weaving word, that may be said to hover over this abyss.

Navette is the word.

The word – *la navette* – is absolutely necessary . . . First, because it is a church term and everything here is hatched against a church. It concerns a small metal vessel in the form of a boat (*navis, navetta*) . . . And then the weaver's *navette* [shuttle] . . . Isn't elaboration a weaver's movement?

Yet we have mistrusted the textile metaphor. This is because it still keeps – on the side of the fleece, for example – a kind of virtue of naturality, primordiality, cleanliness [*propreté*].   (*Glas*, 207–8b)

[Real clouds] look like fleeces . . . not in the least like women. (Aristophanes, *The Clouds*)

The *navette* is singled out as a 'key' term – or more exactly, the exact term – in its precise polysemia – for considering the (irreverent, transvestite, migrant) comings-and-goings of/in the text(s) of Genet. Yet it is also almost discarded or treated with some reservation (and the *navette* can indeed serve as the cursor of suspended or withheld disbelief or of reserved, doubtful, agreement). Derrida's mistrust of the textile metaphor has already been touched on in 'Plato's Pharmacy', as regards the 'dissimulation of the woven texture', that disavowal of artifice. Here, weaving seems to be associated with *veiling* as a modesty and propriety or lack of artifice on the side of the feminine. In both of these formulations, it is a so-called fetishism that is *being disavowed* or covered up, whereas usually fetishism is given to us *as disavowal*. That is, here, 'fetishism' is not so much a form of disavowal (of difference) but that which is disavowed, refused – a refused undecidability, contamination, play, entrancement, pretence, hybridity, and so on – and this supposedly for the sake of an acknowledgement of a 'difference' (especially sexual) that turns out not to be so. If the textile metaphor does serve to support a disavowal of fetishistic undecidability, this would give us good reason to mistrust it. Yet this remains too one-sided or insufficiently cross-eyed in its focus, for the *navette* or shuttle would seem to be that which goes between a virgin immediate maternity and an immaculate paternity. (The bi-columnar layout of *Glas* necessitates that the discussion of the *navette* appear in the right hand column, the column of an admitted homosexuality and, also, of sexual undecidability). And yet, the shuttle could be said to operate across the gaps in and between two disavowals of artifice: a conceptuality that would transcend fabrication, and a naturalization that would feign artlessness. Artfully capable of rising above the purely natural without transcending nature, this go-between *navette* would have wings. It is often ideogrammatically a bird. The connection between the weaver's shuttle and birds is made by Scheid and Svenbro in their consideration of the *Ciris*, a poem attributed to Virgil, in which Scylla cuts a magic lock of hair from her father's head and is transformed into a bird. The bird she is transformed into is a halcyon, kingfisher, *keiris*: ' "Shuttle" moreover is *kerkis* in Greek, a word that is a paronym of *keiris*; and we might also note the common expression *keirkis aidos*, "singing or twittering shuttle"' (Scheid and Svenbro, 1996, p. 139). In order further to bring out the significance of the shuttle-bird in relation to Immaculate Conception, the poetry of Yeats will now be cut and patched into the discussion.

WORLD PICTURES

Yeats seems to have been fascinated by the 'phantasm', as Derrida calls it, of Immaculate Conception, writing three poems, intended as a triptych, on what could roughly be said to be this theme. The sequence begins in terms of its own chronology with 'Leda and the Swan', and this poem begins with the utterly surprising event of the entrance of the swan, its coup: 'A sudden blow'. The poem goes on to represent the rape of Leda by the swan, and it can be suggested that this bird is but a 'winged phallus' ('winged prick' is a phrase of Genet's that Derrida cites) or, retrospectively, the penile prosthesis of Zeus (to whom the origination of the event is supposed to be attributed, although he does not *himself* participate in it in his own proper body or form). The poem goes on to state that the rape 'engenders' the cataclysmic history of the Trojan War and ends with the lines: 'Did she put on his knowledge with his power / Before the indifferent beak could let her drop?' The answer is presumably 'No – being only caught up in the worldly immediacy of the event, she could not have shared any knowledge of its true significance'. She, Leda, would remain a virgin as far as knowledge is concerned. However, as far as 'immaculate conception' is concerned, this poem would constitute a false or impermissible representation. For a start, the objection to this quasi-pictorial representation would be that Immaculate Conception cannot be thus represented. Furthermore, the content of the representation here offers us a rape which would seem to be the antithesis of Immaculate Conception (IC). In *Glas*, Derrida points out that it would be silly to attempt to discredit IC through the positing of the sexual experience. While 'reality' could not prove IC untrue, its revelation would be phantasmatic, where the phantasm would be the truth of the truth (224a). This implies that the origination of IC would be a ghostly one and that it would arise in the form of a repetition (the phantasm as copy of the origin or original copy). Put another way, a speculative necessity – he *must* be the origin – repeats the 'must' or necessity of an originating blow. Derrida writes: 'who would dare say that the phantasm of the IC has not succeeded? Two thousand years, at least, of Europe, from Christ to Sa [*Savoir Absolut*] . . . of all that could be called the imperialism or the colonialisms and neocolonialisms of the IC' (224a). This, I think, could be regarded not as a colonization by what is given as the origin, but a colonization of the origin: the origin is colonized, laid claim to, in an auto-colonization. Could what from one side is conceived of as IC, be from another side conceived of as *phantasmatic rape*? This might concern what comes to be in being silenced – be it the mystery and mutuality of an encounter or its unauthorized violence – once the origin is colonized. In postcolonial discourse (especially), colonialism is often referred to in terms of rape where this rape is not necessarily the literal experience of rape but where, also, the violence and violation is not then merely metaphorical. Assia Djebar depicts this in her picturing of the capture of Algiers:

As the majestic fleet rends the horizon the Impregnable City sheds her veils. . . . The scene is suddenly blanketed in silence, as if the intense silken light were about to be rent with a strident screech. . . . As if the invaders were coming as lovers! . . . And the silence of this majestic morning is but the prelude to the cavalcade of screams and carnage which will fill the ensuing decades.   (Djebar, 1993, pp. 6–8)

'Two thousand years, at least'. 'Leda and the Swan' pictures the inauguration of a two-thousand-year cycle of history, which comes to an end with the birth of Christ. For Yeats, the birth of Christ repeats the earlier moment of historical inauguration whilst reversing it, producing an antithetical historical age. This moment of repetition–reversal is commemorated in Yeats's poem, 'Mother of God', a poem through which 'Leda and the Swan' may be palimpsestically glimpsed. We are given the lines: 'Wings beating around the room; / The terror of all terrors that I bore / The heavens in my womb'. 'Wings beating around the room'? Could this be another 'brute blood of the air', as the swan is described? This immaculate phantasm inaugurates another two-thousand-year cycle, which leads to the prophesied Second Coming. The third poem in the series (although written prior to 'Leda and the Swan'), 'The Second Coming' marks this. The poem begins: 'Turning and turning in the widening gyre / The falcon cannot hear the falconer'. What is thus envisioned is that the bird (shuttle?) no longer responds to the falconer, and what is further envisioned is a godless, anarchic age lacking true leadership. The Second Coming is to be of an Anti-Christ imaged in hybrid, cross-species terms (a beast-man/woman-machine), somewhat reminiscent of Plato's shape-shifting Sophists. What threads Yeats's three poems together, three world pictures, is not only the motif of periodic, repeated phantasmatic IC/rape, but his theory of the gyres. Simply speaking, in Yeats's system, the gyres (or spindles) are inter-penetrating cones, one primary and objective, the other, antithetical and subjective, which in a whirling or spinning motion produce a conflict or contradiction between subjective and objective states. As one winds down the other winds up. Or, as Yeats puts it: 'I see the gyre of "Concord" diminishes as that of "Discord" increases, and can imagine after that the gyre of "Concord" increasing while that of "Discord" diminishes, and so on' (Yeats, 1969, p. 64). Yeats refers in passing to the fact that there may be certain similarities between his thought and that of Hegel (a linking that Yeats, himself, is unsure of). Yeats's theory of the gyres can at least be traced to Plato's *Statesman*. In the *Statesman*, the very necessity of having to address an ideal of leadership arises because a cosmic crisis has initiated, in a movement of reversal, a new historical epoch. It is said: 'There is an era in which God himself assists the universe on its way and guides it by imparting its rotation to it. There is also an era in which he releases his control. . . . Thereafter it begins to revolve in a contrary sense under its own impulse . . . when it has been released, it moves by its innate force and it has stored up so much momentum at the time of its release that it can revolve in the reverse sense for thousands of revolutions . . .' (269–70). This is parodied by Aristophanes:

> *Strepsiades*:　Awhirl! – ah, I get you! . . . Zeus is dead and now Awhirl is the new king.
>
> 　　　　　　　　　　　　　　　　　　　　　　　　(*The Clouds*, p. 129)

We could also exclaim: 'Ah, that's it, the gyres!' Although at this point Plato is yet to speak of weaving and spinning, the rotating movement can, especially given the similarities with Yeats's notion of reversible historical cycles, be seen to be specifically a *spinning* operation. Thus, the royal weaver could be said to be subject to a subjectless or innate cosmic spinning, whilst deriving his necessity from this. And, in Yeats's system, what generates history, prior to any gods and incarnations, is the whirling movement of the gyres. In 'The Second Coming', no divine transcendental cause is given, the predestined incarnation being only attributable to a rocking cradle, one that uncannily rocks itself.

What Yeats may be said to envisage is a mechanical, feminine yet sexless, indifferent, auto-generation as an alternative to a masculine auto-hetero-generation.[7] A mindless autonomous automaton would thus seem to substitute for and duplicate a spectral paternity or a paternal spectre. In *Specters of Marx*, Derrida reads Marx's fetishized commodity as a spinning autonomous automaton that could be the displaced repetition of a paternal spectre. What of the favoured examples of weaving and tailoring in *Capital*? Briefly, weaving is given as an example of specialized labour that loses its specialness in submitting to the abstraction required by exchange value. While other examples of specialized labour could be used here, the fact that Marx selects weaving interestingly serves to make its specialness somewhat paradigmatic of the specialness of (all) labour, of the specificity of work itself in its 'elabo(u)ration'. In addition, in the context of a discussion of work that is not subsumed by capitalism, Marx states: 'Milton produced *Paradise Lost* as a silkworm produces silk, as the activation of *his own* nature' (Marx, 1976, p. 1044). With this, I will move on to a consideration of 'weaving itself' in 'A Silkworm of One's Own'.

FINALLY A SILKWORM

'A Silkworm of One's Own' speaks of its own belatedness and while this belatedness need not be tied down to the exigencies of weaving, it does offer an intricate and attentive treatment of weaving. The text interweaves

an attention to the writing and writings of Hélène Cixous with an obser-
vance of the tallith, most specifically, Derrida's very own prayer-shawl,
and concludes with a memory of looking after silkworms. My treatment
of this text will here be, unfortunately, too selective and abrupt.

What is the thread to follow? Let us say, it is that of a returning–arriving, not of the there-and-yet-not-yet-there untouchability of a spectre, but
what in the text is called both (a) 'touch ground' and a 'quasi-resurrection'.

Derrida reads Cixous's account in *Savoir* (1998) of an eye operation performed on her, in which what is lost is a loss of vision, necessarily of
course her own myopia, what Cixous writes as 'my-myopia'. Thus, that
which has marked her out, so to speak, or been given to her as a sign of
election or of her specialness, here this myopia, could be regarded as a
sacrifice which is to be sacrificed – as Derrida goes on to speak of 'the sac-
rifice of sacrifice, the end of sacrifice' (p. 38). The sacrifice of sacrifice suggests both a re-sacrificing and a de-sacrificing. If sacrifice may be
considered in terms of inheritance through loss, the sacrifice of the sacrifice would recapitulate the necessity of an initial and initiating loss
(acceptance of a tragic yet donating and provocative necessity) at the
same time that there would be a transformation of the condition of loss, a
beginning again, anew. This could be more simply glossed with reference
to the *Odyssey*. Odysseus' journey, which begins by his being cut off from
his origins, can be seen in terms of an exilic working back so as to emerge
from – sacrifice – a condition or period of haunting and being haunted,
to shed a sentence of mourning. The return to Ithaca is not a return to lost
origins, given the acceptance of exile, but it is the moment at which it
becomes possible to begin again. This quasi-resurrection is the miracle of
the yet down-to-earth return; the wonderful comeback to ordinary life
anew. Loss operates the journey of coming back, but the operation of
coming back transforms the virtuality of returning into actuality. Reading
in *Savoir* of the operation that serves to 'recover' a vision that would hitherto have only been virtual not actual, Derrida comments: 'Thanks to
mourning the fire of the New World at last and touch ground' (p. 25).

This uplifting grounding differs from the raised up (ag)grandiosity of a
royal weaver. One thing 'A Silkworm of One's Own' serves to effect is 'a
restitution in size',[8] and the royal weaver is only mentioned in it in passing, much minified from this end of the telescope. But its 'working back'
also differs from that in Plato's text, for Plato's text works back to an origin that would omnipotently assume no loss or lack, disavowing any
indebtedness.[9]

What Derrida finds interesting in Cixous's account of the loss of
myopia is that it is not given to us in terms of the usual figure of unveil-
ing, which would bring along with it the exhausting, would-be exhaustive, tired old thought-grooves of 'revelation', of 'the truth' of sexual

difference in the sight of genital endowment or deficiency, and so on. Derrida directs our attention to how, instead, the text serves to transform sight into touch, citing: 'The continuity of her flesh and the flesh of the world, touch then, was love, and there was the miracle, the giving. . . . She had just touched the world with her eye . . .'   (p. 25). This understanding of eyes that touch and can be touched is also to be found in a poem by Ama Ata Aidoo, 'On Seeing a Small US Airforce Plane at Luanda Airport, June 1987' (Aidoo, 1992):

  Our eyes broke through their curtains and
  Wrung their hands
  Over our heads

Compared with this poetry, could we say that philosophy is blind to touch? That is, it might be that it can only see sight as *sight*, and if not sight, there would only be blindness. If so, we could call this cyclopean, one-eyed, and one-I'd, narcissistic. From Plato's one-and-only weaver to the one-sidedness of immaculate conceptions to Freud's one-eyed reading of weaving, and beyond, it is this I have been trying not to follow but agitate beside. It is, of course, one-eyed just to see this one-eyedness – the texts are always there to be re-read, thankfully, allowing us to disagree with ourselves – but this is a through-thread here. Philosophy, if blind to touch, may also be blind to or insensible to what it might touch upon or what might touch upon it.

The poem *Savoir*, a 'tight weaving of all the given threads', is not detached from the reality that gives it its realization, and is spoken of in terms of: 'an operation of writing which indebts itself to a "real" operation "in the world", right on the body. . . .' With this said, another voice in the text states: 'When you refer thus to the irreducible reality of an event (outside discourse but not outside text). . . . It looks so unlike you, you look so unlike yourself' (p. 43). This emphasis on reality (not outside text) would only be unlike deconstruction if deconstruction were thought of in terms of textual disembodiment. Against this, we should note that when Derrida avows himself, he confesses precisely to a writing of the body. In *Circumfession*, he writes:

  I am still weaving the cloths of an affabulation that I have first to date from *Spurs*, 1972 . . . For example, and I'm dating this, this is the first page of the notebooks, '*Circumcision, that's all I have ever talked about, consider the discourse on . . . the sacrifice, the writing of the body . . . unless, another hypothesis, circumcision itself were merely an example of the thing I was talking about, yes, but I have been, I am and always will be, me and not another, circumcised . . . (12–20–76)*'   (Derrida, 1993, pp. 69–73)

The 'unlike you', referred to in 'A Silkworm of One's Own', is vaguely reminiscent of an Odysseus who on his return is almost unrecognizable, for he is much changed but secretly or strangely the same.[10] Would this be like the silkworm become moth? Let us turn to Derrida's memory of the silkworms that he cultivated as a child.

Derrida's memory is of closely observing the caterpillars in *'the invisible progress of the weaving'*, of the secretion of threads from bodies of indiscernible sex. What is being observed, taken note of, whilst there is not much to be seen with the eyes, is weaving itself. Unlike Plato, for whom 'weaving itself', in its lowly literality, is without any conceptual interest, for Derrida the actuality of the weaving is important, even if it is hard actually to see it. He attests that the silkworms weave, that they themselves weave. It is their own thing, not just there to be capitalised upon by man, by philosophy, while it is still possible to read and learn from these silkworms. Although the literality of weaving is given (as Derrida has earlier spoken of the 'literality' of the tallith), it still serves as a metaphor, and thus is a literal metaphor (as at the outset I suggested that the textile metaphor should be considered), that is, it signifies its actuality and it actually signifies.

I think a slightly strange thing happens in the account of the silkworms. First there are several of them – 'silkworms', a plurality – and then there is just one – 'the silkworm'. What happens to the others? This invisible transition (I think it takes place between the bottom of page 49 and the top of page 50), this transition from more than one to one, even if a collective or representative one, serves to separate the account of the act of weaving from the discussion of the odyssey of the silkworm wrapped up in its cocoon. Not only this, it is at this stage or disjuncture that the question of appropriating a meaning from the operation of weaving arises, set on a hinge so it can be answered either way: 'I cannot say that I appropriated the operation, nor will I say anything other or to the contrary' (p. 50).

What is said on the cocoon-side of the question, in what follows from the above, sounds somewhat philosophical. In particular, the little silkworm and the great Hegel would seem to have some knowledge of each other without knowing it:

The living, tiny but still divisible formula of absolute knowledge. (p. 50)

[A] philosophy of nature for a shoebox . . . namely, that the silkworm buried itself, came back to itself in its odyssey, in a sort of absolute knowledge. (p. 50).

In addition, 'A Silkworm of One's Own' is given as written during a journey and said to constitute a true dream, but a bad one – 'enough to make you thrash about like a wounded devil in an invisible straitjacket, when you can't stop crumpling the sheets around you to make a hole in the violence and find the way out' (p. 47). A cocoon experience? I would like to gloss this together with the references to a Hegelian odyssey, as follows: the self-exteriorization, self-burial, this selfless self-absorption, may be seen or felt as what is called 'a dark night of the soul', a tormented melancholic exile, suffered for the sake of coming back to oneself in a moment of awakening. Such a seemingly solitary odyssey stirs and disturbs me.

Derrida's memory of keeping silkworms jogs my memory. I also kept some silkworms – in Zimbabwe rather than Algeria – me too, it was a school craze. Only I had forgotten this and might never have remembered it, if not for Derrida's memory. That is, his memory coincidentally makes my 'memory', that which might never have come back, finally come back to me. Derrida's memory makes me see the caterpillars more observantly than I saw them at the time, while I remember being rather fixated on the cocoon-stage. My anxiety was that the moths might not hatch together. I feared that only one would make it, or that they would each emerge at different times to find no others there, for the thought of an utterly solitary resurrection seemed and seems truly terrible. I wondered if and how they could time the preparations not only for their rebirths but for their reunion, their arriving together. This is a question of timing as coincidence, co-incidence. This timing would not be just the same as timing as spacing and deferral, although it would necessarily depend on and, if possible, be alert to that. Maybe it could be thought of as 'the question of a cocoon', as might be heard in Aidoo's 'June 7, 1989 on Tiananmen Square', which ends, timing itself wonderfully (although the whole poem needs be read for this):

after a millenium in a coma,
when do we wake up?

Mo Nua, when shall we wake up?

At the outset of 'A Silkworm of One's Own', Derrida considers that 'Penelope's ruse' (only pretending to weave the shroud) has little to do with the diminishment in the casting off of knitting, the anticipation of a shedding. Penelope, whilst certainly deceiving the suitors, at the same time engages in a struggle renewed day by day to survive their greedy impositions, and she also keeps beginning again in the sustained hope or anticipation of meeting up with, catching up with or being caught up with by Odysseus, before it is too late. So the long odyssey which can but take its time, even as it is always urgent, may yet be accompanied by potentially attuned yet other work, needing to try and calculate with its own urgencies and delays.

And so perhaps what this has been preparing to say all along, alongside others, and I am sorry that it took so long, is that deconstruction can and should be given its time with seemingly distant work in mind. This work, which may not be deconstruction, in that – like deconstruction – it has its own compulsions, perhaps often those particularly of beginning again, re-composing, re-habilitating, re-developing, and so on, nonetheless can be seen to have concerns which touch on the concerns of deconstruction. Deconstruction and – and Hélène Cixous's *Savoir* and Ama Ata Aidoo's *An Angry Letter in January* and Bessie Head's *A Question of Power*, for a start.

What is then hatched from the cocoon or cocoons? Well, the moth could be seen as a 'winged prick', but not only that. You can also see it, as one voice in 'A Silkworm of One's Own' says, as a 'bewinged signature' (in the *Odyssey* we find 'winged words') or as a helicopter, as another voice suggests, or we could say as a *navette*, a shuttle, a weaver-bird, a butterfly and – a moth. Bessie Head's *A Question of Power*, a novel very much about emerging from a dark night of the soul, comes to its moment of casting off with the protagonist writing a poem and being given a poem by her young son on which she reflects:

It seemed impossible that he [the son] had really travelled the journey alongside her. He seemed to summarize all her observations. . . .

That's what she felt about people's souls and their powers; that they were like sky-birds, aeroplanes, jets, boeings, fairies and butterflies; that there'd be a kind of liberation of these powers, and a new dawn and a new world. She felt this because the basic error seemed to be a relegation of all things holy to some unseen Being in the sky.

. . . she placed one soft hand over her land.   (Head, 1974, pp. 205–6)

New world and touch ground?

NOTES

1. See Forbes Morlock, 'The Story of the Ignorant Schoolmaster / The Adventures of Telemachus' in *The Oxford Literary Review*, **19** (1997).
2. Jacques Lacan, 'The Mirror Stage as Formative of the I as Revealed in Psychoanaltylic Experience', in *Écrits: A Selection*, trans. Alan Sheridan (London: Tavistock/Routledge, 1977). Malcolm Andrews has also discussed the significance of this fortress symbol in a paper on 'Dickens and his Performing Selves' (publication forthcoming).
3. See Janet A. Kaplan, *Unexpected Journeys: The Art and Life of Remedios Varo* (London: Virago, 1988), p. 21.
4. Sándor Ferenczi, 'Obsessional Etymologizing' in *Further Contributions to the Theory and Technique of Psychoanalysis*, ed. John Rickman, trans. Jane Isabel Suttie *et al.* (London: Karnac, 1994). Ferenczi comments that this could support theories of the sexual origin of language. In *Finnegans Wake*, Joyce writes: 'Where do thots come from?' Maud Ellmann in noting this comments on the

play of 'thoughts' and 'children/tots'. See Maud Ellmann, 'Polytropic Man: Paternity, Identity and Naming in *The Odyssey* and *A Portrait of the Artist as a Young Man*', in *James Joyce: New Perspectives*, ed. Colin MacCabe (Sussex: Harvester Press, 1982), p. 76. There could also be a further reference to Thoth, the winged, bird-headed Egyptian god of writing, that Joyce refers to in *A Portrait of the Artist as a Young Man*, reference to which is also made by Derrida in 'Plato's Pharmacy', p. 84. This is of relevance to the discussion of the shuttle further on in my essay.

5. Sigmund Freud, 'Femininity', in *New Introductory Lectures on Psychoanalysis*, trans. James Strachey (New York: Norton, 1965), p. 132. Derrida discusses this in 'A Silkworm of One's Own'. It can also be noted that Anna Freud had a strong interest in weaving and knitting, as I have discussed in a paper entitled 'Knitting Machines' which, as part of a further reading of weaving, is to appear in my forthcoming book *Literature, Animism and Politics*.
6. In 'Resistances', Derrida speaks of the *sumplokē*, interlacing, that remains in the single but not homogenous trace (p. 30).
7. This feminine yet sexless, subjectless origination could well be thought of in terms of the *chora*, spoken of in Plato's *Timaeus* and discussed by Derrida in both 'Plato's Pharmacy' and *Khōra* in *On the Name*, ed. Thomas Dutoit (Stanford: Stanford University Press, 1995).
8. For a discussion of relevance to this, see Gayatri Spivak, 'Acting Bits/Identity Talk' in *Critical Inquiry*, 18 (Summer 1992).
9. For the logic of 'back' with respect to deconstruction, see Nicholas Royle, 'Back', in *The Oxford Literary Review*, vol. 18 (1996).
10. He is identifiable by the touch of his scar, as well as by his capacity to be hurt by Penelope's seeming coldness towards him and by the shared secret of their shared bed.
11. The work of Gayatri Spivak is an on-going inspiration and reminder here, while it has, of course, its own itineraries. I would also like to mention that one starting point for this work on 'deconstruction and weaving' was in coming across a Jewish-Berber carpet in Marrakesh. Amongst its other coincidences is that most of it was being written up when the person I usually live with happened to be travelling along the Silk Road.

WORKS CITED

Aidoo, A. A. (1992), *An Angry Letter in January* (Coventry, Sydney and Aarhus: Dangaroo Press).
Aristophanes (1973), *Lysistrata and Other Plays: The Arnachians/The Clouds/ Lysistrata*, trans. and introd. Alan H. Sommerstein (Harmondsworth: Penguin).
Cixous, Hélène, *Savoir*, in Hélène Cixous and Jacques Derrida, *Voiles* (Paris: Galilée, 1998), pp. 9–19.
Derrida, Jacques (1981), 'Plato's Pharmacy', in *Dissemination*, trans. and introd. Barbara Johnson (London: The Athlone Press).
—— (1986), *Glas*, trans. John P. Leavey and Richard Rand (Lincoln and London: University Nebraska Press).
——(1987), *The Post Card: From Socrates to Freud and Beyond*, trans. Alan Bass (Chicago and London: University of Chicago Press).
—— (1988), *Limited Inc.* (Evanston, IL: Northwestern University Press).
—— (1993), *Circumfession*, trans. Geoffrey Bennington in *Jacques Derrida* (Chicago, IL: University of Chicago Press).

—— (1994), *Specters of Marx*, trans. Peggy Kamuf (London and New York: Routledge).

—— (1995), *Khōra* in *On the Name*, ed. Thomas Dutoit (Stanford, CA: Stanford University Press).

—— (1996), 'A Silkworm of One's Own', trans. Geoffrey Bennington, in *The Oxford Literary Review*, **18**.

—— (1998), 'Resistances' in *Resistances of Psychoanalysis*, trans. Peggy Kamuf, Pascale-Anne Brault and Michael Naas (Stanford: Standford University Press).

Djebar, A. (1993), *Fantasia: An Algerian Calvacade*, trans. Dorothy S. Blair (Portsmouth: Heinemann).

Ellmann, M. (1982), 'Polytropic Man: Paternity, Identity and Naming in *The Odyssey* and *A Portrait of the Artist as a Young Man*', in *James Joyce: New Perspectives*, ed. Colin MacCabe (Sussex: Harvester Press).

Ferenczi, S. (1994), 'Obsessional Etymologizing', in *Further Contributions to the Technique and Theory of Psychoanalysis*, ed. John Rickman, trans. Jane Isabel Suttie *et al.* (London: Karnac).

Freud, S. (1955), *Beyond the Pleasure Principle*, in *The Standard Edition of the Complete Psychological Works of Sigmund Freud*, vol. XVIII (London: Hogarth Press).

—— (1965), 'Femininity' in *New Introductory Lectures on Psychoanalysis*, trans. and ed. James Strachey (New York: Norton).

—— (1991), *Group Psychology and the Analysis of the Ego*, in *The Penguin Freud Library*, vol. 12 (Harmondsworth: Penguin).

Head, B. (1974), *A Question of Power* (London: Heinemann).

Homer (1991), *The Odyssey*, trans. E.V. Rieu (Harmondsworth: Penguin Books).

Kaplan, J. A. (1988), *Unexpected Journeys: The Art and Life of Remedios Varo* (London: Virago).

Lacan, J. (1977), 'The Mirror Stage as Formative of the I as Revealed in Psychoanalyic Experience', in *Écrits: A Selection*, trans. Alan Sheridan (London: Tavistock/Routledge).

Marx, K. (1976), *Capital*, vol I, trans. Ben Fowkes (London: Penguin).

Morlock, F. (1997), 'The Story of the Ignorant Schoolmaster/The Adventures of Telemachus', in *The Oxford Literary Review*, **19**.

Naas, M. (1996), 'The Time of a Detour: Jacques Derrida and the Question of the Gift', in *The Oxford Literary Review*, **18**.

Plato (1961), *The Collected Dialogues*, ed. Edith Hamilton and Huntingdon Cairns (Princeton, NJ: Princeton University Press).

Pynchon, T. (1979), *The Crying of Lot 49* (London: Pan Books).

Royle, N. (1996), 'Back', in *The Oxford Literary Review*, **18**.

Scheid, J. and Svenbro, J. (1996), *The Craft of Zeus: Myths of Weaving, and Fabric* (Cambridge, MA and London: Harvard University Press).

Spivak, G. C. (1992), 'Acting Bits/Identity Talk', in *Critical Inquiry*, **18**.

Woolf, V. (1929), *A Room of One's Own* (London: The Hogarth Press).

Yeats, W. B. (1989), *Yeats's Poems*, ed. A. Norman Jeffares (London: Macmillan).

—— (1969), *A Vision* (1925: London: Macmillan).

15

Et Cetera . . .
(and so on, und so weiter, and so forth, et ainsi de suite,
und so überall, etc.)

Jacques Derrida

And in the beginning, there is the *and*.

——'And . . .', you say? What is there in an 'and'? And when I say 'an *and*', does the conjunction 'and' become a noun, a name? What's in a name, in this name? And I wonder what a deconstruction can do with such a little, almost insignificant word.

——Here we have a proposal, and decision, and our friend will confirm this, to treat in all modes of 'Deconstruction and . . . *et cetera* . . .'? And it depends, doesn't it, on what follows? How to suspend such a syntagm? And the '*syn-*' of such a syntagm? Together with this 'with' (*cum, syn, mit, avec* . . .), and with this 'and', here we are exposed to so many dangerous liaisons . . .

——And why not? To all sorts of *déliaisons* too. But rest assured. If only you knew how independent deconstruction is, how alone, so alone, all alone! And as if it had been abandoned, right in the middle of a colloquium, on a train platform – or in an airport lounge which would look like this one, changing planes or leaving for I know not what destination . . .

——And well no, I believe on the contrary that nothing is less lonely and thinkable on its own. And deconstruction is also like a way of thinking set-theory. It would always be necessary to say, if we were to believe them, 'deconstruction and . . . et cetera . . . etc.' And 'deconstruction' would always go *with*, together with *something* else. And in this way you would get different taxonomic tables according to the name of this 'thing'; and according to its presumed concept, and according to the play of the definite article, and according to the type of contiguity and the conceptual structure of this X which, consequence or consecution, follows the *and*.

——And without counting the fact – I'd like to come back to this later – that deconstruction introduces an 'and' of association and dissociation

282

at the very heart of each thing, rather it recognizes this self-division within each concept. And all its 'work' is situated at this juncture or this dis-juncture: there is writing and writing, invention and invention, gift and gift, hospitality and hospitality, pardon and pardon. A hyperbole comes along each time to recall and decide this undecidability and/or this *double bind* between X and X: there is X and X, which always comes down to thinking X without X, we shall come back to this law; moreover 'bind' signifies a liaison, a conjunction, like 'and'. A double bind always takes the form of a double obligation: *and . . . and.*[1]

——And thus, for whoever wanted to put some order into all the sentences or all the texts which would come forward in the name of 'Deconstruction and X', the conjunction tables, if I can call them that, and the 'logic' of their titles would be different, or even radically heterogeneous in the following series – in which, as much as the categorial substantives, the syncategoreme *and* is affected, in truth profoundly modified in its sense and in its function:

1. deconstruction *and* critique, deconstruction *and* philosophy, deconstruction *and* metaphysics, deconstruction *and* science, etc.
2. deconstruction *and* literature, deconstruction *and* right, or architecture, or management, or the visual arts, or music, etc.
3. deconstruction *and* the gift, or the pardon, or work, or technics, or time, or death, or love, or the family, or friendship, or the law, or the impossible, or hospitality, or the secret, etc.
4. deconstruction *and* America, deconstruction *and* politics, deconstruction *and* religion, deconstruction *and* the university etc.
5. deconstruction *and* Marxism, deconstruction *and* psychoanalysis, deconstruction *and* feminism, deconstruction *and* new historicism, deconstruction *and* postmodernism, etc.

And one could go on, and it would be quite easy to show that in each of these series, in each of these great sets, the conjunction 'and' is resistant not only to association but also to serialization, and it protests against a reduction which is at bottom absurd and even ridiculous . . .

——And indeed, one starts laughing, and I'm tempted to add 'deconstruction and me, and me, and me . . .', to parody the parody of a famous French song – '50 million Chinese and me and me . . .'.[2] And faced with this rhapsodic 'Chinese' classification and this falsely rigorous accumulation, I must repeat that depending on the type of categoreme thus conjoined with deconstruction by the grammar of what is called a conjunction ('and'), it is not only the sense of each of these categoremes which begins to be determined (and it will have to continue being completed in a sentence and through a discourse, etc.), it is also the enigmatic fate of the little word 'and' itself, that is the syncategoreme, as you were saying, 'and'. . . . And the *syn*, the *with* of the *syn*-categoreme, like the *cum* of *con*junction, also has the sense of a conjunctive liaison, it is a sort of 'and' in general. . . .

——And so what does our friend mean to suggest, then, by his allusion to a 'Chinese' rhapsody? An example would be that classification of animals by a 'certain Chinese encyclopaedia' mentioned by Borges and recalled by Foucault at the very start of his Preface to *The Order of Things* (*Les mots et et le choses* [*Words and Things*]). And what's more the *and* in the title, *Les mots* et *les choses*, is quite different from any *and* that would associate only words or only things. Between words *and* things, there can be no conjunction or homogeneous collection, there can be no simple enumeration or addition, etc. Words and things cannot be added together and cannot follow in the same series . . .

——Except (and 'except' is, like 'without', a conjunctive preposition which conceals the work of a certain 'and', is it not?) – except if one consider, which is not necessarily illegitimate, that words are also both words and things [*et des mots et des choses*] (and there I've just made a use of the *et* which it seems to me can only be French, putting an *et* before the first term of the enumeration, and one can wonder whether this first 'et' is still translatable); and unless one consider, further, that any discrete unit of *being* (word *and* thing, word *or* thing) can be taken into account in a collection. As Husserl recalls, very early, in his debates with psychologism, one can, under the category of 'something in general' (*etwas überhaupt*) associate numerically, and therefore enumerate, from one *and* to the next, arithmetical units and objects as different as a group of trees and a feeling and an angel and a shade of red and the moon and Napoleon. And one can also associate, for they then become, *qua* concepts, more homogeneous, 'concepts' of words and 'concepts' of things, even if a word, in principle, is no more than the designation of a thing through its meaning. A word is 'some thing' in general. These elementary precautions and distinctions would be indispensable for anyone wishing to treat of 'deconstruction [in the singular] and X . . .' (X: the thing, the word, the concept, the meaning? And can one distinguish them in this case? And each time in the singular?)

——What seems to matter to those we are following here, before even the discussion about a deconstruction [in the singular], is it not the *and*? Now listening to the strange conversation that has just begun, let us merely note in the text cited by Foucault, a double word. I insist on its being the double of a word rather than just one thing. In the disorder of this accumulative enumeration (and . . . and . . . and . . .) which would, according to Foucault, indicate to us the 'limit' of *our* thinking, and for us 'the bare impossibility of thinking *that*', there suddenly appears, like the abyss at the heart of things, an '*et cetera*', a category of the '*et cetera*' which in one go swallows everything into its gulf. One thinks of some Jonah's whale transformed into a Noah's ark for all the animals in the list, or of an insatiable *Bocca della Veritá* which would threaten to engulf both [*et*] any identity and even the very concept of concept:

> The animals are divided into: (a) belonging to the Emperor, (b) embalmed, (c) tame, (d) sucking pigs, (e) sirens, (f) fabulous, (g) stray dogs, (h) included in the present classification, (i) frenzied, (k) drawn with a very fine camelhair brush, (l) *et caetera*, (m) having just broken the water pitcher, (n) that from a long way off look like flies.[3]

——Did you notice the omission of (j)? Deliberate or not? On the following page, Foucault reinscribes it where it belongs, between (i) and (k), in the alphabetical order of which he had just said: 'What transgresses the boundaries of all possible imagination or thought, is simply the alphabetical series (a,b,c,d) which links each of these categories to all the others.' Now the letter he had missed out, and which he is going to reinstate as though there were nothing wrong, as though he did not even realize that he was repairing an oversight, is, as we said, j, and it announces a single word in the classification: '(j) innumerable'. Which is the more abyssal and/or more comprehensive collection? That of the 'innumerable'? That of the *'et cetera'*? Or that of 'included in the current classification'? As Foucault says quite rightly: '. . . if all the animals divided up here can be placed without exception in one of the divisions of this list, then aren't all the other divisions to be found in that one division too? And then again, in what space would that single, inclusive division have *its* existence? Absurdity destroys the *and* of the enumeration by making impossible the *in* where the things enumerated would be divided up.'[4]

——As Foucault no doubt realizes, each *and* is not necessarily to be reduced to its enumerative function, even if that function can remain discretely implied in every other semantic or pragmatic modality of the *and*. Such as that of the *and* he himself uses to speak of the *and* ('And then again, in what space would that single, inclusive division have *its* existence?'). This inclusion of the whole in the part, this series which inscribes itself entire in one of its terms, appears, perhaps, from a certain point of view, 'absurd', and of an absurdity which 'ruins the *and* of the enumeration'. But does it not also attest to other, much more powerful resources, which would make of the very ruin of the 'and' an all but invincible force? Wondering what the *'and'* is, what *and* – and even a syncategoreme in general – means and does not mean, does and does not do, that is perhaps, before any enumeration of all the possible titles of the type 'deconstruction *and* . . .', the most constant task of any deconstruction. Those participating in the conversation we're listening to no doubt know this. But will they say it?

————And in passing, and returning to Europe, this Chinese story can also recall the well-known Jewish joke: the sign 'best tailor in the street' will be the most powerful way of getting the better of all the other signs *in the same street* ('best tailor in town', 'best tailor in the country', 'best tailor in the world'). For is the 'best tailor in the street' not better than the one who claims to be the 'best tailor in the world', if that one has a shop in *the same street*?

————And on the subject of the *et caetera* in the Chinese encyclopedia, let us remind ourselves that Borges entitled 'Etcetera' a set of short texts he added to a second edition of *A Universal History of Infamy*: 'In the "Etcetera" section, I have added three new texts',[5] is the last sentence of a Prologue to the 1954 edition. And this Prologue opens with a definition of the baroque, that is of itself, of its very writing, a definition of the baroque having in all conscience to be baroque. Beginning of a prologue, first word of what is written at the beginning: 'I should define as baroque that style which deliberately exhausts (or tries to exhaust) all its possibilities and which borders on its own parody.'[6] The Prologue to the first edition names, among the procedures over-used by these 'exercises in narrative prose', 'random enumerations'.[7]

————And we must no doubt complicate things a little. We must temper both [*et*] this rather confident allusion by Borges to what he calls 'random enumerations' and the interpretation which allows Foucault to speak of a 'laughter which shattered'[8] on reading Borges's text. Further on he will speak, too, of an 'uneasiness that makes one laugh'.[9] For the laughter becomes less euphoric, and above all less communicative, more uneasy indeed, when the *object* of division or classification stops being *read* in a naively realist way (taxonomy of the things themselves, of the animals *themselves*, animal individuals or species) but rather as the series of the characters, attributes, modes of apprehension, qualities of activity or intentional experience that can be referred to animals. It wouldn't then be animals that were being classified, but, like a number of possible themes or noemata, the *experiences* of relation to animals. Borges's list would then remain incomplete, of course, an alphabet would not be long enough for all its entries, but it would no longer be laughable, uneasy or aberrant. It could even lay claim to a certain phenomenological scientificity. And as for the deliberately flagged absence of logical or ontological hierarchy in the simple juxtaposition of themes, unless it correspond to a hidden (for example baroque) principle of composition, that also does interesting work, if only to make us attentive to all that is artificial in any ordering, to its historical and non-natural character. This is of course the direction – a new problematic of order and its constitution – in which *The Order of Things* advances, and inscribes in this way this moment of uneasy laughter in its preface.

——And yet let us not hasten to subscribe to Foucault's *double* diagnosis about this 'table.'

1. For he asserts that 'Absurdity destroys the *and* of the enumeration by making impossible the *in* where the things enumerated would be divided up'.[10] Now not every 'and' is enumerative through and through; and not every enumeration enumerates 'real' things or 'words' that exist. An 'and' can place in a certain order, an *other* order, intentional phenomena, and do so after or within that *phenomenological reduction* which can, of course, be subjected to deconstructive questions at a certain point, but without the discipline of which no deconstruction would begin. And no challenging of an order given as natural (and that is why one might assume that a certain phenomenological reduction is implicitly at work in Foucault's project, even if he misrecognizes it, believes it necessary not to accredit it, or thinks it a smart move never to assume it under this name). This discipline of phenomenological reduction, this placing in parentheses or brackets of naive realism or the natural attitude, is on the contrary the *abc* of deconstruction. But not its *alpha* and its *omega*, its first or its last word, for it also questions the axiomatic of phenomenological reductions along the way – and the way counts, nothing operates in a deconstruction without taking into account a work or a path, a road that must nonetheless be distinguished from the *hodos* of a method.

2. And Foucault goes on immediately: 'Borges adds no figure to the atlas of the impossible, nowhere does he strike the spark of poetic confrontation . . .'. But is this so certain? Who can attest to it? In the name of what? Of what already legitimated poetics? And what if this 'spark' was Borges's text itself? Borges putting to work the poetics (baroque or not, for example) that he is always expounding and describing – and thus simultaneously (this simultaneity or synchrony is one of the values of the 'and', and in Arabic – we'll need to come on to this, the *waw* – 'whereas', 'however', 'thereupon', etc.)?

——How and how many times does the 'and' impose itself upon us, in its own name or under some pseudonymous figure? What would happen if, thanks to some computer mechanism, we were to erase at a stroke all the 'ands' in our discourse? Difficult to calculate. More and less than one imagines at first blush, no doubt, for not all 'ands' have the same value, and such an operation would be naive so long as it was to be limited to the 'ands' that were marked and explicit. But there are so many others, between all the words, more clearly between some than between others, and sometimes even within certain words. *Etcetera*, for example. And one could wonder, moreover, if one might not discover exciting secrets if one subjected a text, a discourse, a book to a spectral analysis – stylistic or pragmatic, and statistical – of all uses of 'and'. . . . And each writer, each poet, each orator, each speaking subject, even each proposition can put to work a different 'and', different as to its modality, as to its number, and sometimes to say the same 'thing', at least to say what realists in a hurry would call the same 'thing', where we should have to distinguish at least between thing, object, sense and meaning, etc. And do so precisely by appropriate reductions.

——And beyond the text cited by Foucault, the whole of Borges's *oeuvre* plays with these impossible possibilities, especially his *Ficciones*. Reread especially 'An Examination of the Work of Herbert Quain'[11] and Funes the Memorious'.[12]

——'Deconstruction and . . .', suggests, then, that this thing called 'deconstruction' is always associated, completed, supplemented, accompanied, if only by what does not accompany it, and with, and without this and that, this or that . . . But also opposed to this or that, disjointed from this or that, as though it was always necessary to distinguish or even choose between deconstruction *and* X and Y.

——Necessarily, since it is neither a philosophy, nor a doctrine, nor a knowledge, nor a method, nor a discipline, nor even a determinate concept, only what happens if it happens [*ce qui arrive si ça arrive*]. And yet, and for this very same reason, how lonely deconstruction is, if only you knew! And it must be alone! Perhaps this is why it multiplies of its own accord and one must say deconstructions, always in the plural, and always *with* this or that, and with this or with that. For lonely as it is, or as it be, you must realize that there is deconstruction *and* deconstruction. And which adds itself to itself, and divides itself and multiplies itself . . .

——And then what? Do you mean it *is* lonely, and/or that it *be* lonely? Constative, ontological theorem and/or optative, performative? Promise or threat?

——The one and/or the other, neither the one nor the other, impossible to decide. Try to measure the thought of the 'and' to this double being-alone, to what is called solitude on the one hand *and* singularity on the other, to the loneliness but also to the isolation of the unique (for among all the implicit values of the 'and', there is also, sometimes, the value of a 'but also', and 'for' and 'now' and 'therefore' and 'not only X but also Y', 'not *only* X but *also* X . . .'). If you were thus to subject the possibility of the 'and' to the test of everyone, if you were to take it into account to the measure of *every one* (*singuli*, one by one, one *and* one, and one *plus* one), you would perhaps see surge up and sink at the same moment the possibility of the 'and' in general. There is addition or seriality (and . . . and . . . and . . .), there is supplementarity only where discrete units hollow out [*creusent*], in some sense, or rather indicate negatively [*en creux*], the possibility of being-alone and being-singular, of separation, of distinction, i.e. also of being-other, and therefore of a certain disjunction, and also of an unbinding, of a relation without relation. To the extent that the matrix usage of the 'and' would always be some 'the one *and* the other', even if the one *and* the other are identical and are other only numerically, *numero*, as they say, and like clones, a series of clones which would each be both the exemplary example of the other and the example-sample of the series. Even 'the one *or* the other' (disjunction or alternative) presupposes some 'the one *and* the other'. Even the oblique bar of the opposition, and for example *and/or* between *and* and *or*, or between *and* or *or*, still presupposes an 'and'. Or *or*. How could one speak or write without *and*? 'Without' itself presupposes 'and', etc.

——And there would thus be an 'and' in general, an autonomous concept, one namable with a name, there would be a sense, an essence, a meaning, a grammar of the 'and'. And what would deconstructions (in the plural, then) have to do with this 'and' in general?

——Everything and nothing. And wait – it is not certain that one can speak here of a concept, and above all, as you just have so hastily, of an 'autonomous concept', and of a noun. Thus, for example, and before even interrogating the possibility of having such a concept of the *syncategoreme* 'and' ('If we wish to be clear as to the meaning of the word *and* . . .', says a subordinate clause in the *Logical Investigations*[13] that we shall have to re-read and complete), Husserl would make every possible effort to distinguish here between a general grammar and a pure logical grammar of the 'and'. What are the limits of this grammar? Does it extend, following 'both . . . and' [*et . . . et*], to its apparently negative form, the *neither . . . nor* [*ni . . . ni*]? You were just saying: deconstruction is neither this nor that, etc. And all the reproaches concerning a supposed negative theology in deconstruction (we have explained ourselves on this issue elsewhere) presuppose that some light has been shed on the 'both . . . and' and/or the 'neither . . . nor'.

——The *neither . . . nor*. Some would say that supposedly singular deconstruction makes use and abuse of it, repeating it to infinity, and especially in its attention to undecidables, to double binds and aporias of all sorts. Deconstruction indeed looks like a repeated reaffirmation both of the *neither . . . nor* and of the repeated reaffirmation (*neither . . . nor*, but *yes, yes*; yes *and* yes, the second *yes* being both called for or promised by the first, therefore allied with it, but necessarily alone too, and disjoined, and again inaugural, the 'and' in the 'yes and yes' then signifying just as much collection or addition as dissociation, just as much memory as amnesia). Is the *neither . . . nor*, then, only a case, a negative modality of the *both . . . and* or again of an *either . . . or* [*ou . . . ou*] itself in turn modifying a *both . . . and*? And what would you do with the *'et non'* and the *sic et non*?

——You can see that to do justice to the 'and', those who are speaking here have had to privilege, within the most open polylogue, an aphoristic or diaphoristic form. These interlocutors proceed by distinctions, disjunctions, interruptions, conjunctions and juxtapositions, bindings and unbindings, seriality and exemplarity, samplification – and simplification: and . . . and . . . and . . . etc . . . *et ceteri omnes, et cetera*, and all the others, and the others whatever they be. But is this interruption which condemns one to the aphorism not the condition of every conversation? What would a conversation or a polylogue be without interruption and without some juxtaposition, without a somewhat arbitrary or aleatory linking, without an 'association of ideas' that only the insignificance of an 'and' would come to say or imply? You have noticed that so many sentences, whatever their author, begin with 'and'. Is this deliberate? Is it done on purpose so as to recall that any sentence could begin by 'and', even if that 'and' were to remain inaudible or invisible? Let's carry on listening to them talking.

——And what else? I still do not know what I have to do with the *et non* any more than I know what language to speak, I mean to what idiom grant a privilege – or an unquestionable hegemony. Deconstruction is also that, if it is anything: an attention paid to the irreducible plurality of signatures and an ethico-juridical vigilance, a political one too, to the effects of hegemony of one language over another, between one language and the other. There are languages, and there is language and language. You notice how easily we begin our sentences with this little word 'and' . . .

——*Et oui*, and yet by an 'and' that most often has a different logical value or a finality proper to it (scansion, spacing, quasi-punctuation, respiration, exclamative opening, neutral addition, linking or following on, disjunction or simple scansion, upping the ante, objection, concession, etc.), to the point at which one could replace or translate it, without much semantic damage, by so many other conjunctions, depending on the case, by 'but', 'now', 'for', 'therefore', 'thus', 'finally', and/or by adverbs: 'then', 'next', 'here', 'now', 'also' – adverb and conjunction – and just as easily by 'immediately', 'what's more', 'thus' – which can also be conjunction and adverb, etc. And you know that in Biblical Hebrew a sort of 'and' signals the beginning of many sentences, just as a punctuation mark would. And as a principle of discernment between sentence-units, of course, but also as link and following on (prefix and not conjunction), the letter *vaw* is added or agglutinated to the beginning of the first word in the sentence the beginning of which it thus marks. And the same letter can modify what is called the 'aspect' of a verb (from accomplished to unaccomplished and vice versa). In Arabic, the 'and', the *wa* (or *waw*), the linking letter, which can mean 'also' also, along with 'with', or at the same time 'at the same time', and simultaneously a sort of simultaneity, well, *waw* can also be defined, I am told, as the 'letter of tenderness',[14] as if, through this very linkage, though this grammatical magnet, a gathering, some gesture of bringing together, a loving movement always left in it the trace of an affect, a communitarian connotation, in the very place at which it would seem to be the opposite (opposition, contradiction, disjunction, incompatibility, privation: 'to the exclusion of', 'against', 'without' or 'for want of', for 'without' always signifies, you guessed it, 'without-with' or 'with-without', 'and-without'. This is a general law of formal logic: a conjunction slips and insinuates itself into every disjunction, and *vice versa*).

——And then one could wonder whether the function thus marked in Hebrew or Arabic is not at work, silently, or otherwise, and differently, in all languages, in all texts, between all units to be cut up or linked together. But is what we call deconstruction not above all a taking into account of forces of dissociation, dislocation, unbinding, forces, in a word, of difference and heterogeneity, such that a certain 'and' itself can translate them? And above all, the forces of hierarchized opposition which set up all the conceptual couples around which a deconstruction busies itself (speech *and* writing, the inside *and* the outside, spirit *and* matter, this *versus* that, etc.)?

——Yes, but the 'and' can also maintain the differences together *as* differences, and *différance* is also this insistence of the same in opposition, or even in infinite heterogeneity. Whence the interminable debate with *Versammlung*, with the thinking of gathering upon which Heidegger insists so much. And I conclude from this that one of the difficulties of metalanguage, the *necessity* of the *effects* of metalanguage and the *impossibility* of absolute metalanguage (and therefore of deconstruction itself, you see?) hangs on the logic of this constraint. One cannot describe and formalize a unit of language, in the broad sense, for example 'and', without *already* making use of it *in* the formalizing definition itself. One must make an at least implicit use of the 'and' to say anything whatsoever about the 'and'; one must *use* it to *mention* or *cite* it in quotation marks.

——And indeed, this is just what happens to Husserl, since he was mentioned a moment ago. In Husserl, it is always a question of a difference between the fullness and emptiness of an intuition of meaning, between a more and a less in the plenitude of intuitive presence, in what Husserl calls (a strange figure which would pose so many problems!) the fulfilment (*Erfüllung*) of the intuition. One could also translate *Erfüllung* by 'accomplishment', execution, realization, or even performance. And then it is a question of responding to what Husserl calls a 'serious difficulty'. How to understand syncategoremes 'detached from all connection (*als jeder Verknüpfung herausgerissene*)'? Husserl first encounters this 'serious difficulty' in asserting first of all how and why, according to him, there can be no *detached* (*herausgerissene*) and therefore independent syncategoreme in a concise and consistent categorematic discourse. For he then objects to himself: if that were the case, how then could one even 'consider' these syncategoremes separately, as such, outside any connection, as Aristotle did? How, for example, could one interest oneself, as we are here, in the *and* for itself and in itself? Response to this objection: we must distinguish between the more or less full and/or the more or less empty. And to this difference in the 'fulfilment' of a meaningful intention there corresponds a difference between 'authentic representations' and 'inauthentic representations':

> We could first reply to this objection by referring to the difference between 'authentic' and 'inauthentic' representations (*auf den Unterschied der 'eigentlichen' und 'uneigentlichen' Vorstellungen*), or, what comes to the same thing, to the difference between simply intended meanings and fulfilled meanings (*der bloss intendieren und der erfüllenden Bedeutungen*).[15]

——And you have noticed that, in order to say so, Husserl must himself use more than once, precisely in order to mark the differential disjunction, the conjunction *and* (twice: difference between X and X) and the conjunction *or* to mark on the contrary the associative, non-disjunctive equivalence ('or, what comes to the same thing', etc). He must *use* what he also *mentions*. In the same sentence.

——The *Logical Investigations* try, then, to demonstrate that detached (*herausgerissene*), dissociated syncategoremes, freely mobile, 'such as "like" (*gleich*), "together with" (*in Verbindung mit*), "and" (*und*), "or" (*oder*)' can in themselves give rise to 'no intuitive understanding' (*kein intuitives Verständnis*), to 'no fulfilment of meaning' (*Keine Bedeutungserfüllung*), except in the context (*Zusammenhang*) of a wider meaning-whole (*unfassenderen Bedeutungsganzen*). And already we can describe and analyse the totalities, the linkings and the contexts which will provide 'and' with a greater plenitude of meaning, only as liaisons, connections, associations, in other words as the putting to work of a certain 'and'. And Husserl himself, as you have just noted, will have regularly to make use of the word 'and' to designate the irreducible incompleteness of all the intuitions of 'and' (phonic phenomenon, expression, meaning or sense), when a more comprehensive linking does not come to determine it. And once the contrary of the aforementioned 'fulfilment' of intuitive presence is 'frustration', one will have to

say, if one follows Husserl, that the 'and' is *in itself*, and if it is abandoned to itself, essentially frustrating.[16] Let us then distinguish in Husserl's analysis between the *used* 'ands' (I will underline them) and the *mentioned* ands:

> If we wish to be clear (*uns klarmachen*) as to the meaning (*Bedeutung*) of the word 'and' (*und*), we must actually carry out (*wirklich vollziehen*) an act of collection (*irgendeinen Kollektionsakt*), <u>and</u> bring to fulfilment in the aggregate thus genuinely presented (<u>*und*</u> *in dem so zu eigentlicher Vorstellung kommenden Inbegriff*) a meaning of the form *a and b* (*eine Bedeutung der Form* a *und* b *zur. Efüllung bringen*). <u>And</u> so in every case (<u>*Und*</u> *so überall*).

——If one follows here the logic of this demonstration, the <u>and</u> thus *used* to speak of the *mentioned and* would give rise to a meaning intention fulfilled by intuition only to the extent that the context provided by the sentence or sentences surrounding and linking with it is sufficiently comprehensive and determining. But is it ever totally so? And if it never is so to the point of intuitive saturation, will there not remain in every discourse, in every text, an irreducible portion of this 'dependency', this non-independence, this non-fulfilment for which the syncategoreme *and* figures at least as the example? And let us leave aside for now the thorny question of knowing whether *and* is one example of a syncategoreme among others, in the series of others, (besides, as Husserl says of *gleich*, for example, and of *in Verbindung mit*, *oder*), or rather, on the contrary, whether it is the quasi-transcendental, the syncategoreme *par excellence* silently implied in every syncategorematic liaison or conjunction between all possible categoremes; for the catalogue of syncategoremes seems to presuppose some *and* between all the discrete units thus classified, just as a certain *and* conjoins too all the categoremes.

——And do not deconstructions always appeal to this necessary and rigorous taking account of context, of course, but of a context that, as has been said and repeated for a long time now, is never fully saturable? Is it not in this non-saturability that undecidability opens up ('both . . . and' [*et . . . et*], 'neither . . . nor' [*ni . . . ni*], 'either . . . or' [*ou . . . ou*], but also the double bind, i.e. both the source and the condition of any decision, or any responsibility (ethical, juridical, political – and in place of each comma, in a list such as this, one could read an *and*))? Does one not see signalled here one of the reasons why deconstruction pays the greatest interest to syntax, no less than to semantics, to syncategoremes (conjunctions, prepositions, adverbs: *not*, *without*, *save*, *yes* etc.), to the interminable becoming-categorematic or becoming-nominal of syncategoremes? And does one not see more clearly why all this had to begin with a questioning of intuitionism? Of phenomenological intuitionism, before all else, and of Husserl's confidence in fulfilment and in the adequation between intention and fulfilment?[17]

——Of course, and Husserl is still not out of difficulty. He begins by refusing to all syncategoremes, for example 'and', a knowledge-function. This can only be conferred on it in the context of a categorematic meaning.[18] 'And' gives nothing to be known by itself. But it retains some meaning and we must here dissociate the apprehension of *meaning* from the function of *knowledge*. After stressing that 'even empty meaning-intentions – the "non-authentic", "symbolic" presentations which give meaning to an expression apart from any knowledge-function – reveal a difference between independence and non-independence',[19] Husserl asks himself a crucial question. This question stands at the joint and/or the disjunction between meaning and/or knowledge and it will have played a determining strategic role, I believe, in the history of 'deconstruction and . . . all its others': how can one *understand* a syncategoreme in itself (for example 'and') and why is there meaning in it, thinkable meaning, where knowledge is lacking? 'And' teaches us nothing, makes us know nothing, and yet we understand a certain meaning of the word or noeme 'and'. We can even nominalize it, as Husserl will make clear later. Become a categoreme, the 'and' of conjunction is designated like a noun, it operates as the name of the conjunction, and we can, then, cite it, recognize it and identify it outside any knowledge context.

But Husserl is determined to resolve the question he formulates courageously in the following terms: 'How can we explain the indubitable fact that isolated syncategoremes, e.g. the isolated word "and", are understood? They are non-independent as regards their meaning-intention, and this surely means that such intention can exist only in categorematic contexts: the isolated "and", the particle torn from its context, ought therefore to be a hollow noise. We can only resolve our difficulty in the following manner:'[20] And there follows a very awkward paragraph. It is organized by a logic of the virtual complement or by an opposition between *normal* functioning and *abnormal* functioning: *either* the syncategoreme 'and' does not have the same meaning as in a categorematic context *or else* it will have received a 'completion of meaning' which will have transformed it into an incomplete expression, yes, but an incomplete expression of a virtually 'living and complete' meaning:

> We understand an isolated 'and' either because the indirect, verbally unexpressed thought of *a certain familiar conjunction* gives it an abnormal meaning, or because vague, unverbalized presentations of things help us to form a thought of the type *A and B*.[21]

——In this latter case, concludes Husserl, the 'and' performs its function both normally and abnormally: normally to the extent that it is linked to an internal virtual completion, and abnormally to the extent that that completion is not incorporated into external expressions. The difference between *normal* and *abnormal* will play a major role a little further on, on the subject of the *suppositio materialis*, i.e. the possibility for any expression (syncategoreme *or* categoreme) to become its own name, for example when it names itself as a grammatical phenomenon. For Husserl, that is an 'abnormal' meaning, for – and this is an axiomatic proposition which is both powerful, necessary, obvious, and quite stupefying for anyone who wishes to follow all its consequences – 'logically considered, all shifts of meaning (*aller Bedeutungswechsel*) are to be adjudged abnormal'.[22]

> If we say ' "And" is a conjunction', the nuance of meaning normally corresponding to the word 'and' is not put into the position of subject: this is occupied by an independent meaning directed to the *word* 'and'. In this abnormal meaning, 'and' is not really a syncategorematic, but a categorematic expression: it names itself as a word.
>
> We have an exact *analogon* of *suppositio materialis* when an expression has, *instead of its normal meaning, a presentation of this meaning* (i.e. a meaning directed to this meaning as object). This is the case, e.g., if we say '*And, but, greater than* are non-independent meanings'. Here we should generally say that the meanings of the *words* 'and', 'but', 'greater than' are non-independent. Just as in the utterance '*Man, table, house*, are thing-concepts', presentations of these concepts function as subjects, and not the concepts themselves. In these, as in the previous cases, the change of meaning (*Die Bedeutungsänderung*) regularly shows itself in our written expression: quotation marks, or what might suitably be called other *heterogrammatical modes of expression* (*heterogrammatische Ausdruckmittel*), are employed.[23]

——If I understand aright, deconstruction, or at least what was called 'deconstruction' at a given moment, is a gesture which does not appear to be frontally opposed to this logic of Husserlian phenomenology. Its business would rather be one of drawing rigorous consequences from an impossibility of total saturation for so-called categorematic contexts, and of a context in general, or again, more precisely, of the always open possibility of these incomplete, syncategorematic functionings that Husserl calls in themselves 'abnormal', 'inauthentic', 'symbolic', and, later, 'critical' (in the sense of 'crisis', of the crisis of European sciences and philosophy, which always has at its origin, according to Husserl, this loss of intuitive and living plenitude in the experience of meaning, of language in general, of sign or expression). Whence 'deconstruction's' interest in the syntax of syncategoremes (*not, without, save, neither . . . nor, both . . . and, either . . . or*), that is in all that Husserl determines as incomplete or abnormal in itself, in a detached state, and that 'deconstruction' also holds to be a chance as much as a threat (the threat is also a chance, there would be no chance without threat, that's an axiom that recurs frequently). Whence, too, the investment of 'deconstruction' in procedures of 'detachment' and in quotation-marks, in the intrinsic possibility for any mark to be repeated, or even mentioned or cited. It is, moreover, curious that Husserl, who often describes the phenomenological reduction by use of the figure of placing in parentheses, brackets or quotation marks, should come to judge these signs as the signs of an anomaly the destiny of which is linked to writing, a heterogrammatical writing. And from this point of view, 'deconstruction' marks still an excess of fidelity, as is often the case, to a certain phenomenological inspiration. As you know, for Husserl there is more than one reduction (eidetic and phenomenological). The transcendental reductions themselves pluralize themselves, radicalize themselves in a sort of hyperbolic upping of the ante. And once they carry themselves off abyssally, link onto or interrupt each other, one can think of this multiplicity as of a polyphony – more than one *alter ego* in the same *ego*, etc. If all language, as was suggested elsewhere,[24] is in itself a sort of spontaneous eidetic and transcendental reduction, and therefore also 'natural' and more or less naive, the multiplicity of reductions can be carried by the more or less discordant concert of several voices. Deconstruction, through all these reductions, is not only more than one language, it is already more than one voice . . .

——Often in a daydream I wonder 'how many times?' for something or other in my life. And how many times have I done this? And how many times has that happened to me? And how many times have I gone home? And how many times did I stop, or not stop, at a red light? And made love? And begun a seminar or given a lecture? (And I leave you to multiply the series of possible examples, but you know, this is not just a game, I really and often ask myself these questions, again and again). And how many times have I spoken or written such and such a word? And there we are changing the order of repetition, for the words themselves open up an original field to serial repetition, to iterability, to exemplarity, etc., and the 'and' itself is a word. For example, how many times have I used (or avoided, which is another way of using), in speech or writing, the word 'deconstruction'? And the word 'and'?

——And how funny they are! Are they not funny? And they ceaselessly mix up learned and linguistico-philosophical references (see that stuff about Husserl), etc., and personal confiding, and narrative style in the fictitiously dialogic exchange, as though there were some link between them. Strange ways . . .

——But will you keep the title 'La déconstruction et . . .' ['Deconstruction and . . .'] in French? Is it not the only language in which the 'and' [*et*] sounds as the homophone of the 'is' [*est*]? First of all, one could say nothing about 'deconstruction and . . .' without implying some definitional presupposition of the type 'deconstruction is . . .' And then again, the 'and' means something (complete or incomplete), but 'something' (*etwas*) (binding, unbinding, conjunction, disjunction, opposition, addition, complement, supplement, etc.) and therefore something about which one ought to be able to say 'this is', 'here is "and"'. . . Husserl was just reminding us of this possibility of categorematic nominalization. What is more, between 'et' and its French homophone (or even homonym) 'est', an equivocal liaison has sprung up on the French scene, and therefore an obscure and untranslatable signature (abnormal, a stranger to all knowledge-functions and to all truth, Husserl would say) of deconstruction. For deconstruction, or what is called by that name, begins by calling into question the question 'what is it?', the question that sets itself up under the authority of the 'is'. i.e. of a determination of Being, and of Being thus nominalized on the basis of the indicative or the present participle of the verb 'be'. From the being [*l'é-tant*] of this 'is' (or of being as an object in general) is organized a fundamental ontology or a transcendental phenomenology which, in principle and *de jure*, dominates vertically the pyramid of ontologies, of phenomenologies or the so-called regional disciplines. By placing this hierarchical schema in question, displacing it without necessarily discrediting it, 'deconstruction', or what is called by that name, opens up space for another organization of the (not necessarily pyramid-shaped) relations between the series of the 'ands' which coordinate horizontally the said 'regions' (a name to be rethought) and the onto-phenomenological order of the 'is'. This is why there is no *encyclopaedia*, no circular principle of pedagogy and 'greater logic' of the University which does not allow itself to be deconstructed. Once it affects the ontological hierarchy, a deconstruction touches on everything, it dislocates the self-identity of an 'is' and an 'and', it introduces everywhere, between all the disciplinary fields or domains, a principle of contamination, of transference and even of translation, but a translation without transparency and without adequation, without pure analogy. Whence the mixture of attraction and intolerance that it provokes in institutions in general, and especially in the University.

——The traditional order, which is thus disturbed down to its hierarchical principle, is the one which, at bottom, subordinates the 'and' to the 'is'. And Husserl, him again, gives it a remarkably dense form in the *Appendix 1* of *Formal and Transcendental Logic*.[25] The forms of conjunctive liaison ('that of the *and* and the *or* (*die des* Und *und* Oder)', he says; but he could have said 'that of the *or* or the *and*') do not have the privileged relation to judgement *par excellence*, the 'predicative' or 'apophantic' judgement. For this judgement, it is the 'mode of liaison' of the copula, or again of the 'is-form' (*die Ist-form*) which is the best 'functional form'. For it 'sets up the members as members of the propositional totality (*des Satzganzen*)'. Re-read the rhetoric of this passage. In it, Husserl distinguishes firmly, with emphasis, between what is situated *on one side* (*Einerseits*), i.e. the 'and', and what is situated *on another side* (*Ander-seits*), i.e. the 'is'. But there is in this neither horizontal symmetry nor commensurability. For a logic, an ontology, a phenomenology, what is *on the side of* the 'and' is ordered and subordinated to what is *on the side of* the 'is'. Classical. That's the most decisive strategic place for 'deconstructive' questions, with the displacements that follow, in the relations of 'deconstruction and . . .' according to all the syntagmatic 'sets' we invoked at the start.

——So what does it mean, 'deconstruction and . . . etc.'?

——Nothing before it's made into a sentence, of course, or an organized discourse. Let's see now, deconstruction in the singular – has anyone ever known what that meant? And wasn't the issue one of returning to that point of 'thought' at which there would be 'thought' a 'thought' that to start with, or to end with, would not mean anything? And the lexicon of 'thought' (thought, to think, thinking thought, thought thought) would be determined and take its sense only from the point of origin of signification, of meaning, i.e. where signification *and* non-signification, meaning *and* non-meaning – some, those who identify meaning and sense, would say sense and non-sense – are articulated, adjoined, joined and disjoined (still the 'and' and the 'or') together. Together and separately. But is this not still more necessary for 'deconstruction and . . . X (whatever other thing)'? For the other of deconstruction, I mean the other in all its forms, the opposite, the associate, the friend or the enemy, the complement or the supplement, is then affected by the same necessity: to let itself be reduced, i.e. led back to the point where 'it' does not mean, not yet or already no longer. Moreover 'and', all on its own, does not mean anything. One can have of it no full intuition. Husserl was not wrong to say that it is one of the 'incomplete' syncategoremes, even if we do not follow him in what he does with this incompleteness.

——So will no-one some day write the history, the autonomous and specific history of the 'and'? Of its logic or its system, or even of the very idea of system, of organized multiplicity, of synthesis, the 'syn' (*cum, avec, apud, hoc, with, mit*) representing either a narrower modality or else, on the contrary, a more powerful category of the syncategoreme '*kai*', 'and', '*und*', '*e*', '*et*', et cetera, which one could even *also* say of the *etcetera*, and *even* (*etiam*) of the *also*, and even of *even*. Who will one day write the history of the taxonomy of all the values of the 'and' – among which one would also find the very idea of taxonomic order: classification, hierarchical or not, by disjunction, conjunction, juxtaposition, opposition (and thus first of all of 'position')? And if deconstruction has something to say in the idea of such a history, of its possibility or its impossibility, who will one day write the history of the 'and' which, in a way which is no doubt unique, will not have named but joined, adjoined, conjoined or disjoined (because this is a grammar of binding and unbinding), deconstruction 'and' X (the letter for so many unknowns)? Before dreaming of this history, one would have to interrogate its system. But what is a system? At least an order of conjunction, but one which remains a determinate form in the history of all the 'conjunctions' and all possible consistent 'sets'. There is 'and' and 'and', as there is 'deconstruction' and 'deconstruction'. The *and* itself cannot gather itself up; it fails, but that's its chance, to be one with itself, it deconstructs itself or rather lets itself be deconstructed, against its will, and disjointed, by what happens to it, what follows or precedes it, coming upon it from elsewhere ('. . . and X') or from the very series, homogeneous or heterogeneous, of the *ands* (*and . . . and . . . and . . . etc.*) . . .

——You often take refuge, perhaps for want of time and space, in this minute word 'and'. The shelter looks secure, the formalization economical, and therefore powerful. *Before* prowling round the 'is' or the question 'what is it?', *before* the whole history of philosophy as ontology, *before* the philosophical definition of deconstruction ('deconstruction is this or that, or nothing or everything', etc.), *before* speculating on the problematic distinction between the theoretical, constative or descriptive 'is' and the performative power to create the event, *before* even the pre-performative event, the one that arrives, like every other, *before* any expectation and possible performativity, there will have been – a word still shorter than the 'est', at least in French – the homophone 'et' (one letter less). Without the 'meaning' of some 'and', nothing would happen, neither linking nor break, neither consequence nor consecution, neither conjunction nor disjunction, neither connection, nor opposition, nor strategic alliance, nor juxtaposition, nor being-*with*, being-*without*, being-together, being-save, not-being, etc.

——If we must formalize to move quickly (and deconstruction, like the very movement of difference, calls for a thinking of economy, therefore speed), we must say more about a certain law which seems to govern every relation of the type: 'deconstruction and . . .'. If my hypothesis is right, and if there is indeed a law there, we can record a recurrence, a regulated *series* of repetitions of which each must be *exemplary* of all the others (still the question of the 'and' – index of seriality and/or exemplarity, two privileged themes for every deconstruction). Each time I say 'deconstruction and X (whatever the concept or the theme)', it is the prelude to a very singular division which makes of this X, or rather makes appear in this X, an impossibility which becomes its own sole possibility, so that between the X as possible and the 'same' X as impossible, there is no longer anything but a relation of homonymy for which we have to account (philosophically, this time, following the principle of reason implied in every attempt to explain, to account for, etc). For example, to refer to demonstrations already attempted in books or seminars, an invention (and therefore an event), a gift, a pardon, a hospitality, even death (and therefore so many other things) can only be possible *as impossible*, as the im-possible, i.e. unconditionally. If one is convinced by these demonstrations that we cannot repeat here, then (and I'll stick with this consequence here), there is, between X *and* X (gift *and* gift, pardon *and* pardon, etc.), between the X as possible *and* the X as impossible, only a relation of homonymy, and therefore a semantic or synonymic non-relation, a relation without relation. There is gift *and* gift, two heterogeneous uses of the same word, and yet, in spite of this incommensurability, we must still account for this homonymy. For it is not fortuitous, one of the two concepts bearing the same name as the other because it is its aim or hyperbolic tension (the only gift, the only invention, the only pardon, the only hospitality worth their name are im-possible gift, pardon, hospitality). That's when there is 'deconstruction and X', but first of all 'X and X', and therefore 'deconstruction and deconstruction'.

——Have I understood properly? So there's something like a rule, a privileged procedure in a deconstruction which is, however, neither a method nor an appropriable technique, but an event or a style. The recurrence, the probability of this quasi-rule (a rule without rule since each time the example is absolutely other) would often go via a sort of disjunctive conjunction at the threatened heart of each conceptual or verbal atom: this and this, this without this, this save this, love and (without) love, God and (without) God, being and (without) being, religion and (without) religion, faith and (without) faith, pardon and (without) pardon, gift and (without) gift, the one getting itself deconstructed in the name of itself, or rather in the name of what, quite other, becomes its simple homonym. And the 'and' would then mark both difference and indifference. There is deconstruction and deconstruction.

——One should never say (and I try never to say) 'deconstruction' in the singular. And yet, if deconstruction is always plural, if there are only deconstructions each time signed otherwise, then the Socratic question insists: what have they in common? What makes of these deconstructions deconstructions which deserve to bear and justify the same name, even if it is in the plural? What justifies the name 'deconstruction'? Unless one has to ask oneself 'who' justifies this name, who authorizes it, what exemplary signature? All the aporias of the 'and' that we have just evoked (and they are also those of the undecidable as condition of the possible-impossible decision, of the passive decision as decision of the other in me, and of the *double bind*, and of the supplement: *both . . . and, either . . . or, and/or, neither . . . nor,* etc.) reappear between each (deconstructing) event and its signature ('deconstruction and me, and me, and me'). A question of the proper name. It was on the subject of the proper name, but also of aphorism and contretemps, that he spoke some time ago of a certain 'theatre of the "and". . .'[26]

——I'll add one more thing, before I forget: deconstruction is not only plural, both possible *and* impossible, because possible *as* impossible. It does not only take into account, above all to formalize it, the 'and' of all the additions and all the 'dangerous supplements', and all the hierarchies which are more or less secretly at work in the enumerative and/or oppositional order of the 'and'. It also tries to think (and that would be thought itself, if some such thing exists) the 'and' of the ambiguous excess, the 'and' which places all collective order on the way to dissemination. The disseminal 'and' is the 'plus d'un',[27] and the 'more than one voice',[28] the 'more than one language'[29] and the 'more than two',[30] and the 'more than three',[31] etc.

——Yes, and as the signature of a proper name is always a *yes*, an affirmation that promises to repeat itself, to confirm and countersign itself, therefore both to recall and forget itself in order to re-sign each time the first and only time (*yes, and yes, and yes*), we must add *yes* to the list of these minivocables which slip in and insinuate themselves between deconstruction and any possible X.

——Yes and no, then! Otherwise, and without the no [*sinon, et sauf le non*], a yes would never be possible. Yes, you say, but also no, no?

——Yes, yes. And yes . . .

Translated by Geoffrey Bennington

NOTES

[Translator's notes are enclosed in square brackets.]

1. [*Et . . . et . . .* in French also means 'both . . . and . . .', as we shall see.]
2. [The reference is to a song by Jacques Dutronc.]
3. Michel Foucault, *Les mots el les choses: une archéologie des sciences humaines* (Paris: Gallimard, 1966), p. 7 [trans. anon., *The Order of Things: An Archeology of the Humam Sciences* (London: Tavistock, 1974), p. xv. The translation in fact silently corrects Foucault's omission of the letter (j), as do subsequent French editions, and uses the form *et cetera*]. Some, like Foucault, write *et caetera*, oth-

ers *et coetera* (and this is in fact the case in the French translation of the fragment Foucault cites without giving the reference: Borges, 'La langue analy-
tique de John Wilkins', in *Enquêtes, 1937–52*, trans. P. and S. Bénichou (Paris:
Gallimard, 1957), p. 144). Others, whom we shall follow here, write more
securely *et cetera*.

4. Ibid., pp. 8–9 (p. xvii).
5. *A Universal History of Infamy*, trans. Norman Thomas di Giovanni (London:
   Allen Lane, 1973), p. 12.
6. Ibid., p. 11.
7. Ibid., p. 13.
8. *Les mots el les choses*, p. 7 (p. xv).
9. Ibid., p. xviii.
10. Ibid. p. xvii.
11. In it, it is a question of a work comprising thirteen chapters. And as could eas-
    ily be the case here too, 'The first reports the ambiguous dialogue of certain
    strangers on a railway platform. The second narrates the events on the eve of
    the first act. The third, also retrograde, describes the events of *another* possible
    eve to the first day; the fourth, still another. Each one of these three eves (each
    of which rigorously excludes the others) is divided into three other eves, each
    of a very different kind. The entire work, thus, constitutes nine novels; each
    novel contains three long chapters. (The first chapter, naturally, is common to
    all.) The temper of one of these novels is symbolic; that of another, psycho-
    logical, of another, communist, of still another, anti-communist, and so on.
    Perhaps a diagram will help towards comprehending the structure [. . .]
    Concerning this structure we might well repeat what Schopenhauer declared
    of the twelve Kantian categories: everything is sacrificed to a rage for sym-
    metry' (trans. Anthony Kerrigan, in *Ficciones* (London: Everyman's Library,
    1993), pp. 52–7 (pp. 54–5)).
12. Before the days of 'the cinema and the phonograph', the narrator learns from
    'the voice of Funes' that he had 'devised a new system of enumeration'. To say
    signs and words, instead of 'seven thousand thirteen, he would say (for exam-
    ple) *Máximo Perez*; in place of seven thousand fourteen, *The Train*; other num-
    bers were *Luis Melián Lafinur, Olimar, Brimstone, Clubs, The Whale, Gas, The
    Cauldron, Napoleon, Agustín de Vedia* . . . I attempted to explain that this rhap-
    sody of unconnected terms was precisely the contrary of a system of enumer-
    ation . . . Funes did not understand me, or did not wish to understand me.
       Locke, in the seventeenth century, postulated (and rejected) an impossible
    language in which each individual object, each stone, each bird and branch
    had an individual name . . . He [Funes] was, let us not forget, almost incapable
    of general, platonic ideas. It was not only difficult for him to understand that
    the generic term *dog* embraced so many unlike specimens of differing sizes
    and different forms, he was disturbed by the fact that a dog at three-fourteen
    (seen in profile) should have the same name as the dog at three-fifteen (seen
    from the front).' Etc. (Ibid., pp. 88–9).
13. '*Wollen wir uns die Bedeutung des Wortes und klarmachen* . . . *Logische
    Untersuchungen*, IV, 'Der Unterschied der selbständigen und unselbständigen
    Bedeutungen und die Idee der reinen Grammatik', §9, 'Das Verständnis her-
    ausgerissener Synkategorematika', trans. J. N. Findlay, 2 vols (London:
    Routledge, 1970), vol. II, pp. 508–9. [In what follows I have occasionally mod-
    ified the translation slightly in view of Derrida's literal attention to the
    German text.]
14. Thanks to Mounira Khemir (see *Retrats de l'ànima: fotografía africana*
    (Barcelona: Fondació la Caixa, 1997). She tells me that this letter is apparently

also the 'travellers' letter'. In the Coran (for example at the beginning of one of the sourates that begin with this letter), it marks that in the name of which one swears or gives oath, what one invokes and by which one commits oneself: '*In the name* of Allah the all merciful, the merciful one' (Sourate LXXXIX).

15. Op. cit., p. 508.
16. 'In our whole exposition "fulfilment" (*Erfüllung*) must of course be taken to cover the opposed state of "frustration". This frustration comes about when the expected fulfilment becomes impossible, either because of a contradiction, an incompatibility, or else because the incomplete or dependent meaning remains deprived of any possible intuition, for want of a sufficiently determined context. It then remains a meaning-intention without full meaning.'
17. This teleological optimism is no doubt irreducible, and it is explicit at the end of the passage we are reading. For Husserl concludes: '<u>and</u> we have a situation (<u>und</u> *dass somit Sachlage wirklich besteht*) which the possibility of an adequate fit between intention and fulfilment necessarily requires.' (p. 508; My underlining, naturally, on the *use* of the 'and').
18. '. . . no syncategorematic meaning, no act of non-independent meaning-intention, can function in knowledge outside of the context of a categorematic meaning. And instead of "meaning", we could of course say "expression", in the normal sense of a unity of verbal sound *and* meaning or sense' (ibid). Husserl himself underlines the second *and*, but the two 'und' in these lines have an operational and not thematic value: they are used, not mentioned.
19. Ibid., p. 509.
20. Ibid.
21. Ibid.
22. Ibid., p. 513.
23. Ibid., p. 514.
24. Jacques Derrida, *Introduction à 'L'origine de la géométrie' de Husserl* (Paris: PUF, 1962), p. 56 ff. (trans. John P. Leavey, Jr, University of Nebraska Press, 1978, pp. 66 ff.). On the 'and so on' as fundamental form of idealization, cf. ibid., p. 148, n. 1 [p. 135, n. 161].
25. *Formale und transzendentale Logik* (Niemeyer, 1929), Beilage I, §5, p. 264.
26. 'Romeo *and* Juliet, the conjunction of two desires which are aphoristic but held together . . . The *and* of this conjunction, the theatre of this 'and', has often been presented, represented as the scene of fortuitous contretemps, of aleatory anachrony: the failed rendezvous, the unfortunate accident, the letter which does not arrive at its destination . . .' (Jacques Derrida, 'L'aphorisme à contretemps', in *Psyché: Inventions de l'autre* (Paris: Galilée, 1987), p. 522, trans. Nicholas Royle, in Derek Attridge (ed), *Acts of Literature* (London: Routledge, 1992), p. 419. On the double bind and the double stricture of bond or conjunction, cf. *Glas* and *The Post Card* (*passim*). On the passive decision as decision of the other in me, cf. especially *Politiques de l'amitié*. On the supplement, cf. especially *Of Grammatology* (*passim*). The logical resources of the 'and' are also analysed in *Otobiographies: l'enseignement de Nietzsche et la politique du nom propre* (Paris: Galilée, 1984), p. 26 ff. [trans. T. Keenan and T. Pepper, 'Declarations of Independence', *New Political Science*, 15 (1986), pp. 7–15], around a particular passage of the Declaration of Independence '". . . solemnly publish and declare, that these united Colonies are and of right ought to be free and independent states . . ."' . . . *Are and ought to be*: the "and" here articulated and conjoins the two discursive modalities, is and ought, constative and prescriptive, fact and right. *And* is God: both creator of nature and judge, supreme judge of what is (the state of the world) and of what refers to what ought to be ("the rectitude of our intentions") . . . for this Declaration to have

a meaning and an effect, there must be a last instance. God is the name, the
best name, for this last instance and this ultimate signature.'

27. [Translator's note. 'Plus d'un' can translate as 'more than one', but also as 'no
longer any one'. More idiomatic attempts to capture this ambiguity might be
'not one', 'not half', 'no end' . . .] Since '*La différance*' (1967) (in *Margins*), so
many formulations of 'the One different from itself', more and less than itself,
seem to lead to the most economical statements of *Mal d'archive* (Paris: Galilée,
1995), such as, for example, 'L'Un se garde de l'autre' (p. 124) or 'L'Un se fait
violence' (p. 125) (trans. E. Prenowitz as *Archive Fever* (University of Chicago
Press, 1995), p. 78).

28. Cf. for example the last words of 'Psyché: Invention de l'autre' (in *Psyché*, p.
61): '. . . that only happens with several voices'.

29. When the expression 'more than one language' appears as an ironic definition
of deconstruction in *Mémoires for Paul de Man* (Columbia University Press,
1986), p. 15, it is followed by a development and a question which resonate
here: 'How many sentences can be made with "deconstruction"'?

30. Especially around the question of the third party. Cf. *Adieu à Emmanuel Lévinas*
(Paris: Galilée, 1997), *passim*, and especially pp. 63 ff. (trans. Michael Naas and
Pascale-Anne Brault, Stanford University Press, forthcoming).

31. On the beyond of the three, on the relation between the three and the four, cf.
Dissemination, *passim*.

WORKS CITED

Borges, Jorge Luis (1973), *A Universal History of Infamy*, trans. Norman Thomas di
Giovanni (London: Allen Lane).
—— *Ficciones*, trans. Anthony Kerrigan *et al.* (London: Everyman's Library).
Derrida, Jacques (1962), *Introduction à 'L'origine de la géometrie' de Husserl* (Paris:
PUF) [trans. John P. Leavey, Jr., University of Nebraska Press, 1978].
—— (1972), *La différance'*, in *Marges: de la philosophie* (Paris: Minuit) [trans. Alan
Bass in Margins of Philosophy (Brighton: Harvester, 1982)].
—— *La dissémination* (Paris: Seuil, 1972) [trans. Barbara Johnson (University of
Chicago Press, 1981)].
—— (1984), *Otobiographies: l'enseignment de Nietzsche et la politique du nom propre*
(Paris: Galilée) [trans. T. Keenan and T. Pepper, 'Declarations of Independence'.
New Political Science, **15** (1986), 7–15].
—— (1986), *Memoires for Paul de Man*, trans. Lindsay, Culler and Cadava (New
York: Columbia University Press).
—— (1987), Psyché: Invention de l'autre', in *Psyché: inventions de l'autre* (Paris:
Galilée), pp. 11–61.
—— (1992), L'aphorisme à contretemps' (*Psyché*, pp. 519–33) [trans. Nicholas
Royle in D. Attridge, ed. *Acts of Literature* (London: Routledge), pp. 414–33].
—— (1995), *Mal d'archive: une impression freudienne* (Paris: Galilée) [trans. Eric
Prenowitz (University of Chicago Press, 1995)].
—— (1997), *Adieu à Emmanuel Lévinas* (Paris: Galilée 1997) [trans. Michael Naas
and Pascale-Anne Brault (Stanford, CA: Stanford University Press)].
Foucault, Michel (1966), Les mots et les choses: une archéologie des sciences
humaines (Paris: Gallimard), p. 7 [trans. anon., *The Order of Things: an
Archeology of the Human Sciences* (London: Tavistock, 1974)].
Husserl, Edmund (1970), *Logical Investigations*, trans. J. N. Findlay, 2 vols (London:
Routledge). *Formale und transzendentale Logik* (Niemeyer, 1929) [trans. Dorion

Cairns (The Hague: Martinus Nijhoff, 1969)].
Khemir, Mounira (1997), *Retraits de l'ànima: fotografía africana* (Barcelona: Fondació la Caixa).

Index